# Contents



MW00572014

# THE STOKES GUIDE TO FINCHES OF THE UNITED STATES AND CANADA

## BIRD BOOKS BY DONALD AND LILLIAN STOKES

*The Stokes Field Guide to the Birds of North America*
*The New Stokes Field Guide to Birds: Eastern Region*
*The New Stokes Field Guide to Birds: Western Region*
*The Stokes Essential Pocket Guide to the Birds of North America*
*Stokes Field Guide to Warblers*
*Stokes Field Guide to Birds: Eastern Region*
*Stokes Field Guide to Birds: Western Region*
*Stokes Guide to Bird Behavior,* Volumes 1-3

*Stokes Beginner's Guide to Bird Feedings*
*Stokes Beginner's Guide to Birds: Eastern Region*
*Stokes Beginner's Guide to Birds: Western Region*
*Stokes Beginner's Guide to Hummingbirds*
*Stokes Beginner's Guide to Shorebirds*

*Stokes Bird Feeder Book*
*Stokes Bird Gardening Book*
*Stokes Birdhouse Book*
*Stokes Bluebird Book*
*Stokes Hummingbird Book*
*Stokes Oriole Book*
*Stokes Purple Martin Book*

## OTHER BOOKS BY DONALD AND LILLIAN STOKES

*The Natural History of Wild Shrubs and Vines*
*Stokes Beginner's Guide to Bats* (with Kim Williams and Rob Mies)
*Stokes Beginner's Guide to Butterflies*
*Stokes Beginner's Guide to Dragonflies* (with Blair Nikula and Jackie Sones)
*Stokes Butterfly Book* (with Ernest Williams)
*Stokes Guide to Animal Tracking and Behavior*
*Stokes Guide to Enjoying Wildflowers*
*Stokes Guide to Nature in Winter*
*Stokes Guide to Observing Insect Lives*
*Stokes Guide to Amphibians and Reptiles* (with Thomas F. Tyning)
*Stokes Wildflower Book: East of the Rockies*
*Stokes Wildflower Book: From the Rockies West*
*Stokes Backyard Bird Book*

THE

# STOKES GUIDE TO FINCHES

OF THE UNITED STATES AND CANADA

LILLIAN STOKES & MATTHEW A. YOUNG

LITTLE, BROWN AND COMPANY
New York Boston London

Copyright © 2024 by Lillian Q. Stokes and Matthew A. Young

Hachette Book Group supports the right to free expression and the value of copyright. The purpose of copyright is to encourage writers and artists to produce the creative works that enrich our culture.

The scanning, uploading, and distribution of this book without permission is a theft of the author's intellectual property. If you would like permission to use material from the book (other than for review purposes), please contact permissions@hbgusa.com. Thank you for your support of the author's rights.

Little, Brown and Company
Hachette Book Group
1290 Avenue of the Americas, New York, NY 10104
littlebrown.com

First Edition: September 2024

Little, Brown and Company is a division of Hachette Book Group, Inc. The Little, Brown name and logo are trademarks of Hachette Book Group, Inc.

The publisher is not responsible for websites (or their content) that are not owned by the publisher.

The Hachette Speakers Bureau provides a wide range of authors for speaking events. To find out more, go to hachettespeakersbureau.com or email hachettespeakers@hbgusa.com.

Little, Brown and Company books may be purchased in bulk for business, educational, or promotional use. For information, please contact your local bookseller or the Hachette Book Group Special Markets Department at special.markets@hbgusa.com.

For photo credits, see page 327.

Designed by Ashley Prine, Tandem Books

ISBN 9780316419932
LCCN 2023949235

10 9 8 7 6 5 4 3 2 1

IM

Printed in China

*From Lillian:*

To my beloved husband, Don

What a journey we had! Through thirty-five Stokes guides, two PBS TV series, hundreds of talks, and more, we have been so fortunate to bring joy and a deepened connection to birds and nature to millions. I will carry on.

---

*From Matt:*

To my Mom, Joan

When I was five years old, my first student was my mother. I would discover a treasure like a spring peeper or a patch of strawberries, or point out birds singing and she would always wonderfully indulge my budding abilities and encourage me. Thanks, Mom!

# Preface

***August 2020***

It started with Red Crossbills.

A friend called Lillian and told her that Red Crossbills were coming every morning at 8 a.m. to a nearby nature center parking lot to get grit. Lillian eagerly went there and for over a month recorded their calls, photographed and studied them, was drawn deeper into their world, and bonded with them. To learn where they came from (Red Crossbills are grouped by their flight calls and each call type lives in a different core area) she sent her recordings to Matt Young, an expert at decoding Red Crossbill call types from spectrograms. Thus, the paths of Lillian and Matt met over Red Crossbills, and that crossing became the genesis of this book.

Realizing there was no extensive book devoted exclusively to the finches of the United States and Canada, Lillian and Matt joined forces and created a mutually supportive partnership to bring you this guide to all things finch! From the introductory Quick Takes designed to engage and entertain, through the complete identification, language,

distribution, life histories, feeder information, irruptions and migrations, deeper dives into scientific discoveries, and beautiful photos, we hope this book will further your love and understanding of finches.

This book is also about more than finches. Both Lillian and Matt are social workers (Lillian was a psychiatric social worker for 10 years, and Matt has been a program director or care manager supervisor at the William George Agency for 12 years) who strongly believe that the wellness and healing power of a connection to birds and nature is available to all. That message is infused throughout this book, and it personally sustains them.

---

*From Lillian:*
I produced 35 Stokes guides with my beloved husband, Don, in which our goal was to inspire people to love, understand, and conserve birds and nature. The opportunity to write this guide was thrilling for me, but bittersweet because it had to be without him. Don was first misdiagnosed with Parkinson's disease for 5 years, then during the writing of this guide was diagnosed with Lewy body dementia and needed to go live in a dementia care facility. The strength to be a caregiver for someone with dementia, as well as the strength to bring you another beautiful Stokes Guide, comes from the enduring wellness power of my connection to birds and nature. Immersion in finches and the writing of this guide was a therapeutic gift. Red Crossbills came calling, I listened, and the path opened for me to bring you a book of which I am immensely proud!

---

*From Matt:*
I have had a love of finches since that very first moment of watching Red Crossbills land and feed above me at the Lower Falls of the Yellowstone River in the summer of 1995. And of course, I didn't know it at the time, but that seminal moment changed me at my core, and changed the course of my life. Ah, the power of birds and nature is about as motivating and healing as anything on earth. In the birding circles, we call this a spark bird, but that moment was much more—it was a spark event. Now almost 30 years later, finches have always been there, from that time out west in 1995, to when I first moved to Ithaca and the great finch superflight of 1997–1998 occurred, to when my father was dying in 2002 and I had a daily flock of 150 Evening Grosbeaks and Common Redpolls at the feeders to get me through, to the next great finch superflight that coincided with the launching of the Finch Research Network in 2020 during the early months of the Covid-19 pandemic. The opportunity to bring this book to you with the wonderful Lillian Stokes is both a dream and a life's work coming to fruition.

---

We both thank our wonderful publisher as well as all those listed in the acknowledgments for helping us to bring you this historic first: *The Stokes Guide to Finches of the United States and Canada*. We hope you enjoy it!

# How to Use This Guide

***AREA COVERED***

This guide covers the fifty United States and the provinces and territories of Canada.

## WHAT IS A FINCH?

Before genetics and the phylogenetic species concept became prominent, a finch was known as a bird with a short, stout, conical bill used for cracking or crushing seeds. But some finch bills aren't conical in shape at all, as is most evident in the finches of Hawai'i—the honeycreepers—some of which have long, thin bills. So, it's complicated, and genetics are now used to define a finch. Phylogenetically, finches are placed in the family Fringillidae and divided into three subfamilies: Fringillinae (contains one genus of the chaffinches), Carduelinae (contains 183 species, including most of the finches in this guide), and Euphoniinae.

There are birds in other families called "finches," such as Darwin's finches of the Galapagos, but Darwin's finches are in the tanager family. Some people think House Sparrows are finches, but they are in the sparrow family, Passeridae.

## SPECIES ACCOUNTS

We have placed the finches in this guide into three groups: the eighteen main breeding finches, the eight vagrant finches, and the seventeen endemic finches (a.k.a. honeycreepers) of Hawai'i. The birds are arranged, within each of the three groups, in phylogenetic order, as determined (as of the writing of this guide) by the American Ornithological Society Checklist Committee. Phylogenetic order is the order in which birds are believed to have evolved, from the earliest to the most recent.

***THE MAIN BREEDING FINCHES***

Because these are the finches most often seen by our readers, including those that visit backyard feeders, we have provided the most thorough information on these species: identification, language, distribution, subspecies, habitat and diet, feeder behavior, breeding behavior, movements and irruptions, and conservation status.

***THE VAGRANT FINCHES***

These are the very rare finches that most readers will not see. We focused on what we considered most relevant to these vagrant finches: identification, calls, subspecies, habitat and diet, and status and distribution. We indicate each species' rarity with an American Birding Association Checklist Code (Version 8.11—August 2022), which appears next to its status and distribution section. Code 3 are "rare, species that occur in very low numbers, but annually, in the ABA Area [North America north of Mexico plus the Hawaiian Islands]." Code 4 are "casual, species not recorded annually in the ABA Area, but with six or more total records—including three or more in the past 30 years—reflecting some pattern of occurrence." Code 5 are "species that are recorded five or fewer times in the ABA Area, or fewer than three records in the past 30 years." In the status and distribution section we occasionally refer to eBird records. eBird (ebird.org) is a worldwide database of bird distribution and abundance, collected in a scientific framework, consisting of birders' checklists of when and where they saw birds. eBird is managed by the Cornell Lab of Ornithology.

When referring to an eBird record, we generally mean a sighting of an individual bird (unless we specify more than one) even if it was reported on multiple checklists. (Sometimes it may be impossible to know whether it is the same individual.) When referring to an individual checklist, the name of the eBird observer is listed in the citations at the end of the guide.

### *THE ENDEMIC FINCHES OF HAWAI'I*

These beautiful finches came to Hawai'i five to seven million years ago and through adaptive radiation became more than fifty species. Now they number only about sixteen with some on the brink of extinction. We felt it important to create a separate section for these species to spotlight their plight and to give readers a greater appreciation and understanding of them. The species accounts in this section are shorter since many of the species are not that well known or studied, or even accessible to birders. In each species account we give their identification, distribution, language, habitat and diet, conservation, sometimes a fun fact, and a quote from the people or organizations working to save them. In the Research and Conservation chapter, we offer detailed information on the work being done by dedicated conservation groups to save these beautiful birds.

## INFORMATION INCLUDED IN SPECIES ACCOUNTS

### *NAME*

Each species has a common name as well as a scientific name that is agreed upon by the American Birding Association Checklist Committee, which in turn, as of the writing of this guide, follows the lead of the American Ornithological Society's North American Classification Committee (NACC). On November 1, 2023, the American Ornithological Society committed to change all English-language names of birds within its geographic jurisdiction that are named directly after people. Three species in this guide may have their English common names changed: Cassin's Finch, Lawrence's Goldfinch, and Pallas's Rosefinch.[1] For more information, see https://americanornithology.org.

The scientific name for each species has two parts. The first is the genus, or group, to which that bird belongs; the second is the species within that genus. The scientific name of a subspecies has three parts: genus, species, subspecies.

### *QUICK TAKE*

This introductory creative essay, written by Lillian and unique to each main breeding species, is meant to engage, make memorable, and bring to life the personality and essence of that species.

### *IDENTIFICATION*

#### LENGTH

The length of the bird from the tip of the beak to the tip of the tail, given in inches. In most cases, this is an average measurement, for length can vary within a species and between sexes.

#### SHAPE

Shape is extremely useful and a first step in bird identification. Becoming good at observing and describing shape will fast-forward your bird identification skills. Plumage varies with feather wear, sex, age, and season, but through all of these plumage variations, shape often remains the same. Shape can be helpful in distinguishing between species with look-alike plumages.

There are two types of shape description: qualitative and quantitative. Qualitative uses general impressions to describe the "quality" of a bird's shape using familiar descriptive adjectives (e.g., "stocky," "bulky," "chunky," "compact," "slim"). But we take a quantitative approach in this guide, using comparative measurements within the bird (e.g., "wing length 3 x wing width") and precise language to describe shape. For example, quantitative words for the shape of birds' bodies include "deep-chested," "deep-bellied," "broad-necked," "defined neck"; quantitative words for bills include "blunt-tipped," "deep-based," "decurved," "conical."

Shape descriptions in this guide refer to adults; immature and juvenile birds may have slightly different proportions. Bill length is from the tip of the bill to the base of the culmen (the lengthwise ridge of the upper mandible); head length is from the base of the culmen to the back of the nape. The lore is the distance between the front of the eye and the base of the bill.

The primaries are the outermost and longest feathers of the wing. On a perched bird, they can be seen on the lowest edge of the folded wing and may extend out over the rump or tail. Primary extension (also called primary projection) is best seen on perched or sitting birds. There are two measurements of primary extension: how far the primaries project past the tail and how far they project past the tertials. This measurement can then be compared to other parts of the same bird, such as the length of the lore or bill or to the length of the longest tertial.

The tertials are important features to observe on birds because their length can be compared to other parts of a bird and because they often help in identification and determining age. They are the innermost feathers of the wing and, on a perched bird, tend to lie over the folded secondaries in a widely overlapping fashion. Estimating the length of the longest tertial can be a useful measurement to compare with the bill length or length of primary projection past tertials.

## *AGE AND SEASONAL PLUMAGE DESCRIPTIONS*

In describing birds at various ages and times of year, we have tried to keep terminology simple yet accurate. There are several systems for describing the plumages and ages of birds. In this guide, we have used the life-year system. It describes birds' ages much like we describe our own—a bird's first year is roughly its first twelve months, its second year the next twelve months, and so on. In general, plumages are described on a seasonal basis, which roughly reflects molt timings: summer (which mostly coincides with breeding) and winter (which coincides with nonbreeding). There are exceptions, however—among them the Red Crossbill and White-winged Crossbill, which may breed in any season of the year—so this needs to be taken into account.

Below are the headings we have used in the identification sections of the guide and brief explanations of their meaning.

**Adult** Adult bird without seasonal plumage change.

**Adult Summer** Adult bird that has seasonal plumage change from roughly March to August.

**Adult Winter** Adult bird that has seasonal plumage change from roughly September to February.

**Juv** Juvenile plumage, the first full plumage of a bird after it leaves the nest. Some birds keep this plumage only until fall, when they molt into 1st-winter or adult plumage; others keep it for as long as the first year. (Juv. is also used in the text to mean a juvenile, a young bird in juvenile plumage.)

**1st Winter** This term is used when the juvenile plumage is partially molted in fall and the resulting new plumage is not yet like the adult.

**Imm.** Immature. Any distinct plumage between juvenile and adult.

**1st Year** The plumage kept for roughly the first twelve months of a bird's life.

### *PLUMAGE DATES*

Where applicable, we give a range of months in which that plumage can be seen. It is important to remember that plumages change gradually, so that at either end of the range you may see a bird molting as it transitions out of an old plumage and into a new one. Also, individuals vary in timing; thus, at either end of a date range you may see one bird still mostly in the previous plumage while another is fully molted into the new plumage. Note again that some species, such as the Red and White-winged Crossbills, can breed in any season, so the range of months may be broader than our estimate.

### *SUBSPECIES*

The subspecies designation is given to consistent regional variations in a species' appearance and/or behavior. A subspecies is often defined by physical characteristics as well as by the geographic region in which it breeds. Subspecies are decided upon through careful examination of birds in the wild and in museum collections, and also through field studies of breeding behavior, ranges, and visual and auditory clues.

Differences between subspecies can be subtle and clinal (changing gradually over a geographic area), and there can be disagreement on the presence or number of subspecies within a species. The American Ornithological Society (AOS) maintains an authoritative list called the *Checklist of North American Birds,* which is periodically revised. Although species classification is fairly regularly updated, the last time subspecies were comprehensively updated was in 1957. So much additional research has occurred since that time that we felt compelled to reflect it in our guide, so we looked for a consistent and more current approach to subspecies classification.

One of the most thorough reviews of subspecies has been done by Peter Pyle in his *Identification Guide to North American Birds, Part I* and *Part II,* revised in 2022. It is detailed, dense with information, and thoroughly documented. It is designed primarily for bird banders and people studying birds in the hand, but it is also a thorough guide to the aging of birds and the sequence of their molts and can be extremely useful to any field birder. Pyle aims to "standardize the treatment across all species and to adhere to a rule by which 75% of individuals of each subspecies could be separated from 100% of individuals of similar subspecies."

In this guide, we have followed Pyle's classification of subspecies in his new revision. We have summarized his ranges and descriptions in a way we hope will be useful for the field birder, but encourage all interested birders to consult Pyle for more thorough descriptions of the ranges and differences between subspecies.

There are two species for which we did not follow Pyle's classification of subspecies. In the case of the Evening Grosbeak and the Red Crossbill (especially the latter), Pyle's subspecies designation is not a good fit. For these two species we follow the call type designation, which refers to the acoustical differences in the call the birds make in flight. The Red Crossbill has eleven to twelve different call types (Cassia Crossbill = Type 9), and the Evening Grosbeak has five call types. Five different subspecies of Evening Grosbeak largely overlap with the ranges of the five call types; for more information, see the Evening Grosbeak account. With the Red Crossbill, the call types are more nomadic and commonly overlap.

Below the Subspecies heading, the number of subspecies that occur in the area covered by this guide is given in parentheses or a narrative description. Monotypic means there are no subspecies in the world.

For certain birds with many subspecies, the subspecies are joined into groups that have similar characteristics. In these cases, we describe the characteristics of the groups and then list the subspecies and their ranges.

Identification of subspecies in the field can often only be done reliably by seeing a bird in the heart of its designated subspecies breeding range during breeding. Since there may be a gradual blending of characteristics where subspecies meet and often quite a bit of variation within the range of a subspecies, and since ranges are inexactly known and defined, identification in the field to the subspecies level outside the heart of the breeding range and outside the breeding period is frequently inexact. We often have included photographs of subspecies when they show a marked variation in appearance or are representative of a group of subspecies. In a few instances, a subspecies not occurring in North America is shown as an aid to identification.

### *SIMILAR SPECIES*

In this section we include information on how to distinguish the species in the account from other similar or look-alike species.

### *DISTRIBUTION*

For each species (except the vagrant finches, whose breeding ranges are not in the United States and Canada) we include a description of their breeding range, often their winter range, and also a distribution map.

### *RANGE MAPS*

We include up-to-date range maps, color drawn by Matt Young and transferred to vector files by Ken McEnaney.

PURPLE FINCH

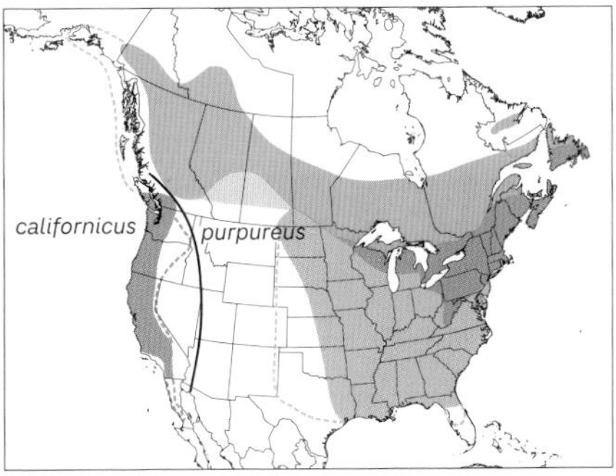

californicus
purpureus

Year Round
Breeding
Non-Breeding
Migration

When relevant, maps show summer range (red), winter range (blue), year-round range (purple), and migration routes (yellow). The maps occasionally include dotted lines to indicate regular extralimital occurrences during the respective season (winter, summer, or on migration). Solid blue dots indicate locally known to breed, and solid black dots indicate vagrant occurrences. An exception to the usual range maps are the call type maps in the Red Crossbill, Cassia, and White-winged Crossbill sections.

## RED CROSSBILL TYPE 2

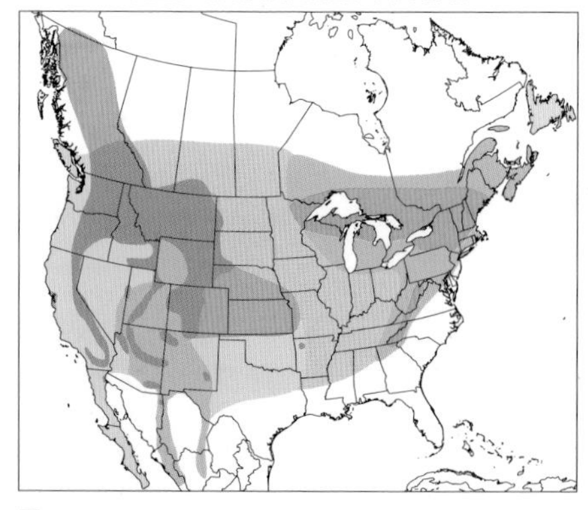

Core Zone of Occurrence
Secondary Zone of Occurrence
Primary Zone of Irruption
Secondary Zone of Irruption
Tertiary Zone of Irruption

Here, these unique White-winged Crossbill, Cassia Crossbill, and Red Crossbill call type maps created by Matt follow this map key:

**Core Zone of Occurrence (purple):** Crossbills are found here most years eating seed of key conifers and breeding.
**Secondary Zone of Occurrence (red):** Crossbills present in fewer numbers most years, and small numbers breed. Type 3 breeds in the Northeast, represented with dashed lines indicating that it occasionally acts as a secondary zone of occurrence.
**Primary Zone of Irruption (blue):** Crossbills flee to these areas when key conifers in their core zone fail, and may stay and nest rarely in small numbers. (The dashed line indicates where small numbers may irrupt and breed.)
**Secondary Zone of Irruption (yellow):** Crossbills flee to these areas when key conifers in their core zones and primary zone of irruption experience widespread failure of many conifers. They very rarely nest here, only Type 2 appearing to do so.
**Tertiary Zone of Irruption (gray):** Only Type 2 goes here rarely, and may breed locally, as this would be more aptly named the Eclectic Crossbill.
● **Solid Blue Dots:** Locally known to breed.
● **Solid Black Dots:** Vagrant occurrences.

For species in the Vagrant Finches section, there is no range map but a description of when they tend to show up and how often they occur. Many of these species wander into our area from other continents such as Europe and Asia. Some arrive only once or a few times in the United States and Canada, others come irregularly every few years, and some show up regularly but in no one predictable place. These vagrant species without maps have ABA birding codes of 3, 4, or 5.

### *CHARTS*

These proposed seasonality foraging charts were created by Matt with the assistance of David Yeany II. See page 131 for more information.

For the Red Crossbill, we present food charts that take the reader through the cone cycle year, which runs approximately July 1–June 31. Crossbills usually start the cone cycle year foraging on the seed of softer-coned conifers such as spruces, hemlocks, larches, and firs, shift to semisoft conifers like eastern and western white pines, limber pine, and Douglas fir (inland variety), eventually ending late winter into spring feeding on hard-coned pines such as lodgepole, ponderosa, Jeffrey, and others in the West, and red, jack, pitch, Virginia, and loblolly to name a few in the East. They are constantly looking for the best rich patches of conifers with seed throughout the year.

Conifers in the area covered by this guide produce cones in a cycle that begins in May and June and start to ripen around the first of July. If there's enough available food on their preferred trees, and this means even green cones (on white, Engelmann, or red spruce), then crossbills will begin breeding shortly thereafter, with this first breeding cycle extending from about July 1 to early September for the Red Crossbill call types, and from July 1 into October for the White-winged Crossbill.

### *LANGUAGE*

Sound is a key feature in identifying birds. We have included written descriptions of calls and songs for males only, females only, and sounds made by both males and females. We generally attempt to describe the quality of the call as well as give a mnemonic rendition of the sound. Calls are usually innate sounds and tend to be short; song in finches is learned, more complex vocalization. In some cases, such as the Red Crossbill, we give spectrograms of the calls, which are visual representations of the spectrum of frequencies of a signal as it varies with time. It is a signature of the bird's voice in the simplest terms.

### IMITATION/MIMICRY

Some of the finch species are accomplished mimics or imitators of sound, which we discuss in this section.

### *HABITAT AND DIET*

This section describes the key elements of the breeding and often wintering habitat for each species. When a species uses a wide range of habitats, we try to characterize that variety. Since diet is tied to a bird's habitat, we include it here and list the major foods the species eats. This may not be a complete list of all the foods a bird eats. Finches are primarily seed eaters and feed regurgitated seeds to their young. For some species, insects are an important part of their diet, especially during breeding, as is the case with Evening Grosbeaks, which eat spruce budworms and feed them to their young. Most finches also eat grit and are attracted to salt, although we may not say this for all species that do. Finches are also attracted to water, especially Lawrence's Goldfinch. In this section we frequently describe the method of feeding, particularly when it is unusual, as in the case of the crossbills, whose unique crossed bill makes them experts at extracting seeds from conifers.

### *AT YOUR FEEDER*

Bird feeding is one of the main ways people enjoy and connect to birds. Finches are one of the largest groups of feeder birds in the world, and this special section is meant to enhance people's enjoyment of these species. We include tips on what seeds and feeders to use, and also what interesting behavior to look for. More complete information is given in the Feeding and Attracting Finches chapter.

### *MOVEMENTS AND IRRUPTIONS*

Finches are well known for their irregular migrations, called irruptions, which are tied to population size and whether variable food sources can support those populations. If they cannot, these "boreal finches" irrupt southward. In this section, we tell which finches move or irrupt where and when.

### *BREEDING BEHAVIOR*

For the main breeding finches, we describe their breeding behavior, including territory, courtship, and nesting.

### TERRITORY

The concept of territory in birds is often thought of as a fixed geographic area, defended by the male and sometimes the female, in which nesting takes place. But that does not apply to certain finch species, whose territorial behavior instead includes the male defending, from other males, a floating space around the female.

### COURTSHIP

This includes pair formation, pair maintenance, and mating. Pair formation, the initial contact between a male and female in breeding condition, may include some of the most elaborate behavior of that species, with the male displaying with postures, flight, and singing. Female finches choose the male to pair with based on their evaluation of the male's condition and ability to provide food to her and the offspring. In most cases the male finch provides the female with almost all, or a majority, of her food while she incubates the eggs and takes little time to leave the nest.

Mating refers to copulation and displays that come before or after it. Copulation is similar in all finches. The female usually tilts forward and raises her tail feathers while the male steps onto her back and lowers his tail feathers. Their cloacas (the opening through which sperm or eggs are discharged, as well as digestive waste) touch, and sperm is transferred. Copulation may last for only a few seconds but may be repeated many times.

### NESTING

This includes timing of nesting, description of the nest and its construction, number of eggs laid, length of incubation and nestling periods, and number of broods. It also includes behavior that occurs during this time, as well as information, if known, about the fledgling period of the young.

### *MOLT*

The molt section of this guide is simple and focuses on adult birds and changes in plumage the reader could actually see. In some cases, we describe the dynamics of molt, such as how the American Goldfinch acquires its yellow color through carotenoid pigments in its diet.

Molt schedules vary among birds, but a few general patterns are helpful to know. The majority of molting for finches takes place after breeding, in late summer and early fall. American Goldfinches molt twice: before breeding, when they acquire their bright yellow breeding plumage, then again after breeding, changing to subtle brownish-gray winter plumage. For Red Crossbills, which can breed at almost any time of year, timing of molt can vary. Juveniles, in their first fall, often molt only their body feathers and retain most of their wing and tail feathers until their second fall. This results in a clue to recognizing birds in their first year: their wing and tail feathers are more worn and faded and often slightly lighter in color than those of the adults (sometimes discernible in a photo).

For a complete account of molt in finches, we refer you to Peter Pyle's *Identification Guide to North American Birds, Part I* and *Part II*.

### *CONSERVATION*

In this section we give the main conservation status of the species and sometimes their population trend as well as threats to their conservation.

We use the Partners in Flight (PIF) Avian Assessment Database scores. The PIF databases were developed with the input of dozens of ornithological experts from many countries. They are managed by Bird Conservancy of the Rockies and form the scientific basis for the PIF Landbird Conservation Plan, other bird conservation plans, and State of the Birds reports. The PIF species Continental Concern score indicates the status of that species' vulnerability. We also report PIF Watch List Species of greatest concern, Yellow Watch List being of moderate concern, and Red Watch List being at risk of extinction without significant action. We report the International Union for Conservation of Nature (IUCN) designation for species that are endangered.

The Research and Conservation chapter covers this topic in greater depth.

***FUN FACTS AND DEEPER DIVE***

These are bits of interesting information about a species that are complementary to the text.

## FEEDING AND ATTRACTING

Bird feeding can be a great joy, and studies have shown that engagement and connection with birds can bring all of us health and wellness benefits. We provide readers with the keys to feeding and attracting finches successfully, including which seeds and feeders to select, how to cope with feeder issues such as deterring squirrels, and how to keep finches safe. We hope this information will encourage our readers to connect in a positive and healthy way with this beautiful group of birds—the finches!

## MOVEMENTS AND IRRUPTIONS

When finches irrupt, especially in the eastern part of Canada and the United States, where this dynamic plays out on a much greater scale, it's a thrilling event for birders. Just seeing an Evening Grosbeak or Common Redpoll in one's backyard can be a magical experience. The flip side for finches, though, is that an irruption is an indication of too many finches and not enough food, and that the birds have been forced to flee to find food for survival.

We take the reader through what an irruption is, covering the different landscapes of western and eastern Canada and the United States where irruptions vary greatly in scale. We highlight the food that drives irruptions and offer some historical perspective on when the first irruptions were documented and how they have changed over the last sixty-plus years. We also discuss superflights—defined as at least seven species of finch in the East moving en masse—and the role that budworm events have played in those superflights.

## RESEARCH AND CONSERVATION

While finch species are relatively common across the globe, many are endangered. And without continued research, how would we even approach saving some of the most threatened species? In this chapter, we highlight three major conservation efforts: the finches of Hawai'i (the honeycreepers), of which now only about sixteen of fifty-three species continue to exist; the gregarious Evening Grosbeak, which has declined 92% over the last seventy years; and the rosy-finch group, which comprises three species, two of which are listed as endangered due to climate change. We also cover research topics of interest that apply across the Fringillid finches and identify several organizations and agencies conducting research and/or working on conservation efforts to save these species.

## LOOK-ALIKES

This is a mainly visual comparison of look-alike House, Purple, and Cassin's Finches to help identify these confusing species.

# MAIN BREEDING FINCHES

# EVENING GROSBEAK*

*Coccothraustes vespertinus*

> *Clothed in the most striking color-contrasts of black, white, and gold, he seems to represent the allegory of diurnal transmutations; for his sable pinions close around the brightness of his vesture, just as the night encompasses the golden hues of the sunset; while the clear white space enfolded in these tints foretells the dawn of the morrow.*
>
> —Elliott Coues, 1879

## QUICK TAKE

Spring 2021. She flew in, and stuck her landing on the white spruce branch, which bounced down slightly under her weight. She had come with her small flock into this breeding area in the boreal forest of Ontario.

---

* The North American Classification Committee (NACC) of the American Ornithology Society (AOS) is considering a 2024 proposal to transfer Evening Grosbeak (*Coccothraustes vespertinus*) and Hooded Grosbeak (*Coccothraustes abeillei*) into the genus *Hesperiphona*. If passed, the Evening Grosbeak would become *Hesperiphona vespertinus* (as it was in the second through fifth editions of the AOS Checklist).

With a lightning move, she plucked a plump, cream-colored caterpillar off the branch with her ample bill. She lifted off and headed back to what observers have described as a "flimsy" nest with waiting babies. Her mate followed closely. They had a strong pair bond, and she had been with him before in other seasons. This was no flimsy nest. The nest's looseness was intentional, a disguise among the conifer needles, and its location gave her the perfect surveillance point to watch for predators in this open forest. Birds often live on the edge; what we see as "flimsiness" may be their winning ticket to survival in the evolution lottery.

During breeding, her mate brought morsels for her; she would quiver her wings, accepting the gift. Facing her, he too would flutter his wings. She would rotate away from him, wings still fluttering, tail high, breast thrust forward, and he would mount on top of her, transferring sperm as they copulated with a cloacal kiss.[1] She had then produced five light-blue eggs marked with purplish splotches, like an abstract impressionist painting. Now five little, naked, bowling-ball-headed babies that only a mother and father Evening Grosbeak would find beautiful were in the nest.

As she flew in with her caterpillar food prize, several tiny, white-rimmed, violet-and-red mouths shot up on stalks like jack-in-the-boxes to greet her. She poked her large bill into one of the mouths and regurgitated the masticated little caterpillar, an infant formula just right for these under-one-week-old nestlings.

The little spruce budworm caterpillar she had plucked had been munching on the tender tips of white spruce. Budworms prefer balsam fir, then white spruce, and sometimes other spruces and tamarack. The nutritious spruce tips are a kind of

power boost for successful procreation when it's time for the caterpillar to mate as an adult moth. Spruce budworm caterpillars emerge from their overwintering state and feed from May through June or July. The caterpillars will go through several molts and then form pupae. Emerging later as medium-sized, gray-and-rust-colored adult moths in July, they will live for only two weeks and have sex that lasts about three hours each time. If a male moth has an excellent nutritional background, he will grow bigger and when mating, transfer to the female a "nuptial gift," a spermatophore containing additional nutrients, a big plus for females who may have only a few mature eggs. The female moth will lay eggs, the new larvae hatch, disperse, and overwinter in hibernacula.[2]

The eastern spruce budworm (*Choristoneura fumiferana*) is highly destructive to the boreal forest, yet highly productive for bird procreation. Once a spruce budworm outbreak occurs, it can remain in an area for a decade or more. Tree mortality starts after about four or five years of severe defoliation.[3]

This spring Evening Grosbeaks were feeding growing babies, and budworms were reproducing. But not all was peaceful in the boreal forest. There was a sense in the background, like the beginning drumbeats of "Bolero," but ominous, as if something might go terribly wrong.

Male with small caterpillar

## DEEPER DIVE

How the Evening Grosbeak (formerly called *Hesperiphona vespertina*) got its name:

> "Its generic name is derived from the Greek, referring to the Hesperides, 'Daughters of Night,' who dwelt on the western verge of the world where the sun goes down. It was discovered in 1823 by Henry R. Schoolcraft and named in 1825 by W. Cooper from a specimen taken at Sault Ste. Marie, Michigan. It was called the Evening Grosbeak as it was then observed to sing only at evening. Whatever may have been its distribution and habits then, it is no longer a distinctly western bird nor does it sing only at sundown."[26]

The female Evening Grosbeak suddenly looked up toward the sun, which had turned eerily orange. A light haze of gray smoke began to fill the air, and minuscule particles of burned forest drifted down on her nest.

Unknown to her, 360 miles away, terrible fires were burning the boreal forest.

At 1.2 billion acres, the North American boreal is the largest intact forest remaining on earth, home to 1–3 billion birds of 325 species that arrive there to breed in summer, including Evening Grosbeaks.[4] The forest stores twice as much carbon as tropical forests, which helps to slow climate change.

Record-setting numbers of fires, over one thousand, exacerbated by the warming effects of climate change, raged in northwest Ontario that year, sending smoke as far away as the Eastern Seaboard. The fires did not reach the budworm outbreak where she was, at least not that summer.

What is known is that Evening Grosbeaks fuel their population growth by feeding on budworms. Budworms boost their populations by feeding on spruce trees. Spruce trees become budworms, budworms become Evening Grosbeaks in the interconnected web of life.

The unknown is the drumbeat of climate change, increasing fires, and potential destruction—of boreal birds, budworms, and the boreal forest whose trees mitigate global warming. Evening Grosbeaks already have suffered a population decline of 92% since 1970, making them about the steepest declining landbird species on the continent. Will there be continuing dawns for Evening Grosbeaks, or a final sunset?

## IDENTIFICATION

**Size:** L 8"

**Shape:** Medium-sized, short-legged, large-headed bird with a very deep-based conical bill and relatively short, notched tail. Line of culmen fairly continuous with flattened forehead and shallow.

**Both Sexes:** Bill pale greenish in spring and summer, paler cream/yellow in winter.

**Adult Male:** Bright yellow eyebrow and forehead, contrasting with the rest of dark head; underparts (including undertail coverts) deep yellow; wings and tail black except for white tertials, inner secondaries, and inner greater coverts.

**Adult Female:** Grayish head and back separated by dull yellowish collar; pale gray to buffy-gray chest and belly; white undertail coverts; blackish wings with grayish tertials, inner secondaries, and inner greater coverts; white patch at base of primaries conspicuous in flight.

**Juv:** (June–Oct.) Like adult female but browner overall and with a yellow wash to inner greater coverts; as in adult, juvenile female has white patch at base of primaries; male has none.

### *SUBSPECIES*

Here we follow Grinnell's 1917 assessment of 5 subspecies based on recordings over the last several decades[5] and new information published by Sewall et al. in 2004[6] showing 5 call types that largely match the ranges of the 5 subspecies. Extensive recordings over the past 50+ years support the recognition of the 5 subspecies.

The American Ornithological Society last recognized 3 Evening Grosbeak subspecies, *C. v. brooksi, C. v. vespertinus,* and *C. v. montanus* in 1957 (at that time, the American Ornithologists' Union) as they combined 2 other subspecies *C. v. warreni* and *C. v. californicus* under *C. v. brooksi*. The reason was that *C. v. brooksi* is a widely ranging irruptive in much of the West, occurring in the ranges of *C. v. warreni* and *C. v. californicus,* something that was not known at the time ornithologists were determining subspecies designations. Since the morphological differences of those subspecies are slight and even somewhat obscured by individual variation, ornithologists grouped them under *C. v. brooksi*, thereby subsuming *C. v. warreni* and *C. v. californicus* under *C. v. brooksi*.

Adult m. NY/11

Adult f. NY/05

Adult m. BC/06

Adult f. NY/11

Adult m. CA/06

Adult, partially leucistic WI/12

The following is a list of the subspecies, morphology, call types, and ranges. A study on Types 1, 2, and 4 found no differences in body size, but statistically significant differences were found in females' bill measurement.[7]

1. *brooksi*/Type 1 (coastal AK, mainly BC to s. AZ, NM, w. TX, and to MX border and east to MO): Bill long and thick; female back darker and sooty, male frontal yellow bar broad.

2. *californicus*/Type 2 (Sierra Nevada and to Cascades of OR, rarely to WA to north and to UT): Bill intermediate in thickness between Type 3 and Type 5; female back light brown-gray, male frontal bar relatively narrow.

3. *vespertinus*/Type 3 (maybe AB and northeastern BC, ON, QC, MN, to east coast North America): Shortest and thickest bill; female back tinged gray, male eyebrow broad.

4. *warreni*/Type 4 (southern Rockies of WY to UT, CO and south to central AZ and NM): Bill of intermediate thickness, but more slender than Type 3; female back slightly paler, male frontal bar broad.

5. *montanus*/Type 5 (s.e. AZ, NM and MX): Least common call type; more slender, longer, and more curved bill than any of the other call types, female back medium-pale brown with buffy tinge, male frontal bar thin.

### *SIMILAR SPECIES*

Male Hooded Grosbeak (*Coccothraustes abeillei*) of Mexico is distinguished by entirely black head with no yellow supercilium as in male Evening Grosbeak. Female Hooded Grosbeak is distinguished by a black forehead and crown; female Evening Grosbeak is grayer. The Hawfinch (*Coccothraustes coccothraustes*) of Eurasia, a vagrant in the United States and Canada, is a rich brown, with a distinctive black pattern enclosing eye, lore, base of bill, and chin, and lacks any yellow in plumage like Evening Grosbeak.[8]

## DISTRIBUTION

Breeding range is across Canada, the northern tier of the Great Lakes states, into the Northeast, and the western mountainous areas of the United States and Mexico.

Since Evening Grosbeak is a nomadic species, more research and recordings are needed to determine exactly where different flight call types occur and co-occur. See the Research and Conservation chapter to learn where to contribute recordings. The map shows where the call types most commonly occur. However, there is some overlap, and the area across Canada between Types 1 and 3 is not fully understood. During irruptive years, Type 1, which is widely irruptive in the West, can be found with Type 2 in southern Oregon into California, with Type 4 in the southern Rockies, with Type 3 in Alberta, and potentially with Type 5 in southern Arizona and New Mexico. During large winter irruptions, Type 3 can be found southward to Florida, and Type 1 southward to near the Mexico border in Arizona and New Mexico, touching or overlapping in range with Type 5.

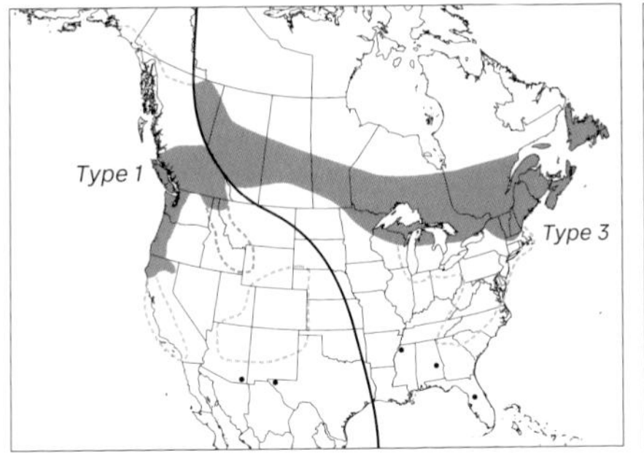


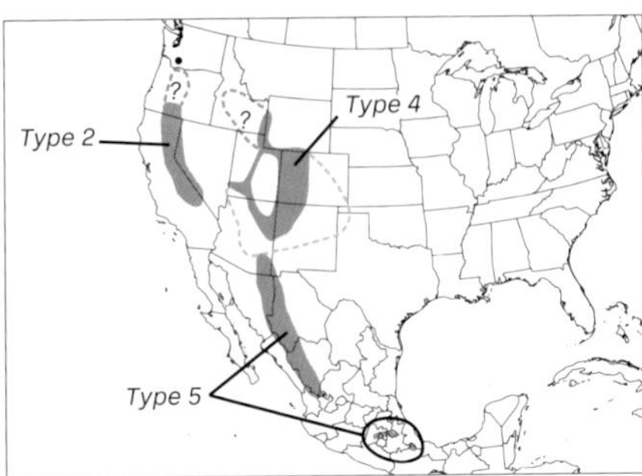


Year Round
Non-Breeding

## LANGUAGE

### *MALE*

Evening Grosbeaks do not appear to have the well-developed song consisting of a long series of melodious, warbling vocalizations that is typical of many finch species. What may function as song for Evening Grosbeaks is a repetitive, stereotyped pattern of one or several *breet* notes, sometimes with *pzeer* or *peer* type notes given in a series by perched birds.[9] Can be given in the first couple of hours after dusk. Song is given mainly April to June by males. More study of song is needed for the five call types.

### *MALE AND FEMALE*

The main diagnosable Evening Grosbeak flight/contact call is variations on the *peer* or *pzeer* call given by each of the five call types, specific to that type and thus likely aiding individuals in recognition of their group and even potential mates.

Evening Grosbeaks also give trill calls near their nest, soft *chirp* calls in flocks, and chatters[10] or chuckles (Tom Hahn, personal communication). A soft, rising alarm *wink* call is also given (Laura Erickson and Ryan Brady, personal communication).

Below are descriptions of each call type.

The call types were first described by Sewall, Kelsey, and Hahn[11] and were mostly geographically distinct, approximately matching the ranges previously described for the 5 subspecies of Grinnell 1917.

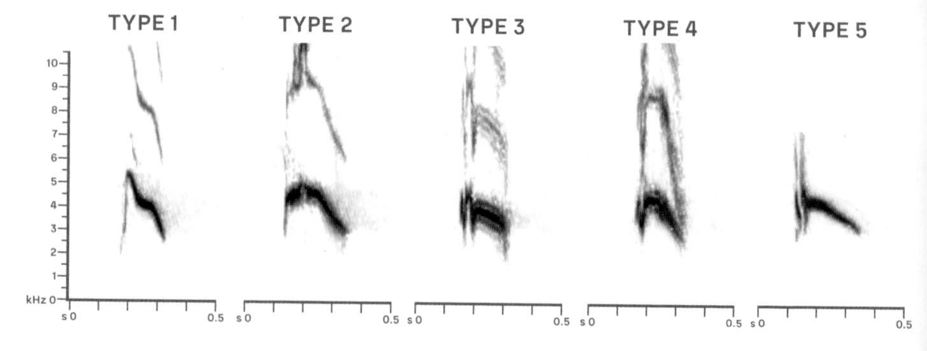

Call types 1, 2, 3, 4, 5

**Type 1** (ssp. *brooksi*) *chee-er* is a rich, pure tone that begins high, rises, strongly descends, then plateaus midway and descends farther. Most distinctive.

**Type 2** (ssp. *californicus*) *tee-oo* distinctively rises, then drops gradually. Calls are high, thin, and clear.

**Type 3** (ssp. *vespertinus*) *prree* starts with a harsh, trilled burst, then descends slightly. Sounds a bit like the call of a House Sparrow. There could be a second eastern call type, but more study is needed.

**Type 4** (ssp. *warreni*) *p-teer* drops rapidly, rises, then drops slowly. Separated from similar Type 2 by burrier sound.

**Type 5** (ssp. *montanus*) *chee* starts with short drop, then loud peak, and slow decline. Has a ringing, piercing quality.

## HABITAT AND DIET

Across the boreal, Evening Grosbeaks occur in a variety of mixed-conifer forest types, and during breeding, often in areas of spruce budworm outbreaks. In western areas they are found in mixed deciduous-conifer, spruce-fir and pine habitats. In eastern areas of North America and Canada, they breed primarily in coniferous woodland habitat, especially with spruce and balsam fir, and in the Northeast also in mixed deciduous-coniferous forests. Wintering habitat includes coniferous or deciduous remote woodlands and sometimes northern suburban areas, especially with bird feeders.

During summer, Evening Grosbeaks often consume insects, especially spruce budworm larvae when outbreaks occur. Grosbeaks eat a wide variety of buds and tree seeds of box elder, black locust, maples, tulip poplar, ash, apples, and pines. They eat fruits such as winterberry, hawthorn, cherries, and apples, consuming the pits but not so much the flesh. Their large, powerful bill can crack open a big fruit pit and extract the cotyledon (the first leaf within the embryo of a seed plant). Salt-laden sandy soils, and sanded and salted roadways are used for gritting in winter. Such areas can be dangerous because of traffic. Grosbeaks quench their thirst in winter by eating snow, and they may sip sap from maples in spring. Call Type 5 (ssp. *montanus*) frequent pine forests, and thus appear to feed on pine seeds more frequently than the other call types.

Female eating box elder seeds

A study on call types that included bill measurements of length (length of culmen) and width (width between distal tips of nares) found bill-width differences in males between call types but, perhaps more interestingly, statistical differences in female bill width and length. Since differences in bill measurements may be associated with different diets, it's possible that Evening Grosbeak call types differ in their foraging efficiency on certain foods—much like Red Crossbills, which also have different call types and bill measurements and perform better on different foods. This is an area for further study in Evening Grosbeaks.[12]

## AT YOUR FEEDER

Everyone who has had a large flock of "Evebeaks" descend on their bird feeder and consume large quantities of sunflower seeds knows why their nickname is "grocery-beaks" or "grosspigs." Bill Sheehan in northern Maine estimated he went through almost two tons of sunflower seed during the winter of 2021–2022. Black oil sunflower seeds are a favorite, either hulled or in-shell, and because of their big, powerful beaks, grosbeaks can even eat the large gray-striped sunflower. Due to their beak and body size, grosbeaks prefer hopper and platform feeders or large tube feeders with longer perches.

You may see aggression at feeders, with crown feathers raised and bills jabbed toward subordinates. Adult males are dominant over young males, and both are dominant over females at feeders in winter. In a large feeding flock, often you'll see mostly males on the feeder, with the females on the ground. Young females dominate adult females, especially in late summer.[13] The Evening Grosbeak would have been more aptly named the Morning Grosbeak since birds at feeders are primarily seen morning to early afternoon under most conditions.

## MOVEMENTS AND IRRUPTIONS

The history of Evening Grosbeak movements and irruptions involves a magic carpet ride along what Tavener 1921 in Bent[14] called a "baited Highway" of box elder trees. Starting in the mid to late 1800s, Evening Grosbeaks began appearing in the East. By 1965 they were found in Newfoundland and the eastern range expansion was complete. These Evening Grosbeaks are believed to be Call Type 3 since no other call type (up to the writing of this guide) has ever been recorded in East Coast states.

Food scarcity likely prompted these grosbeak irruptions. Box elder, widely planted throughout the prairie pothole region of central Canada and the American Midwest and the East, holds its seeds in winter, providing a refueling stop for wave after pulsing wave of hungry grosbeaks riding east across Canada to—eventually—the eastern shores of North America. Plantings of pin cherry, another favorite grosbeak food, and increasing numbers of bird feeders also provided fuel.

The magic carpet rides may have moved grosbeaks, but what really allowed them to stay and breed in new areas in the early 1900s was the burgeoning spruce budworm outbreaks they encountered. While destructive to boreal forest trees, spruce budworms were like manna, a sudden advantage, to Evening Grosbeaks who must feed their growing young a protein source.

Large spruce budworm infestations occurred in "1910–1920, 1945–1955 and 1968–1985 decimating 10, 25, and 55 million hectares."[15] The current spruce budworm outbreak, which started in eastern Canada around 2011–2012, is estimated to be around 23 million hectares (Tyler Hoar, personal communication). The massive budworm infestation in the 1970s began in the late 1960s, diminished in the mid-1980s and resulted in the defoliation of large amounts of boreal forest from Lake Superior to the Atlantic.[16] Many Evening Grosbeak irruptions coincided with these outbreaks. Christmas Bird Count data from the 1960s to early 1990s showed the percentage of sites reporting Evening Grosbeaks had increased high values between 1968 and 1985 from Ontario through the Great Lakes, eastern Canada, and New England.[17] They were even witnessed every year on the Ithaca Christmas Bird count, which is south of the boreal forest, between 1967 and 1991.

Since 1960, Type 3 has irrupted in the East in numbers in 1962, 1964, 1969, 1970, 1972, 1973, 1976, 1978, 1981, 1984, 1986, 1991, 1992, 1994, 1996, 1998, and 2021.[18] There were small irruptions in 2007 and 2019 and other years between 1998 and 2021, including the 2020–2021 irruption, the largest in nearly 25 years, but these were still of a much smaller magnitude than those reported during the spruce budworm outbreak of 1965–1988.

Noteworthy eBird reports in 2021 included Type 1 recorded in Iowa and Minnesota.[19] After many decades' absence, eBird reports indicated Type 3 recorded in the superflight irruption of 2020–2021 to the Gulf States of Mississippi, Alabama, Georgia, and Florida.[20]

As the spruce budworm outbreak continued to expand, another large irruption occurred during the winter of 2022–2023, likely the third largest in the East since the late 1980s, but still smaller than the 2020–2021 irruption.

## EVENING GROSBEAK CALL TYPE MOVEMENTS AND IRRUPTIONS

**Type 1.** Based on recordings we know Type 1 of the Pacific Northwest is by far the most abundant, widespread, and irruptive call type in the West, irrupting to areas throughout much of the West even to the Mexico border. Rarely occurs north to coastal Alaska or east to Iowa. Type 1 would be the most likely to co-occur with Type 3 in the East.

**Type 2** is seemingly quite sedentary, staying mostly in the Sierra Nevada and southern Cascades. This less common call type rarely wanders north to southern Washington or east to Utah where it overlaps with Call Type 1 and rarely Type 4.

**Type 3,** the boreal forest call type, is the big irruptive call type found in the East, which can irrupt south as far as Florida, as it did in the 2020–2021 superflight. Before its population dropped after the 1980s it made often biennial irruptions even as far as Georgia, but irruptions have been much smaller and infrequent south of Pennsylvania in the last 20+ years.

**Type 4,** which has a core range in the southern Rockies, occasionally irrupts altitudinally to foothills of the Rockies. Small numbers were seen in the lowlands of the Rockies in 2017, and again to the foothills and even to the panhandle of Texas in 2022–2023, but more recordings are needed to know the periodicity of such events.

**Type 5** appears to be quite uncommon, even in its core range in Mexico. Appears to be rare and erratic in Arizona and New Mexico in the United States. Hard to find even in apparently ideal habitat, though the area around Cofre de Perote, Veracruz, does seem to offer the best chance of finding it.

## BREEDING BEHAVIOR

### *TERRITORY*

Evening Grosbeaks break down into smaller flocks from their large, gregarious wintering flocks for the breeding season. They arrive at breeding areas, where they sometimes nest semicolonially, and pairs quickly begin nesting activities. Grosbeaks can be quite tolerant of one another during breeding, and other grosbeaks near their nest tree are not driven off. There is no territoriality as such, and no defense of an area containing food resources. Their food may be distributed in sometimes very abundant patches. A large outbreak of spruce budworms can be a magnet for grosbeak nesting.

### *COURTSHIP*

Evening Grosbeaks cement their pair bonds through courtship feeding, touching bills, and the male displaying with wings spread and quivering. The male delivers tree buds and seeds while courting the female. While reportedly monogamous, rarely males can be polygynous and breed with two females at a time. In a study in the Colorado mountains, polygyny was documented in one of 64 nests.[21] This needs more research.

### *NESTING*

**Timing:** June to August
**Nest:** Sparse, flattened saucer, outside diameter 4.5–5.5 in., with a base of twigs, roots, and mosses lined with grasses, rootlets, and pine needles. Placed in shrubs, or coniferous or deciduous trees, such as pines, spruces, firs, maples, beech, willows, and oaks, usually at 60–80% of the tree's height at 10 ft. or less from the trunk. Nest can be 15 ft. off the ground in shrubs to 100 ft. higher up in trees.
**Eggs:** 2–5, light blue or blue-green with splotches of purplish
**Incubation:** 12–14 days
**Nestling period:** 13–14 days
**Broods:** 1–2

Evening Grosbeaks are very secretive about nesting, quietly collecting nest materials and laying eggs. The female constructs the nest, with the male occasionally bringing in material, and they may give calls, soft calls, trills, and soft trills during building. Nests placed in open areas in larger trees near the trunk, facing south, are more successful.[22]

Males call from perches near the nest tree. Females lay 2–5 eggs, and males feed females by regurgitation while they are on the nest. Females do all the incubation and most of the feeding of young during the nestling stage. Both adults keep the nest clean by removing fecal sacs.

The female broods the young for most of the nestling period, ending brooding as soon as one nestling fledges. The nestlings do not fledge simultaneously but leave the nest at 13–14 days. Both adults feed the fledglings, the male feeding them more.

The fledglings stay in the nesting area for 2 to 5 days and beg for food with trilling calls when parents are evident. Parents often bring their young to sunflower feeders, if accessible. The adults feed the young into August or September. At 3 months of age, the young move around with the adults in flocks, and as winter sets in, birds may number in the hundreds.

In adult Evening Grosbeaks, the sex ratio may depend on geographic location,[23] but more study is needed during the breeding season. Like many finch species, males appear to winter more north of females.

## MOLT

The Evening Grosbeak is a species that differs little in appearance between seasons for either sex. They fully molt once at the end of breeding. Prebreeding molt includes some head and neck feathers. As they prepare for the breeding season, the most striking difference in their appearance is when male and female beak color changes in spring from yellow to a beautiful lime green.

## CONSERVATION

Evening Grosbeaks were listed as a species of special concern in Canada in 2016, due to long-term and significant declines in their population. Partners in Flight estimates the overall population of this grosbeak has declined 92% since 1970, and these declines have only deepened since 1985. Project FeederWatch indicates a significant range-wide decline in Evening Grosbeak populations from 1988 to 2006.[24] The 2022 State of the Birds report lists the Evening Grosbeak as an urgent action

Adult m. with green beak

Leucistic Evening Grosbeak

"tipping point" species—birds that have lost 50% or more of their populations during 1970–2019 and are on a trajectory to lose another 50% if nothing changes.[25] Evening Grosbeak is ranked 13 out of 20 on the Partners in Flight Continental Concern Score and is a "D" Yellow Watch List species with a declining population. Population declines have been attributed to habitat loss, management reduction of spruce budworm populations, car collisions, and possibly disease.

Efforts are underway to understand the Evening Grosbeak declines, including gaining a better understanding of grosbeak breeding, migration, and wintering areas.

Ornithologists from the Pennsylvania Natural Heritage Program at the Western Pennsylvania Conservancy (WPC) and Powdermill Avian Research Center at the Carnegie Museum of Natural History (CMNH) began Evening Grosbeak tracking studies in 2017. In 2021 WPC and CMNH teamed with the Finch Research Network (FiRN), expanded their Evening Grosbeak project, and secured additional resources from the Knobloch Family Foundation through the Road to Recovery initiative. The tracking project continued in 2022 through March 2023, and much is being learned. Read the Research and Conservation chapter for the complete story of what the project is finding and implementing to help this severely declining species.

# PINE GROSBEAK

*Pinicola enucleator*

> *Do birds come to you, or do you come to birds? What is the spark that ignites the fire that becomes the destiny of human-animal bonding in nature? What is the moment in time and space, like the long football pass that becomes the touchdown, when you know in your soul you connect and are hooked?*
>
> —Lillian Quinn Stokes

## QUICK TAKE

I crouched down in the crowded commercial parking lot as trucks whizzed by. Adrenaline pumping, my entire being was focused on a beautiful red bird that had just landed on the gray pavement at the edge of a small island planted with crabapples. I lifted my handheld camera, locked the autofocus on my prize, and fired away. Touchdown! Through the lens, I had connected with this stunning avian species and received the ninety-nine-yard pass. I was hooked. A large truck then barreled by and flushed the flock of forty Pine Grosbeaks, who disappeared over the roof of the auto parts store into the blue horizon.

Pine Grosbeaks are beautiful, and also a dichotomy: close and easily seen during irruptions versus far and difficult to see in remote breeding areas. Seed, conifer bud, and fruit eaters, they breed in the boreal forests of North America (also in western montane coniferous and coastal Alaskan and British Columbian rainforests), rarely venturing far. However, when winter food supplies crash in the boreal, especially in big irruption years, they flee to southern Canada and the northern United States.

One of the best places to find them then, in the East, is in ornamental fruit trees, especially crabapples, in commercial parking lots and residential areas. These "parrots of the north" are large birds with large bills, who slowly climb, often using their beak, around the crabapples, chomping off and discarding bits of pulp to access the seeds inside. The ground below the trees becomes a red-orange mosaic.

There are nine subspecies of Pine Grosbeaks, five breeding in North America (and one a casual vagrant), and four breeding in Eurasia.[1] The main subspecies found in the East and across most of Canada, and the one that is most irruptive in the upper part of the eastern United States, is *P. e. leucura*. In the Rockies, it's *P. e. montana;* in California, *P. e. californica;* in the Pacific Northwest, *P. e. flammula;* and in the Queen Charlotte Islands of British Columbia, *P. e. carlottae*. Research into their physiogeographical history shows another dichotomy: two branching ancestral lines. The Pine Grosbeak subspecies in North America are more closely related to one another than they are to the birds in Eurasia. Thus, Pine Grosbeaks have

Pine Grosbeak eating crabapples on the ground in the parking lot

Male LQS photographed in the parking lot

divergent lineages in each of the northern continents, perhaps because the boreal forests of those continents have been isolated since the Pliocene epoch, 5.33 million to 2.58 million years ago.[2]

North American Pine Grosbeak subspecies differ in size and bill dimensions and in tones of male plumage from pinkish to deeper red. Individual males in the boreal vary in the redness of their plumage, but those in coastal Alaska have more orangish plumage, and those in the Queen Charlotte Islands are darkest. Different subspecies also have different flight/contact calls to keep the flock together. Flight call genetics and variation need more study.

The above experience was a magical day for me. Determined to see all eight of the irruptive finch species in the superflight 2020–2021 year, I especially wanted to photograph an adult male Pine Grosbeak, something I had never done. I searched many areas that day, then encountered another birder who gave me a tip that some irruptive finches were in a town twenty-five miles away. I took the same leap of faith a receiver does when he heads downfield to the end zone, being open to what the universe would deliver. Faith paid off. The adult male Pine Grosbeak and I connected. If I had come ten minutes later, I would have missed him.

The intersection of time and space that delivers the spark of a magical connection to birds and nature is open to all. You just have to take the leap.

## FUN FACT

The Pine Grosbeak is closely related to bullfinches of the genus *Pyrrhula*, which mostly occur across Asia.

## IDENTIFICATION

**Size:** L 9"

**Shape:** Medium-sized, deep-chested, deep-bellied, broad-necked bird with a fairly long notched tail and short, deep-based bill with a curved culmen.

**Both Sexes:** Two broad white wingbars on blackish wings (upper wingbar may be hidden); broad white edges to tertials and secondaries; blackish bill.

**Adult Male:** Variable shades and extent of pinkish-red to red to orangish-red on the head, back, breast, and sometimes below (see Subspecies); rest of body gray.

**Adult Female:** Body mostly gray with olive, bronze to orangish or reddish-brown on head and rump (sometimes a hint on breast).

**1st Year:** Like adult female (Sept.–Mar.); in 1st summer (Apr.–Aug.), male can have a few pink or reddish body feathers.

**Juv:** (June–Sept.) Mostly brown with buffy wingbars.

### *SUBSPECIES*

There are 9 subspecies worldwide; 5 subspecies breed in North America: *P. e. flammula, P. e. leucura, P. e. carlottae, P. e. montana* and *P. e. californica*. Subspecies *P. e. kamtschatkensis* is a casual vagrant to the western Aleutian Islands and Pribilofs. The bills of subspecies found in North America are shorter, broader, and deeper, with ssp. *leucura* in the East the broadest and deepest.[3]

*P. e. leucura* (cent. AK–n.e. BC east to NF–CT) variably sized, m. breast and flanks pale red to red, varying individually with no consistency geographically; *P. e. montana* (cent. BC–AZ and NM) large, m. breast dark red, flanks mostly gray; *P. e. californica* (e. CA) medium-sized, m. breast dull red, flanks mostly gray; *P. e. flammula* (s. cent. AK–n.w. BC) medium-sized, m. breast and flanks bright red; *P. e. carlottae* (w. cent.-s.w. BC is.) small, m. breast and flanks dark red; *P. e. kamtschatkensis* (vag. to w. AK) medium to small, m. breast and flanks bright red.

### *SIMILAR SPECIES*

White-winged Crossbill is similar in that it's the same general shade of pinky-red (males), but Pine Grosbeak is a stockier bird with gray underparts, less bold white wingbars, and the bill is conical and not crossed.

Adult m. MN/01
F./imm. NH/11
Adult m. AK/02
F./imm. NH/01
M. MN/01
F./imm. NH/01

## DISTRIBUTION

Breeds from Alaska east to Newfoundland and Nova Scotia, south in the western mountains to California, and down to Arizona and northwestern Maine. Winters south to the Dakotas and New York, and very rarely to Pennsylvania and New Jersey.

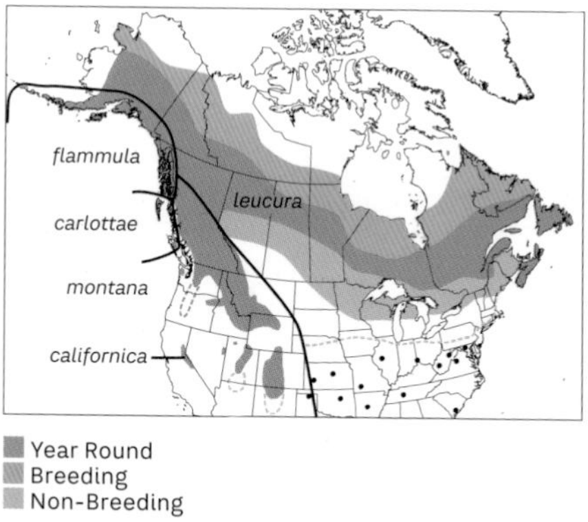

flammula
carlottae
montana
californica
leucura

Year Round
Breeding
Non-Breeding

### *SUBSPECIES DISTRIBUTION*[4]

#### PACIFIC NORTHWEST

*P. e flammula* breeding—Alaskan Peninsula coastal rainforests, Kodiak Island to s.e. Alaska, n.w. British Columbia (Stikine River); wintering—occasionally south to Vancouver Island, northern British Columbia coast.

#### QUEEN CHARLOTTE ISLANDS

*P. e. carlottae* resident in Queen Charlotte Islands, British Columbia, and may occur on northern Vancouver Island and nearby coastal British Columbia. This subspecies needs more study as it could be monophyletic, thus warranting species status.

#### ROCKY MOUNTAINS

*P. e. montana* breeding—from Rocky Mountains in northern British Columbia to New Mexico and Arizona; wintering—to lower elevations of Rocky Mountains.

#### CALIFORNIA

*P. e. californica* resident Sierra Nevada, California.

#### CANADA AND UPPER UNITED STATES

*P. e. leucura* breeding—boreal and taiga zones from Newfoundland, Nova Scotia, southern Quebec, and northwestern Maine across to Alaska; wintering—irrupts at irregular 4–7 year intervals south of the boreal with records as far south as Arkansas and South Carolina.

## LANGUAGE

### *MALE*

Song during breeding consists of rich warbled sequences, with few repeated notes, reminiscent of Purple Finches, may include imitations of other species. Can be stereotyped or grade into a longer version. Male also sings a softer, almost ventriloquist song near female and while she's incubating. The different subspecies may have similar songs, but this needs more study.

### *FEMALE*

Females rarely sing.[5] Note that first-year males, which look like adult females, can sing. Female also gives loud rising call when fed by the male.

***MALE AND FEMALE***

Flight calls are highly variable and differ geographically, and more whistled *tee-tee-tew* resembling Lesser yellowlegs in eastern *leucura* subspecies to often more modulated two-parted *pew-pew* in western subspecies, but vocal similarities with modulated and whistled calls occur where subspecies *leucura* meets subspecies *flammula* and *montana* in western boreal. Subspecies *P. e. montana, P. e. californica,* and *P. e. carlottae* have modulated call notes with less whistles.[6] Birds seem to share the same call as the other members of their flock and do not mix with other call types, which needs more research.

Other calls: Alarm call is whistled and slightly rising, trills and pips are given in close contact,[7] and a longer *tiu tiu-tiu tiu-tiu tiu-tiu* when flock departs.

Juveniles give loud one-note calls as fledglings that transition to same flight calls as parents.

***IMITATION/MIMICRY***

Song can include imitations of other nearby species, including Pine Siskin, Lesser Goldfinch, Lawrence's Goldfinch, Purple Finch, and Cassin's Finch.

## HABITAT AND DIET

Prefers open coniferous forests, especially pine, fir, and spruce, and forest edges, also subalpine areas. Habitat for subspecies *californica* is the only one that doesn't include some species of spruce. Winters in mixed coniferous-deciduous forests. Pine Grosbeaks feed primarily on a variety of spruce and pine buds and the buds

Pine Grosbeak at feeder with Evening Grosbeaks

and seeds of mountain ash, box elder, ash, and maple. They sometimes eat insects and feed insects to their growing young. During irruptions, they may occur in suburban and urban environments and eat fruits such as cherries, crabapples, and more. In some irruptions they may feed more on ash seeds and conifer buds. Pine Grosbeaks usually can be found feeding in small flocks, or, during big irruptions, in larger flocks. During the breeding season, they feed as pairs.

## AT YOUR FEEDER

Pine Grosbeaks will come to feeders for sunflower seeds, particularly in the breeding part of their range and at the northern edges of their irruptive range. Feed them black oil sunflower, in-shell or hulled, at hopper, platform, or tube feeders that accommodate their size.

## MOVEMENTS AND IRRUPTIONS

The subspecies *P. e. leucura* is the most likely to irrupt into southern Canada, the border states, and the Northeast. These irruptions seem to take place approximately every 4–7 years but can occur more frequently given increasingly unknown factors of food availability in a world of changing climate. In irruption years *P. e. leucura* may occur with subspecies *P. e. flammula* in British Columbia and Alaska and with *P. e. montana* in British Columbia, Alberta, and perhaps northern states where ranges meet.

*P. e. flammula* and *P. e. montana* are moderately irruptive in the West, but other subspecies in the West do not irrupt nearly as much. Rather than the big irruptions seen with *P. e. leucura*, and to a lesser extent *P. e. flammula* and *P. e. montana*, the other subspecies, *P. e. californica*, can move in winter altitudinally to lower areas. The Rocky Mountain subspecies, *P. e. montana*, may descend to lowland riparian thickets and aspen groves.

In the East, Pine Grosbeaks have irrupted in numbers southward during 1962, 1966, 1969, 1970, 1972, 1973, 1978, 1981, 1982, 1986, 1990, 1994, 1996, 1998, 2002, 2004, 2005, 2006, 2008, 2009, and 2013. There were irruptions that were decidedly eastern in origin in northeastern New York and the New England states in 2021 and 2023.[8]

## BREEDING BEHAVIOR

### *TERRITORY*

A study in the Uinta Mountains of southeastern Utah reported Pine Grosbeaks on territories.[9] One territory had an approximate mean diameter of 1,200 feet. Territory defense includes treetop singing from conifers. Males drove off other males who too closely approached their mates. In this study, however, a nesting pair fed with another pair in a spruce 30 yards from their nest tree.

### *COURTSHIP*

A study in Finland had Pine Grosbeaks arriving as a flock to their breeding grounds in February or March if the food was not covered with snow, but they did not form pairs or territories until May.[10] In another case, pairs formed while in flocks in Michigan in March.[11] The Utah study had a pair arriving and feeding with a mixed flock of Red Crossbills, Pine Siskins, and juncos in June.

Pine Grosbeak eating crabapples

Pine Grosbeak at nest

The male sings songs incorporating imitations of other species during breeding, and a soft song to the incubating female. Mated pairs have similar flight calls. Precopulation displaying males sway their bodies with ruffled breast feathers, wings out and tails fanned.[12] As with other finches, the male feeds the female during courtship and through part of the nestling stage when she is brooding.

### *NESTING*

**Timing:** May to July
**Nest:** Cup outside diameter, 5.9–8.6 in., bulky, of conifer twigs, roots, small and large twigs with lining of lichens, conifer needles, grasses, feathers. Concealed in conifer foliage near trunk, usually placed 6.5–13 ft. high.
**Eggs:** Usually 3–4, pale blue with large end decorated with lavender, and reddish-brown dots and splotches
**Incubation:** 13–14 days
**Nestling period:** 13–18 days
**Broods:** Unknown if more than 1

The female broods the nestlings until they are about 10 days old. Both parents feed the young mainly seeds, and also insects such as caterpillars. Similar to the rosy-finches, food is carried back to the young in gular sacs; in the Pine Grosbeak, these are slit openings along the side of the tongue about 1 mm long that go to a pouch.[13] The sacs develop only when the adults are feeding young. Pine Grosbeaks feed their young a regurgitated paste of insects and plant matter.

After leaving the nest, the young gather with family groups into small flocks and feed together. The young become independent at about 3 weeks.

## MOLT

Pine Grosbeaks molt once a year in summer and fall, the color of subspecies males varying as noted in the identification section. During winter, the plumage's lighter tips wear off so that by spring the reds and other colors appear darker. First-year males and females look very similar. It can be difficult to age and sex those birds, although females average a little duller on crown and rump, with a lighter russet on head or olive tinge on the breast than first-year males. Once those males molt in their second year, they look like adult males.

The red and yellow plumage colors on Pine Grosbeaks come from the deposition of dietary carotenoid pigments into their plumage, with processes likely similar to the well-studied House Finch, but this requires more study in the Pine Grosbeak.

## CONSERVATION

Subspecies *P. e. carlottae* of the Queen Charlotte Islands of British Columbia ranks as a species of conservation concern (Blue list, BC Conservation Data Center 2020).[14] This subspecies needs more study, as it could be monophyletic, thus warranting species status.

On the Continental Concern Score, the Pine Grosbeak rates 10 out of 20. It is listed as Least Concern on the IUCN Red List of Threatened Species.

Subspecies *P. e. californica,* at least, is estimated as vulnerable to climate change, based on research modeling the projected impact of the ongoing climate crisis.[15]

# GRAY-CROWNED ROSY-FINCH

*Leucosticte tephrocotis*

> *Their beauty in flight is enthralling. Their movements stirring and rousing, their spirits intrepid. They face gale force winds, frigid temperatures, and driving snow with aplomb. These stout birds seem to know everything about how easily to survive what is harsh and difficult for most.*
>
> —Dr. Lynne Spriggs O'Connor, "The Finches of Cloudland" from *Elk Love: A Montana Memoir*[1]

## QUICK TAKE

When it comes to survival, these hardy finches quite literally have their heads in the clouds. Theirs is not a fantasy world, but a world of cumulonimbus reality. Towering vertical giants, cumulonimbus clouds go way up there, from two thousand to fifty-two thousand feet, occurring at the mountaintop nesting levels of this remarkable finch at ten thousand feet and above.

Gray-crowned Rosy-Finches (along with their cousins, Brown-capped Rosy-Finches and Black Rosy-Finches) are likely the highest elevation breeding birds in North America. Gray-crowns even nest on the slopes of mountains such as Denali, the highest mountain on the continent at 20,310 feet. Of these rosy-finch cousins, Gray-crowned Rosy-Finches also have the broadest range. They breed at high elevation in the Brooks Range, Rocky Mountains, Cascades, and Sierra Nevada—but also breed at sea level on the Aleutian and Pribilof Islands of Alaska.

Nesting locations also vary according to the area. Nesting spots may have in common overhead protection and nearby feeding areas for seeds and insects on snowfields, glaciers, or the ground. When nests are in alpine locations, high cliff placements give protection from rodents and are in cracks and holes or under overhanging rocks. Nests can be in old, abandoned buildings on the Aleutians and Pribilofs.[2]

Gray-crowned Rosy-Finches have protections in place to thrive in their harsh environment. In the rarefied air of this mountaineering survivalist, humans might get hypoxia (low oxygen levels in their blood). But rosy-finches have adapted to survive in these conditions due to the high blood-oxygen affinity of the hemoglobin in their red blood cells.[3] This is not true for bird species that breed at lower elevations.[4]

Are Gray-crowned Rosy-Finches the complete package and secure in their future survival? Their conservation status is Least Concern, perhaps due to their wide range and numbers.

However, cumulonimbus clouds can become threatening thunderheads portending dangerous weather. So too can the climate change that would melt glaciers and destroy habitat threaten the cloudlands of these hardy finches' home. Then none of these adaptations, however magnificent, would save it.

Snowcapped Denali

## IDENTIFICATION

**Size:** L 6.25"

**Shape:** Fairly small, deep-bellied, small-headed with a short conical bill and moderate-length notched tail. Long primary projection past tertials; crown peaked when crest raised. Bill longest among rosy-finches.

**Both Sexes:** Breast feathers warm brown to cinnamon-brown without blackish centers and with variable thin pale fringes; blackish forecrown; pale silvery-gray hindcrown, which extends to the eye and sometimes through the cheek (see Subspecies), contrasts strongly with surrounding warm brown back; limited rose on brownish rear belly.

**Adult Male:** Bright pink on wings and more extensive bright pink on belly.

**Adult Female:** Duller less extensive pink on wings and belly; forecrown less extensively black. Both sexes have blackish bill in summer, yellowish in winter (f. bill color changes to yellow about 1 month earlier than m.).

**1st Year:** Like ad. But greater secondary coverts and primary edges mostly to all whitish (ad. pink in these areas); little or no pink on underparts.

**Juv:** (June–Aug.) Grayish-brown overall with pinkish to buff wingbars.

### *SUBSPECIES*

Morphologically, 4 taxa separate into 2 smaller alpine-interior brown-cheeked subspecies and 2 larger coastal, also smaller montane-dwelling, gray-cheeked subspecies.

**Brown-cheeked Group:** Medium-small; brown cheek includes *L. t. tephrocotis*; black of forecrown extends >0.66 in. from bill and contrasts with gray hindcrown; slightly dark centers to breast feathers. Birds of montane n.e. Oregon (*"wallowa"*) smaller on average with distinct dark centers on feathers of breast. *L. t. dawsoni*, black on forecrown extends <0.66 in. from bill and merges less distinctly with gray hindcrown; breast feathers with little or no dark centers.

Adult m., *tephrocotis* NM/12

Adult f., *tephrocotis* NM/12

Adult m., *dawsoni* CA/03

Adult f., *dawsoni* CA/03

Adult m. OR/06

**Gray-cheeked Group:** *L. t. griseonucha* and *L. t. littoralis*. Large to medium-small; characterized by uniformly gray auriculars and hindcrown; *L. t. griseonucha* very large (largest taxa in genus *Leucosticte*, length about 6.6–8.2 in.; mass 1.5–2 oz.); upperparts and breast chocolate brown. Birds in the Pribilof Islands (*"umbrina"*) are darker on average with dark streaks on upperparts. *L. t. littoralis* ("Hepburn's" Rosy-Finch) are slightly brighter.

### *SIMILAR SPECIES*

Black Rosy-Finch has shorter bill, black-centered breast feathers, little or no rose on underparts. While both Black and Gray-crowned Rosy-Finches have gray crowns, some subspecies of Gray-crowneds have gray cheeks, unlike Black, which always has blackish cheeks. Brown-capped Rosy-Finches are browner overall and don't have the gray crown of Black or Gray-crowned.

## DISTRIBUTION

Breeds in Alaska and mountainous regions of British Columbia, Yukon, and Alberta south to Washington, Oregon, northwest Montana, northern Idaho, and the high mountains of California. In autumn and winter, distribution shifts and includes Saskatchewan, southern Alberta, Manitoba, Wyoming, Idaho, Nevada, Utah, Colorado, New Mexico, and rarely Arizona. The wintering Alaska Islands subspecies, *L. t. griseonucha,* is resident; the California Gray-crowned Rosy-Finch, *L. t. dawsoni*, moves to lower elevations; and *L. t. littoralis* and *L. t. tephrocotis* move farther from their breeding areas.

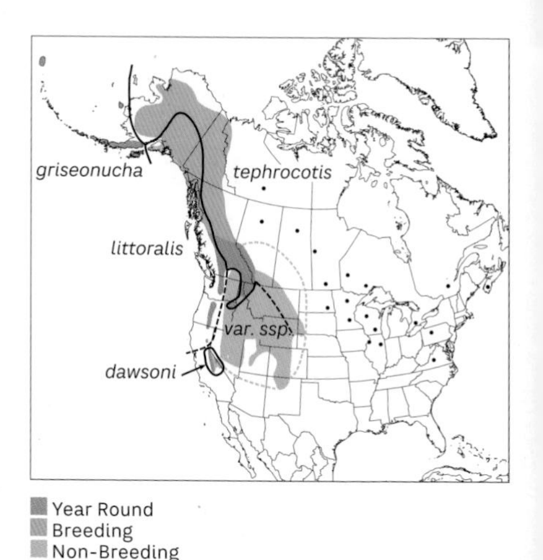


### *SUBSPECIES DISTRIBUTION*

### GRAY-CHEEKED GROUP

*L. t. griseonucha* breeding and wintering, Aleutian-Kodiak and Pribilof Is. AK.
*L. t. littoralis* breeding montane w.c. AK–s.w. Yuk, n.c. CA, wintering to c. MT–n. NM.

### BROWN-CHEEKED GROUP

*L. t. tephrocotis* breeding montane c. Yuk–n.e. OR to n.w. MT, wintering to n.e. CA–AZ–NM.
*L. t. dawsoni* Resident montane e. CA.

Adult m., *littoralis* "Hepburn's" NM/12

Adult f., *littoralis* "Hepburn's" NH/12

Adult m. St. Paul, AK/08

Adult m., *griseonucha* Adak, AK/05

Juv. St. Paul, AK/08

## LANGUAGE

Note: The vocalizations of all three species of rosy-finch are extremely similar. More research is needed on the breeding grounds to reveal what vocalization differences exist, if any, across the three rosy-finches.

### *MALE*

Song is thought to consist of *chew* calls delivered in loud, long series of notes, but the lines between songs and calls in the rosy-finches blur. Song of *chew* calls are strung together and vary in pitch and intensity, and are interspersed at times with other call notes. May have a courtship song of rapid *chews* with high-pitched notes included, like those of other rosy-finches. Song is given from perches, circling flights, and at the end of the day near cliffs where they nest.

### *FEMALE*

Female reported to sing quietly and infrequently in Aleutians, but more study is needed.[5]

### *MALE AND FEMALE*

The most conspicuous call of this species is *chew* used extensively as part of song. This call ascends briefly, then loud, buzzy, and descending in pitch. *Chew* calls vary considerably in pitch within and among individuals. A soft *chuh-chuh-chuh,* varying in repetitions, is often given (Tom Hahn, personal communication). Additional calls include *che-er, vreer, chirp, cheep,* and *peent*. Calls may be used in different

situations such as chases, flight, roosting, predator mobbing, and alarm. Phrases consisting of a variety of strung-together calls could also serve as different songs. Different calls are thought to serve separate functions and are an area that remains in need of more study.

Worth looking into is whether calls differ between the mountaintop Brown-capped Rosy-Finch (*weu* has three bands of frequency) and the Aleutian Islands breeding Gray-crowned Rosy-Finch, *L. t. griseonucha*, (*see-ew* more of a pure tone with a narrow, concentrated frequency) due to higher background noise and windy climatic conditions along the Alaskan islands. Shreeve[6] makes mention of this, but his sample size is small.

## HABITAT AND DIET

Gray-crowned Rosy-Finches inhabit maritime tundra areas in the Aleutian and Pribilof Islands of Alaska, and high alpine tundra areas above timberline in mountain ranges in North America. Breeding habitats include rocky areas, talus substrate, and cliff areas near snowfields and glaciers, especially in habitat lacking conifers.[7] Uses similar habitats in winter but will also move nomadically in response to snow levels to lower elevation in mountain valleys, open environments with a variety of vegetation, and feeders in towns and villages.

Adult male feeding at edge of snowbank, OR

Gray-crowned Rosy-Finches feed on a wide variety of plant matter, including leaves, buds, berries, seeds, depending on the areas where they nest. In summer, they and their young eat more insects such as cutworms, beetles, weevils, and gnats. Mayflies are a very important part of their diet, constituting 38% of their food in summer.[8] In a study in the Sierra Nevada, there were 5.9 times more Gray-crowned Rosy-Finches at fishless lakes than lakes with introduced nonnative trout that eat mayflies.[9] Gray-crowns can pick insects from the ground or foliage and even fly out to grab an insect in midair. Insects blown onto the snow are important in the early summer diet. In winter seeds are the predominate food.

## AT YOUR FEEDER

Gray-crowned Rosy-Finches flock to winter feeding stations in mountain areas and ski resorts, sometimes in very large numbers. A study in Montana of banded rosy-finches at two different feeding stations 25 miles apart showed they moved between the stations in winter. Their preferred foods are black oil sunflower and Nyjer®. Moving about winter feeding areas in mild weather may help them know where alternate food sources are located when the weather turns severe, and a known food source is covered.[10]

## MOVEMENTS AND IRRUPTIONS

Movements of the subspecies vary and are altitudinal, latitudinal, and mainly facultative—forced because of lack of food due to harsh winter conditions and snow cover. Movements usually occur from breeding areas in mid-October to mid-November and then back again in March and April. Rosy-finches on the Aleutian and Pribilof Islands are largely resident in winter. The California subspecies, *L. t. dawsoni,* moves to lower elevations. *L. t. littoralis* and *L. t. tephrocotis* move latitudinally, often some distance from their breeding grounds.

## BREEDING BEHAVIOR

The breeding behavior of Gray-crowned Rosy-Finches needs more study, including differences in the subspecies.

### *TERRITORY*

Gray-crowned Rosy-Finches spend the winter in flocks, and pairing with females may occur in those flocks, even before migration occurs. As spring approaches, males may become less tolerant and chase one another. Males show aggression and hop toward other males with ruffled body plumage, head retracted, and body crouched. Males fight with other males and defend females without there being a defined geographic territory.

### *COURTSHIP*

Males woo females with a variety of complex overtures. In the "wing-wave," the male may sleek his plumage, elevate tail and head, ruffle the feathers at the back of his head and droop, then slowly raise and lower wings, and walk or hop unevenly, one foot in front of the other, toward the female while giving the *chew* call. A variant of this display has the male more vertical, spreading stationary wings, exposing the underwings. The male's song is directed at females, and can increase in

Nest in cliff crevice, OR

Abandoned building, Adak Island, AK, nest site of *griseonucha*

Nest of *griseonucha* on shelf in the abandoned building, Adak Island, AK

tempo and intensity and culminate in copulation. The female engages in mutual bill touching and nibbling as part of courtship. She invites copulation by crouching with ruffled feathers, tail raised, head in, wings vibrating, irresistible to a male Gray-crowned Rosy-Finch.[11]

### *NESTING*

**Timing:** From early April through July, depending on geographic location.
**Nest:** Cup, outside diameter 2.75–6.5 in., of grasses, lichens, mosses, lined with fine grasses, fur, feathers placed in protected hollow in a cliff, in old buildings, rarely on the ground.
**Eggs:** 2–6, usually 3–5, white or creamy, sometimes with reddish or yellow-brown specks
**Incubation:** 12–16 days
**Nestling period:** 14–22 days
**Broods:** 1–2

The male does not let the female out of his sight during nesting, and he defends her and the nest site. The female will also chase intruders from the nest site. However, when the young are in the latter part of the nestling stage, the male starts guarding the nest more than guarding the female. He will stay behind after both have fed the young and perch above the nest and even roost nearby at night.

As mentioned in the Quick Take, nesting sites vary depending on geographic location and subspecies. In alpine locations Gray-crowned Rosy-Finches nest on cliffs in cracks or holes with overhead protection. In a study on Amchitka Island in the Aleutian Islands, Alaska, habitat is wet maritime tundra, and rosy-finches have a long nesting season, late April to July. They double-brood and nest in old buildings. There were 13.9 nests per 100 hectares on those islands. Protected nest locations plus few predators like hawks led to a nesting success of 54.9.[12]

The male feeds the female at the nest, but she sometimes leaves to feed on her own. After hatching, both parents feed the young. They can carry more significant amounts of food from distances, made possible by the special buccal pouches in their mouth. Fastidious parents keep the nest and the area around it clean by carrying off the fecal sacs of the young and dropping them at a distance. Once fledged, the young are fed by the parents for 2–3 weeks and follow the parents around, begging and quivering their wings. Later the young may form into same-sex flocks by fall.

Of note is a skewed sex ratio of more males than females, noted also in Black Rosy-Finch and Brown-capped Rosy-Finch.[13] A study of *L. t. griseonucha* on Adak Island, Alaska, captured more males than females in every month, with the average sex ratio of 4 males per female.[14] Even though in nestlings the ratio was 21 males to 23 females, by November the estimate of the sex ratio in juveniles showed an excess of males. Thus, long before females bred, they were scarce by their first autumn of life. Researcher D. Shreeve noted in the study, "I believe the sex differences in mobbing behavior may affect the rate of recruitment into adult flocks, and therefore explain the greater survivorship of juvenile males. Since males are more active in mobbing behavior, flock survivorship might be enhanced by the preferential selection of the relative active juvenile males (over juvenile females). Males might be accepted more readily into flocks of adults in later summer and autumn. In my observations at nests, one or more males typically mobs an approaching predator, while a single female remains concealed or assumes a stationary position."

In winter Gray-crowned Rosy-Finches can form extremely large wandering flocks of 1,000 and reportedly even 10,000 birds. They will flock with other rosy-finches and Horned Larks. Rosy-finches roost together for warmth and protection in winter in a variety of natural and built areas such as caves, cracks in cliffs, and buildings.

## MOLT

Gray-crowned Rosy-Finches molt once per year postbreeding. Pink wash on feathers of fall plumage wears off by spring, making birds more brownish. The male's bill that is black during breeding becomes more yellowish in winter, a month later than a similar change in females.

## CONSERVATION

Their conservation status is Least Concern according to the 2020 IUCN Red List. Partners in Flight rates the species 12 out of 20 on the Continental Concern Score, indicating low conservation concern. Widespread range and large numbers aided by low human disturbance at remote breeding areas, winter bird feeding, and food in agricultural fields help their populations. However, global warming remains a threat to their alpine habitats.

### FUN FACT

**Gray-crowned Rosy-Finches can drink on the wing. They hover in front of a cliff with running water, place their bill against it, and the water trickles into their mouth.**

# BLACK ROSY-FINCH

*Leucosticte atrata*

> *Although humans see reality in colour, for me, black and white has always been connected to the image's deeper truth, to its most hidden meaning.*
>
> —Peter Lindberg, photographer

## QUICK TAKE

In the high-altitude air of western mountains lives a mysterious finch whose stunning dark plumage can read black as night against the blinding whiteness of high-albedo (reflective) snowfields.

The Black Rosy-Finch may be the least known and least studied species of bird in North America. Between 1925 and 2002, only four authors reported reaching the species' nests.[1] Nests are in vertical rock cliffs and inaccessible to all except researchers with mountain-goat climbing abilities.

The Black Rosy-Finch is a beautiful species. Breeding males have a silver hind-crown, black body, bill, and face, and rose wings. Females are beautiful, too, a slight silver wash adorning their bodies as if their feathers were edged with stardust. Black Rosy-Finches nest in the high mountains of northwestern Wyoming and the nearby states of Montana, Idaho, Utah, and Oregon. In general, their breeding range lies between the ranges of their close relatives, the Gray-crowned Rosy-Finch to the north and west, and the Brown-capped Rosy-Finch to the south and east.

From 1983 to 1993, Black Rosy-Finches, along with Gray-crowned and Brown-capped Rosy-Finches, were thought to be one species with the Asian Rosy-Finch (*Leucosticte arctoa*), but further biological and genetic study has shown that they are separate species.[2]

In an October 2019 article in *Wyoming Wildlife,* Robin Kepple describes what researcher Carl Brown endured to survey Black Rosy-Finch nests as part of his master's thesis and a study for Wyoming Game and Fish and the Wyoming Cooperative Fish and Wildlife Research Unit.[3] Expert climbing and rappelling ability are essential. "Typically, Carl and his three techs were hiking several miles in and thousands of feet up just to get to the nesting habitat. These were not day hikes. They were weeklong backpack trips, done one after the other to take advantage of those handful of weeks when the weather is somewhat tolerable at those elevations in Wyoming. It really is impressive that these little birds choose to make their living in such a hostile environment."

Teton Range, WY

The results of all this work so far are substantial: Brown's study located three new Wyoming breeding areas in the Salt River, Wyoming, and Snake River Ranges, and identified fifteen Wyoming nests, raising the count nationwide from twenty-three to thirty-eight.[4]

Knowing where they breed might seem all that is needed to protect Black Rosy-Finches, a simple matter of black and white. But deeper truth plays out in shades of gray. In the punishing environment of their harsh alpine breeding area, shelf space is abundant for nest locations. But fuel is what matters to nourish bodies driven by reproductive urges. When the Black Rosy-Finches arrive in early spring, they seek the moist edges of melting white snowfields, virgin territory that uncovers succulent insects and seeds of survival.

Enter climate change, and a harsh disconnect could occur between expectations and reality. Alpine environments are especially vulnerable to rising temperatures and changing precipitation patterns.[5] What if the snow melts too early? What if there is no snow? What if there is no abundance of insect food when it is most needed for Black Rosy-Finch breeding arrivals and then their progeny? Dust from climate events can also darken the snow, making it melt. When the high-albedo (reflective) white snow and ice melt, sunlight is then absorbed by the darker ground, further heating the planet. White will become black, potentially spelling doom for a species. It will ultimately be up to humans to determine the Black Rosy-Finch's direction on the ladder to extinction and whether climate change can be mitigated. The clock is ticking.

## IDENTIFICATION

**Size:** L 6.25"

**Shape:** Fairly small, deep-bellied, small-headed bird with a short conical bill and fairly short notched tail. Long primary projection past tertials. Bill medium-length among the rosy-finches.

**Both Sexes:** Breast feathers with blackish centers and gray to brown fringes; blackish forecrown; pale silvery-gray hindcrown extends to eye and contrasts strongly with surrounding dark gray to black collar and cheek; little or no rose on belly.

**Adult Male:** Forecrown and body very black with bright rose on wings.

**Adult Female:** Forecrown and body feathers broadly edged with gray, creating a cool gray wash overall; paler pink on wings. Both sexes have blackish bill in summer, yellowish in winter (m. bill turns black sooner than f.)

**1st Winter:** Like adult but greater secondary coverts and primary edges mostly to all whitish (adults pink in these areas); little or no pink on underparts.

**Juv:** (June–Aug.) Grayish-brown overall with pinkish to buff wingbars.

### *SUBSPECIES*

Monotypic

### *SIMILAR SPECIES*

Both Black and Gray-crowned Rosy-Finches have pale gray napes that contrast strongly with the rest of the body, and as a result may be confused for each other. The Gray-crowned Rosy-Finch differs from the Black Rosy-Finch in having a longer bill, warm-brown-centered breast feathers, and more rosy underparts, and some subspecies also have gray cheeks. Brown-capped Rosy-Finches lack a pale gray nape.

## DISTRIBUTION

Breeds above tree line in mountaintop habitat from northeast Idaho and west-central Montana southward through southeastern Oregon, north, and east Nevada to southern Utah and west and north-central Wyoming (including the Wyoming, Salt River, and Snake River Ranges). The winter range extends outward south through Colorado to Arizona, the Sandia Mountains of New Mexico, and California in the southern Sierra Nevada.[6]

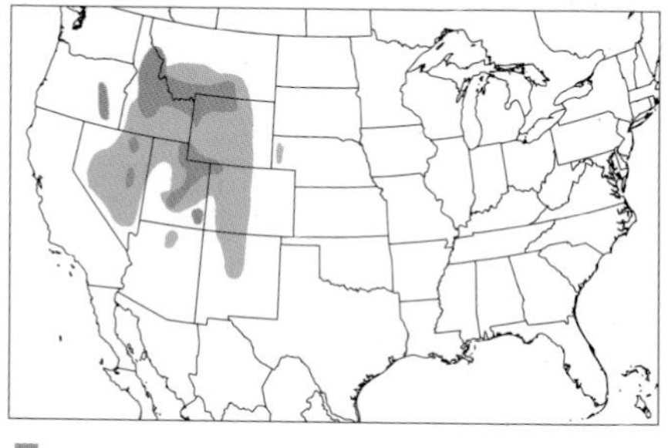

Year Round
Non-Breeding

Adult m. NM/12

Adult f. NM/12

Adult m. UT/07

Juv. UT/07

## LANGUAGE

Note: The vocalizations of all three species of rosy-finches are extremely similar. More research is needed to distinguish what differences might exist.

### *MALE*

Song is thought to consist of *chew* calls and is delivered in loud, long series of notes, but the line between songs and calls is blurry. Song of *chew* calls are strung together and vary in pitch and intensity, and are interspersed at times with other call notes. May have a courtship song of rapid *chews* with high-pitched notes included, like those of other rosy-finches. Song is given from perches, circling flights, and at the end of the day near cliffs where they nest.

### *MALE AND FEMALE*

The most conspicuous call of this species is *chew,* used extensively as part of song. This call ascends briefly, then loud, buzzy, and descending in pitch. *Chew* calls vary considerably in pitch within and among individuals. *Chew,* along with calls such as *che-er, vreer, chirp, cheep,* and *peent,* may be used in different situations such as chases, flight, roosting, predator mobbing, and alarm.[7] Some phrases consisting of a variety of strung-together calls could also serve as different songs. Different calls are thought to serve separate functions and need more study.

## HABITAT AND DIET

Black Rosy-Finches breed above timberline at 8,600 feet or more, where crevices in cliffs and rockslides provide protected nooks for nest sites, and nearby tundra snowfields and glaciers provide feeding locations. They winter in valleys, high desert plateaus, and open areas between mountain ranges when the weather turns bad, then return upward when winter winds uncover feeding spots.

Black Rosy-Finches eat a wide variety of seeds and insects blown into the area (aeolian insects), which they glean off snow surfaces or often the wet ground and meadows at melting edges of snowfields and glaciers. They may also take seeds directly from standing stalks. During breeding, insects are a big part of their diet and the main food they feed to their young in the early nestling stage. By the end of summer, adults and older nestlings switch to seeds. If foraging trips require going some distance from the nest, no worries: Black Rosy-Finches are prepared. They, like the other rosy-finches, have paired pouches under the floor of their mouth to carry food, enabling trips of up to several miles from the nest.

Black Rosy-Finches, Sandia, NM/12

## AT YOUR FEEDER

Severe winter weather will drive Black Rosy-Finches down into valleys near mountain ranges, ski resort areas, towns, and farms, and they can arrive in very large numbers at feeders. Black oil sunflower, Nyjer®, and mixed seed are preferred, but they will also eat cracked corn and millet.

## MOVEMENTS AND IRRUPTIONS

Migration and movement are largely weather dependent. In fall the birds move downslope mostly during October to mid-November. In good weather, they will sometimes remain at high-altitude mountainous areas throughout winter.[8] During windy, wet, snowy inclement weather and when deep snowpack covers food supplies, they may be forced to descend to valleys until the weather improves. There is some evidence that the sexes migrate differentially, but this needs further study.[9]

Black Rosy-Finches leave valley floor wintering sites to the east of mountains from mid-March to mid-April and probably migrate to alpine tundra breeding habitat in April. After arrival in spring, they will periodically move up and down slopes, depending on the weather.

### FUN FACT

**Rosy-finches store enough food in their crops to get them through the night in their protected roosts, with enough fuel left for foraging the next day.**

## BREEDING BEHAVIOR

### *TERRITORY*

In late winter, males become less tolerant of one another and charge and chase. Flocks arrive in early spring on their breeding grounds, and the agonistic behavior ramps up. Males threaten one another with displays such as hopping toward each other with head forward and body feathers ruffled, or running with head high and a sleeked upright posture.[10]

### *COURTSHIP*

Males turn their attention to attracting females, and some pairing may have occurred on the wintering grounds. A skewed sex ratio has been documented, with more males than females. The result is intense competition among males for a mate. Males may chase females, and courting males approach females with elaborate displays designed to wow. With head high and tipped back, front of body lowered, tail perpendicular, wings vibrating, the male holds grass in his bill and rapidly chirps.[11] He may dance back and forth in a semicircle while displaying in front of the female.[12] An interested female assumes a similar posture, chirping and elevating the rear of her body. The male then mounts her and copulates.

### *NESTING*

**Timing:** June to August
**Nest:** Cup, outside diameter about 5 in., with a base of mud and moss, woven of grasses, plant stems, lined with grasses, feathers, hair, and even fur from marmots and bighorn sheep and placed in protected holes or cracks in vertical cliffs or talus slopes.
**Eggs:** 3–6, white
**Incubation:** 12–14 days
**Nestling period:** About 18–20 days
**Broods:** 1

During nesting, the male defends a floating territory around the female, not letting other males near her, especially near the nest site. She selects the site, looking for a spot in cliffs or talus protected from the elements and out of reach of ground predators. The nest is completed quickly, and the female begins incubating about when the third egg is laid. She takes breaks to feed herself during the day, the male her constant companion on feeding trips, and he chases away other males. But the male does not spend time at the actual nest during this period. At night he roosts on nearby cliffs and does loud territorial chirping, driving away any male visitors.

The female broods and also feeds the young by herself until they are about 5 days old. Then both parents feed the nestlings, insects at first, then later seeds, and carry the fecal sacs away. The parents continue feeding the fledglings until they become independent in about 2 weeks. Fledglings follow parents, uttering piercing begging notes.

Research on the parentage of young in Black Rosy-Finch nests found that 25% of young in three nests were the result of the female mating with males other than the male who attended the nest and helped her raise the young.[13] Family groups congregate, including adults still feeding young. The young seem to form flocks at the end of the summer before the adults have flocked up.

Research by French 1959 found a skewed sex ratio of more males than females in Black Rosy-Finches,[14] also noted in Gray-crowned and Brown-capped Rosy-Finches by other researchers.[15] French reported 5.6 males per female in banded Black Rosy-Finches in winter and an estimate of 6 to 8 males per female on the breeding grounds. He even found an unbalanced sex ratio in birds in juvenal plumage—only 2 of 7 birds he collected were female.

In winter, Black Rosy-Finches often roost together, sometimes in the hundreds,[16] for warmth in protected areas like caves, mine shafts, abandoned buildings, amusement park piers, and old Cliff Swallow nests.

## MOLT

Adults have a complete molt postbreeding, and their bills turn from black to yellow with a dark tip in winter. In summer, adults do not have a prebreeding molt. Their summer plumage has more saturated shades of reddish-pink due to feather wear and the effects of solar radiation.

## CONSERVATION

Listed as Endangered by the IUCN Red List, which notes that "this species has been undergoing an extremely large decline over the last decades." Partners in Flight lists them as Red Watch List with a Continental Concern Score of 17 out of 20, since they have a small population and restricted breeding area. Black Rosy-Finches have been designated a Species of Greatest Conservation Need in Wyoming's State Wildlife Action Plan, or SWAP—a comprehensive wildlife conservation strategy to maintain the health and diversity of wildlife within a state. While they breed in many protected national parks and wilderness areas, climate change poses a threat. Large winter roost sites may also need protection.

# BROWN-CAPPED ROSY-FINCH

*Leucosticte australis*

*"Rocky Mountain High"*
—Song by John Denver and Mike Taylor

## QUICK TAKE

John Denver recorded his classic "Rocky Mountain High" in 1972, now one of the two official state songs of Colorado. It was inspired by the sense of wonder and peace he experienced in the mountains of his new home. In the lyrics, the stars are other worlds Denver observed from the Rockies. Brown-capped Rosy-Finches sing their own songs high in the Colorado mountain peaks they call home. This sociable, undaunted, beautifully rose-tinted, almost endemic species might qualify as the Colorado state bird (the Lark Sparrow officially holds that position).

Nesting at ear-popping heights of up to 14,200 feet in their summer range, they have the distinction of breeding (along with their cousins, Black and Gray-crowned Rosy-Finches) at the highest altitudes of any bird species in North America. A tight cup of roots and grasses anchored with mud is most often located in fissures and ledges of cliffs overlooking glaciers. You might need serious rock-climbing equipment and skills to reach some of the more remote nests. Due to the out-of-the-way nature of their breeding location, not many studies have been done.

Brown-capped Rosy-Finches feed on seeds in open areas at the edges of snowbanks and dine on insects plucked from the snow surface—an insect snow cone! They can travel a distance and then transport food back to their nests in twin suitcases, special paired buccal sacs beneath the floor of their mouth.

When severe winter weather moves in, most rosy-finches move out and retreat to lower elevations and feed along roadsides, in pastures, and at bird feeders. Their survival strategy is to feed heavily during the day, and huddle together at night for warmth in sheltered locations such as caves, buildings, and old Cliff Swallow nests. Nighttime temps can hit -22 degrees Fahrenheit. Brrrrr![1]

An inaccessible alpine home does not guarantee safety. This species is listed by the IUCN as Endangered, since population numbers are said to have declined by 95% between 1970 and 2014. Of concern is what a warming climate will do to this species. Models predict that if the earth warms just 2 degrees Celsius by 2050, 99% of the Brown-capped Rosy-Finch's range will be lost.[2]

Where will Brown-capped Rosy-Finches go then? Will they fly to the stars of Denver's song? And what does it mean to us to know this will be one more loss, this time of a beautiful species that thrives up high in the Rocky Mountain air?

## IDENTIFICATION

**Size:** L 6.25"

**Shape:** Fairly small, deep-bellied, small-headed bird with a short conical bill and fairly short notched tail. Long primary projection past tertials. Bill shortest among the rosy-finches.

**Both Sexes:** Breast feathers cold brown without blackish centers and with variable gray to buffy fringes; extensive rose on lower breast and belly.

**Adult Male:** Blackish forehead blending to dark gray of hindcrown, which extends to eye; this gray area on face does not contrast strongly with brown cheek. Extensive pink on belly; deep pink on wings.

**Adult Female:** Brownish forehead that blends to grayish-brown hindcrown and rest of face; little or no contrast on face; dull pink on belly, less extensive than on male; pale pink on wings. Both sexes have blackish bill in summer, yellowish in winter.

**1st Winter:** Like adult but greater secondary coverts and primary edges mostly to all whitish (adult pink in these areas); little or no pink on underparts.

**Juv:** (June–Aug.) Grayish-brown overall with pinkish to buff wingbars.

### *SUBSPECIES*

Monotypic

### *SIMILAR SPECIES*

Black and Gray-crowned Rosy-Finches have pale gray napes that contrast strongly with the rest of the body.

## DISTRIBUTION

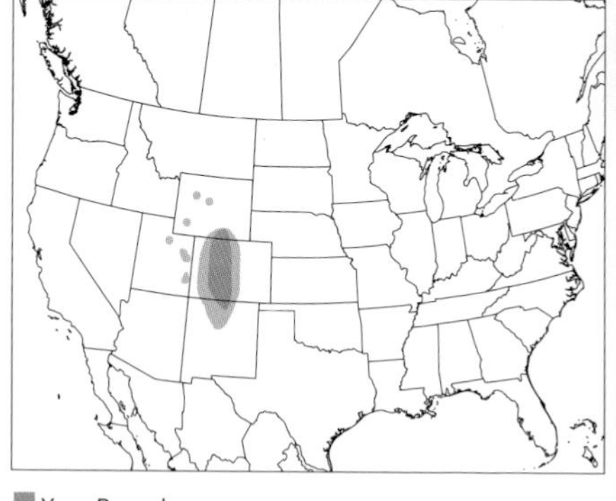


Mapping rosy-finch ranges continues to evolve since locating them is limited by their inaccessible breeding locations and their nomadic wandering during nonbreeding. Limited distribution of Brown-capped Rosy-Finches makes them the most range-restricted of the North American rosy-finches, and they breed largely on Colorado mountain peaks. They also occur in southeastern Wyoming on Medicine Bow Peak and in New Mexico in the Sangre de Cristo Mountains of Santa Fe and Taos Counties. Their distribution expands in winter and finds them in Colorado down to north-central New Mexico, and a few areas of Wyoming, including Laramie.[3]

Adult m. MN/12

Adult f. NM/12

Adult m. CO/06

1st winter NM/12

## LANGUAGE

Note: The vocalizations of all three species of rosy-finch are extremely similar, and more research is needed on their differences.

### *MALE*

Strung-together *chew* calls function as song and are given in a loud, long series that can vary in pitch, but the distinction between calls and song is blurry. Brown-capped Rosy-Finches can include high frequencies in their song during high-arousal courtship. They most commonly give song near their nest area.[4]

### *MALE AND FEMALE*

*Chew* is the most common call of this species. This call consists of broad frequencies that decrease in pitch over time and can be variable among individuals. Other calls include *chirp, che-er, vreer, churt,* and *peent* used in different situations such as chases, flight, alarm, and roosting. A *weu* call may be given from birds in flocks and when a predator approaches.[5] Different calls are thought to serve separate functions and need more study.

## HABITAT AND DIET

In a study in the San Juan Mountains of Colorado, altitude-loving Brown-capped Rosy-Finches preferred breeding habitats with very low woody vegetation (no trees or shrubs above a foot high) with less than 75% snow cover and usually within 1,300 feet of cliffs.[6] Brown-capped Rosy-Finches also inhabit shaded, colder enclaves on northeast-facing mountains below timberline. Breeding habitat must be close to or within commuting distance of feeding areas on tundra, rockslides, and snow surfaces. In winter with deep snow, Brown-capped Rosy-Finches retreat to open tundra, mountain valleys, and towns, returning to higher elevations even in severe cold, when the wind has exposed feeding spots.

Brown-capped Rosy-Finches take seeds and insects blown onto snowfields and at the margins and surfaces of frozen lakes. They also feed in meadows close to snowbanks where melting snow has exposed insects and seeds. In summer, about mid-June through July, the majority of their diet includes insects. By August and September, they feed largely on seeds, especially high-calorie newly ripened seeds still attached to plants.[7] Later stage nestlings and fledglings are fed mostly seeds.

## AT YOUR FEEDER

In winter Brown-capped Rosy-Finches feed, sometimes in huge flocks, with Black and Gray-crowned Rosy-Finches, visiting feeders at lower elevations and also at higher elevation towns and ski areas. Their bird seed preferences include black oil sunflower, millet, Nyjer®, and finch mixes. The Colorado Avian Research and Rehabilitation Institute in Estes Park hosts thousands of the three species at winter feeders and offers sunflower seed and millet. In 2004, they documented over 10,000 rosy-finches on a single day.[8]

Brown-capped Rosy-Finches in mixed flock with Black Rosy-Finches

## MOVEMENTS AND IRRUPTIONS

Brown-capped Rosy-Finches are largely restricted to Colorado and a few nearby states and do not make the wide-ranging irruptions seen in other species such as Pine Siskin and Red Crossbill. Brown-capped Rosy-Finch movements are lateral as well as altitudinal. In spring they return to breeding grounds around March through April. Starting in late September, but mainly from mid-October to mid-November, they migrate during the day, moving to lower elevation valleys or southward beyond their usual breeding range. Joining flocks with other rosy-finch species, they can winter together at places like Sandia Crest, New Mexico, and go to feeders. Banding studies at Sandia Crest show that the species composition of those flocks varies from year to year.[9] In spring and winter, Brown-capped Rosy-Finches make altitudinal movements to escape bad weather and find food.

## BREEDING BEHAVIOR

### *TERRITORY*

Territorial activity does not occur as we usually think of it in birds, where a species defends a defined geographic area. Instead, Brown-capped Rosy-Finch males defend a floating territory surrounding a female, not letting other males get within a certain distance of her.

### *COURTSHIP*

Pairing and courtship activities may occur in winter flocks, or in spring. There reportedly is a skewed sex ratio, with more males than females.[10] Females watch and assess males. Courtship activities take the form of males supplanting each other with ruffled plumage, counter-singing, and chasing females. Males also perform song flight displays in a "large horizontal arc or circle traveling several hundred meters while chirping,"[11] which helps locate and attract available partners in an open, windy alpine environment.

Males sing at the nest area and display with tails high, feathers fluffed, and wings fluttering, while holding a piece of grass and chirping. In a similar display, males approach females with sleeked plumage, tail and head high, ruffled back-of-head feathers with wings slowly raised and lowered, or wings spread and held stationary, body posture vertical.[12] Males and females engage in mutual bill-nibbling. Receptive females ruffle their plumage, crouching with head and tail up, wings vibrating, then copulation occurs.

### *NESTING*

**Timing:** June to August
**Nest:** Cup, outside diameter 4.7 to 5.7 in., secured with a base of mud and moss, consists of roots and fine grasses surrounded by a thick layer of coarse grasses, roots, and mud, lined with grasses, fur, feathers, and cloth. Placed most frequently in holes in cliffs or protected under rocks. Also nests in rocks in moraines and in buildings, caves, and abandoned mines.
**Eggs:** 3–6, white
**Incubation:** 12–14 days
**Nestling period:** 14–20 days, more likely 17–20 days
**Broods:** 1

The female selects the nest site while the displaying male follows her. During incubation, she spends a majority of her time at the nest and is fed there by the male but may also leave to feed herself. Both male and female chase intruders from the nest site.

When the young hatch, they are fed by both parents. The nestlings are mostly fed by regurgitation. Nest cleanliness is maintained by the parents eating or carrying off the fecal sacs.

The young leave the nest and are capable of flight in about 17–20 days. They spread out over slopes, pursue

Nest with nestlings in rock crevice, CO/07

adults, and beg for food. After about 2 weeks of care by adults, they become independent. Little is known about the immature stage, but they reportedly form medium-sized flocks themselves before joining adult flocks in fall.

## MOLT

The timing and sequence of molt needs more study. Adults molt once per year after breeding. The rosy color on adults becomes darker in summer due to wear and the effects on color pigment from solar radiation. Similarly, body color fades to a lighter brown. The bills of adults are yellow in winter and dark in summer; the bills of the males are blacker than those of females.

## CONSERVATION

Listed as Endangered by the IUCN Red List. Endangered species are plants or animals that are at great risk of extinction unless rapid action is taken. Partners in Flight puts the Brown-capped Rosy-Finch on its Red Watch List and rates the species 16 out of 20 on the Continental Concern Score. A recent study by DeSaix et al. showed that "the Brown-capped Rosy-Finch faces climate threats across their breeding range from changing habitat suitability and disruptions of genetic-environment associations. Future persistence may depend on rapid adaptation to novel climate conditions in a contracted breeding range."[13]

# HOUSE FINCH

*Haemorhous mexicanus*

> *The Hollywood Sign is more than just nine white letters spelling out a city's name. It's one of the world's most famous monuments and a universal metaphor for ambition, success, glamour . . . for this dazzling place, industry and dream we call H-O-L-L-Y-W-O-O-D.*
>
> —Hollywood Sign Trust[1]

## QUICK TAKE

The 1940s sign in the Long Island, New York, pet store read "Hollywood Finches," a marketing ploy by pet dealers to make imported finches glamorous. Who would have dreamed that label disguised the trojan horse of a small population of imported western finches? Once released in the East, they would take over and become one of the most successful range expansions in US ornithological history. In only fifty years, House Finches colonized the eastern half of the United States. How did that happen?

Worthy of a Hollywood movie plot, the mystery began at Jones Beach on April 11, 1941, when Richard B. Fischer and Robert Hines discovered, to their amazement, the first House Finch in the eastern United States, a brightly colored male. This first record was published in an ornithology column edited by John Elliott. A year later, in March 1942, Elliott found seven House Finches twelve miles northeast of Jones Beach at a tree nursery in Babylon, Long Island. By 1943 the finches were breeding there. In a few years, like champagne bubbles rising, large colonies had popped up at several other Long Island locations. By 1953 the bubbles had spread to New Jersey, New York, and Connecticut.[2] Members of the local ornithological community scratched their heads. How did the House Finches get here?

Sleuthing revealed that Dr. Edward Fleisher of Brooklyn had written in the Linnaean News-Letter (1(4): 1–2) that in January 1940 he discovered in a bird store in Brooklyn a large cage with twenty House Finches for sale as "Hollywood Finches." Fleisher sprang into action and campaigned to end the trafficking of protected American passerine birds. He contacted the National Audubon Society, but Richard Pough, who would typically handle such matters, was out of town. Undeterred, Fleisher pursued his mission with the Bureau of Biological Survey (a precursor of the United States Fish and Wildlife Service) which informed him House Finches were on the list of migratory birds protected by "the convention between the United States of America and the United Mexican States" (the Migratory Bird Treaty Act) so trapping, transporting and selling them without a federal permit violated the law."[3] Fleisher was visited by a US Game Management agent. In their conversation, Fleisher said he strongly opposed releasing the House Finches in the area, and they should be disposed of in some other way. The bureau then sent him a letter declaring that based solely on Fleisher's information, the bureau had stopped the trapping, transportation, and sale of House Finches in the United States. Victory! Or was it?

Unfortunately, further investigation by Pough and the National Audubon Society revealed that a wholesale dealer had been supplying local pet shops for years, selling them for thirty-five dollars per hundred. Elliott and Arbib also investigated and found California bird shippers who trapped House Finches. One said he thought dealers had been shipping thousands, maybe as many as one hundred thousand, to many eastern states for a long time. However, the 1940 ban, initiated by Fleisher's actions, put a big damper on dealers' business and essentially shut down the trade. "Circumstantial evidence, at least, indicates that the surplus unsalable birds were released, perhaps by a single New York dealer, when the ban was effected in 1940."[4]

With this get-out-of-jail-free card, the newly released House Finches had no problem settling into their eastern environment. Seed eaters with the ability to nest on human structures and in plantings, they found food and breeding habitat. Their phenomenally strong adaptive abilities allowed them to spread, and by 1990 they blanketed the East and southern Canada.

Thus, the Hollywood tale is a success story for a glamour-labeled western finch who got a free ride due to the ambition of pet dealers who, when caught in illegal trade, turned the finches loose.

Now ubiquitous, House Finches are among the best-studied finch species and have additional fascinating stories worthy of Hollywood plots. There's the red-hot leading male, dating circles, mate-swapping, and more. Read on.

## IDENTIFICATION

**Size:** L 6"

**Shape:** Fairly small, slender, small-headed bird with a generally short stubby conical bill (see Subspecies) and relatively long slightly notched tail. Culmen noticeably curved (mostly straight in Cassin's and Purple Finches). Similar Cassin's and Purple Finches have a deeper belly, longer bill, less curved culmen, and are larger-headed and more broad-necked with a shorter, deeply notched tail.

**Both Sexes:** Lack pale eye-ring.

**Adult Male:** Variable bright red to orange-red (occasionally yellow) on head, breast, and rump and generally brownish auriculars; whitish belly and flanks strongly streaked with brown; back brownish with indistinct streaks.

**Adult Female:** Head finely streaked with brown; weak facial pattern; dusky streaking on underparts blurry and not strongly contrasting with dull whitish background; no distinct orange-red on plumage, (but a few may show faint tinge of pinkish, yellow, or orange).

**1st Winter:** Male often has reduced or mottled red on head and upperparts, some reportedly may lack any red; female like adult female.

**Juv:** (Apr.–Oct.) Brownish with buffy wingbars.

### *SUBSPECIES*

(2) *H. m. frontalis* (most of N. Am–Baja CA and n.w. Mex). Has on average small bill and duller whitish underparts with less distinct streaking. M. with dull orangish-red or yellow on head and breast. Birds on the Channel Is., CA (*"clementis"*) have large bill. *H. m. mexicanus* (res. s.c. TX–e. Mex to s. Mex) have large bill, whiter underparts with more noticeable brown streaking. Birds in c. TX to C–e.c. Mex (*"potosinus")* on average are less orange. Note: some 1st-yr. males may lack any reddish, orange, or yellowish coloration, particularly in the Great Basin. More study is needed on plumage maturation in regard to geographic variation.

### *SIMILAR SPECIES*

Purple and Cassin's Finches have deeper belly, longer bill, less curved culmen, and are larger-headed and more broad-necked with deeply notched tail that is shorter than that of House Finch. House Finch male lacks reddish color on back, nape, and has heavy streaking on lower breast, flanks, belly. Female House Finch has plain face, lacks the indistinct whitish eyebrow of Purple and Cassin's Finch females. Cassin's Finch has a thin pale eye-ring.

Adult m.
TX/06
Adult f.
NM/01
Adult m.
NH/05
M.
CA/11
M.
NM/01
Juv.
MA/05

## DISTRIBUTION

Can be found from the southern parts of the western Canadian provinces through the western United States and down to Chiapas, Mexico. House Finches from California were sold to pet dealers in the East, but were released on Long Island in 1940. The species can now be found from s. Ontario and the s. Maritime Provinces to the Gulf Coast states. Western populations have also expanded over the last decades, and the two populations have met. There is greater genetic diversity in western versus eastern populations.[5] House Finches have also been introduced to the Hawaiian Islands.

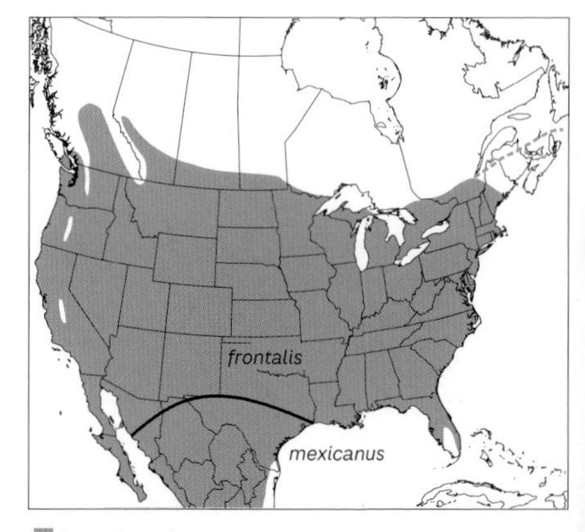


Year Round

## LANGUAGE

### *MALE*

Song consists of complex, rambling, melodiously warbled phrases. Courting males may sing a long, fast version and include high-pitched squeaks. Songs often include buzzy *tzeep* notes mixed in at the end.

House Finch song similarity varies geographically. In New York, males of one geographic area shared similar song dialects (repertoires of themes or types of songs containing syllables sung in a stereotyped sequence) distinct from males in other areas.[6] In California, males had more songs and syllable variety but no geographic dialect areas.[7] Song takes place perched or in flight, including during a stiff-winged "butterfly flight" courtship display. Males learn songs during their first months of life and may also learn from other males after they disperse.

***FEMALE***

In the New York study, where House Finches had regional dialects, "female singing was widespread . . . breeding males and females sing the same set of song themes . . . and the song patterns of female House Finches are like those of neighboring males."[8] Females may sing alone or near mate but sing primarily during copulation and courtship feeding, especially intensely when the male approaches and then at the end of incubation and brooding. In the California study, females and males sang a shorter song version during breeding, and females sang mainly in March and April.[9]

***MALE AND FEMALE***

The most frequent call, given singly or in twos, from both males and females, is variable *cheep* or *chirp* calls, sounding similar to a House Sparrow *cheep* call. It is given in flight or perched and functions as a contact call. *Cheep* calls can be confused with Evening Grosbeak and Red Crossbill call-type flight calls. In aggressive encounters, loud *chit-chit-chit* calls are given.

## HABITAT AND DIET

Originally a species of the arid Southwest, House Finches now occur across North America in an extensive range of habitats. In western areas, they are found in desert areas, chaparral, shrublands, subalpine areas to 11,500 feet, open deciduous and coniferous woodlands, and suburban and urban areas. In the East, House Finches mainly inhabit human-settled areas, nesting in conifers and evergreens, on houses and other structures, even high-rise buildings. House Finches feed in flocks, singly, or in pairs, and their diet is as varied as their habitats. Mostly they consume tree and weed seeds, buds, and fruits. The young are mainly fed regurgitated seeds and sometimes aphids and insect larvae.

House Finches eating ocotillo, AZ

## AT YOUR FEEDER

House Finches rank in the top 10 feeder birds in all areas of the country according to Project FeederWatch, a database of abundance at feeders based on the reports of feeder-watcher participants. Black oil sunflower seed is preferred. They enjoy safflower seed and will occasionally eat Nyjer® seed finch mixes, and cracked corn. Generally tolerant of one another while feeding in flocks in the wild, House Finches may show aggression toward each other at feeders, with supplanting attacks and head-forward displays, indicating a flock dominance hierarchy. In one study, females were dominant over males in a captive flock but not so much in a wild flock. During breeding, females were dominant over their mates.[10] House Finches may also dominate other species, and in a study at feeders, House Finches were dominant 90.9% of the time over Purple Finches.[11]

More so than other birds, House Finches are susceptible to the eye disease mycoplasmal conjunctivitis caused by a strain of poultry pathogen (and does not affect humans). Eastern populations are more susceptible than western, which are more genetically diverse, and an outbreak in 1994 caused a significant population decline in eastern birds. Feeder cleanliness is vitally important; see Feeding and Attracting Finches for information on all aspects of feeding birds, including cleanliness, safety, and finch diseases.

## MOVEMENTS AND IRRUPTIONS

Mostly non-irruptive, but some migration may occur in the most northern populations. The rest of the population seems mostly resident, including western birds, but movements to lower elevations are noted in the West, especially during snowstorms, with birds seeking out areas with feeders and less snow cover. Young birds that are dispersing have been recorded moving as far as 500 miles.[12]

House Finches copulating; female has nest material

## BREEDING BEHAVIOR

### *TERRITORY*

Males become less tolerant of one another as spring breeding begins. House Finches do not exhibit much territorial behavior and nest semicolonially. Males defend a floating space around the female, and then their nest, rather than defend a larger territory as traditionally defined. Females too will drive away other females from their mate and nest. Once the nest is complete, defense wanes.[13]

### *COURTSHIP*

House Finches pair up while still in winter flocks or soon after arriving at breeding grounds. Some may have remained paired all winter. Males may begin singing frequently but do not counter-sing in any agonistic encounters with other males. When males are near females, they sing at a greater rate, indicating that song functions to attract a mate. In a Montana study of banded wild birds, males that sang louder songs with more syllables at a faster rate had greater reproductive success, judged by their earlier nesting and bigger clutches. Thus, male song may be a criterion for female mate choice.[14]

Research in New York showed both male and female House Finches in a local area had song dialects and sang the same songs, suggesting that these function to sexually stimulate each other, synchronize their sexual cycles, and aid in individual recognition.[15]

Female and two males, AZ/05

In House Finches the ratio is more males to females, up to 2.5:1 depending on the location studied.[16] Thus, there is heavy competition for a mate during breeding. Males sing frequently and chase other males. Courtship displays include "butterfly flight" with males flying stiff-winged, gliding the last 20 feet with wings held slightly above horizontal and singing intensely. In another display, the male—head up, chin feathers ruffled, wings drooped—hops toward the female, pivoting side to side, singing a loud song version ending with *tzeep* note. Billing (touching and grabbing bills) leads eventually to the male feeding the female.

Copulation is by female invitation, and the male hops onto her back. About 5% of the time, in a position reversal, the female then will mount the male.[17]

Plumage color of males is a component of female House Finch mate choice; females often prefer colorful males, the redder the better, and those may be more viable males with perhaps better genetic quality. Research done on the eastern population of House Finches in Michigan[18] found that breeding female House Finches select the reddest males. Those males were better at providing food at a higher rate to females and young during nesting (a huge plus since males may provide much of the female's food at this time), plus the male's winter survivorship was superior to less colorful males, a sign of viability.

However, it's not always the case that females prefer the reddest males and that those males are better at parental care. There can be conditional and individual variation in reproductive strategy as to the color of a male, parental investment, and which males the females choose. House Finches in eastern studies were redder with a narrower range of color than male House Finches in a Montana study, where male breast plumage ranged from red to yellow to intermediate. In that study, the most successful males (had the most surviving offspring to 40 days of age) were of intermediate plumage color, nested early, and had high levels of feeding females and young. Older, experienced females avoided pairing with redder males more than did younger, less experienced females.[19]

Southwestern House Finches in the Sonoran Desert have their own courtship traditions. In late winter, mixed-sex flocks of 10–15 finches gather in circles on the tops of giant saguaro cacti, with the birds facing into the circle. New arrivals form an outer circle or try to access the inner circle. This can go on for 20 minutes, on multiple cacti, with pairs sporadically flying off together from the inner circle, apparently bonded. There can be nearby circles on other saguaros. Northwestern House Finches similarly form mate-selection circles on the tops of utility poles or roofs.[20]

While House Finches are mainly socially monogamous, fidelity is another story. Both males and females may perform extra pair displays when their mate is out of sight. Even when their mate is present, House Finches may copulate with partners other than their social mate, without that mate protesting. In a Montana study, females solicited extrapair copulations by carrying a piece of nesting material and enticing other males to mate with her. Her social mate observed from a distance, and most of these copulations did not result in fertilization.[21] In southwest Arizona, males solicited copulations from other females while their females were incubating, and females solicited other males while their females were nest building. "Overall," the study concluded, "6–10% of offspring are a result of extrapair fertilizations."[22]

### *NESTING*

**Timing:** As early as late February to August
**Nest:** Cup, outside diameter about 4.5 in., of plant stems, twigs, rootlets, string, feathers, wool, hair, paper, cigarette filters, etc. lined with finer materials. Placed in conifers, palms, cacti, on buildings and structures, anywhere that provides a ledge or base with overhead cover.
**Eggs:** 2–7, light blue with purple speckles on end
**Incubation:** 13–14 days, by female
**Nestling period:** 13–14 days up to 17 days in cold weather
**Broods:** Usually 1–3 successfully, but has attempted upwards of 5

Pairs that were together in a previous breeding season may start nesting earlier. House Finches explore different places and even construct sometimes large preliminary nests, then change their minds and start a new, final nest. Nest sites vary widely: trees, cacti, planters, wreaths on doors, and even ivy on buildings. More than one person has been surprised when watering a hanging planter to discover a House Finch nest with babies in that planter! The male escorts the female as she gathers nest material, and may even carry bits, but does not construct the nest. Nest building

can take up to 29 days and is a learned skill, with first-year females closely watching older females. The female is usually, but not always, fed on the nest by the male. In southwest Arizona, 56% of males did not feed incubating females.[23]

After the young hatch, the female broods them for about 5 days, or longer in the Southwest if the nest is exposed to direct sun. Both parents feed the young mainly seeds by regurgitation. The young fledge and, depending on the geographic location, may remain nearby, not able to fly well for a few days, or fly out immediately. Young birds are fed up to 18 days, then feed on their own by 3 weeks of age. The male may feed the fledglings himself until they can feed independently while the female proceeds to nest again.

Juvenile birds form flocks at feeding areas, and males may dominate females in those flocks. After 120 days these large flocks move away from nesting areas and disperse.[24]

## MOLT

Much research has been done on carotenoids in plumage, and House Finches are one of the best-studied passerine species in the function and control of plumage coloration.[25]

House Finch adults have a complete molt once a year, after breeding. Any brightening of plumage during the year is a result of wearing off of buffy feather edges. Plumage color, ranging from red to yellow, is the result of access to dietary carotenoids at the time of molting. House Finches deposit pigments from the carotenoids in their feathers. They "convert yellow dietary carotenoids to red carotenoids in an oxidation process."[26] The proportion of red and yellow carotenoid pigments in feathers varies widely, and there is no consistency between different ages and populations of House Finches.[27]

According to research by Hill in 2019, "plumage coloration signals mitochondrial function, and hence core cellular functionality, in the house finch.... Linking the ornamentation used in mate choice to function of core respiratory processes provides a novel mechanistic explanation for why carotenoid coloration relates to a range of aspects of individual performance and why females use plumage redness as a key criterion in choosing mates."[28]

## CONSERVATION

Their conservation status is Least Concern. Partners in Flight ranks House Finch a 6 out of 20 on the Continental Concern Scale.

# ID TIPS TO COMMON RED FINCHES

**PURPLE FINCH** ***Haemorphus purpureus***
**SHAPE**: Broad neck, large head, relatively thick, short bill with slightly curved culmen, relatively short, notched tail.
**COLOR: Male:** Purplish-red wash over most of body, although don't use color hue alone to distinguish red males of all three species. Paler eyebrow and brownish cheek show through wash. No or faint streaks on flanks.
**Female/imm.:** Females and immatures of both sexes brownish streaked, white undertail converts, white eyebrow and moustachial region. Note: Western subspecies *H. p. californicus* female/ imm. has less distinct white eyebrow (more like female/imm. Cassin's Finch) and all sexes have streaked undertail coverts.

**PURPLE FINCH**

californicus
purpureus

**HOUSE FINCH**

frontalis
mexicanus

**CASSIN'S FINCH**

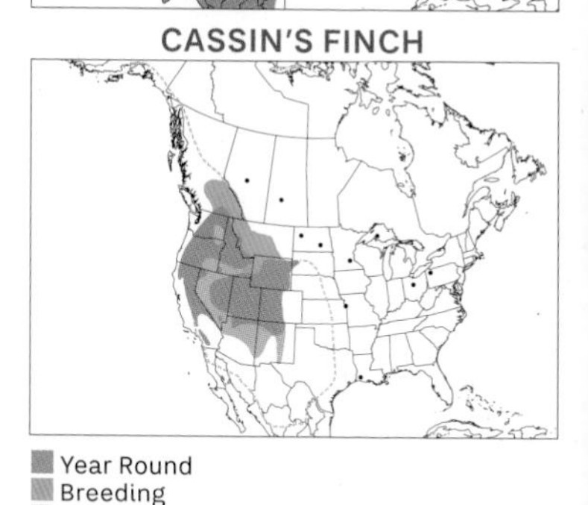

Year Round
Breeding
Non-Breeding
Migration

**HOUSE FINCH** ***Haemorphus mexicanus***
**SHAPE:** Rounded, smaller head with generally thinner neck (depending on posture), longer tail and more elongated body than Purple Finch. Tail rounded or with slight notch. Short bill with noticeably curved culmen. Shorter wing tips (primary project past tertials) than Purple or Cassin's Finch.
**COLOR: Male:** Red or orangey-red (rarely yellowish) confined to head, breast and rump, not all over body as in Purple Finch. Strongly streaked flanks differentiate it from Purple and Cassin's Finch.
**Female:** Plain brown face differentiate it from female Purple and Cassin's Finch.

**CASSIN'S FINCH** ***Haemorphus cassini***
**SHAPE:** Crown is peaked and noticeably so when raised. Long bill with very straight culmen differentiate it from House and Purple Finch. Long notched tail.
**COLOR:** Both sexes have thin, pale eye-ring.
**Male:** Red is most pronounced and noticeable on crown and contrasts with paler pinkish-red on breast. Lacks dark brown streaks on flanks (although streaked undertail coverts, white undertail coverts on Purple Finch).
**Female:** Females and immatures both streaked brown, whitish eyebrow somewhat less distinct than on Purple Finch female/imm. subspecies *H. p purpureus*.

## PURPLE FINCH

**Male:** Overall purple-red color, short slightly curved bill, no dark streaks on flanks

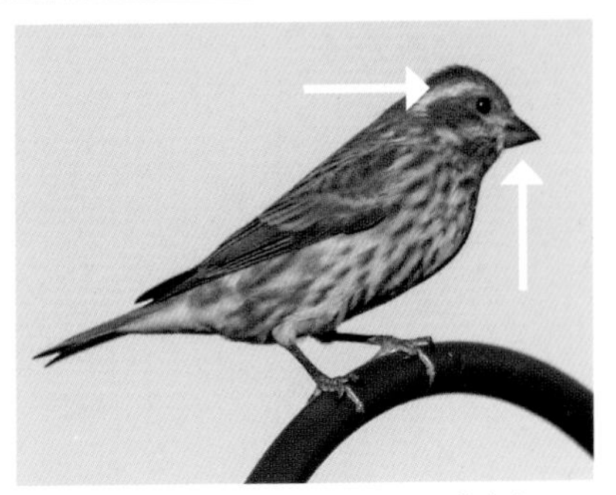

**Female/imm:** White eyebrow, short, slightly curved bill

## HOUSE FINCH

**Male:** Red mostly on head, breast, rump, heavily streaked flanks, short curved bill

**Female/imm:** Plain face, short curved bill

## CASSIN'S FINCH

**Male:** Red most prominent on crown, long straight bill, unstreaked flanks

**Female/imm:** Peaked crown can be raised, long straight bill

**Note** : Range maps can be a clue to identifying which finch you see.

# PURPLE FINCH

*Haemorhous purpureus*

> *Who in the rainbow can draw the line where the violet tint ends and the orange tint begins? Distinctly we see the difference of the colors, but where exactly does the one first blendingly enter into the other? So with sanity and insanity.*
>
> —Herman Melville, *Billy Budd, Sailor*

## QUICK TAKE

The Purple Finches' species name, *purpureus,* comes from the Latin meaning "crimson" or other reddish color. Is it really purple? Describing this bird's hue might just drive a birder insane.

One person's "purple" is another person's "raspberry" because people may not always see colors in the same way. One study found that men and women perceive and describe the colors of the same objects differently. Women perceived more color nuances, especially in the yellow and green hues; men needed longer wavelengths to see the same hues and perceived warm colors as a little redder.[1] One might quibble about the color of an adult male Purple Finch, whether purple, raspberry, red, dusky rose, maraschino, carmine, cayenne, maroon, eggplant, strawberry, fuchsia, or merlot spilled on the tablecloth. But it gets even more complicated since there are three red look-alike finches in North America—Purple Finch, House Finch, and Cassin's Finch. Males all have red on their plumage, and females and immatures have brown streaks.

Now add two recognized subspecies of Purple Finch, *H. p. purpureus* and *H. p. californicus*. Each looks a little different (*californicus* m. less bright with more brownish underparts, f. greenish above, duskier below), sounds a little different, and behaves slightly differently. A study of their genetic structure indicates their story goes back to the last ice age when much of North America was covered with an ice sheet.[2] However, there were open areas with suitable food, or refugia, where species were able to survive. *Californicus* survived in the Pacific coast refugia, *purpureus* survived in refugia east of the Rockies. The two subspecies now remain in separate genetic lineages, except in southwest British Columbia where they may intermix.

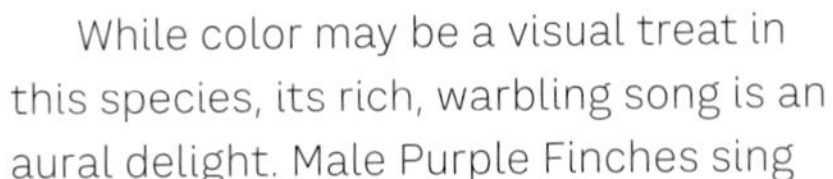

While color may be a visual treat in this species, its rich, warbling song is an aural delight. Male Purple Finches sing several versions of song; females sing too, and so do immature males, who look like adult females.

Purple Finches breed in cool coniferous and mixed forests, riparian and suburban areas. In winter, migratory eastern Purple Finches may occur in many habitats in the eastern United States and southeastern Canada down to the Gulf Coast states. The more sedentary West Coast *californicus* moves to lower elevations.

Like many irruptive finches, Purple Finches periodically leave northern areas due to cone-crop shortages, and much to the delight of birders in the southern United States, they grace feeders in areas where they don't usually occur. But it's not always a peaceable kingdom when they show up. Purple Finches that look female-plumaged (adult females and young males and females look alike) dominate adult males at feeders, and their House Finch cousins dominate when feeding together.

Regardless of who's winning, watch for Purple Finches at your feeders. When they arrive, get out your color wheel and decide for yourself their hue.

## IDENTIFICATION

**Size:** L 6"

**Shape:** Fairly small, deep-bellied, broad-necked, fairly large-headed bird with a short conical bill with slightly curved culmen and a relatively short notched tail.

**Both Sexes:** Lack pale eye-ring.

**Adult Male:** Bright raspberry wash evenly over head, breast, and rump; weakly contrasting brownish streaking on maroon back; a few blurry streaks on flanks, otherwise belly, flanks, and undertail coverts white to pinkish and unstreaked. Rarely plumage may be orange or yellowish instead of red.

**Adult Female:** Distinct to indistinct whitish eyebrow and moustachial streak (see Subspecies) on brown face; thick brown streaking on white to creamy underparts; slightly darker brown streaking on brown back; undertail coverts streaked or unstreaked (see Subspecies). Rarely may be tinged pinkish or yellowish, especially on rump.

**1st Year:** Both sexes like ad. f., but some 1st-yr. m. may have pinkish or yellowish tinge on plumage.

**Juv:** (June–Sept.) Streaked brown.

### *SUBSPECIES*

(2) *H. p. californicus*/Type 2[3] (BC, s.w. WA–s.w. CA) small; culmen generally straight. f. with less contrasting whitish eyebrow and moustachial region than f. *purpureus*/Type 1[4] (thus, more like f. Cassin's Finch or even House Finch), faint olive tinge overall, blackish streaks on undertail coverts; m. head dull red. *H. p. purpureus* (rest of range to north and east) large; culmen generally curved; f. with bold and contrasting white eyebrow and moustachial region, grayish tinge overall, few or no streaks on undertail coverts; m. head bright red.

### *SIMILAR SPECIES*

Cassin's Finch has thin pale eye-ring; longer bill with straight culmen; female with indistinct whitish eyebrow and moustachial region, blackish streaking on underparts (including undertail coverts), contrastingly black streaking on brown back; male with rosy wash brightest and darkest on crown. House Finch has shorter bill with curved culmen; distinct streaks on sides; male generally, not always, more orangish-red, less colorful overall, especially on back and wings, with color confined to front of crown, throat, breast; female has a plain face, lacks whitish eyebrow of *purpureus* subspecies.

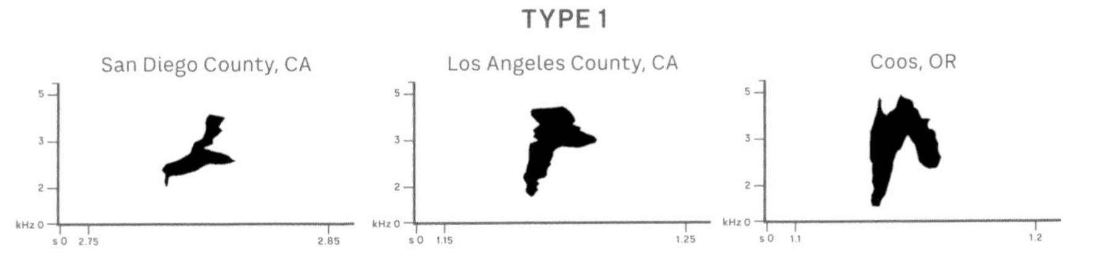


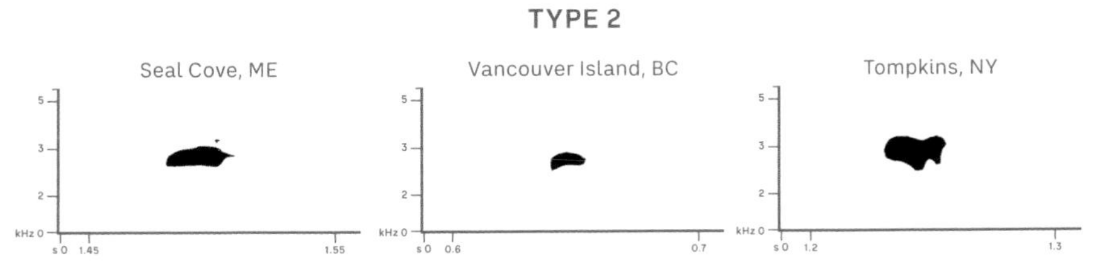


Flight calls fall into at least two clear call types, with Type 1/western birds on the top, and Type 2/eastern birds on the bottom. The Type 2 spectrograms are shorter in duration and occupy a narrower frequency range than those of Type 1. *(Spectrograms courtesy of Yuyan Kuang)*

## DISTRIBUTION

Moderately common across much of its range. Ranges of eastern *H. p. purpureus* and western *H. p. californicus* meet in south-central British Columbia. Purple Finches breed across central and southern Canada, along the West Coast, in the north-central and northeastern states, and southward in the Appalachians to Virginia. In winter the eastern subspecies *purpureus* can be found to the Gulf Coast states and even rarely in interior parts of the mountain west.

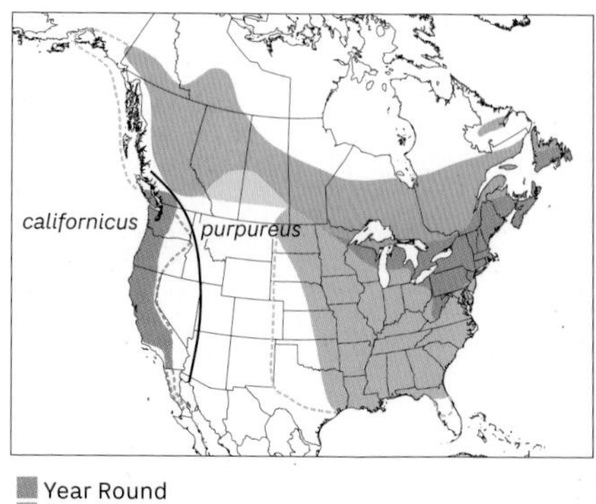


Year Round
Breeding
Non-Breeding
Migration

## LANGUAGE

### *MALE*

A long song of rich, loud warbling, sometimes with buzzy repeated notes in the middle, especially when given in flight. May include imitations of other birds. Given more in early spring while birds are in flocks. Also gives a disjunct song (sometimes referred to as "the vireo song") of spaced, distinct phrases of 1–3 syllables, clear or burry, heard all year.[5] Eastern and western subspecies show some differences; for example, eastern birds give a more varied song with a wider range of warbling notes than western birds.[6]

### *FEMALE*

Females are reported to sing. Several times one researcher witnessed a female, who was fed by the male then returned to the nest, "sing a little song for a minute or two . . . The song was finch-like but quite different from that of the male."[7] Female gives a *whit whewe* from nest.[8]

Since females and first-year males look similar, it may be difficult to identify the sex of the singer when song is given by these birds. Female song is an area for future research.

### *MALE AND FEMALE*

A brief, low-pitched *pwik* (Type 1) or *tik* (Type 2) call is the most common call and mainly given in flight. Flight calls of the two subspecies are different. The eastern subspecies *H. p. purpureus tik* call is a little squeakier and softer than the western subspecies *H. p. californicus pwik* call (Matthew Young, personal observation). More recordings of western interior Purple Finches are needed. Short repeated sounds such as *wheew* and *tidilip* given by all ages and sexes need further defining.[9]

### *IMITATION/MIMICRY*

Masterfully includes imitations of other birds in its song on occasion[10]—Barn Swallow, American Goldfinch, Pine Siskin, American Robin, Eastern Towhee, and many others. Imitation across the finches needs further research.

## HABITAT AND DIET

Purple Finches mostly breed in moist coniferous and mixed forests, often at the edges of wetland corridors, in orchards, and suburban and developed areas with conifers. In winter they live in a very broad range of habitats including deciduous and coniferous forest types, fields, urban and suburban areas, and just about anywhere they can find adequate food.

Purple Finches eat a variety of seeds and buds of trees such as maples, elms, tulip poplars, ash, and others. They also eat seeds of conifers. Their menu includes fruits and even flower nectar, which they access by biting the base of a blossom. Purple Finches eat insects and large amounts of spruce budworms.

## AT YOUR FEEDER

Purple Finches will show up at well-stocked bird feeding stations offering Nyjer® and finch mixes, but black oil sunflower, in the shell or hulled, is a favorite. Safflower is also at the top of their list. Try offering multiple tube feeders of safflower to mitigate intraspecific and interspecific competition. In one study, House Finches were dominant over Purple Finches at feeders 90.9% of the time.[11] Some think that competition from House Finches at winter feeders, and to some extent House Sparrows, may help explain the drop in Purple Finch populations in the East.

Another study showed female-plumaged Purple Finches dominated adult male Purple Finches in 63 of 64 encounters at feeders.[12]

Purple Finch males and female/imms. and American Goldfinch

## MOVEMENTS AND IRRUPTIONS

Western *H. p. californicus* is largely resident with occasional altitudinal movements to lower elevations, but eastern *H. p. purpureus* is highly migratory and irruptive, and birds can move in numbers as far as the Gulf Coast states. Fall movements occur from late July to even February in the East with birds starting to return as early as February and spring migration continuing into May. Eastern birds are occasionally noted in the western states.

Largest irruptions by *H. p. purpureus* over last 60 years were 1965, 1967, 1969, 1970, 1972, 1973, 1974, 1975, 1976, 1977, 1978, 1981, 1982, 1985, 1991, 1993, 1995, 1996, 1997, 2001, 2004, 2005, 2006, 2008, 2009, 2011, 2016, 2017, 2019, 2020, 2021, and 2022. Averages every 2–3 years but can go several years without irrupting during minimal budworm outbreaks, as in the 1980s, or can irrupt several years in a row as in the ongoing budworm outbreaks of the 1970s and in recent years.[13]

## BREEDING BEHAVIOR

The complete breeding biology of Purple Finches needs more research, including differences in the subspecies.

### *TERRITORY*

During breeding, pairs are solitary. Male Purple Finches may establish a territory that they defend from other males. This differs from House and Cassin's Finch males, who guard a female rather than a specific territory.[14] Lone males sing a version of song with rapid notes near the beginning, and strongly accented notes near the end, and may include a song flight display with wings held at an angle.[15]

### *COURTSHIP*

Male Purple Finches have fairly elaborate courtship displays consisting of hopping with tail cocked; drooped, vibrating wings; puffed chest; raised bill; then elevating into the air. Sometimes two males may display and sing in competition after chasing a female. Females assess them and, when interested, respond with fluttering wings and crouched posture, inviting copulation.

### *NESTING*

**Timing:** Early April through August
**Nest:** Cup, outside diameter 7 in., of twigs, grasses and rootlets, bark strips, lichens, lined with grasses, moss, feathers, fur, hair, rootlets, placed out on a branch of conifers or deciduous trees, 3–50 ft. high.
**Eggs:** 2–7, light blue-green with dark marks
**Incubation:** 12–13 days
**Nestling period:** 13–14 days
**Broods:** 1–2

The female builds the nest, the male possibly participating. Nests of the western subspecies, *H. p. californicus,* are placed in trees other than conifers more often than the nests of the eastern subspecies *H. p. purpureus.* There are reports of the male frequently feeding the female during incubation. After hatching, both parents feed regurgitated seeds to the young. Once they leave the nest, the young may remain in the vicinity for about a week until they develop better flying ability. Presumably, they then move around with their parents and join wintering or migrating flocks.

There may be a skewed sex ratio in Purple Finches; 3 banding studies found a ratio of 57% males to 43% females, but another study found a closer ratio of 52% males to 48% females.[16] This is an area for further study.

## MOLT

Purple Finch adults undergo a complete molt postbreeding from July to November. Adult females and first-year birds look very similar, and are streaked brown and not reliably sexed in the field. Some first-year males might have a pinkish tinge. Young males will molt into their adult red color in their second year. Some older adult females, very rarely, will become tinged pinkish or yellowish. Males at first have whitish edges to feathers on head, back, and wings that gradually wear off, making them appear brighter toward breeding. In April, adult males may molt some feathers on the front of their heads.

## CONSERVATION

IUCN status is Least Concern. However, northern and eastern populations have declined (perhaps less so recently), so monitoring is important. According to the North American Breeding Bird Survey, Purple Finches declined by 0.8% a year between 1966 and 2019. Some declines in the East might be due to competition over food with House Finches but can also be tied to large infestations of spruce budworm in North American boreal forest, which peaked 1945–1955 and 1965–1985. Partners in Flight indicates Purple Finch rates a 9 out of 20 on the Continental Concern Score.

# CASSIN'S FINCH*

*Haemorhous cassinii*

> **Essence** *(Latin:* essentia*) is . . . used in philosophy and theology as a designation for the property or set of properties that make an entity or substance what it fundamentally is . . . The concept originates . . . with Aristotle who used the Greek expression* to ti ên einai*, literally meaning "the what it was to be" . . . or the shorter phrase* to ti esti*, literally meaning "the what it is" . . . Latin translators coined the word* essentia *(English "essence") to represent the whole expression.*[1]

* On November 1, 2023, the American Ornithological Society committed to changing all English-language names of birds within its geographic jurisdiction that are named directly after people, and that may affect this species. For more information, see How to Use This Guide, page xii.

## QUICK TAKE

What is the essence of a Cassin's Finch?

Is it the red-and-brown plumage that sends birders scrambling to field guides to differentiate it from look-alike Purple and House Finches?

Is it the flocking penchant to wander together, feed together, breed together?

Is it the dominance of females in winter flocks at feeders, which may aid winter survival?

Is it the warbling, variable song that may imitate other species such as Red Crossbill, Evening Grosbeak, and Pine Siskin?

Is it the singer—both males and females sing, or do they?

Is it the love of salt, a hypertensive diet no-no?

What is the essence of a Cassin's Finch? It is all of the above and more, kept in a DNA lockbox.

Essentially, a Cassin's Finch is a species whose gene expression makes it uniquely adapted to its conifer habitat, a wandering lifestyle, and to breed and produce fertile offspring with its own.

But how do we really know what we know about a bird species? Is it the accumulated knowledge, over the centuries, from scientists who do research, genetic testing, observations of behavior of color-banded birds, dissecting of spectrograms of songs and calls, and so much more? Is it the data from birders, including eBird reports of distribution and abundance, Christmas Bird Count information, migration tracking, backyard observations, and so much more? Yes, it is all of that and more. Often, we know birds because of a special bond and their meaning in our lives, a connection that lifts our spirits and touches our soul.

As to the whole "what it is," the *to ti esti* of a Cassin's Finch, we are only scratching the surface. The combination to that DNA lockbox eludes us—we have much more to learn about this beautiful finch.

## IDENTIFICATION

**Size:** L 6.25"
**Shape:** Fairly small, moderately slim birds with relatively short notched tail and a fairly short conical bill with a straight culmen, making it look very pointed. Bushy crest often raised.
**Both Sexes:** Thin, pale eye-ring.
**Adult Male:** Pale rosy wash over head, breast, and rump, brightest and darkest on crown; fairly contrasting dark-brownish streaking on pinkish-brown back; underparts white with variable fine dark streaking on flanks and undertail coverts.
**Adult Female:** Streaked brown overall; indistinct whitish eyebrow and moustachial region on brown face; fine blackish streaking on white underparts; undertail coverts finely streaked. Compare with female Purple Finch.
**1st Year:** Both sexes like adult f., but some 1st-yr. m. may have pinkish or yellowish tinge.

### *SUBSPECIES*

Monotypic

### *SIMILAR SPECIES*

Red color is concentrated on cap of adult male Cassin's Finch versus Purple or House Finch adult males. Similar Purple Finch has deeper belly, shorter bill with a curved culmen, shorter primary projection: similar House Finch has slimmer belly, shorter, decurved bill, shorter primary projection, and longer tail.

## DISTRIBUTION

Breeds in open coniferous habitat in mountains of western North America, usually between 3,200 and 9,800 feet, from southern British Columbia and western Alberta to southern California interior mountains and northern Arizona and New Mexico.[2] A small population is in western South Dakota. Winters in most of breeding range and down to northern Baja California and northern mountains of Mexico.

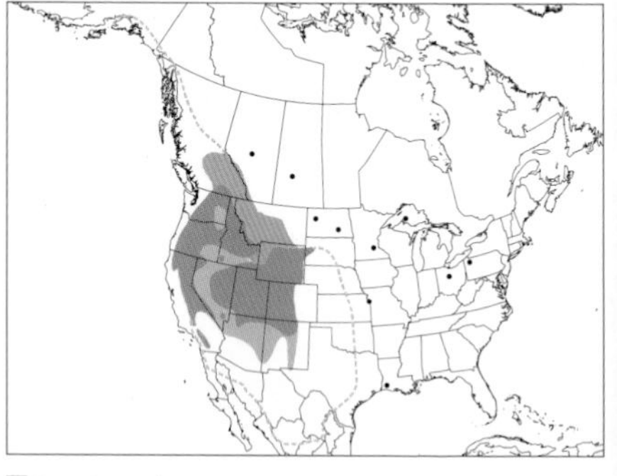

Adult m. OR/06

F./imm. CA/03

## LANGUAGE

### *MALE*

Song is a complex, long, fast, variable warble that may include imitations of other bird species and sometimes high *seets*. Songs can also be shorter with spaces between phrases.[3] Songs of males are learned and may vary geographically. In a study of male Cassin's Finches in northern Utah, males at each of several geographically close sites "sang a characteristic theme sharing only the initial sequence of three or four figure types that appeared unique to a locale," suggesting "a system similar to a dialect that may aid in behaviorally isolating breeding populations to increase ecological flexibility in an environment subject to frequent and dramatic changes."[4] Male House Finches in local areas in New York also shared song dialects and had clear boundaries between groups with a similar dialect.[5]

### *FEMALE*

Females also sing. The northern Utah study "recorded 11 songs during copulation of three pairs, all involving older males. Both sexes sang during copulation." The songs of the males (not females) were analyzed and found "the introductory triplet was shared by the males, songs were continuous prior to and during copulation."[6]

More study of female song in Cassin's Finches is needed. Since yearling males sing and look like females, identification of song in brown-plumaged Cassin's Finches should be made with caution and when the sex of the singer can be verified.

### *MALE AND FEMALE*

Calls include a typical, less musical *tidilip* sound and a *weew* call. A fast, chittering call can be given in close or agonistic circumstances.[7]

### *IMITATION/MIMICRY*

Song can include imitations of birds such as Red Crossbill, Pine Siskin, Western Tanager, Evening Grosbeak, Pygmy Nuthatch, Northern Flicker, Steller's Jay,[8] and Townsend's Solitaire (Tom Hahn, personal communication).

## HABITAT AND DIET

Cassin's Finches live in coniferous forests of the interior mountains of the West with a variety of conifer types such as ponderosa, lodgepole, Jeffrey, limber, bristlecone, and pinyon pine, and juniper. They are also found in habitats with Douglas fir, Engelmann spruce, red, subalpine, and grand fir, and quaking aspen. In Washington they can occur in open ponderosa pine forest and moist subalpine forest.[9] In the eastern Sierra Nevada, they occur in dry mid-elevation Jeffrey pine forest at 7,000–8,000 feet and in cooler lodgepole pine forest around 10,000 feet (Tom Hahn, personal communication). In winter they generally occupy the same habitat but frequently at lower elevations.

The Cassin's Finch diet is mainly a vegetarian buffet. They feast on a wide range of seeds, tree buds, especially of quaking aspen, and also fruits. Occasionally they will get animal protein from insects, including moth larvae.

They are highly attracted to salt and minerals in earth. A study that tested the preferences of Cassin's Finches, Red Crossbills, Pine Siskins, and Evening Grosbeaks for sodium chloride ($NaCl$) over calcium chloride ($CaCO_3$) found those species are attracted to salt but preferred the calcium chloride.[10] One research paper concluded that species in the Carduelinae subfamily eat salt because of an increased need for sodium during egg production and because feeding young through regurgitation depletes their sodium.[11]

## AT YOUR FEEDER

Cassin's Finches readily come to bird feeders, especially during winter months, often in the company of other finches such as House Finches and Pine Siskins. They prefer black oil sunflower seeds, millet, and finch mixes offered in appropriate feeders. A study showed that female Cassin's Finches were dominant over adult male and first-year males at bird feeding stations in winter.[12]

Cassin's Finch habitat, Boulder, CO

Cassin's Finches at feeder with Pine Siskins

## MOVEMENTS AND IRRUPTIONS

Cassin's Finches can move altitudinally and laterally in their range,[13] but more study is needed on their migrations. Although thought to be weakly faithful to breeding sites, one study indicated the same birds overwintered where they bred.[14] Movement to breeding areas is mostly in April and May.

### FUN FACT

**The House, Purple, and Cassin's Finch genus was changed from *Carpodacus* to *Haemorhous* because new genetic information found the 3 species are more closely related to one another than they are to the *Carpodacus* rosefinches. The European Common Rosefinch (*Carpodacus erythrinus*) is a vagrant to North America.**[25]

## BREEDING BEHAVIOR

### *TERRITORY*

Males defend a zone around a female from other males with threat postures and chasing. This defense does not occur until a nest site is selected. In one study, the researcher found that song was not territorial in function; it was not used in aggressive encounters with other males but only to attract a female. Mated males stopped all singing when nest construction began and ceased defending females when incubation began.[15]

### *COURTSHIP*

Cassin's Finches may form pairs in flocks or right after their arrival on the breeding grounds. There is some speculation that pairs remain together in winter. Two different studies showed differences in fidelity to a breeding location. In a study in Utah, populations were nomadic to breeding grounds, with different birds returning year to year.[16] All females and adult males, and only a small number of yearling males paired and bred. There was an excess of first-year males. Males arrived to breeding areas already singing, and sang while gliding during moth-like flight displays, flying slowly in a straight line during courtship. They also sang while perched atop conifers. First-year unmated males, however, continued singing into August.

The northern Utah study found that females only responded to the call of their mates, a system of mate recognition that "would aid integration of reproductive behavior of nesting pairs of Cassin's Finch."[17]

Another study in southern Oregon, in an isolated area of ponderosa pines, found about the same-sized population of Cassin's Finches returned to the same breeding site year after year, each spring, with females being slightly more faithful to the site than males. Adults as well as most yearling females and males there bred.[18]

### *NESTING*

**Timing:** May and June, sometimes into July
**Nest:** Cup, outside diameter 3 in., of plant stems, twigs, rootlets, lined with finer material such as grasses, plant fibers, rootlets, bark, feathers. Placed over 49 ft. high on end of lateral branch of conifers near top of tree, or close to trunk.
**Eggs:** 3–6, light blue-green with purplish, brown, or black speckles
**Incubation:** 12 days, by female
**Nestling period:** Little is known, can be 16 days
**Broods:** 1–2

Nesting is semicolonial, and nests are spaced enough, or constructed at different times, to mitigate aggression.[19] Females construct the nests and are followed closely by males. Both sexes are reported to sing during copulation.[20] Once incubation starts, males stop defending the female and may just perch some distance away and remain watchful.

The male feeds the female on or near the nest during incubation, until the nestlings are about 4 days old. He will give a loud call when arriving near the nest, and she may call back. A study showed these calls were pair specific, allowing mates to recognize one another, an advantage for maintaining a pair bond during winter, then arriving to a breeding area ready to begin nesting.[21]

Both parents feed the young, but little is known about the young's diet. Soon after they fledge, the young depart the nesting area with their parents. In southeastern Oregon, in July, finches formed flocks of up to 30 or more birds and wandered, migrating usually by September.

In a Utah study, males "significantly outnumbered females in 2 of 3 years and the female is considered the limiting resource for reproductive effort."[22] In a study of banded Cassin's Finches in winter flocks there was a higher proportion of males: "Females were outnumbered by all males 203:85 in 1972–73 and 43:16 in 1973–74. These sex ratios are similar to the disparities favoring males reported by Samson in 3 breeding populations of Cassin's Finch in northern Utah."[23]

Another study in Oregon at Hart Mountain found that in the Camp Creek breeding area the sex ratio was approximately 50/50, although they noted "it is not worthwhile to discuss these full-season male/female ratios, usually in the order of 60/40 because our sample periods varied substantially among years." Additionally, they noted a small surplus number of males in the larger Hart Mountain area.[24]

After breeding, Cassin's Finches complete their molt before moving from the breeding areas. In fall, they gather into flocks and spend the winter foraging, often with other finches such as Red Crossbills.

## MOLT

Cassin's Finches molt from their juvenile plumage into their first-year plumage, and at this point both males and females resemble the streaked-brown adult female. At age 14 months (usually in July), they molt into their adult plumage, and males acquire their red color for the first time.

The male's red plumage comes from eating carotenoid pigments in plants, which are then deposited during a feather's growth. Rarely, male Cassin's Finches can have pale yellow to yellowish-orange plumage, depending on the carotenoid content of their diet.

## CONSERVATION

The Cassin's Finch rates a 13 out of 20 on the Continental Concern Score. Moderately rapid declines over the past decades seem to have slowed. This species has therefore been down-listed from Near Threatened to Least Concern on the 2019 IUCN Red List.

# COMMON REDPOLL (REDPOLL COMPLEX*)

*Acanthis flammea*

> *Standing there . . . I am reminded of the incredible phenomenon of small birds in winter, that ere long amid the cold powdery snow, as it were a fruit of the season, will come twittering a flock of delicate crimson-tinged birds, . . . redpolls, to sport and feed on the seeds and buds now just ripe for them on the sunny side of a wood, shaking down the powdery snow there in their cheerful social feeding, as if it were high midsummer to them. These crimson aerial creatures have wings which would bear them quickly to the regions of summer, but here is all the summer they want.* What a rich contrast! tropical colors, crimson breasts, on cold white snow!
>
> —Henry David Thoreau, "Autumn," December 11, 1855

---

* We refer to the Redpolls as "Redpoll Complex" to reflect the potential changing taxonomic status of Hoary Redpoll and Common Redpoll merging into a single species.

## QUICK TAKE

Irruptive finches are known for their mystery. Some come from where the farthest land meets the frozen sea. These northern visitors flee their hinterlands when food is scarce, on a schedule tied to the rhythms of ecology, and move south, trusting to waiting nourishment.

Common Redpolls are ch-ch-ch chatterboxes that irrupt and create their own snowstorm, swirling over the landscape, as they flit in unison seeking vital food resources. While they can feast on a variety of weed, conifer, and other seeds, their quest is for favored birch and alder seeds. They grasp a birch catkin base in one foot, releasing the seed-protecting bract with their finely pointed bill and eating the seeds. The tiny hawk-shaped bracts litter the snow below.

Common Redpolls (also known as Mealy Redpolls) breed in the arctic tundra and taiga forests from Alaska through Canada to Labrador. There are two subspecies in North America. The nominate subspecies, *A. f. flammea,* is small, and the larger, darker subspecies, the "Greater Common Redpoll," *A. f rostrata,* has several rows of dark flank streaks with a notably extensive black bib.

These irruptive redpoll finches still thrill birders as much as they did in Thoreau's day. Henry David Thoreau did not have binoculars—they were invented in 1893, and he died in 1862—but Thoreau was highly skilled at observing and recording the birds and nature he saw. In today's world, birders seek and document finches using new tools such as the internet and binoculars and hope to be as enchanted as Thoreau by the sight of a redpoll.

Redpolls usually irrupt every two to four years, sometimes alternating between the eastern and western United States. One of the biggest redpoll irruptions was during the finch superflight of 2020–2021. Common Redpolls moved in their largest numbers in the East in a decade. By early October 2020, a couple of rare Common Redpolls at feeders in New Mexico sounded an alert. By November, redpolls had moved into Delaware, Ohio, Indiana, and some of the northern areas of the Great Plains, then eventually reached Arkansas, Tennessee, and North Carolina in the East (per eBird reports). In the future redpolls will irrupt again in numbers; the question is when.

Finch prognostications arrive each fall in the form of the Winter Finch Forecast, officially begun in its online version in 1999 by legendary founder Ron Pittaway. It's eagerly awaited by the birding community because it predicts which finches, how many, and where they will be seen that winter. Once out, the forecast spreads like wildfire through birding media. The torch has been passed, and since 2020 the Winter Finch Forecast, now assembled by Tyler Hoar, is released through the Finch Research Network (founded by the coauthor of this guide, Matt Young).

Armed with the forecast, birders also tap into sources such as eBird, state bird listservs, bird organizations, and other birders for where the finches may be seen. Common Redpolls are often best found by searching every large-sized clump of heavily seed-laden birches from a birder's location to the Canadian border. Ha ha, just kidding, but birders keeping an eye out for likely birch habitat in their home patch could be rewarded with these crimson-tinged avian snow ornaments. The biggest payoff of all might be to locate the redpoll holy grail—a rare, prized Hoary Redpoll in with a bigger flock of Commons. That story is continued in the Hoary Redpoll chapter . . . read on.

## IDENTIFICATION

**Size:** L 5.25"

**Shape:** Small, deep-bellied, small-headed, broad-necked bird with a relatively thin-based, sharply pointed conical bill and moderate-length strongly notched tail. Distinguished from very similar Hoary Redpoll (with caution and adding plumage clues) by slightly longer and proportionally narrower-based bill, creating a more acute point; slightly more sloping forehead; and rounded crown (when crest is relaxed).

**Adult:** Both Common and Hoary Redpolls have red forecrown, black chin and lore, 2 white wingbars. Key clues to distinguishing the species (besides shape) are undertail coverts, rump, flank streaking, wingbar width, and color of scapular edges. Common Redpoll has white undertail coverts with 2 to many broad dark streaks; a dusky or whitish rump with extensive dark streaking (except older male, which can have bright pinkish-red rump); extensive broad dark streaking on the flanks; moderately wide white tips to greater secondary coverts; and brownish edges to scapulars, creating a dark-brown back.

**Adult Male:** Pinkish-red to bright red on breast and flanks, feathers tipped with white when fresh and wearing away over the year, revealing deep red.

**Adult Female:** Little or no pink on breast and flanks; generally darker than male on back. Similar female Hoary Redpoll paler overall; whitish undertail coverts with 0–3 thin dark streaks; whitish rump with little or no streaking; a few thin dark streaks on flanks; broad white tips to greater secondary coverts; grayish edges to scapulars, creating a frosty look to back; adult male with wash of pink on breast and flanks; adult female with essentially no pink.

**1st Year:** Often shows molt limits, with inner greater coverts fresher, darker, and more broadly tipped with white than older outer coverts. M. usually with wash of pink on breast and flanks; f. with no pink.

**Juv:** (July–Aug.) Generally streaked brown overall without red or black on head; buffy wingbars.

### *SUBSPECIES*

Two subspecies in North America; the subspecies *A. f. rostrata,* "Greater Common Redpoll," from northeast Canada, Greenland, and Iceland, is significantly (10%) larger and heavier.[1] Broader necked; darker face; bill deep-based with slightly curved culmen; streaking on flanks heavy and dark brown; extensive black bib quite noticeable especially when viewed head-on. The more widespread subspecies *A. f. flammea* from Alaska, Canada, northern Europe, and Siberia is smaller, bill slender, streaking on underparts thinner and medium brown. Subspecies *A. f. islandica* has a dark and a pale form and is restricted to Iceland.[2]

Adult m., *flammea* MN/01

Adult m., *flammea* NH/04

Adult f./1st yr. m., *flammea* MN/01

1st yr. f., *flammea* NH/10

Adult m., *rostrata* NH/03

Adult f., *rostrata* NH/03

### *SIMILAR SPECIES*

The North American Classification Committee (NACC) of the American Ornithology Society (AOS) recognizes 3 separate species of redpolls: Hoary Redpoll (*A. hornemanni*), Common Redpoll (*A. flammea*), and Lesser Redpoll (*A. cabaret* in Eurasia and introduced to New Zealand). That could change in the future, and they could be lumped as 1 species. For more on this and thorough tips on how to tell Hoary Redpoll from Common Redpoll, see the Hoary Redpoll account.

## DISTRIBUTION

Breeds in tundra and taiga forests across Alaska and Canada to Labrador, generally more south of Hoary Redpoll, although there is considerable overlap in their ranges. During the nonbreeding season, redpolls may retreat a bit from the farthest areas of their range, but during irruption years they move down to the middle or even southern areas of the United States.

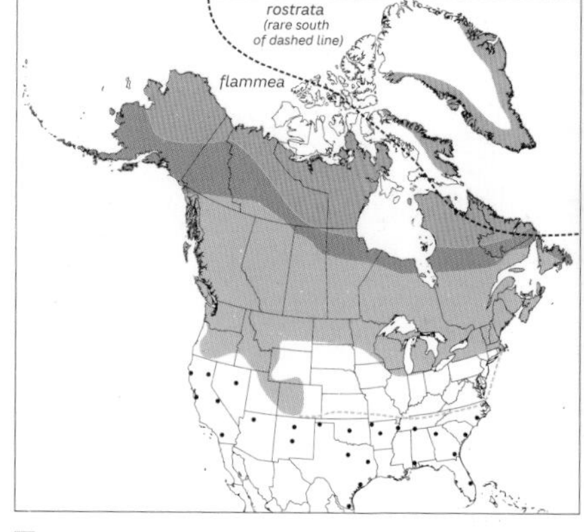


## LANGUAGE

### *MALE*

Common Redpoll song is believed to be largely indistinguishable from Hoary Redpoll song. Song is a long series of repeated short calls and trills, sometimes with single notes mixed in. Can be continuous or, more often, a disjunct version that can intergrade. Flight calls and trills may be mixed in a song.[3] Song given perched or in flight.

### *MALE AND FEMALE*

A variable, complex flight call, described as *che, che, che, chew, chew, chew,* or *jirp, jirp, jirp,* is the most common call given in redpoll flocks. A rising in pitch described as *zree, sweeee,* or *drweee* call, singly or in series, is given in alarm, to call the group together, or when birds are excited. Also, a buzzy trill is given by flocks in winter, and can be incorporated in song.[4]

## FUN FACT

**The redpoll's name is derived from the Middle English name for head, called "pol." So redpoll means redhead.**[14]

Common Redpoll subspp. *rostrata* (middle) is larger than the subspp. *flammea*

## HABITAT AND DIET

Common Redpolls are found in open woods with conifers, and in birch, willow, juniper, and alder in wetland areas. They also breed in protected places on the tundra with stunted trees, shrubs, and conifers. Subspecies *rostrata* breeds on rocky slopes on Baffin Island, and, in Greenland, away from the foggy coast in drier areas with birch, willow, and alder shrubs.[5]

Common Redpolls forage on a diversity of foods including seeds of bog, paper, yellow, gray, black, and river birches, speckled and red alder, conifers, grasses, weeds, and buds. In the breeding season, they eat a number of insects and spiders and feed them to their young. During irruptions, redpolls follow large mast crops found on birches, alders, and to a lesser extent spruces and other trees.

Highly gymnastic redpolls can feed upside down on the tippy ends of twigs to extract seeds from catkins and even shake catkins to retrieve the seeds from the ground. Birch seeds are at the top of the preferred food list for good reason: in the most extreme winter weather, they deliver high energy, helping redpolls adapt to severe arctic temperatures. Both redpoll species can store seeds in an esophageal pouch before dark and digest in a sheltered location later or at night.

## AT YOUR FEEDER

Feeders stocked with Nyjer®, finch mixes, and black oil sunflower will attract chatterbox redpolls. While thrilling to see, redpoll flocks will sometimes overtake a feeder by the hundreds, so accommodate them with multiple feeders.

Common Redpoll flock in weedy field

## MOVEMENTS AND IRRUPTIONS

Redpolls generally irrupt from their breeding range, in times of food shortage and high population numbers, not necessarily because of cold temperatures, which they are well-adapted to survive. Biennial irruptions occurred southward into the northeastern states for several years from 1992 to about 2004, but irruptive movements haven't been nearly as regular in the last decade.

Although more of an irruptive in the East than the West, in some years redpolls irrupt across the northern half of the United States. A large irruption including the West occurred in 2012–2013. As mentioned, one of the biggest redpoll irruptions in a decade took place in the East during the 2020–2021 historic superflight. This irruption was notable for large numbers of Common Redpolls and other finches such as White-winged Crossbills arriving in Oregon earlier than usual (in November) and in some of their best numbers on record.[6] Other western states such as Idaho, Wyoming, and Colorado also saw good numbers.

Common Redpolls have irrupted in the East during 1960, 1962, 1966, 1969, 1970, 1972, 1976, 1978, 1981, 1982, 1986, 1987, 1992, 1994, 1996, 1998, 2000, 2002, 2004, 2005, 2008, 2009, 2013, 2020, and 2021.[7]

## BREEDING BEHAVIOR

Given the possibility that redpolls are all one species, more study is needed on their breeding grounds. Genetically there is evidence of low levels of interbreeding between the two species, but field observations also point to high levels of assortative mating (they can tell each other apart).

### *TERRITORY*

Common Redpolls do not seem to have territorial behavior; it's more aptly described as weakly defending an area around the nest at certain breeding stages. Nests singly or in loose groups.[8]

### *COURTSHIP*

During courtship, the male feeds the female regurgitated, partially digested seeds. Males may fly in slow circles or with undulating flight while vocalizing. Other courtship displays include the male quivering his wings with head raised while hopping toward a female, and a "moth flight" of hovering with shallow rapid wingbeats. If females respond with crouching and wing fluttering, copulation follows.[9]

Common Redpoll males in aggressive interaction

A study of captive birds showed that redpolls established a dominance hierarchy and had a variety of displays to communicate agnostic intent such as crouching with body sleeked, pointing head forward, and lifting chin up and down, showing the black chin. During nonbreeding, males were dominant over females. Things changed during breeding; females selected mates and became dominant over them.[10]

### *NESTING*

**Timing:** April to September
**Nest:** Cup, outside diameter about 4 in., of grasses, twigs, rootlets, moss, thickly lined with ptarmigan or grouse feathers, hair, wool; placed up to 5.5 ft. high out on a branch of conifers like spruce, or crotch of alder, willow, or other trees or low shrubs; on tundra in driftwood, rock ledges, or other cover.
**Eggs:** 4–7, light green to turquoise with dark or lilac speckles or swirls at end
**Incubation:** 11–12 days
**Nestling period:** 10–16 days
**Broods:** 1–3

The female builds the nest, collecting grasses and rootlets or even material from an old nest, while the male follows her closely. The female is fed by the male during incubation but may sometimes leave to feed herself. At one monitored nest in Finland, the female spent 96.6% of the incubation period on the nest.[11]

After the young hatch, the female broods them until they are about 5 days old. At first, the male may deliver food to the female who then feeds it to the young, then both male and female feed them. Both adults dispose of fecal sacs until near the end of the nestling phase. After fledging, the young remain in family groups for an unknown period.

There is some evidence of polyandry (female mating with more than one male during breeding) in Common Redpolls. A study in Churchill, Manitoba, showed through DNA analysis that an adult color-banded female and an adult color-banded male had a brood together and the female was the biological parent of one set of young.[12] But while the same female was still feeding almost fully grown young from that brood, she had a nest with a second male. The authors concluded, "We feel that polyandry might be more prevalent in cardueline finches (including redpolls) than is generally recognized."

### FUN FACT

**Redpolls can adapt to cold winter temperatures by tunneling under the protective snow for the night to keep warm. In the morning they emerge, leaving a telltale redpoll-sized hole.[13]**

## MOLT

Adults completely molt at the end of breeding, usually July to September. The reddish color of the male is pale in autumn because it is obscured by the pale edges of the new feathers. Those edges wear off by breeding time, revealing a brighter, more intense red.

## CONSERVATION

Partners in Flight rates them Low Concern, 9 out of 20 on the Continental Concern Score. However, Common Redpolls have still experienced declines, and, as with other northern breeding finches, their boreal and tundra habitat is vulnerable to changes brought about by global climate change.

# HOARY REDPOLL (REDPOLL COMPLEX*)

*Acanthis hornemanni*

*"Fever"*
—Song by Eddie Cooley and Otis Blackwell, 1956

## QUICK TAKE

***July 2020***

Ornithologist Matt Young was sitting in his office. With perfect timing, he was just about to launch the Finch Research Network (abbreviated FiRN, named after the firn ice country of northern finches where it is so cold, the partially compacted névé, a type of snow leftover from past seasons, crystallizes into a substance denser, an intermediate stage between snow and glacial ice: firn). The Finch Research Network aims to officially form a community and network of people interested in observing

* We refer to the Redpolls as "Redpoll Complex" to reflect the potential changing taxonomic status of Hoary Redpoll and Common Redpoll merging into a single species.

and studying finches. Owing to his past love of meteorology-like predictions, Matt knows that the coming finch irruption will be a good flight. What he doesn't know is that it will not be just a good flight, it will become an epic superflight. These "superflights" are defined as southern flights of seven to eight eastern irruptive finches: Pine Siskin, Common Redpoll, Hoary Redpoll, Purple Finch, Pine Grosbeak, Evening Grosbeak, Red Crossbill, and White-winged Crossbill. Superflights are rare, and only when conditions align and food supplies are diminished will all species move in numbers. Hoary Redpolls, it turns out, would move in the largest numbers seen in ten years. Redpoll fanaticism was to become 104 degrees Fahrenheit Finch Fever. I, along with thousands of other birders, was about to get a bad case.

***January 12, 2021***

-67 degrees, I told myself, they live where it's -67 degrees. These beautiful little fluffball "angel pols" come from where the firn ice is. They have extra insulative feathers that enable them to live where few others do. It's cold and windy; this is like a balmy beach day for them. Ignore your cold feet if you want to see one. I was determined to find my grail bird, a Hoary Redpoll, one of the most elusive and hard to identify of the irruptive finches, and I was not going to leave this cold, windswept landscape at Woodmont Orchard, New Hampshire until I not only saw but photographed one.

In the parking lot I got out of the car. A birder appeared; I asked her if she had seen the Hoary Redpoll that was being reported on the local New Hampshire listserv, and she said yes.

"Just go up the farthest hill and keep looking for a flock of redpolls. They move around a lot."

That was the first understatement.

"What's the best path?" I asked, since it was not obvious.

"Well, go straight to the woods and turn left, but you will have to cross some ice."

That was the second understatement.

The path went left and became straight ice. Cradling my big, heavy Canon 1DX pro camera body and lens I walked on the ice in my Oboz fleece-lined boots, placing my feet in what little indentations I could find. I made it across the *looong* icy stretch, like a Lord of the Rings journey, then emerged onto the big path that led up the big hill. Onward!

Then I saw a figure on top of the far hill, dwarfed by the vast landscape. I realized that she was viewing a flock of redpolls in the distance.

For two hours, I kept looking at the constantly moving distant flock and not seeing any whitish bird jump out at me that was a Hoary Redpoll. I kept desperately searching. Was this going to become some sick game of Where's Waldo?

Then Taurus-birth-sign-me kicked in with what is described as Taurus stubbornness, but I prefer to think of it as commitment. No Hoary Redpoll was going to elude me! I did not care how cold I got. The constant lifting up and down of my heavy camera and lens was getting to me and it felt like I had been doing bicep curls for hours. I mentally and spiritually regrouped.

I looked up, and in the distance, saw that two figures—my friends Scott and Rich, excellent birders—were coming up the path. The reserve troops had arrived.

Hoary Redpoll, Woodmont Orchard, NH/01

We worked together for the next half hour, using our combined skills. We would see a lighter, frostier bird in with the Common Redpoll flock, but the flock would then move and locate somewhere else. Suddenly the flock flew to the edge of the enormous field in the taller grasses and weeds under the orchard fruit trees. We very cautiously moved closer, always mindful of not disturbing the birds.

If this were a movie, the cameras would go into slow motion, the lights would rise, and the hallelujah chorus would play. For one, brief, shining, moment the Hoary Redpoll popped up right in front of us, in a tree, and posed. Click, the perfect side angle showing the smaller pushed-in bill and faint side streaking, click, click, click, click, my camera fired at twelve frames per second. The Hoary flew off the perch, rotating at the ideal angle to give a clear view of the almost pure white undertail, then turned on its descent showing the pure white rump. I had just gotten the perfect photos to ID the Hoary Redpoll. Elation does not begin to describe my state.

I was not the only one chasing Hoary Redpolls; thousands of birders were on a finch quest just like mine at this time. For some, the flames were fanned by wanting to add a new life bird (a bird you have seen for the first time in your life), high on a birder's Richter scale of excitement. We may be hard-wired to seek rare birds, as newness activates the "novelty center" of our brain (substantia nigra/ventral segmental area) increasing our dopamine levels which makes us want to go exploring in search of a reward.[1]

During this time the Finches, Irruptions, and Mast Crops Facebook page (administered by Matt Young at the Finchmasters—Finch Research Network) blew up with members wanting confirmation of their sightings and photos of potential Hoary Redpolls.

Hoary Redpoll, Woodmont Orchard, NH/01

Hoary Redpoll, Woodmont Orchard, NH/01

But if a Hoary Redpoll listened to the current discussion among ornithologists as to whether it exists as a separate species, it might face an identity crisis. Is a Hoary separate from other redpolls, or are they all one species? This story took a turn at Matt's home in Cortland, New York in March 2012, when a flock of redpolls descended upon his yard—a flock with plumage diversity he had not seen before. This flock of Common Redpolls (nominate subspecies *flammea*), numbering only about sixty-five or seventy birds, also contained a few big Common Redpolls subspecies *rostrata,* Southern Hoary Redpolls, subspecies *exilipes,* and two or three that many thought could be nominate Hoary Redpolls, subspecies *hornemanni.* Matt invited colleagues Scott Taylor and Nicholas Mason from the Cornell Laboratory of Ornithology over to band birds and take blood samples . . . and a genetic study started.[2]

Using modern techniques of looking at genome sequences, a newer research paper in 2021 surmised that Hoary and Common Redpolls (and the Lesser Redpoll, *A. cabaret,* of Eurasia) may be one species but share a supergene that maintains the plumage difference.[3]

The North American Classification Committee (NACC) of the American Ornithology Society (AOS) is considering a 2024 proposal to merge Common Redpoll, Hoary Redpoll, and Lesser Redpoll into a single species. If passed, the new species would be *Acanthis flammea* (Common Redpoll) and consist of subspecies *A .f. flammea, A. f. rostrata, A. f. islandica, A. f. hornemanni, A. f. exilipes, and A. f. cabaret.*

Meanwhile, Hoary Redpolls do not care. Who are they? These ice angels who fueled fire-hot finch fever are masters of survival who succeed in their arctic home.

## IDENTIFICATION

**Size:** L 5.5"

**Shape:** Small, deep-bellied, small-headed, broad-necked bird with a relatively thick-based sharply pointed conical bill, and moderate-length strongly notched tail. Distinguished from very similar Common Redpoll (with caution and adding plumage clues) by slightly shorter, proportionally deeper-based bill, creating a more broadly angled tip and stubbier look; slightly steeper forehead and flattened crown (when crest is relaxed); head and broad neck blend into body. Shorter bill and steeper forehead create an impression of a "pushed-in" bill.

**Adult:** Both Common and Hoary Redpolls have red forecrown, black chin and lore, 2 white wingbars. Key clues to distinguishing the species (besides shape) are undertail coverts and rump, both difficult to see except at close range. In Hoary Redpoll, both sexes have white undertail coverts with 0–3 thin indistinct streaks and whitish rumps with moderate to no dark streaking. Additionally, upperparts whitish to grayish with grayish-brown streaking; white edges of greater coverts thicker; and flanks variably with a few thin dusky streaks.

**Adult Male:** Pinkish limited to upper breast, feathers tipped with white when fresh (fall and winter) and wearing away over the year, revealing more color.

**Adult Female:** Generally without pink on breast and flanks; generally slightly darker than male. See Common Redpoll account for comparison.

**1st Year:** Often shows molt limits, with inner greater coverts fresher, darker, and more broadly tipped with white than older outer coverts. Male breast, flanks, and rump rarely tinged pink. Some 1st-yr. males indistinguishable in the field from 1st-yr. females.

**Juv:** (July–Aug.) Generally streaked brown overall without red or black on head; bill less stubby than on adult.

### *SUBSPECIES*

Two subspecies, *A. h. hornemanii* (northeast Canada and Greenland) larger (by 10%), large-billed, very broad-necked, more whitish overall with little streaking. *A. h. exilipes* (northern Europe, Alaska, and Canada) smaller, smaller-billed, browner with dusky streaking.

### *SIMILAR SPECIES*

As mentioned, research published in 2015 by Mason and Taylor concluded that redpolls are likely all one species.[4] They compared DNA and RNA from 77 redpolls, several from Matt Young's feeders in New York, and specimens from museums around the world.

More recent research by Funk et al. 2021 titled "A Supergene Underlies Linked Variation in Color and Morphology in a Holarctic Songbird" found that a chromosomally inverted supergene may control how redpolls look.[5] Common and Hoary Redpolls regularly mix genes through interbreeding, but the supergene they share maintains the plumage difference between the more streaked and larger-billed Common and smaller-billed, frostier-appearing Hoary Redpoll.

Adult m., *hornemanni* NF&LB/03

Adult f., *hornemanni* NF&LB/03

Adult m., *exilipes* AK/06

Adult f., *exilipes* AK/06

1st yr., *exilipes* NY/02

## HOARY REDPOLL VS. COMMON REDPOLL ID

Some birds neatly fit typical Common or Hoary Redpoll characteristics, but a lot of birds are intermediate. Identify them by taking time, using caution, getting lots of photos, and, if possible, measurements. Get as many photos as you can from different angles. Also capture several redpolls in the same photo, so the bird in question can be examined in relation to the other redpolls under the same lighting conditions for accurate comparison of size and plumage colors. See also both species' Identification sections in this guide. Hoary Redpoll subspecies *hornemanii* and the Common Redpoll subspecies *rostrata* are generally a good bit larger overall than most Hoary Redpoll subspecies *exilipes* and Common Redpoll subspecies *flammea*.

Difficulty of Hoary Redpoll identification, ranked easiest to toughest, is adult male, adult female, immature male, and immature female (traits overlap with immature female Common Redpoll).

### *BEST*

1. Hoary: white, unstreaked (or up to 3 fine streaks) undertail coverts. Common: undertail with 2 to many broad dark streaks.

2. Hoary: clean white rump. Common: rump whitish or dusky with extensive dark streaking and older males can have bright pinkish-red rump.

3. Hoary: frostier back (especially before late winter and spring) and overall frostier bird. Hoarys will get browner-backed-looking due to feather wear as spring approaches. Common: brownish edges to scapulars create dark-brown back.

Hoary undertail, up to 3 thin fine streaks

Common undertail, many dark streaks

Hoary male, white rump

Common male, dark streaks on rump

Hoary, left, frosty back; Common, right, dark back

Hoary, stubby bill

Common, longer, more narrow bill

Hoary, wispy flank streaking

Common, extensive dark flank streaks

### *SECONDARY*

1. Hoary: short stubby bill giving a steep forehead appearance, but it's mainly only applicable to females because there's overlap in males. Common: in general, slightly longer proportionally narrow-based bill creating a more acute point, slightly less sloping forehead, and rounded crown (when crest relaxed).

2. Hoary: wispy or thinning flank streaking, but immature females can be pretty streaky on flank and on undertail too. Common: flanks with extensive broad dark streaking.

Hoary *hornemanni*, thicker neck

Common, broad neck

Hoary male, whitish chest, pale pink

Common male, red streaked breast

### *TERTIARY*

1. Hoary: buffy wash to face which seems fairly common in both Hoary and Common females.

2. Hoary: whitish chests with only a few streaks and pale pink on upper breast in male. A note of caution: Hoary males can gain in redness and how extensive the red is from fall to spring. Common: more heavily streaked chests with pinkish-red or bright red on breast and flanks of males.

3. Hoary: thicker, generally bull-necked appearance (even much more noticeable in Hoary Redpoll subspecies *hornemanii*). Common: broad-necked. Note appearance can change depending on bird's posture.

4. Hoary: whiter and wider-edged greater covert wing bar. Common: moderately wide white tips to greater secondary coverts.

5. Hoary: smaller size to the red forehead "pol" on head compared to Common. Hoary has feathering down legs.

## DISTRIBUTION

Regularly found in the boreal and taiga regions in Canada at the very northern edge of the Common Redpoll's range. The large subspecies *A. h. hornemani* lives in northeastern Canada and Greenland. In irruption years Hoary Redpolls can be found southward mixed in Common Redpoll flocks across the northern half of the United States. During the 2020–2021 superflight, Hoary Redpolls irrupted as far south as Nebraska, Iowa, Illinois, Indiana, Ohio, Pennsylvania, and New Jersey (per eBird records).

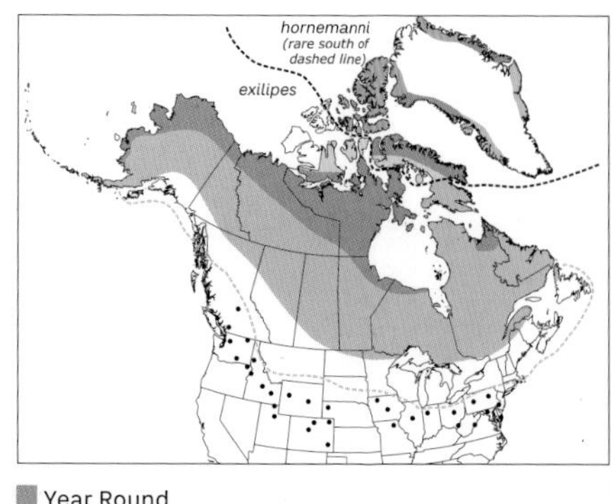


## LANGUAGE

Differences in language between Hoary and Common Redpoll are imperceptible, although a few suggest that the Hoary's calls may be louder, harsher, or sharper and possibly identifiable. A closer study is warranted. See Common Redpoll account for a complete description of redpoll language.

## HABITAT AND DIET

Extending more north than the Common Redpoll, Hoary Redpolls breed in low coniferous or mixed scrub and in tundra shrubs in sheltered areas. In southwest Alaska, their breeding habitat is in riparian shrubs and areas with stunted conifers, dwarf shrubs, and trees such as willows, birch, and alder.[6] In winter, look for Hoary Redpolls mixed with Commons in weedy fields and woodland edges of birch

Hoary Redpoll *hornemanni* with Common Redpolls *flammea*

and alder filled with seeds. Their diet of many kinds of weed, grass, and tree seeds is very similar to the Common Redpoll's. See that account for details.

Hoary Redpolls have adaptations to help them survive in their harsh environment. With a special storage pouch in their throat (called diverticulata, an expandable side area of their esophagus), they can eat then retreat, moving to shelter to process and digest the tiny seeds of their diet. When the temperature drops, Hoary Redpoll's digestive efficiency rises (more than Common Redpoll's). When it gets darker, no flashlight needed—Hoary Redpolls can forage in lower light levels than Common Redpolls.[7]

## AT YOUR FEEDER

Redpolls can descend on feeders in large numbers, especially in irruption years. That provides an opportunity to find the rare, frosty-looking Hoary Redpoll among the Common Redpolls. Offer Nyjer® and sunflower in the appropriate feeders, but separate the specialty finch feeders to lessen competition at the sunflower.

## MOVEMENTS AND IRRUPTIONS

While some redpolls may winter in their breeding range, they usually leave the most northern areas of their range. In the larger irruption years, the Hoary Redpoll irrupts south in singles to small numbers mixed in with Common Redpolls. For more on redpoll movements and irruptions, see the Common Redpoll entry.

## BREEDING BEHAVIOR

The frostier and smaller-billed Hoary Redpoll breeds more north of the Common Redpoll, but genetic evidence shows that they interbreed. However, other studies, plus observations by birders, point to assortative mating: they can tell each other apart. More research is needed.

### *TERRITORY*

Hoary Redpolls may pair before arrival to breeding areas. Males may chase other males from the nest area, but nests have been located close to each other in the same bush clump.[8]

### *COURTSHIP*

In one study 40 miles north of the Arctic Circle at Bathurst Inlet, Canada, a male Hoary Redpoll flew to a female and displayed while vocalizing, flying in several short hovering arcs with rapid wingbeats, then landed on her back and copulated.[9]

### *NESTING*

**Timing:** May to July
**Nest:** Cup of grasses, alder, willow twigs, roots lined with caribou hair, ptarmigan, willow down; placed on ground to 7 ft. high in willows, alders, birch, tamarack, spruce, and even in hollows in driftwood or rocky crevices.
**Eggs:** Average 4–5, range 1–7, bluish or greenish with speckles
**Incubation:** 11–13 days
**Nestling period:** 11–15 days
**Broods:** Unknown if more than 1

The female builds the nest. Ssp. *hornemanii* may reuse nests. Nest sites of Hoary Redpolls may be closer to or over shallow water than those of Common Redpolls.[10] Incubating and brooding females are fed by males, who fly in with loud flight calls and transfer food to the calling, wing-fluttering females.

The female broods increasingly less as nestlings grow. Nestlings are at first fed by the male bringing food to the brooding female, who then feeds the young. By day 10, male and female are equally feeding young. After the young depart their nest, families and their fledglings join together before migrating.

## MOLT

Molts later than most other bird species in its range. Adults have a complete molt after breeding. Plumage appears palest when fresh in autumn because the edges of the feathers are pale. Those edges wear off as the season progresses, by breeding time revealing slightly darker upperparts and more color for males (deeper pinkish but not the red of Common Redpoll) on cheeks, rump, and breast. Females rarely ever show pink color.[11] The Hoary Redpoll's plumage may have higher insulative value than the Common Redpoll's, allowing it to survive more extreme temperatures.[12]

## CONSERVATION

Not well studied, given its extremely remote northern range. Ranked Low Concern, 8 out of 20 on the Continental Concern Score, by Partners in Flight. However, climate change could have a significant negative impact on the habitat in its range.

# RED CROSSBILL (RED CROSSBILL COMPLEX*)

*Loxia curvirostra*

*One of the most difficult and perplexing issues in the systematics of Holarctic birds concerns the morphologically variable red crossbill complex . . . It is currently controversial whether this complex represents a single geographically variable species . . . a series of sibling species . . . or a more complicated combination of these alternatives.*

—Jeffrey G. Groth, June 1993

*I stood at Yellowstone Falls and I heard these birds come in and I saw their bills which were the oddest-looking thing, just a crazy adaptation. I was hooked the minute I saw them. I knew it was special, but what I didn't know was the rest of the trajectory and outlook on my life would be changed forever.*

—Matthew Anthony Young, June 1995

* We refer to the Red Crossbills as "Red Crossbill Complex" to reflect a future potential change in the taxonomic status of Cassia Crossbill being merged back to Call Type 9 and considered a single species with Red Crossbill.

*The Red Crossbills seemed incredibly attuned to one another and often would call before arriving, or when leaving, the flock in tight communication with one another. Their* jip-jip-jip *sounds seemed embedded in my brain. I began to hear their calls in my sleep. I bonded with the flock.*

—Lillian Quinn Stokes, August 2020

## QUICK TAKE

Red Crossbills are the most mysterious finches of an already mysterious group of birds, with a unique bill, their own language, and systematics that defy categorization. They're tied to conifer seeds for nourishment, and their nomadic lifestyle, guided by knowingness, leads to survival in times of seed shortage. And that bill—comparatively large, crossed, but not deformed, looking as though damaged in an accident or gallant endeavor.

Of the ten-thousand-plus bird species on earth, only Red Crossbills and five other crossbill species have a bill that crosses. The lower part (mandible) of a Red Crossbill's curves under the upper part of the bill (maxilla), like the way your fingers look when wishing for luck. Forged on the anvil of evolution with the precision of a Swiss Army knife, the bill is well suited to force the seed from a conifer cone, especially a closed one.

Extraction begins with the Red Crossbill grasping the cone in the foot on the opposite side from where the lower bill crosses the upper, like a dance move from the Argentine Tango. The powerful bill, tips strengthened by curvature, is bite-like inserted into the scales of a closed cone. In a thrusting outward motion of the lower bill, the scales are spread; if not far enough, spreading continues until the seed bounty surrenders to the crossbill's tongue. Then the tongue lifts the seed, securing it in a cradling groove in the upper palate, while the lower bill removes the seed from its seed coat to become crossbill fuel and DNA. Predator and prey are one. The dance of coevolutionary forces dictates morphology and shapes a species' destiny.

Red Crossbills in North America comprise eleven ecotypes; think of them as tribes differentiated by their contact flight call that largely live in their own unique areas, or core zones, until forced to move. They usually respond to only their own call type and mate assortatively with only their tribe members. They don't neatly fit into the category of separate species or even subspecies due to their nomadic behavior. There are times and a small number of situations where cross-breeding does occur at low levels, and they would flunk the species test of fidelity to one's species.

As a mostly conifer seed specialist, they have a nomadic adaptation which has them move to find a new rich patch of food resources to avoid starvation in times of food shortages.

Tribes live in core areas of occurrence with the conifers they primarily feed on—their key conifers. While almost all call types can feed on a variety of conifers, and they do, bill differences, like a tight fit of tool to the task, make many crossbill tribes uniquely suited for efficiently extracting the seeds of the key conifers in their core area.

Red Crossbill pair; female left, male right

But there are two partners in this tango. Conifers have their own agenda, finding fertile ground to pass on their DNA. They can outfox crossbills by evolving thicker cone scales, but, tit for tat, seed-predator crossbills evolve bigger bills to penetrate the cones. Conifers can sometimes boom then bust, cyclically producing a mammoth crop of seeds, stimulating a higher breeding rate and higher population in birds. They may sometimes follow with a low cone production year, forcing crossbills to flee to find a new patch of conifers. Strategy drives strategy, the coevolutionary dance continues.

Each of the eleven crossbill tribes possesses a unique language—their contact flight call—which is part of social bonding, flock cohesion, and communication about the best buffet. That call often needs to be decoded by *Loxia*-phile (crossbill-loving) code breakers. Accurately assigning a type to a recorded Red Crossbill call is best done by an expert through audiospectrographic analysis. The average birder can't discern it in the field, but skilled birders with abilities to detect nuances of sound can learn to tell call types.

Nestlings learn the special language of their tribe by hearing and imitating their parent's calls beginning in their first week in the nest; it's not innate. By about sixty days old they have perfected their family-specific contact call type. Adult Red Crossbills who are mated often take it one step further. The structure of their contact call notes becomes more similar the longer they're together, cementing closeness, coordination, and individual recognition.

Red Crossbills are mysterious birds with unique bill adaptations, language, lifestyles, and questions of whether their tribes are separate species. Ornithologist

Jeffrey G. Groth did the landmark work in 1993, discovering that a Red Crossbill taxon gives a unique call type. Additional research has demonstrated that call types have slight differences in morphology, genetics, and ecological associations.[1]

But crossbills are more than their science. They soar past the edge of science's knowingness, out into our unknown and into their knowingness. They can become a symbolic, even spiritual, force of energy that can spark a transformation in life.

Coauthor Matt Young became hooked on Red Crossbills when he stood at Yellowstone Falls as a young man, his gaze landing on a bird with an iconic crossed bill. He was mesmerized, watching them eat as seed coats rained down on him, baptizing him in his own waterfall of crossbill origin. Matt's life path then took him on to become the recognized Red Crossbill expert he is today.

Lillian Stokes, author of thirty-five bird and nature field guides, was transfixed and recruited by Red Crossbills when she visited them for a month when they came for grit to the parking lot of a nature center. She recorded their calls and sent them to code-breaker Matt Young.

Through luck or destiny, the paths of Matt and Lillian crossed over Red Crossbills and that crossing became the genesis of this book.

This Red Crossbill landed close by when Matt and Lillian first met in person

## IDENTIFICATION

**Size:** L 5.5–7.8"

**Shape:** Fairly small, short-tailed, short-legged, big-headed, broad-necked bird with distinctive heavy bill with crossed tips. Tail deeply notched; primary projection very long (2½ x bill).

**Both Sexes:** Lack bold white wingbars of White-winged Crossbill.

**Adult Male:** Body mostly all red, orangey, or even yellow, sometimes a mix of red and yellowish feathers; wings and tail blackish; throat and breast usually of uniform color.

**Adult Female:** Brownish or yellowish or yellowish green, often brightest on rump, crown, and breast; throat always grayish and lacking color, which is the best way to tell females from younger males; rarely may have thin, indistinct, buffy or grayish wingbar on coverts (but never like a broad, well-defined, white wingbar of White-winged Crossbill, which also has white-tipped tertials). In both sexes, undertail coverts whitish with dark chevrons.

**1st Year:** M. may be yellow, orange, or reddish with some brown; f. usually brownish or greenish with a little yellow but no color on the throat, as with adult f.

**Juv:** (just about any time of year since crossbills breed almost year-round) Brownish overall, with heavy brown streaking on whitish underparts; sometimes thin buffy wingbars. May breed in this plumage.

### *SUBSPECIES*

Jeffrey Groth's 1993 landmark study and monograph of call types was a key advancement in the science of the Red Crossbill.[2] It demonstrated that rather than thinking of Red Crossbills in terms of subspecies, their differences in bill and body size should be categorized by their contact flight call. He first described 8 call types, and in 1999, Craig W. Benkman found Call Type 9 in two isolated Idaho mountain ranges.[3] That type was elevated to species status—the Cassia Crossbill—in 2017. Kenneth Irwin distinguished Call Type 10 in 2010,[4] and a crossbill found mainly in Middle America was designated as Type 11.[5] The newest call type is Type 12 (formerly the eastern Type 10), described by Matthew A. Young et al. in 2024,[6] and is most common in the Great Lakes, Northeast, and Maritimes. Not counting Type 9 (Cassia), owing to its elevation to species status, there are now 11 call types in North and Central America.

The vast majority of the call types occasionally overlap in range even when breeding, violating the basic principle of subspecific designation, in which breeding ranges must be largely non-overlapping geographically. However, a few subspecies at the periphery of the range may be accurately assigned to subspecies: *L. c. stricklandi* (Type 6) in Arizona into Mexico, *L. c. mesamericana* (Type 11) in Central America, and *L. c. percna* (Type 8) in Newfoundland. *L. c. neogaea* is a match for one of the types most commonly found in eastern North America, likely Type 12, the new "Northeastern Crossbill."

Adult m. MA/04

Adult f. NY/01

Adult m. OR/08

1st yr. m. NY/03

1st yr. m. OR/08

Juv. NH/08

### *SIMILAR SPECIES*

Red Crossbill is similar to Cassia Crossbill (formerly Type 9 Red Crossbill) and only accurately distinguishable from that species by the analysis of flight call recordings. Red Crossbill is also similar to White-winged Crossbill, but that species has 2 broad, well-defined white wingbars, with males of more of a pinkish or scarlet red plumage. The Red Crossbill is highly variable in size of body and bill (even somewhat within call type), especially bill depth, which is the most heritable trait not susceptible to wear like bill length.[7] The smallest-billed Red Crossbill, Type 3, has a smaller bill than the White-winged Crossbill, and Cassia Crossbill has the fourth largest bill depth of the crossbill call types and species in North America.

## DISTRIBUTION

Spans North America, inhabiting coastal ranges in the Pacific Northwest; southern taiga forests from Alaska to Newfoundland; montane coniferous forests of the Appalachians, Rockies, Cascades, and Sierras; and higher elevations of Arizona, New Mexico, and Mexico to Nicaragua. They can also be found across much of the conifer forests of Eurasia from the United Kingdom to Japan.[8]

Distribution is intricately tied to habitat and diet, and therefore wherever the best habitat with ample cone crops can be found, crossbills will move, or even occasionally irrupt to those areas. For the sake of clarity, and because distribution is driven by cone crops, we combine these areas in this species account.

See pages 126–143 for range maps and foraging seasonality charts for more details.

## LANGUAGE

Crossbills usually associate and respond to just their own call type. Each type can be determined the vast majority of the time by deciphering the audiospectrographic analysis of its recording. Under Movements and Irruptions, each call type is given its own account, including descriptions and spectrograms. Flight calls are most often given in flight but can be given while perched. In addition to flight calls, Red Crossbills produce other sounds, including songs, which may be unique but as of now are not used to differentiate a call type. Rarely, crossbill mates have changed call type: in 3 instances, Type 2 changed to match the call type of Cassia Crossbill, and Cassia Crossbill, also in 3 instances, changed to match the call of Type 2.[9]

### *MALE*

Gives 2 types of song, a long song that is conversational and rambling and a consistent stereotypical song given when nesting. Males give several variations of these songs. Long song consists of slightly softer, longer series of fast phrases, may include flight notes, even calls of other call types, and isn't necessarily associated with breeding. A more stereotyped short song, often associated with breeding, is of repetitive two- or three-note phrases, and may begin or end with a few single notes.[10] Songs are given perched, or while flying with flapping-gliding wingbeats as a "flight song."

The tonal quality of the songs (especially the stereotyped song) appears to take on the quality of sound similar to described call type. There appear to be diagnostic

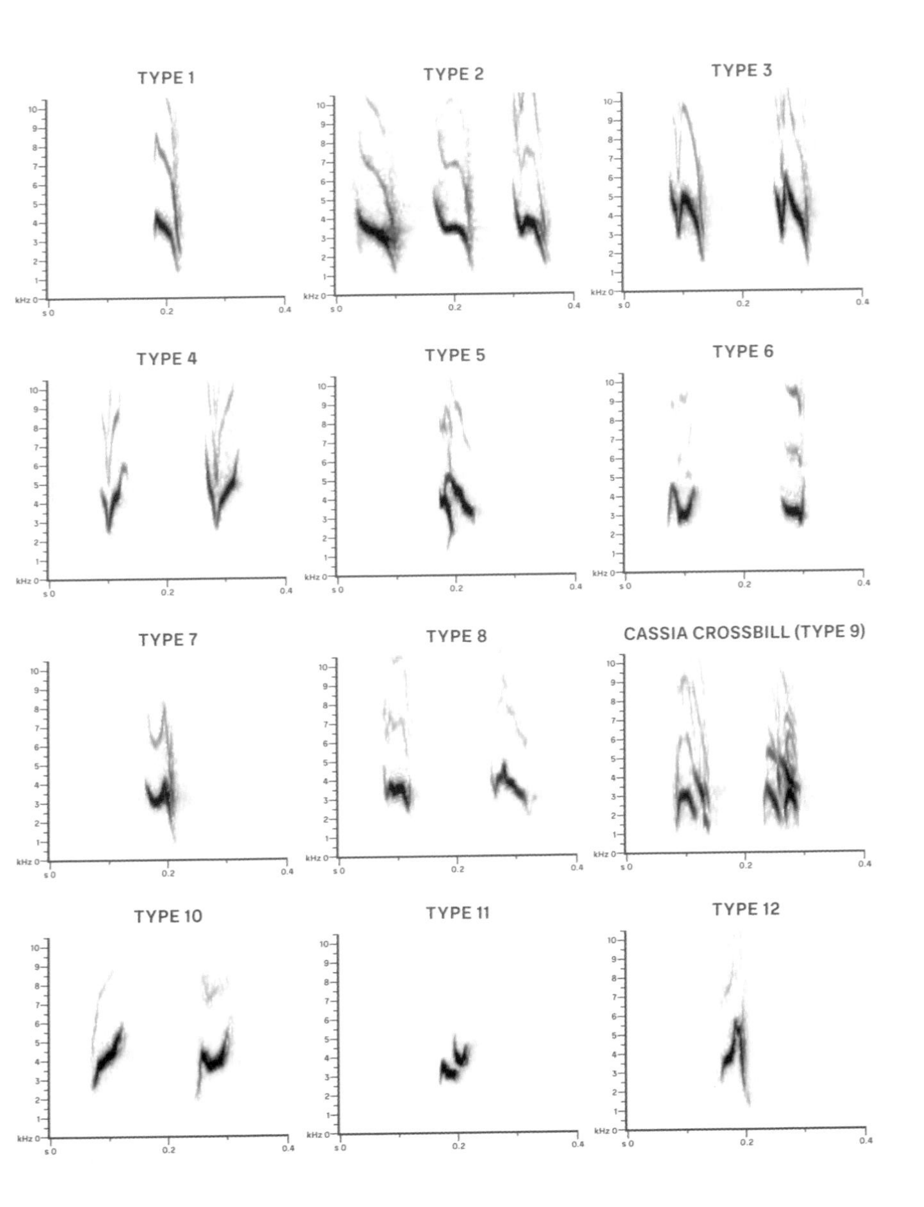


patterns to songs of some of the types: Type 1 seems to incorporate many more whistled and trilling phrases in its song in addition to sharp call notes; Type 10 gives many buzzy sounds in their song's phrases, and the song appears thin, much like their *whit-whit* contact calls; Type 3 song phrases often contain a distinctive modulated ascending note, and their song sounds squeaky, scratchy and weak like their contact call; Type 2 strings together a jumble of contact-like call notes and their songs sound powerful. Although some phrases seem distinct to call type, there is much overlap as well. Type 5 appears to give more consistent song phrases than other types from year to year. More study is needed.

### *FEMALE*

May not sing as often, and without the loud song phrases of male, but can do "conversational" song.[11] Thus, seeing a crossbill singing does not always imply it's a male.

### *MALE AND FEMALE*

In addition to the flight/contact call, males and females commonly give a *toop* or "excitement call," as well as softer alarm calls when a predator is around. (See page 135 for Red Crossbill toop calls.) These calls vary slightly from call type to call type and they are more suggestive of identification but not always diagnostic. Types 2, 4, 6, 8, and 10 can sometimes be identified by the *toop*/excitement call, but Types 3, 5, and 9 (Cassia), and Types 1 and 12 cluster, and are therefore not always diagnostic. Type 3 is a bit more nasally than Type 5 and Cassia, so with lots of practice they are discernible. Excitement calls are also given between nesting pairs, and in aggression within flocks. For more on these calls see the Eastern and Western editions of Nathan Pieplow's *Peterson's Field Guides to Bird Sounds of North America*.

Variable *chitter* calls consist of softer calls given in flocks while feeding or drinking. *Chitoo* calls vary little and are given by juveniles of all call types when begging for food from adults.

## HABITAT AND DIET

Crossbills can feed on seed in open or closed cones (most pines) still attached to branches, or remove the cones (closed hemlock, spruce, Douglas fir, lodgepole pine) to feed on elsewhere. They can also feed on seed in cones that have dropped to the ground. Crossbill bills can cross either left or right. To eat, the bird inserts its partly opened bill into a cone, then closes the bill, which lifts the scales up and apart. The

Red Crossbills coming to grit on dirt road in NY

tongue grabs the seed and tucks it into a special groove in the upper palate that occurs on the opposite site to where the lower bill crosses, then husks the seed.

Bill measurements (morphology) include depth, length, and palate groove width. In some crossbill types, research has shown a performance match between bill measurements and the seed size of their key conifers. Bill depth (curved tips add strength) matters because the crossbill can more effectively force open the scales and reach the seeds. Palate groove width matters because the more closely it fits a seed, the more securely it's held and the faster the crossbill can husk it.

Conifer cones usually open and drop their seeds in the months following seed ripening, and this can happen rather quickly some years when temperatures warm. In other cases, open cones will close again partly due to habitat moisture, retaining some seeds, as in western hemlock.[12] Some conifers are serotinous, meaning they delay cone opening until they receive a blast of heat, usually from fire, though a dry atmosphere or tree death might release seeds; even so, some amount of seeds are shed annually. These serotinous conifers have hard, closed cones, sealed with resin, and crossbills must pry them open using cracks where the cones have already started to open.

Studies by Craig W. Benkman hypothesize that certain call types (Type 2, 3, 4, 5) of Red Crossbills often feed on the conifers to which their bills are most efficiently adapted to extract seed. This measure of feeding performance, not preference, was studied in areas of the western United States. Lodgepole pine, which is used often by Type 5, is serotinous and produces one of the more consistent cone crops from year to year.[13] Lodgepole pine can also be non-serotinous in many areas. However, crossbills of many call types conifer switch and migrate, driven by their finely tuned, almost uncanny instincts to assess "food profitability": how quickly they can extract and consume seeds from their current conifers, or "milligrams of (conifer) kernel ingested per second" as defined by Benkman.[14] Thus, crossbills will change their habitat use and move according to seasonal conifer profitability across the landscape. Ecologists refer to such switching as "optimal foraging."

In times of large-scale cone-crop failure, crossbills may irrupt and migrate great distances in search of cones. In such years they move from a core zone of occurrence, where they're most common, to a primary zone of irruption, where the conifer composition may be similar to conifers in their core zone (for example, Type 3 uses western hemlock in its core zone but will irrupt and use eastern hemlock in eastern North America). Crossbills that inhabit island-like locales, like Cassia Crossbill (formerly Type 9, now its own species), or Types 5 and 6, that live with more stable cone crops, may irrupt less than other call types.

When key conifers disappoint, crossbills readily conifer switch to rich patches of conifers with ample seed. Sometimes crossbills just migrate based on their own assessment of which conifers will provide them with the highest feeding rates according to their needs at the time, including breeding. For example, Type 5's bill fits Rocky Mountain lodgepole pine as its key conifer but frequently munches on Engelmann spruce when nesting.[15] And, within a crossbill call type, bill depth measurements can differ and be even a better fit for feeding on conifers in a rich local patch in a different geographic area.

Crossbills of the same call type may move to a 4-star Michelin conifer tree, highly dense with seeds, by noting the feeding behavior of the other crossbills there.[16] Movement to a new area is a group decision by members of the same call type. When the menu is good, crossbills are busy eating, not "talking" much to one another. But if the feeding is poor for their call type, meaning the food source is inadequate to provide sufficient feeding rates with their specialized bill, then chitter calls from the flock signal it's time to move on, and they fly off.[17] Crossbill researcher Jamie Cornelius also found that after crossbills gather social information from food-restricted neighbors for three days, they will raise their pace of consumption, thus increasing their gut mass to maintain the needed muscles for flight even when limited to two short feeding periods per day.[18]

The cone cycle year starts roughly around July 1 as newly developing cone

Red Crossbill on Norway spruce

| CONIFERS RANKED BY ACCESSIBILITY | | |
|---|---|---|
| SOFT-CONED | SEMI-SOFT-CONED | HARD-CONED |
| Western hemlock | Douglas fir | *Some are serotinous (*denotes at least partial serotiny)* |
| Tamarack | Pines such as eastern white, western white, southwestern white, and limber | Lodgepole pine* |
| Engelmann spruce | Douglas fir (var. *glauaca*) | Ponderosa pine |
| White spruce, the "universal crossbill munchie" per Jeffrey Groth | Blue spruce | Jeffrey pine |
| Red spruce | Norway spruce | Jack pine* |
| Eastern hemlock | | Red pine |
| Sitka spruce | | Pitch pine |
| Douglas fir (var. *menzeisii*) | | Virginia pine* |
| | | Table Mountain pine* |
| | | Short leaf pine |
| | | Loblolly pine |
| | | Black spruce* |

crops are maturing. Crossbills first utilize the soft-coned conifers with seed that are readily accessible, and then switch to increasingly harder cones that hold seed longer as the year goes by.

Crossbills are wily, and therefore quite flexible, especially in spring. A crossbill's bill is just not that suitable for feeding widely on other food sources beside conifer seeds, but they will readily utilize emerging insects like woolly aphids and insect larvae to fatten up in spring before moving (Hahn and Cornelius, personal observations). Moreover, when many conifer seeds have been shed in spring, they will visit feeders for sunflower and also consume seeds and buds from deciduous trees.

## FOREST COMPOSITION IN THE EAST VS. THE WEST

Whether east or west, crossbills prefer forests made of conifers, whether pine, spruce, hemlock, or fir. This habitat is largely found across the boreal forest of Canada, the montane forests of the West, and in the northern-tier states from the West Coast to the Northeast.

There is a big difference in the diversity and density of conifers in the West versus the East. The coastal and montane forests of the Pacific Northwest are particularly strong crossbill-friendly habitat, with many call types co-occurring there, and a crossbill will almost always find something palatable on the menu. Call types that are most common and find their home (core zone of occurrence) in the West are 2, 3, 4, 5, 6, 7, 9 (Cassia), and 10. The other types—minus Type 8, which is largely endemic to Newfoundland—can be found in the West from time to time as well, especially Type 1 along the Pacific Northwest coast to Alaska.

The landscape of the East offers crossbills something different: lower density of conifers but a high diversity, especially in the Northeast and down the Appalachians. In most years a single species of conifer will produce a bumper cone crop in addition to other conifers with different phenologies producing viable crops. This often gives a call type a single species to feast on, but once the bumper crop is depleted it can then jump to other viable crops so it can make it to the next cone cycle year. Call types that are most common and find their home (core zone of occurrence) in the East are 1, 8 and 12. Type 3 irrupts there every 3–5 years; Type 2 locally occurs in areas of the plains states, Great Lakes, New York, Massachusetts, and Ontario, occasionally down the Appalachians; and Type 10 locally occurs in areas of the Great Lakes and Quebec. Type 4 locally occurs in the western Great Lakes and is rare in the Northeast (2023–2024 was an exception), and Type 5 is vagrant anywhere in the East. See maps below for more details.

Crossbills continually move across the landscape looking for the next rich patch of resources, first using softer-coned conifers, then, as the year progresses, switching to increasingly harder-coned conifers, which hold their seed the longest into spring.

| THE RED CROSSBILL CALL TYPES BILL SIZES |
|---|
| Smallest to largest bill size (i.e., bill depth): Type 3 < White-winged Crossbill < Type 10 < Type 1 = Type 12 = Type 4 < Type 7 < Type 5 < Type 2 < Cassia (Type 9) < Type 11 < Type 8 < Type 6 |

## MOVEMENTS AND IRRUPTIONS

Red Crossbills are the ultimate nomads. They move toward food availability, seeking the most profitable habitat with the best seed crops for their needs at the time, from surviving the winter to breeding. As mentioned, food profitability is defined by Benkman as "milligrams of (conifer) kernel ingested per second" at an adequate level.

Sometimes a crossbill call type moves mainly within its core area, but other times massive crossbill movements of multiple call types will move across the landscape, especially in May–July and October–January.

Since crossbills are intimately tied to conifer seeds as their food source, understanding conifers provides a way to understand Red Crossbills. Conifers vary in distribution and diversity and have different schedules of ripening and dropping, or holding on to, their seeds. This intricate, pulsing wave of conifer ripening phenology dictates crossbill movements and habitat use across North America.

### KEY TO INDIVIDUAL CALL TYPE MAPS*

■ **Core Zone of Occurrence (Purple):** Crossbills are found here most years eating key conifers and breeding.

■ **Secondary Zone of Occurrence (Red):** Crossbills present in fewer numbers most years, and small numbers breed. Type 3 breeds in the Northeast, represented with dashed lines indicating that it occasionally acts as a secondary zone of occurrence.

■ **Primary Zone of Irruption (Blue):** Crossbills flee to these areas when key conifers in their core zone fail, and may stay and nest rarely in small numbers. (The dashed line indicates where small numbers may irrupt and breed.)

■ **Secondary Zone of Irruption (Yellow):** Crossbills flee to these areas when key conifers in their core zones and primary zone of irruption experience widespread failure of many conifers. They very rarely nest here, only Type 2 appearing to do so.

■ **Tertiary Zone of Irruption (Gray):** Only Type 2 goes here rarely, and may breed locally, as this would be more aptly named the Eclectic Crossbill.

● **Solid Blue Dots:** Locally known to breed.

● **Solid Black Dots:** Vagrant occurrences.

--- **Dashed Line:** Irruptive migration takes place in this area.

* These specially created maps are based on knowledge of major crossbill audio collections, published literature, observations across the last almost 30 years, documented records, and cone-ripening phenologies across North America.

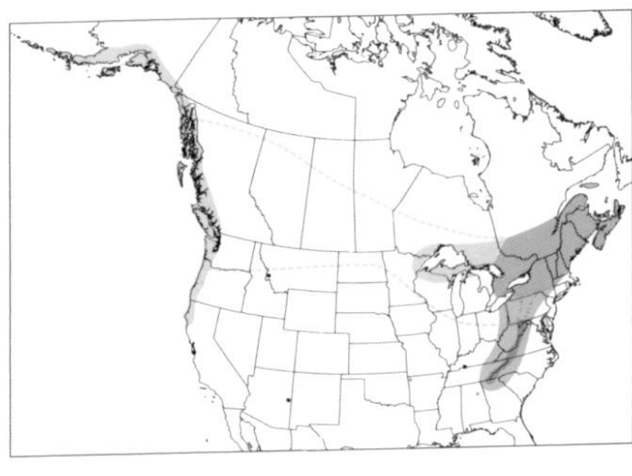


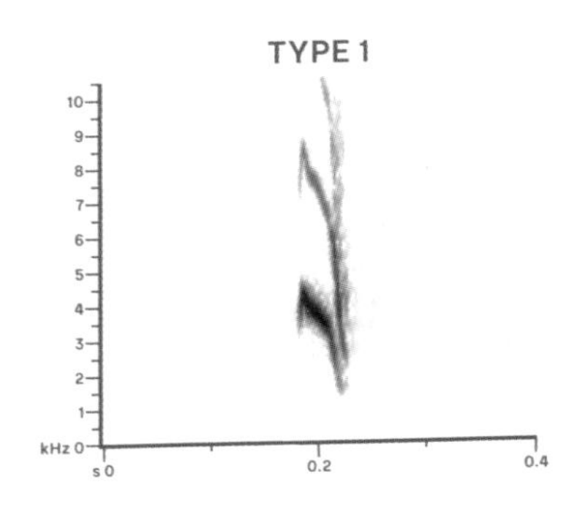


**Language: Type 1 Flight Call**
**Appalachian Crossbill**[19]
Quick, descending, dry *chewt; chewt-chewt-chewt.* Spectrogram usually starts with an upward part, the peak landing between 4.5 and 5kH, then a faster downward part to sonogram than Type 2, which has a similar sonogram. Often has more consistent secondary ending component than Type 2. Compare to Type 2.

**Bill Depth:** Medium

**Distribution:** Core zone of occurrence is the Appalachians of the Virginias to the Carolinas to Georgia. Secondary zone of occurrence is the northeastern United States, Ontario, and southern Maritime Provinces; rare in West most years, but appears to occur occasionally in coastal Washington and can be local in coastal Alaska.

**Movement and Irruptions:** Mainly resident in Appalachians and in lesser numbers the Northeast; appears to irrupt to Pacific Northwest and perhaps coastal Alaska.

**Diet and Habitat:** Red spruce and eastern white and Virginia pine forests of the Appalachians and foothills. Most commonly utilized trees in East appear to be red spruce, white spruce, eastern white pine, Virginia pine, and perhaps eastern hemlock some years; in West, particularly in coastal Alaska, Sitka spruce and western hemlock. Appears to use generalist strategy and utilize what conifers are available when, including using red, pitch (*Pinus rigida*), and Virginia pine (*Pinus virginiana*)[20] in winter months. Feeds and breeds regularly in small numbers in Norway spruce in state forests of southern New York. *(See chart on page 128.)*

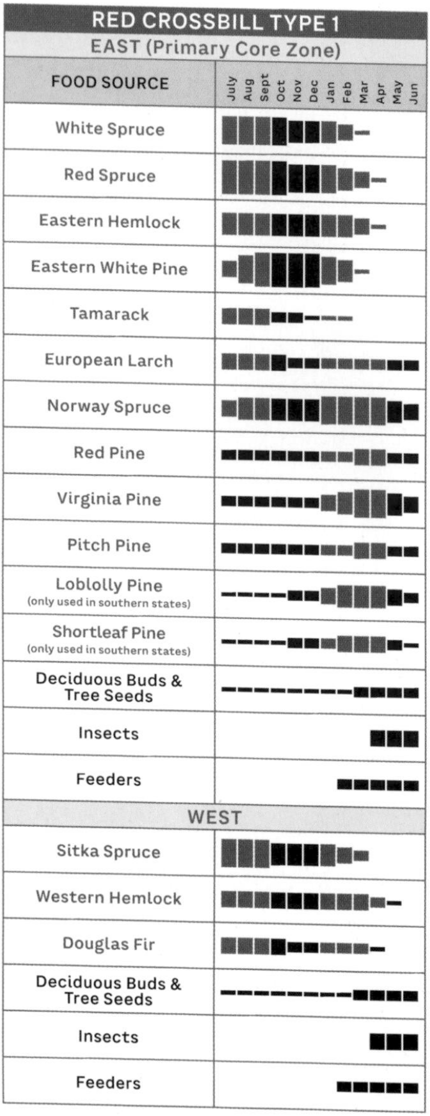

## RED CROSSBILL TYPE 1

### EAST (Primary Core Zone)

| FOOD SOURCE | July | Aug | Sept | Oct | Nov | Dec | Jan | Feb | Mar | Apr | May | Jun |
|---|---|---|---|---|---|---|---|---|---|---|---|---|
| White Spruce | | | | | | | | | | | | |
| Red Spruce | | | | | | | | | | | | |
| Eastern Hemlock | | | | | | | | | | | | |
| Eastern White Pine | | | | | | | | | | | | |
| Tamarack | | | | | | | | | | | | |
| European Larch | | | | | | | | | | | | |
| Norway Spruce | | | | | | | | | | | | |
| Red Pine | | | | | | | | | | | | |
| Virginia Pine | | | | | | | | | | | | |
| Pitch Pine | | | | | | | | | | | | |
| Loblolly Pine (only used in southern states) | | | | | | | | | | | | |
| Shortleaf Pine (only used in southern states) | | | | | | | | | | | | |
| Deciduous Buds & Tree Seeds | | | | | | | | | | | | |
| Insects | | | | | | | | | | | | |
| Feeders | | | | | | | | | | | | |
| **WEST** | | | | | | | | | | | | |
| Sitka Spruce | | | | | | | | | | | | |
| Western Hemlock | | | | | | | | | | | | |
| Douglas Fir | | | | | | | | | | | | |
| Deciduous Buds & Tree Seeds | | | | | | | | | | | | |
| Insects | | | | | | | | | | | | |
| Feeders | | | | | | | | | | | | |

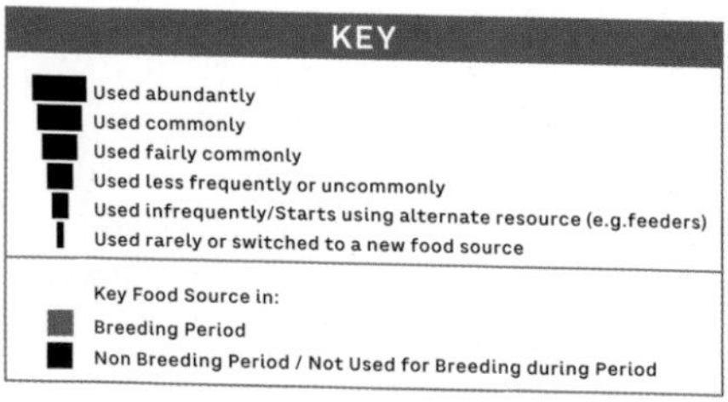

### KEY

- Used abundantly
- Used commonly
- Used fairly commonly
- Used less frequently or uncommonly
- Used infrequently/Starts using alternate resource (e.g.feeders)
- Used rarely or switched to a new food source

Key Food Source in:

- Breeding Period
- Non Breeding Period / Not Used for Breeding during Period

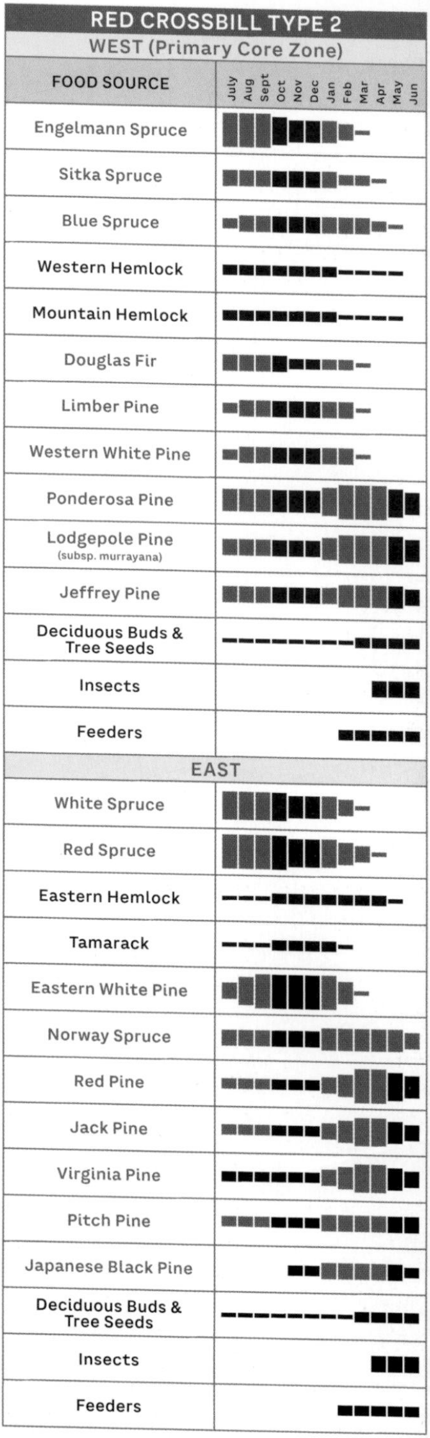

## RED CROSSBILL TYPE 2

### WEST (Primary Core Zone)

| FOOD SOURCE | July | Aug | Sept | Oct | Nov | Dec | Jan | Feb | Mar | Apr | May | Jun |
|---|---|---|---|---|---|---|---|---|---|---|---|---|
| Engelmann Spruce | | | | | | | | | | | | |
| Sitka Spruce | | | | | | | | | | | | |
| Blue Spruce | | | | | | | | | | | | |
| Western Hemlock | | | | | | | | | | | | |
| Mountain Hemlock | | | | | | | | | | | | |
| Douglas Fir | | | | | | | | | | | | |
| Limber Pine | | | | | | | | | | | | |
| Western White Pine | | | | | | | | | | | | |
| Ponderosa Pine | | | | | | | | | | | | |
| Lodgepole Pine (subsp. murrayana) | | | | | | | | | | | | |
| Jeffrey Pine | | | | | | | | | | | | |
| Deciduous Buds & Tree Seeds | | | | | | | | | | | | |
| Insects | | | | | | | | | | | | |
| Feeders | | | | | | | | | | | | |
| **EAST** | | | | | | | | | | | | |
| White Spruce | | | | | | | | | | | | |
| Red Spruce | | | | | | | | | | | | |
| Eastern Hemlock | | | | | | | | | | | | |
| Tamarack | | | | | | | | | | | | |
| Eastern White Pine | | | | | | | | | | | | |
| Norway Spruce | | | | | | | | | | | | |
| Red Pine | | | | | | | | | | | | |
| Jack Pine | | | | | | | | | | | | |
| Virginia Pine | | | | | | | | | | | | |
| Pitch Pine | | | | | | | | | | | | |
| Japanese Black Pine | | | | | | | | | | | | |
| Deciduous Buds & Tree Seeds | | | | | | | | | | | | |
| Insects | | | | | | | | | | | | |
| Feeders | | | | | | | | | | | | |

**Language: Type 2 Flight Call**
**Ponderosa Pine Crossbill**[21]
Lower, slower, richer, less quickly descending *cheewp; cheewp-cheewp-cheewp*. Spectrogram lacks an initial uptick component like Type 1. Gradually descends, leveling a bit, but then can go up then down, making a "kink" in the visual path of the spectrogram. Thus, there are two types of spectrograms: "kinked" and "unkinked." Can sometimes have an ending component. Most of the energy of the call is given below 4.5 kHz. The kinked type is most often heard in the West, and the unkinked type most often heard in the East.

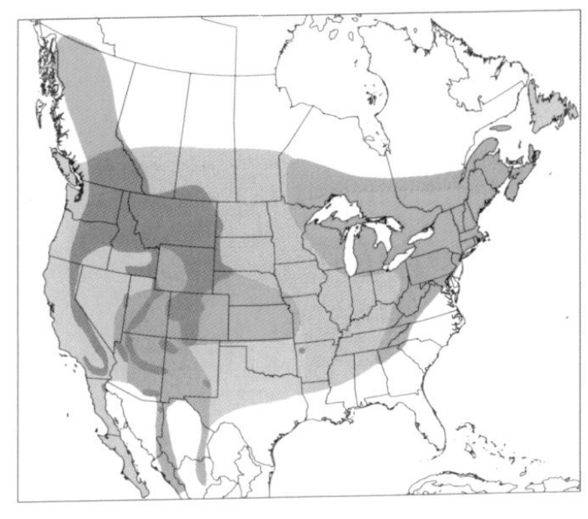


**Bill Depth:** Large
**Distribution:** Across United States into southern Canada and down to n. Mexico. There are two versions of Type 2 call as seen on a spectrogram. Most of the kinked type occurs in the West, whereas the unkinked type occurs mainly in the East, but there is overlap, especially in the western Great Lakes. See map for details on distribution.

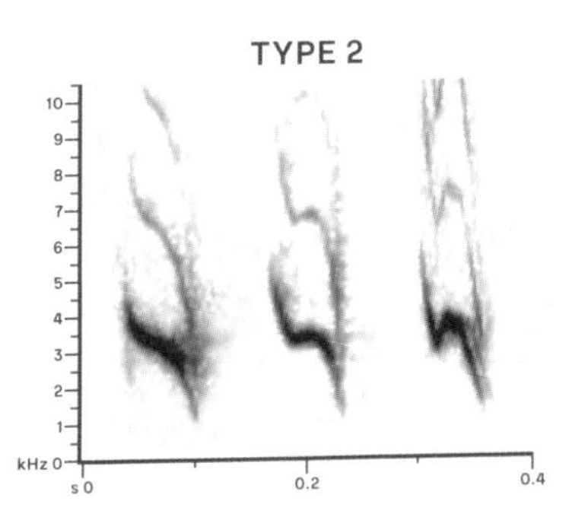


**Movements and Irruptions:** Most widespread across North America, and highly irruptive thus moving around North America in numbers with frequency, sometimes across distances west to east. Only Type 3 irrupts or moves across greater distances. The kinked type of the West sometimes irrupts east in fairly sizable numbers, especially to the Great Lakes.
**Diet and Habitat:** Pine and spruce forest, but can utilize just about any conifer species except perhaps the smallest-coned. Would be better named the Eclectic Crossbill or the "eats-everything crossbill." In the West, where most common, is most efficient feeding on ponderosa pine in the Rockies, Cascades, and mountains of Arizona. Like any crossbill, loves Engelmann spruce and to a lesser extent Douglas fir and blue spruce. In East uses red, jack, pitch, white, Virginia, nonnative Scotch, and Table Mountain pines, but also readily feeds on red and white spruces. Has even been strongly suspected of using more than twelve conifer species when nesting. It mainly eats *P. ponderosa scopulorem* in the US Rocky Mountains but feeds on *P. ponderosa* ssp. *ponderosa* in the Cascades. In the Sierra Nevada it associates with a subspecies of lodgepole pine (*Pinus contorta murrayana*) with easy-to-open seeds from its non-serotinous cones, which differ from the typical serotinous cones of the lodgepole pine subspecies in the Rockies and Cascades. Also eats Jeffrey pine when nesting in the Sierra. *(See chart on page 128.)*

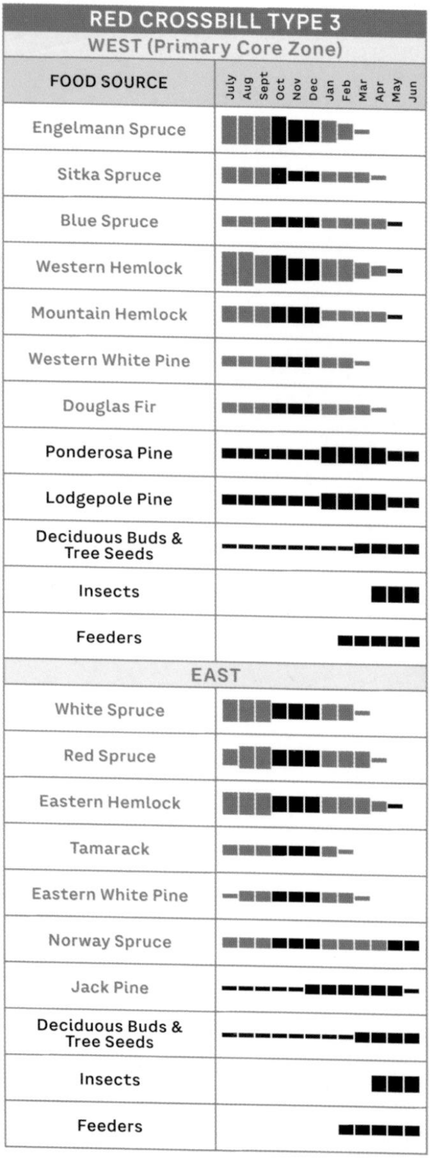

## RED CROSSBILL TYPE 3

### WEST (Primary Core Zone)

| FOOD SOURCE | July | Aug | Sept | Oct | Nov | Dec | Jan | Feb | Mar | Apr | May | Jun |
|---|---|---|---|---|---|---|---|---|---|---|---|---|
| Engelmann Spruce | | | | | | | | | | | | |
| Sitka Spruce | | | | | | | | | | | | |
| Blue Spruce | | | | | | | | | | | | |
| Western Hemlock | | | | | | | | | | | | |
| Mountain Hemlock | | | | | | | | | | | | |
| Western White Pine | | | | | | | | | | | | |
| Douglas Fir | | | | | | | | | | | | |
| Ponderosa Pine | | | | | | | | | | | | |
| Lodgepole Pine | | | | | | | | | | | | |
| Deciduous Buds & Tree Seeds | | | | | | | | | | | | |
| Insects | | | | | | | | | | | | |
| Feeders | | | | | | | | | | | | |

### EAST

| FOOD SOURCE | July | Aug | Sept | Oct | Nov | Dec | Jan | Feb | Mar | Apr | May | Jun |
|---|---|---|---|---|---|---|---|---|---|---|---|---|
| White Spruce | | | | | | | | | | | | |
| Red Spruce | | | | | | | | | | | | |
| Eastern Hemlock | | | | | | | | | | | | |
| Tamarack | | | | | | | | | | | | |
| Eastern White Pine | | | | | | | | | | | | |
| Norway Spruce | | | | | | | | | | | | |
| Jack Pine | | | | | | | | | | | | |
| Deciduous Buds & Tree Seeds | | | | | | | | | | | | |
| Insects | | | | | | | | | | | | |
| Feeders | | | | | | | | | | | | |

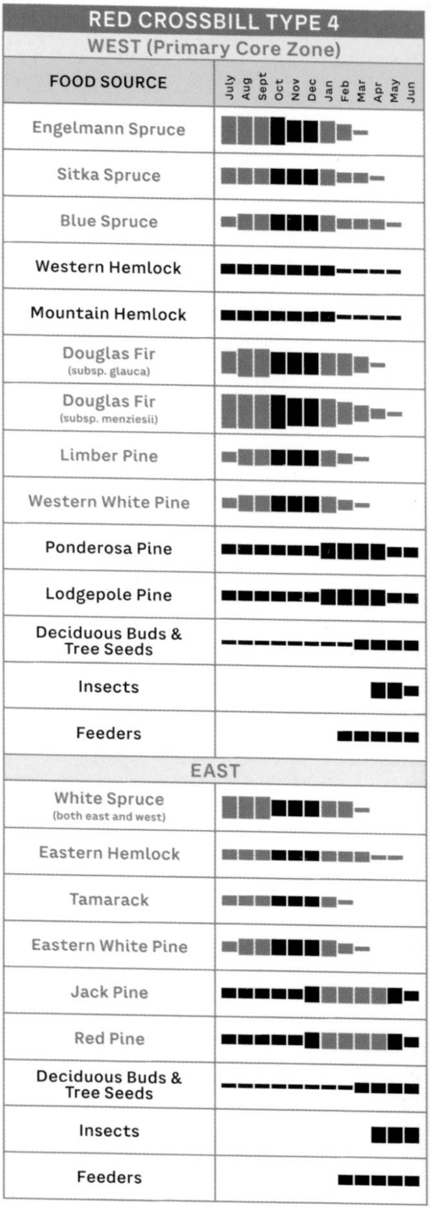

## RED CROSSBILL TYPE 4

### WEST (Primary Core Zone)

| FOOD SOURCE | July | Aug | Sept | Oct | Nov | Dec | Jan | Feb | Mar | Apr | May | Jun |
|---|---|---|---|---|---|---|---|---|---|---|---|---|
| Engelmann Spruce | | | | | | | | | | | | |
| Sitka Spruce | | | | | | | | | | | | |
| Blue Spruce | | | | | | | | | | | | |
| Western Hemlock | | | | | | | | | | | | |
| Mountain Hemlock | | | | | | | | | | | | |
| Douglas Fir (subsp. glauca) | | | | | | | | | | | | |
| Douglas Fir (subsp. menziesii) | | | | | | | | | | | | |
| Limber Pine | | | | | | | | | | | | |
| Western White Pine | | | | | | | | | | | | |
| Ponderosa Pine | | | | | | | | | | | | |
| Lodgepole Pine | | | | | | | | | | | | |
| Deciduous Buds & Tree Seeds | | | | | | | | | | | | |
| Insects | | | | | | | | | | | | |
| Feeders | | | | | | | | | | | | |

### EAST

| FOOD SOURCE | July | Aug | Sept | Oct | Nov | Dec | Jan | Feb | Mar | Apr | May | Jun |
|---|---|---|---|---|---|---|---|---|---|---|---|---|
| White Spruce (both east and west) | | | | | | | | | | | | |
| Eastern Hemlock | | | | | | | | | | | | |
| Tamarack | | | | | | | | | | | | |
| Eastern White Pine | | | | | | | | | | | | |
| Jack Pine | | | | | | | | | | | | |
| Red Pine | | | | | | | | | | | | |
| Deciduous Buds & Tree Seeds | | | | | | | | | | | | |
| Insects | | | | | | | | | | | | |
| Feeders | | | | | | | | | | | | |

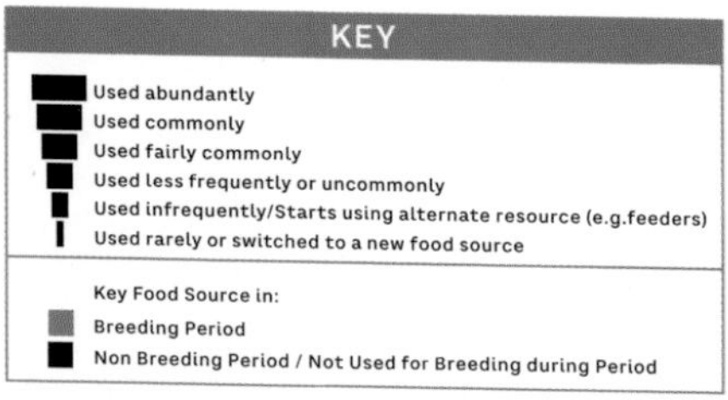

### KEY

- Used abundantly
- Used commonly
- Used fairly commonly
- Used less frequently or uncommonly
- Used infrequently/Starts using alternate resource (e.g.feeders)
- Used rarely or switched to a new food source

Key Food Source in:

- Breeding Period
- Non Breeding Period / Not Used for Breeding during Period

**Language: Type 3 Flight Call**
**Western Hemlock Crossbill**[22]
Squeaky, scratchy, hard, and less musical and distinctively audibly descending *tik-tik-tik*. Spectrogram tops out above 5 kHz, which is at higher frequency than most call types, making it higher than Type 1 and 2. Note the zig-zag or lightning bolt shape of the spectrogram.
**Bill Depth:** Smallest
**Distribution:** Core zones of occurrence are western coastal areas of North America and adjacent interior west. The Northeast is a primary zone of irruption but can also act as a secondary zone of occurrence in years they come east, when the eastern hemlock and spruce cone crop is large.[23]
**Movements and Irruptions:** Highly irruptive in large numbers to the Great Lakes, Northeast, Ontario, and sometimes Maritimes (sometimes with Type 10) about every 3–5 years. Moves to the Intermountain West as well, but much less frequently and in lower numbers.
**Diet and Habitat:** Western hemlock and Sitka spruce forest; more spruce in interior. Most commonly utilized trees in the West appear to be western hemlock, Sitka spruce, Engelmann spruce, and less often Douglas fir. Will also readily utilize ponderosa and lodgepole pines in parts of the West in late winter.[24] In East, readily feeds on eastern hemlock, and white and red spruces. This crossbill usually occurs on the western coast of North America, up through Canada into Alaska, and feeds on the small cones of western hemlock, also on Sitka spruce when its cones open (Tom Hahn, personal communication). The western hemlock cones in this area stay somewhat closed after opening because of the high-moisture habitat, thus some seed is retained and available over a longer period. *(See chart on page 130.*)*

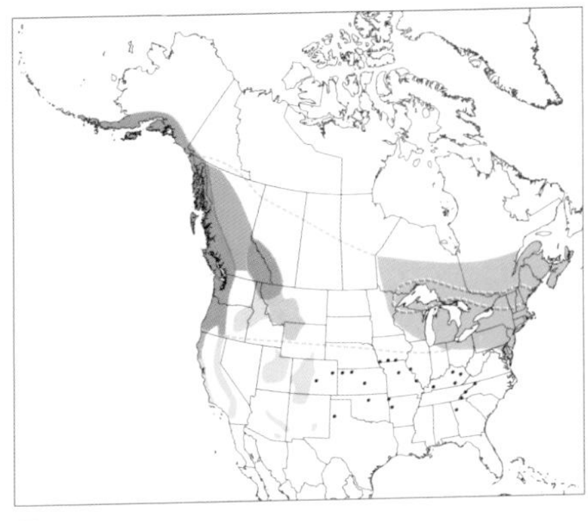


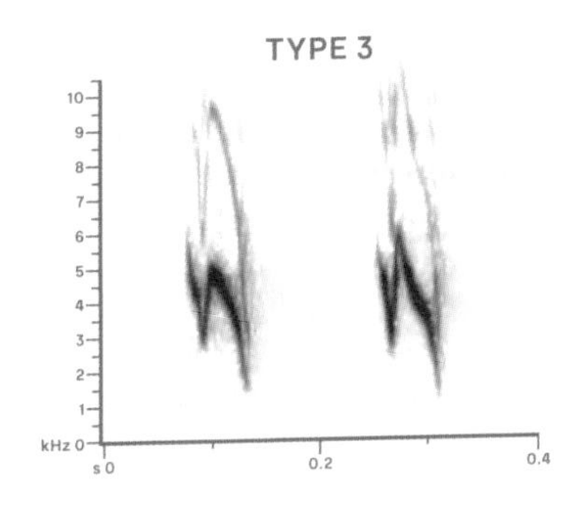


* Foraging charts are meant as a guide to help birders and ornithologists search for crossbills across the cone cycle year of July 1–June 30. These proposed seasonality foraging charts were created by Matt Young based on a combination of existing literature, data, thousands of hours observing crossbills foraging, and cone ripening phenologies and masting crop cycles. David Yeany II assisted in the creation of these charts.

**Language: Type 4 Flight Call**
**Douglas Fir Crossbill**[25]

Bouncy, high *pwit-pwit-pwit* or *jeyip-jey-ip-jeyip* very distinctive. Spectrogram has a V shape element to it. Compare to Types 10 and 6.

**Bill Depth:** Medium

**Distribution:** Pacific Northwest is core zone of occurrence area. Secondary core zone of occurrence is northern Rockies; occasionally to the western Great Lakes but rare to the East.

**Movements and Irruptions:** Occasionally moves to Intermountain West and even Arizona, less commonly to Ontario, Great Lakes, and rarely to Northeast. However, 2023 saw the biggest movement into the northeast in 25–50 years.

**Diet and Habitat:** Douglas fir and spruce forests, and to a lesser degree pine forests. Most commonly utilized trees in the West appear to be coastal variety (*Pseudotsuga m. menziesii*) of Douglas fir, also Engelmann spruce, and Sitka and blue spruce. In East mainly uses white spruce, and eastern white, red, and jack pines, the latter two species somewhat readily utilized in late winter in the pine barrens of Wisconsin and adjacent areas.[26] It does the same in parts of the West, utilizing ponderosa and lodgepole pine in late winter.[27] *(See chart on page 130.)*

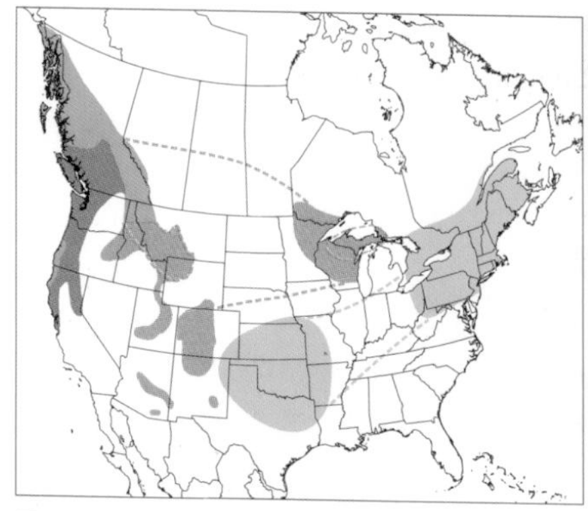


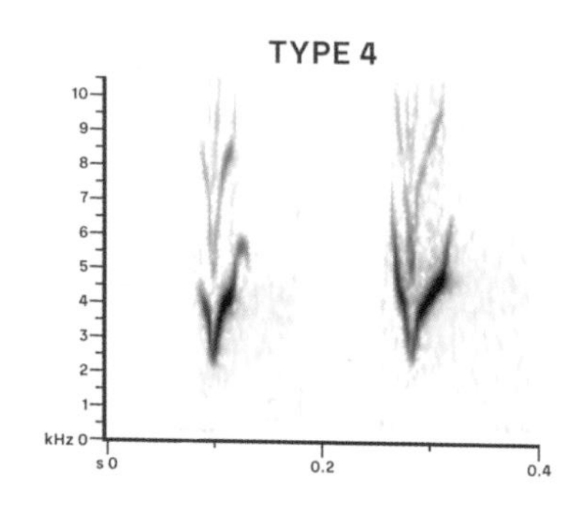

**Language: Type 5 Flight Call**
**Lodgepole Pine Crossbill**[28]

Variable springy or twangy and quite distinctive *klip-klip-klip*. Produces overlapping sounds that give it a polyphonic quality (two or more voices produced simultaneously). The second element has a sharp rise and varies more than the first. The two elements are generally heard singly by the human ear.

**Bill Depth:** Large

**Distribution:** Core zone of occurrence is Rockies of western United States and southern British Columbia; vagrant to Great Lakes and Northeast. Rare in Sierra Nevada where lodgepole pine occurs.

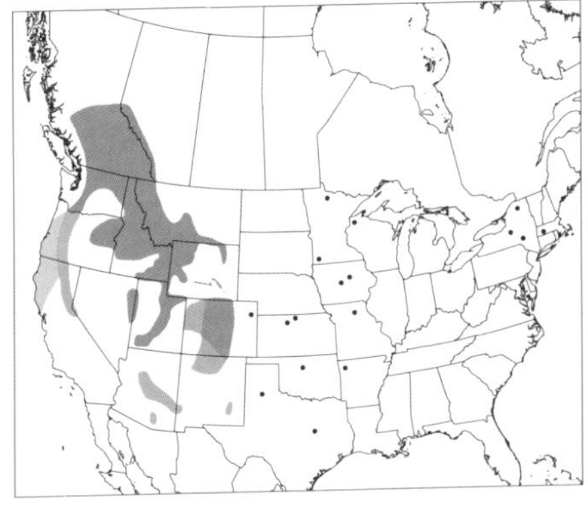


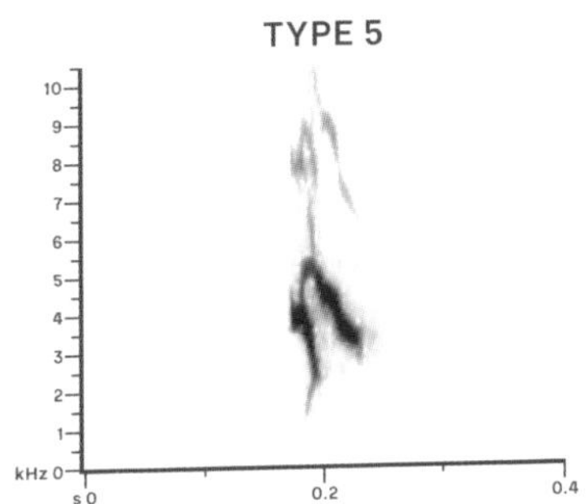


**Movements and Irruptions:** Appears to be more sedentary (or just moves within the Rockies) than most call types owing to lodgepole pine producing a remarkably consistent cone crop from year to year;[29] appears to be mostly an altitudinal migrant in the Rockies and vagrant to the East.[30]

**Diet and Habitat:** Pine forests at mid-elevations and spruce forests at higher elevations and in valleys. Most commonly utilized trees in the West appear to be lodgepole pine and Engelmann spruce (high elevation), less often Douglas fir, blue spruce (in valleys), or other pines like the softer-coned western white and limber. *(See chart on page 134.)*

## RED CROSSBILL TYPE 5

| FOOD SOURCE | July | Aug | Sept | Oct | Nov | Dec | Jan | Feb | Mar | Apr | May | Jun |
|---|---|---|---|---|---|---|---|---|---|---|---|---|
| Engelmann Spruce | | | | | | | | | | | | |
| Blue Spruce | | | | | | | | | | | | |
| Douglas Fir | | | | | | | | | | | | |
| Lodgepole Pine | | | | | | | | | | | | |
| Ponderosa Pine | | | | | | | | | | | | |
| Limber Pine | | | | | | | | | | | | |
| Western White Pine | | | | | | | | | | | | |
| Deciduous Buds & Tree Seeds | | | | | | | | | | | | |
| Insects | | | | | | | | | | | | |
| Feeders | | | | | | | | | | | | |

## RED CROSSBILL TYPE 6

| FOOD SOURCE | July | Aug | Sept | Oct | Nov | Dec | Jan | Feb | Mar | Apr | May | Jun |
|---|---|---|---|---|---|---|---|---|---|---|---|---|
| Engelmann Spruce (rare in area) | | | | | | | | | | | | |
| Douglas Fir | | | | | | | | | | | | |
| Southwestern White Pine | | | | | | | | | | | | |
| Ponderosa Pine | | | | | | | | | | | | |
| Apache Pine | | | | | | | | | | | | |
| Deciduous Buds & Tree Seeds | | | | | | | | | | | | |
| Insects | | | | | | | | | | | | |
| Feeders | | | | | | | | | | | | |

## RED CROSSBILL TYPE 7

| FOOD SOURCE | July | Aug | Sept | Oct | Nov | Dec | Jan | Feb | Mar | Apr | May | Jun |
|---|---|---|---|---|---|---|---|---|---|---|---|---|
| Engelmann Spruce | | | | | | | | | | | | |
| White Spruce | | | | | | | | | | | | |
| Engelmann x White Spruce | | | | | | | | | | | | |
| Douglas Fir | | | | | | | | | | | | |
| Western White Pine | | | | | | | | | | | | |
| Lodgepole Pine | | | | | | | | | | | | |
| Ponderosa Pine | | | | | | | | | | | | |
| Deciduous Buds & Tree Seeds | | | | | | | | | | | | |
| Insects | | | | | | | | | | | | |
| Feeders | | | | | | | | | | | | |

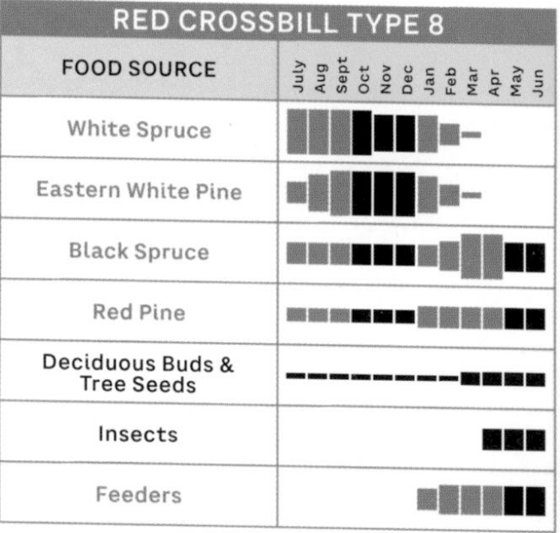


## KEY

- Used abundantly
- Used commonly
- Used fairly commonly
- Used less frequently or uncommonly
- Used infrequently/Starts using alternate resource (e.g.feeders)
- Used rarely or switched to a new food source

Key Food Source in:

- Breeding Period
- Non Breeding Period / Not Used for Breeding during Period

**Language: Type 6 Flight Call**
**Sierra Madre Crossbill**[31]
Variable, ringing, somewhat musical *cheep-cheep-cheep*. Spectrogram resembles Type 4 but can be more variable, starts downward then very suddenly rises.
**Bill Depth:** Largest
**Distribution:** Core zone of occurrence in United States is sky islands (isolated mountain ranges) of southeastern Arizona, southwestern New Mexico, and down through the Sierra Madre de Occidental to south Mexico, Guatemala, and El Salvador.
**Movements and Irruptions:** Unknown
**Diet and Habitat:** Pine forests. Most likely trees utilized while breeding in the Southwest into Mexico appear to be Apache pine and other Mexican hard-coned pines. Within this vast habitat, the diversity of pines is perhaps the highest in the world, so the question remains why only one call type occurs here—surely an area for further study. *(See chart on page 134.)*

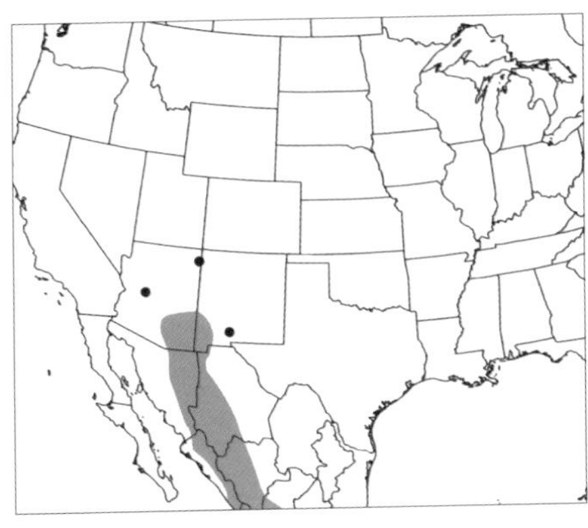


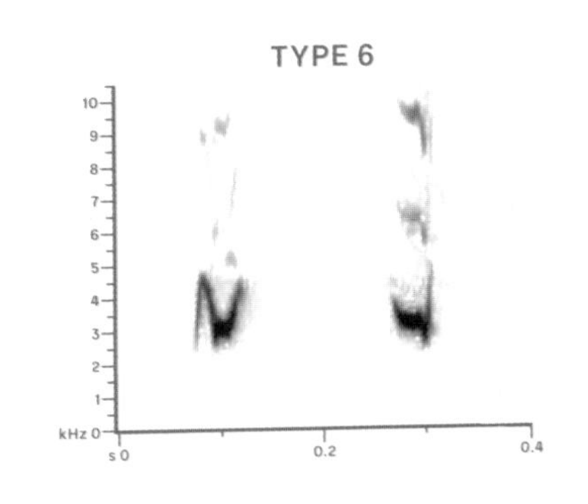


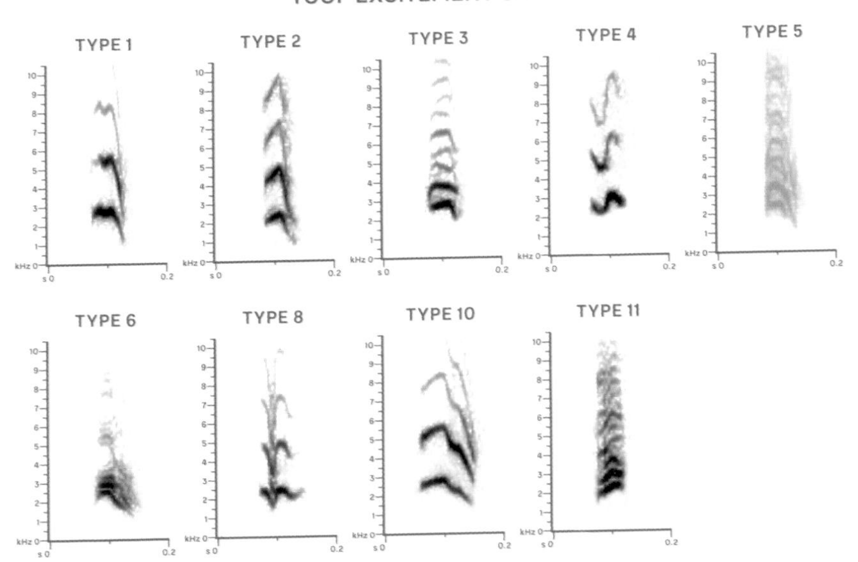

**Language: Type 7 Flight Call**
**Enigmatic Crossbill**[32]
*jit-jit-jit* Not many records exist compared to other call types; more recordings are needed. May sound chirping or a bit between a Type 2 and Type 5 or even Cassia-like. Also shares some similarities with Type 12, hence the name "Enigmatic Crossbill." Spectrogram can have quick downsweep followed by a rise, then a fall, or just a rise with longer fall, thus usually forming a U-shaped spectrogram or a polyphonic (two or more voices produced simultaneously) spectrogram falling between Type 5 and Cassia Crossbill (Type 9).
**Bill Depth:** Medium
**Distribution:** Core zone of occurrence interior areas of Pacific Northwest United States through British Columbia and western Alberta north to Yukon Territory.
**Movements and Irruptions:** Little known, occasional to the western northern-tier states, but likely most reside in British Columbia, and western Alberta north to the Yukon Territory.

Core Zone of Occurrence
Secondary Zone of Occurrence

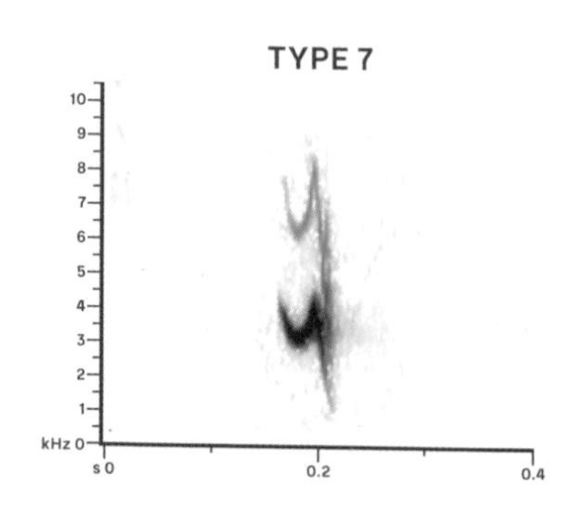


**Diet and Habitat:** Spruce and lodgepole pine forests of western Canada. Most commonly utilized trees appear to be lodgepole pine and white and Engelmann spruce, including the white x Engelmann spruce hybridization zone in British Columbia. *(See chart on page 134.)*

**Language: Type 8 Flight Call**
**Newfoundland Crossbill**[33]
Ringing and complexly modulated *cheet-cheet*. Spectrogram has up down, up down pattern that looks like an *M*.
**Bill Depth:** Large
**Distribution:** Newfoundland
**Movements and Irruptions**: Resident on Newfoundland, and rarely appears to move to Magdalen Islands, Anticosti Island, and possibly nearby maritime coastal areas.[34]
**Diet and Habitat:** Spruce and pine forests. Most commonly utilized trees appear to be black spruce, white spruce, and red and eastern white pines.

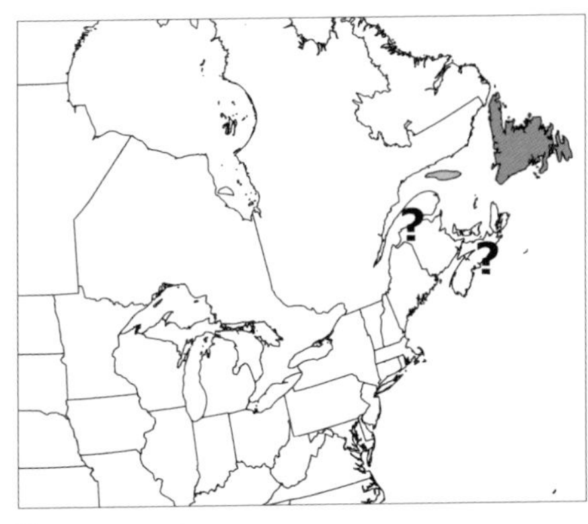


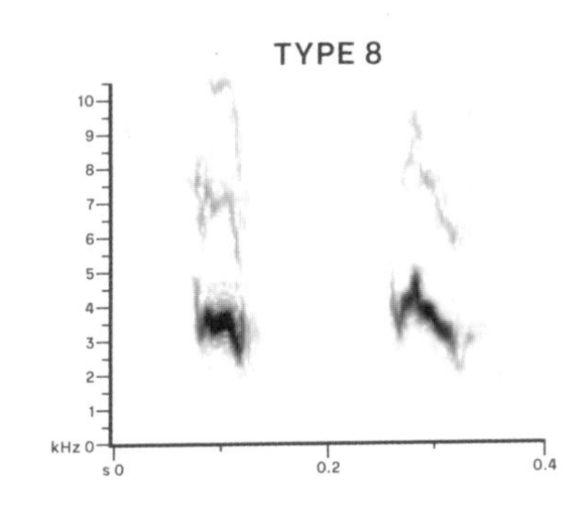


In Newfoundland Type 8 Red Crossbill appears to most closely associate with black spruce (*Picea mariana*) whose cones (large, heavy cones with thick scales that require greater force to pry open) differ from the black spruce cones on the mainland (small, less seed mass per cone mass), which may have to do with the presence or absence of red squirrels who prey on the cones. According to research, it is thought that for about 9,000 years, after the glaciers retreated and spruces colonized Newfoundland but red squirrels did not, the Red Crossbills coevolved with the spruces. The black spruce cones became larger with thicker scales, and crossbills likely evolved bigger, deeper bills that could deliver more force, all the better to pry apart the cones.[35] Red squirrels were introduced as a prey base for the reintroduced pine marten to Newfoundland in 1963 and now deplete a greater percentage of the black spruce cone crop by early fall than on the mainland where the black spruces presumably have greater defenses against red squirrels. Crossbill populations in Newfoundland have plummeted, and they are considered threatened but still persist, especially at feeders,[36] because of the introduction of red squirrels as well as changes in forest ecology, less spruce budworm (also a food source) activity, and forest loss due to logging and forest fire regimes. *(See chart on page 134.)*

| CASSIA CROSSBILL | | | | | | | | | | | | |
|---|---|---|---|---|---|---|---|---|---|---|---|---|
| FOOD SOURCE | July | Aug | Sept | Oct | Nov | Dec | Jan | Feb | Mar | Apr | May | Jun |
| Engelmann Spruce (Albion Mountains) | | | | | | | | | | | | |
| Douglas Fir (Albion Mountains) | | | | | | | | | | | | |
| Lodgepole Pine | | | | | | | | | | | | |
| Deciduous Buds & Tree Seeds | | | | | | | | | | | | |
| Insects | | | | | | | | | | | | |
| Feeders | | | | | | | | | | | | |

| RED CROSSBILL TYPE 11 | | | | | | | | | | | | |
|---|---|---|---|---|---|---|---|---|---|---|---|---|
| FOOD SOURCE | July | Aug | Sept | Oct | Nov | Dec | Jan | Feb | Mar | Apr | May | Jun |
| Mexican Yellow Pine | | | | | | | | | | | | |
| Deciduous Buds & Tree Seeds | | | | | | | | | | | | |
| Insects | | | | | | | | | | | | |
| Feeders | | | | | | | | | | | | |

| RED CROSSBILL TYPE 10 | | | | | | | | | | | | |
|---|---|---|---|---|---|---|---|---|---|---|---|---|
| WEST (Primary Core Zone) | | | | | | | | | | | | |
| FOOD SOURCE | July | Aug | Sept | Oct | Nov | Dec | Jan | Feb | Mar | Apr | May | Jun |
| Sitka Spruce | | | | | | | | | | | | |
| Western Hemlock | | | | | | | | | | | | |
| Douglas Fir | | | | | | | | | | | | |
| Deciduous Buds & Tree Seeds | | | | | | | | | | | | |
| Insects | | | | | | | | | | | | |
| Feeders | | | | | | | | | | | | |
| EAST | | | | | | | | | | | | |
| White Spruce | | | | | | | | | | | | |
| Eastern Hemlock | | | | | | | | | | | | |
| Eastern White Pine | | | | | | | | | | | | |
| Tamarack | | | | | | | | | | | | |
| Jack Pine | | | | | | | | | | | | |
| Red Pine | | | | | | | | | | | | |
| Deciduous Buds & Tree Seeds | | | | | | | | | | | | |
| Insects | | | | | | | | | | | | |
| Feeders | | | | | | | | | | | | |

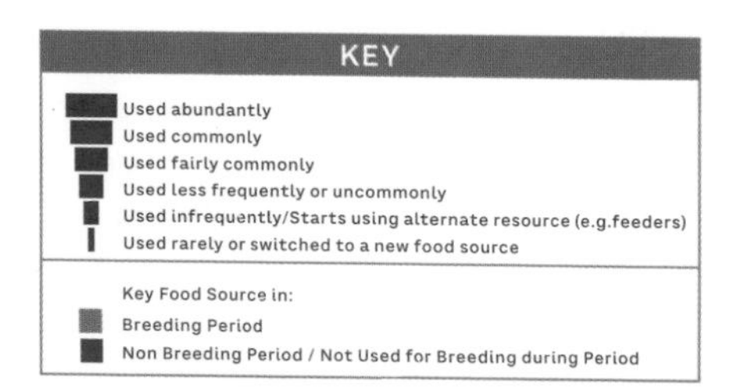

**Language: Formerly Type 9 Flight Call, Now Is Cassia Crossbill**[37]
Very dry, distinctive *dip-dip-dip* or *dyip-dyip-dyip*. Spectrogram may look like Type 1 or Type 5. The downward pattern, however, occurs in a lower frequency, below 4 kHz, than either Type 1 or 2.
**Bill Depth:** Large
**Distribution:** Locally adapted lodgepole pine forest absent of competing tree squirrels in South Hills and Albion Mountains of southern Idaho; also appears to be local in north central Colorado west of Denver 2021–2022 but perhaps back to 2012.
**Movements and Irruptions:** Mainly resident, but may move to mountains to northeast and south and southeast of South Hills.[38] Movement can occur if forced, such as when wildfires destroy large parts of range. The Badger Fire of late summer 2020 in Idaho led to an approximate 40% reduction of Cassia Crossbill habitat, and possibly was the cause for the species to wander beyond its limited home range.[39]

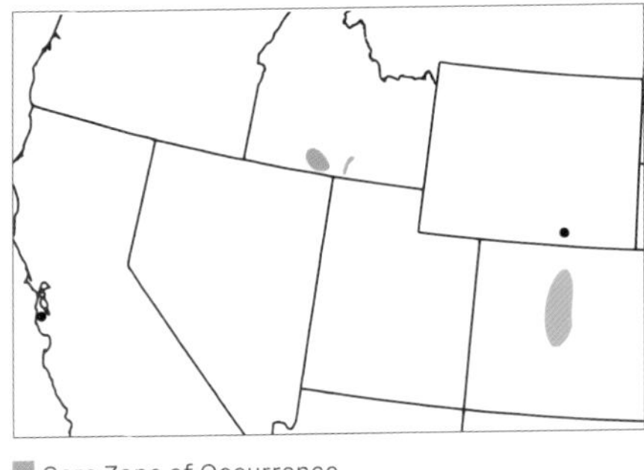


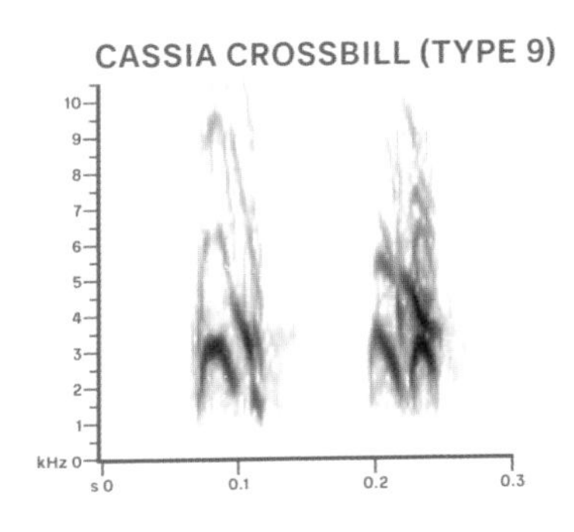


Cassia Crossbills occurred in north central Colorado in 2021–2023 and in the coastal area of Skylawn Cemetery, California, in 2023. A small flock of three adults and a juvenile was recorded and documented 450 miles away from the South Hills, Idaho, in the Colorado Rockies, at Arapaho, Grand County, Colorado, by Christian Nunes on July 16, 2021.[40] In 2022, there were several other records, including photos and recordings of Cassia Crossbills in Colorado, including a report by Ben Sampson and Brian Genge on August 7, 2022, in Summit County, of 16 birds with juveniles noted. Over the course of the 2022 summer, additional records came in three other north-central counties west of Denver. Nathan Pieplow[41] also discovered he had recorded a Cassia Crossbill from the same general area back in 2012. And birds have been confirmed breeding in at least Summit and Grand Counties.
**Diet and Habitat:** Most commonly utilizes lodgepole pine forests, especially a local population lacking tree squirrels in South Hills and Albion Mountains. Tree squirrels outcompete crossbills for seed across much of their range except for in Cassia County, Idaho, where there are no tree squirrels. The crossbills are thought to be coevolving with the local population of lodgepole pine.[42] *(See chart on page 138.)*

**Language: Type 10 Flight Call**
**Sitka Spruce Crossbill**[43]

*whit-whit*, very dry, thin, a bit like *Empidonax* flycatcher *whit* note. Compare with Types 4, 7, and 12. Spectrogram can be somewhat variable but is dominated by an upsweep.

**Bill Depth:** Small

**Distribution:** Sitka spruce and western hemlock forests. Core zone of occurrence is mainly southern coastal British Columbia and coastal Pacific Northwest to northern California; irruptive zone where birds occur locally are Great Lakes, Quebec, and rarely the Northeast.

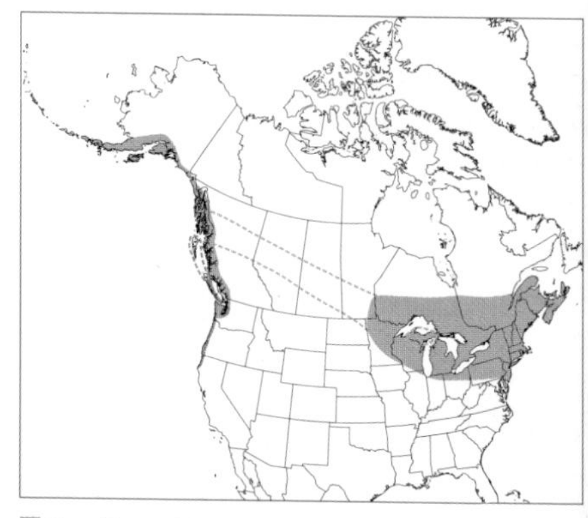

Core Zone of Occurrence
Secondary Zone of Occurrence
Primary Zone of Irruption

**Movements and Irruptions:** Occasionally irrupts into Great Lakes, but even more rarely into the Northeast and southeastern Canada. Likely irrupts in small numbers with Type 3 when they move east in numbers every 3–5 years.

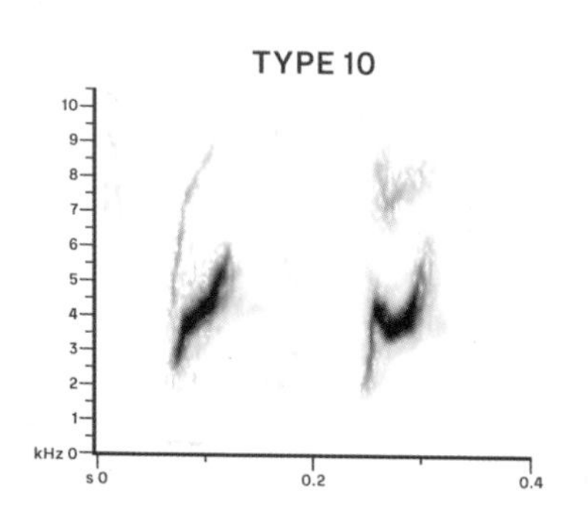


**Diet and Habitat:** Most commonly utilized trees in the West appear to be Sitka spruce and sometimes western hemlock; in East, spruces and eastern white, red, and jack pines. Occurs in Sitka spruce habitat in the outer part of the coastal Pacific especially south of Vancouver Island where spruces more reliably produce seed. *(See chart on page 138.)*

**Language: Type 11 Flight Call Central American Crossbill[44]**
*drip-drip* sounds flat and somewhat similar to Cassia Crossbill. Sonogram compares to lower-frequency variants of Type 5. Often gives flat, polyphonic (two or more voices produced simultaneously) flight call that can sound similar to the Cassia Crossbill or some lower-frequency variants of Type 5.

**Bill Depth:** Large

**Distribution:** Core zone of occurrence Guatemala, Honduras, possibly Belize, Nicaragua, and El Salvador.

**Irruptions:** Unknown

**Diet and Habitat**: Pine forests. Most associated with Mexican yellow pine (*Pinus oocarpa*) (John van Dort, personal communication), other hard-coned Central American pines. Mexican yellow pine is a type of conifer with serotinous closed cones, in which the female cones are egg-shaped, that provides food year-round.[45] *(See chart on page 138.)*

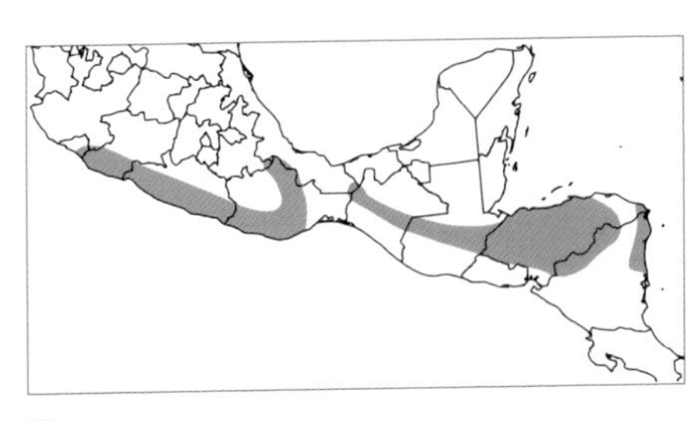

Core Zone of Occurrence

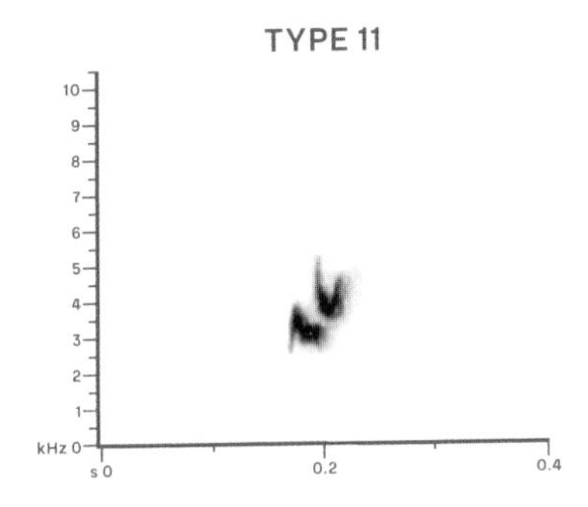

**Language:** **Type 12 Flight Call**
**Northeastern Crossbill**[46]
Overslurred Type 12 (formerly overslurred Type 10) gives a harder, squeakier *kip-kip* with a strong downward inflection at the end, looking like an upside down *V*.
**Bill Depth:** Medium
**Distribution:** The core zone of occurrence appears to be the red and white spruce, and red, jack, and white pine forests of the Maritime Provinces, Maine, New Hampshire, Vermont, and the Adirondack region of New York. Type 12 also occurs with frequency in central and eastern Ontario, Michigan, Wisconsin, and eastern Minnesota. There are a few summertime records for this type all the way across the boreal to Alaska.
**Movements and Irruptions:** This type fairly commonly migrates down the East Coast to Cape Cod, Long Island, New Jersey, Delaware, and in recent years south to Virginia and North Carolina—this is Type 12's primary zone of irruption. Rare records (2020–2021) in the southern Appalachians to Alabama and west to upper Midwest.

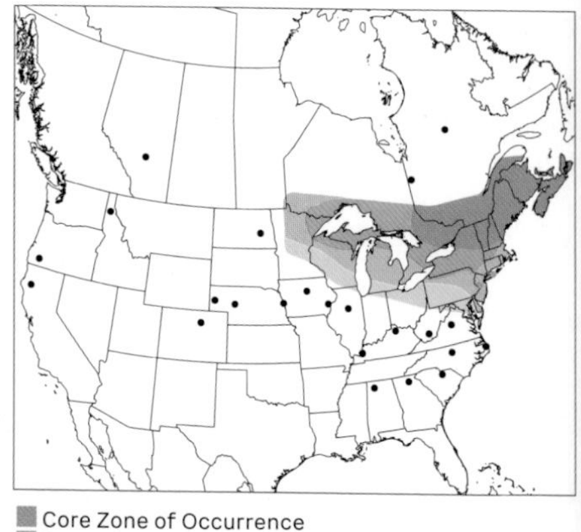


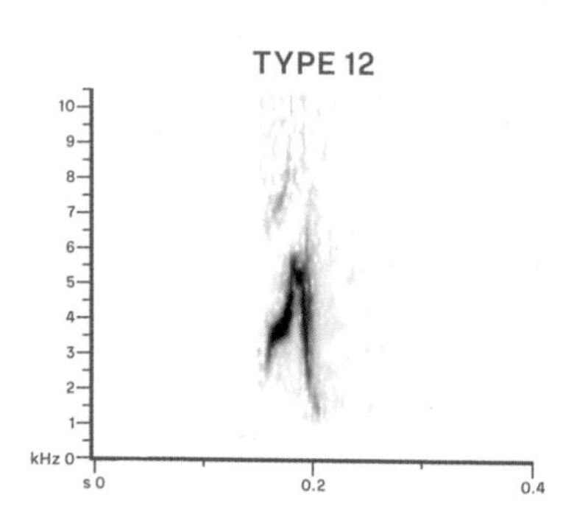


During the late summer of 2020, after a number of very successful breeding cycles, Type 12 migrated down the East Coast in numbers not previously seen, with birds reported and documented south along the coast to North Carolina and in interior Appalachian areas south to Alabama. On its return flight in summer of 2021, many settled into areas of northern Pennsylvania and southern New York to nest, with confirmed breeding from January to May 2022. Many of these forests were plantations of Norway spruce, and in known areas where Type 1 had been breeding for decades, especially in the state forests of southern New York. Type 12 were more common than Type 1, and it will be interesting to track whether these areas become regularly used for nesting. It also has bred regularly in the pitch pine forests of Massachusetts and Maine, and in recent years northern New Jersey, Long Island, and the pine barrens of Albany, New York.

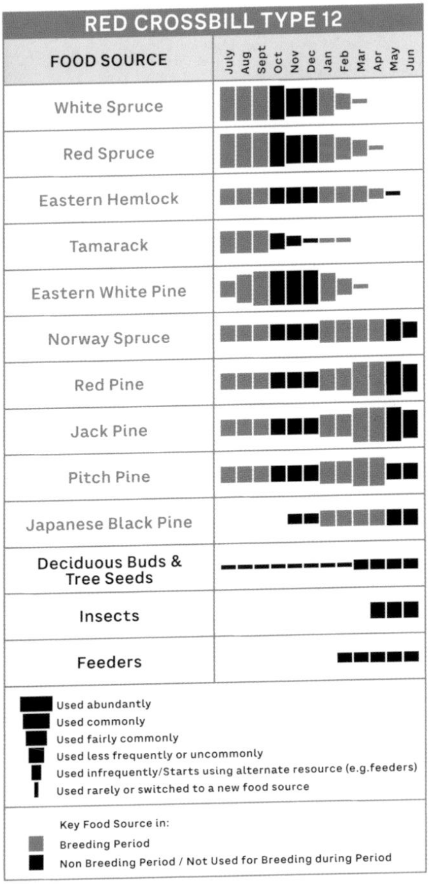

**RED CROSSBILL TYPE 12**

| FOOD SOURCE | July | Aug | Sept | Oct | Nov | Dec | Jan | Feb | Mar | Apr | May | Jun |
|---|---|---|---|---|---|---|---|---|---|---|---|---|
| White Spruce | | | | | | | | | | | | |
| Red Spruce | | | | | | | | | | | | |
| Eastern Hemlock | | | | | | | | | | | | |
| Tamarack | | | | | | | | | | | | |
| Eastern White Pine | | | | | | | | | | | | |
| Norway Spruce | | | | | | | | | | | | |
| Red Pine | | | | | | | | | | | | |
| Jack Pine | | | | | | | | | | | | |
| Pitch Pine | | | | | | | | | | | | |
| Japanese Black Pine | | | | | | | | | | | | |
| **Deciduous Buds & Tree Seeds** | | | | | | | | | | | | |
| **Insects** | | | | | | | | | | | | |
| **Feeders** | | | | | | | | | | | | |

Used abundantly
Used commonly
Used fairly commonly
Used less frequently or uncommonly
Used infrequently/Starts using alternate resource (e.g.feeders)
Used rarely or switched to a new food source

Key Food Source in:
Breeding Period
Non Breeding Period / Not Used for Breeding during Period

**Diet and Habitat:** Owing to a much stronger jaw musculature, Red Crossbill is more of a generalist, as it can feed on, and utilize for breeding, a much wider array of conifers than White-winged Crossbill (Tom Hahn, personal communication). As many types do, it switches from rich patch of conifer seed to rich patch of conifer seed throughout the year[47]; most commonly utilized trees appear to be red, jack, and eastern white pines, and native red and white spruces. Norway spruce plantings are also used where sufficiently large groves are found. Its main diet is red and white spruce in summer and eastern white pine from fall into winter, then in late winter into spring it switches to pitch pine along the East Coast and red and jack pine in the Northeast, Great Lakes, and southern Maritimes. It also readily feeds on conifer seed of Japanese black pine along the coast, and Norway spruce in interior state lands, especially in central New York. The vast majority of sightings between September and January are from eastern white pine, which is very likely the most widespread conifer in total acreage in the northeastern states and the most reliable cone producer as well.

Red Crossbill on pitch pine

## AT YOUR FEEDER

Red Crossbills rarely use feeders, but when they do, it's in spring when the majority of conifer seed has been dropped from cones, at the periphery of their ranges in places like Alaska, Newfoundland, and Yukon Territory, and is a feeder offering sunflower seed. Loss of habitat due to logging, fires, and pest outbreaks of spruce budworm and mountain pine beetle could lead to more feeder visits. When adults bring their young to a feeder, the habit is passed on to the next generation.

## BREEDING BEHAVIOR

### *TERRITORY*

Red Crossbills do not seem to be very territorial, although males may use a treetop perch for singing near the nest and sometimes fight and chase other males. A group of pairs may nest colonially, separated from other groups of pairs.

### *COURTSHIP*

Red Crossbills have close ties within their flocks, establish very close bonds with their mates, and are believed to be monogamous. Mate bonds can last even during the nonbreeding season.

Breeding displays include flapping/gliding flight above trees, loudly singing. Chasing females and then touching and grasping bills occurs. Females choose mates based on call type, not on bill morphology for key conifer foraging.[48] Since young crossbills learn their calls from their parents, mating with someone whose call is slightly different signifies to pair members that each come from different parents, thus preventing inbreeding. The longer pairs are together, the more their calls more closely resemble each other's, cementing their bond and aiding in individual recognition.[49]

Crossbills appear to breed mostly with their own call type but hybridize in a small percentage of cases. One study showed that 6 of 820 pairs involving Cassia Crossbills bred with a call type other than their own.[50]

### *NESTING*

**Timing:** July to September and January to April, even when temps are below zero with many inches of snow on the ground. Breeding generally ceases in autumn in North America (Hahn and Cornelius, personal communication).
**Nest:** Cup, outside diameter 4–5 in., of conifer twigs, lichen, grasses, needles, and finer bark shreds, feathers. Placed 6.5–65.5 ft. high, concealed in dense conifer side branches or near trunk in spruce, Douglas fir, pine, hemlock.
**Eggs:** 2–4, usually 3, white, rose, or greenish with cinnamon or purple speckle marks at end
**Incubation:** 12–16 days, usually 14, by female
**Nestling period**: 15–17 days
**Broods:** Usually 1–2 or up to 4 in prolific, widespread conifer seed crop years

Nesting occurs wherever large cone crops form on spruce (*Picea* spp.), Douglas fir, western hemlock, eastern hemlock (*Tsuga canadensis*), western larch (*Larix occidentalis*), and many species of pine (*Pinus* sp.).

Pairs investigate nest sites together, and males may sing softly when near female. The female builds the nest, incubates, and is fed by the male, especially when she incubates in cold weather. Female broods the nestlings just about continuously for 5 days. The young are fed regurgitated seed kernels from the adults' crops. Fledglings are fed by both parents, but only the male feeds them if the female lays a second clutch of eggs. Young fledgling crossbills do not develop a crossed bill, which would enable them to feed on their own, for some time. Thus, dependency is long, and during this time they perfect their call type by imitating their parents. At 45 days they may effectively have learned seed extraction and shelling. Immature crossbills may associate together but then group with adults.

In winter, crossbills survive cold temperatures by going to roost with food stored in their crop and also have seasonal metabolic body adaptations that allow them to withstand extreme cold.

## MOLT

Red Crossbills can breed throughout much of the year, so molts and plumages vary. Male coloration can be bright red to orange-red to even yellow. Depending on the time of molt, some birds can have mixed red and yellow body feathers.

Molts can be extended over a period, be suspended and partial, or complete. Note that birds in juvenile-type brown plumage can breed. Adult male Red Crossbills in Europe who have bred prior to July can be more yellow, while those molting after July are red. This may also occur in North American birds but needs study (Tom Hahn, personal communication).

## CONSERVATION

Partners in Flight rates Red Crossbill 8 out of 20 on the Continental Concern Score and IUCN lists it as Low Concern for its range in Canada and the United States, but rising temperatures, climate change, and logging could threaten crossbill populations. Diverse conifer species and ages are important to crossbills across North America—for example, older trees produce more reliable cone crops. As global temperatures increase, conifer diversity will very likely decrease, thus changing species distribution, age, and the timing of seed release. This dynamic would have a negative impact on crossbill populations.

In some areas like the Northeast, population numbers (Type 12) are increasing, likely due to maturing forests and conifer plantings.[51] Nonetheless, call types like Type 8 (ssp. *percna*) in Newfoundland and Type 6 (ssp. *stricklandi*) in Central America, which are at the edges of their ranges, appear to be uncommon to rare. Type 8 is listed as threatened in Newfoundland.

### DEEPER DIVE

Female Red Crossbills, in addition to choosing mates based on call type, directly watch, assess, and select males that are faster at foraging.[52] This is advantageous since females obtain supplemental food from males who feed them by regurgitation during egg-laying and incubation, and the males also feed the nestlings.

# CASSIA CROSSBILL (RED CROSSBILL COMPLEX*)

*Loxia sinesciuris*

*"Islands in the Stream"*
—Song by Barry Gibb, Maurice Gibb, and Robin Gibb, 1997

## QUICK TAKE

We might think of spending island time on a tropical oasis island surrounded by turquoise blue water, lying in a hammock sipping a margarita. There is a different kind of island—a sky island. Of another world, sky islands are separated from other mountain ranges by physical distance. The sky islands of southern Idaho's South Hills and Albion Mountains, isolated from the Rocky Mountains, are home to the Cassia Crossbill, who lives in only a small, twenty-seven-square-mile area of a local

* We refer to the Red Crossbills as "Red Crossbill Complex" to reflect a future potential change in the taxonomic status of Cassia Crossbill being merged back to Call Type 9 and considered a single species with Red Crossbill.

variety of lodgepole pine (*Pinus contorta latifolia*) forest. How Cassia Crossbills came to be and how they came to live there is a *Treasure Island*-style tale.

About five thousand to seven thousand years ago, lodgepole pines moved into the South Hills and Albion Mountains. Red Crossbills, conifer seed specialists, sailed into these sky islands and discovered treasure. This local variety of lodgepole pine (*Pinus contorta latifolia*) had an abundance of cones heavily laden with seeds. It was likely beyond anything the crossbills had encountered.

Pirating American red squirrels (*Tamiasciurus hudsonicus*), which devour lodgepole pine seeds, were nowhere to be found. Hesitant to cross the open expanse between mountains and be vulnerable to predators, red squirrels stayed in the Rocky Mountains, and the lodgepole pines there evolved cones with a wider base, higher mass, and fewer seeds to guard their seed treasure against the squirrels. In the squirrel-less South Hills and Albion Mountains, the lodgepole pines needed no squirrel defense and so had many seeds and were just right for Red Crossbills to pry open with their crossed tool of a bill. The crossbills stayed and became sedentary.

Lodgepole pines are not defenseless; trees have their own evolutionary trajectory. Now faced with Red Crossbills as their primary pirate, the lodgepole pines of the South Hills and Albion Mountains began to evolve thicker scales on the distant end of their cones, where the most seeds lie, to hide and protect their genetic riches. The crossbills evolved into larger birds with shorter, deeper, and more decurved bills to access the seeds in the cones. Instead of a duet, the relationship between these pirate crossbills and lodgepole pines became a duel of armament escalation.[1]

In 1996, researcher Dr. Craig W. Benkman visited the South Hills and Albion Mountains and discovered that crossbills were twenty times more abundant there

Cassia Crossbill juvenile with a lodgepole pine cone

than in similar lodgepole pine habitat in the Rocky Mountains where squirrels live.[2] Not only were these Red Crossbills a different size with different-sized bills than other western crossbills, they also sounded different. Red Crossbills are grouped by eleven recognized call types (Type 9 is Cassia Crossbill): specialized flight calls that enable a flock to stay together and communicate locations of good food. Flight calls are categorized by analysis of their recordings by an expert; the average birder cannot discern them by ear. Members of a group of crossbills (ecomorphs) mainly respond just to their own call type and usually mate with one another. The Red Crossbills in the South Hills and Albion Mountains were categorized as Type 9 and called the South Hills Crossbill. An intense 2001–2006 field study by Dr. Benkman found that of 1,704 breeding Cassia Crossbill pairs in the South Hills and Albion Mountains, only 12 bred with other call types (2 and 5), a hybridization rate of only 0.0007.[3]

In a coevolutionary race, these sedentary South Hills Crossbills had evolved different behavior and morphological attributes that seemed to result in reproductive isolation even though there was no geographic isolation from other crossbill types who could fly into these hills. Did the South Hills Crossbills meet the criteria of a new species?

Additional research determined that these crossbills were genetically different from the remaining Red Crossbill call types.[4] Phylogenetic studies showed that Cassia Crossbills were monophyletic (descended from a single ancestral species).

In 2017 the North American Classification and Nomenclature Committee (NACC) of the American Ornithological Society (the AOS Checklist Committee), voted to grant the South Hills Crossbill species status, and it became Cassia Crossbill, the first of the North American Red Crossbill call types to be designated as a new species. The vote to grant species status was 8–2 in 2017, and in 2022 the committee upheld the decision, but only by a vote of 6–4. Two members changed their votes from 2017, citing the potential fragility and possible reversibility of factors separating Cassia and Red Crossbills. For now, Cassia Crossbill remains a species, but that could change in the future.

Although Red Crossbill Call Types 2 and 5 pass through the South Hills and Albion Mountains, they do not have bills as well evolved to open the local lodgepole pine cones, and therefore they occur in lower numbers, and nesting is much less common.[5] The Cassia Crossbills that settled on their treasure islands had seemingly done well as long as they coevolved.

In the summer of 2020, wildfires demolished millions of acres of western forests. The Badger Fire devastated ninety thousand acres in the South Hills, about 40% of Cassia Crossbill habitat, and scientists are assessing the effects on their population, estimated at about six thousand birds. The future is uncertain for the Cassia Crossbill. As the climate warms, the lodgepole pines, whose cones are adapted to open in the heat, could drop their seeds prematurely, depriving the crossbills of treasure. Even worse, devastating fires could, in one stroke, demolish the habitat that seems critical for their survival.

Will these Cassia Crossbills sail away again to another world? With their exquisitely specialized deep bill, will they be equipped to find and mine the treasures of other conifer species at the optimal rate required for survival and reproduction? Or will this new species flicker briefly in time, doomed to extinction almost before it began? However, in 2021 and 2022 (and even an old record discovered by Nathan Pieplow from 2012), Cassia Crossbills have been found in Colorado, with some supposedly breeding there.[6] They turned up in coastal California and Wyoming in 2023 as well. Were they driven out of Idaho by the fires? The tale continues to unfold . . .

## FUN FACTS

**Cassia Crossbills were named after Cassia County, Idaho, the county in which they reside. Their genus, *Loxia*, means "crosswise," and *sinesciuris* means "without squirrels," as red squirrels are absent from the South Hills and Albion Mountains.**

## IDENTIFICATION

**Size:** L 7.25"

**Shape:** Medium-sized, short-tailed, big-headed, short-legged finch with distinctive heavy bill with tips that cross each other.

**Adult Male:** Body mostly all red or reddish-orange; wings and tail deep-brown; flight feathers and short, deeply notched tail both deep-brown. Second-year male's orangish often becomes deeper red with age.

**Adult Female:** Brownish-gray or olive green, often brightest greenish-yellow on rump, crown, and breast; throat pale, distinguishing it from immature male.

**1st Winter:** Males may resemble adult males or adult females. Both sexes have buffy edges to the wing coverts (but not like well-defined white wingbar of White-winged Crossbill).

**Juv:** (June–Sept.) Brownish overall, with heavy brown streaking on whitish underparts.

### *SUBSPECIES*

Monotypic and therefore no geographic variation known.

### *SIMILAR SPECIES*

White-winged Crossbill's bill and body are smaller, and it has 2 white wingbars. Very similar to Red Crossbill, which has highly variable body and bill size, especially bill depth, the heritable trait not susceptible to wear like bill length. Cassia Crossbill has the fourth largest bill depth of the crossbill call types and species in North America. See chart for bill depth measurements in the Red Crossbill account.

## DISTRIBUTION

Seemingly endemic species that occurs in the lodgepole pine forests of the South Hills and Albion Mountains of Cassia County (also occurs just over the county line in Twin Falls County) in south-central Idaho, but there are now several records from Colorado, Wyoming, and California.

## LANGUAGE

### *MALE*

The song of the Cassia Crossbill is long with multiple phrases, basically the same as any Red Crossbill call type but with buzzier notes and more repetition.[7] The repetition suggests it might have a more limited song repertoire.

### *MALE AND FEMALE*

Flight call is *dip-dip-dip,* or *dyip-dyip-dyip* low, very dry, harsh, distinctive.

Since Cassia Crossbill was Red Crossbill Type 9 until elevated to species status in 2017, its call is best identified by its spectrogram (see page 139). The spectrogram may look somewhat like the Type 1 Red Crossbill with an initial upward component, but the downward modulated part occurs in a lower frequency domain below 4 kHz. Similar to Type 5 Red Crossbill as well. For comparisons, see the Call Types with Spectrograms under Red Crossbill account.

An excitement call, *toop-toop-toop,* is given at times of nesting when interlopers are nearby, and likely given at times of stress, alarm, or aggression to others in the flock. Similarity exists to excitement calls of Red Crossbill Types 3 and 5, and identifying them based on this call is not recommended.

Same as Red Crossbill, the *chitter* call is not well studied but seems to be a quiet, communicative call given in flocks when feeding or drinking.

The *chittoo* call is a typical begging call of juveniles seeking food from adults.

## HABITAT AND DIET

Cassia Crossbills tend to be most common on north slopes with open mature stands of lodgepole pines with serotinous cones, which remain closed until fire or high heat melts the resin and the cones open and release their seeds en masse. These cones can accumulate and remain closed for several decades or more and provide a reliable seed bank for the crossbills. As the cones weather, some form small gaps in their scales, allowing access to crossbills.[8]

## AT YOUR FEEDER

Not known to visit feeders, but presumed possible in immediate vicinity of South Hills and Albion Mountains of Idaho. Loss of habitat due to fires and mountain pine beetle could lead to more movements away from the area and therefore visitations at feeders.

## MOVEMENTS AND IRRUPTIONS

Dr. Craig W. Benkman color-banded and recaptured Cassia Crossbills from 1998 to 2017 and determined they were resident in the South Hills and Albion Mountains of Idaho. The farthest any had been known to move until 2021 was a female who moved 35 miles from the Albion Mountains to the South Hills, and a juvenile documented to have moved upwards of 6 miles from capture site.

A record of a small flock of three Cassia Crossbills, including a juvenile, was documented 450 miles away in the Rocky Mountains at Arapaho, Grand County, Colorado, by Christian Nunes on July 16, 2021.[9] A flock of three was then recorded about 20 miles away in Summit County on July 10, 2022, by Luke Pheneger.[10] Nathan Pieplow discovered he had recorded a Cassia Crossbill back in 2012 from Summit County, Colorado.[11] As mentioned, the Badger Fire in the late summer of 2020 was possibly the cause for some individuals to wander beyond their normal limited range. Other Colorado records in 2022 and 2023 include photos and recordings of Cassia Crossbills from Summit, Eagle, Park, Pitkin, Jackson, and Larimer Counties.[12] It appears that Cassia Crossbills have bred in the area.[13] There are also 2023 ebird.org records from Albany County, Wyoming, and San Mateo County, California.

## BREEDING BEHAVIOR

### *TERRITORY*

Not reported to defend a territory. There may be occasional aggression over mates and food resources.

### *COURTSHIP*

Monogamous, and mates seem to be selected from their feeding flock. Courtship activities include males singing from treetops or while doing slow wingbeat display flights. Males chasing females and billing (touching and grabbing bills) are part of the courtship behavior. Females, in addition to choosing mates based on call type, directly watch, assess, and select males that are faster at foraging.[14] Females obtain supplemental food from males, who feed them by regurgitation during egg-laying and incubation, and the males also feed the nestlings. Thus, females choose mates that will be more fit at feeding them and their nestlings. Often when mates stay together for successive nesting events they will ever so slightly change the structure of their calls to match each other's. Cassia Crossbills breed with their own species 99.93% of the time. Extrapair paternity likely does not occur.[15]

***NESTING***

**Timing:** April into August
**Nest:** Likely same as in Red Crossbill, outside diameter up to 5 in., of small conifer twigs, lined with lichens, grasses, feathers. Placed 36–98 ft. high, concealed on south branches near trunk.
**Eggs:** Little information, likely 2–3, pale white, rose, or greenish with speckled end
**Incubation:** Likely as in Red Crossbill, 12–16 days by female
**Nestling period:** Likely as in Red Crossbill, 15–25 days
**Broods**: 1–2

Additional nesting information is likely similar to Red Crossbill. The female Cassia Crossbill builds the nest after the pair searches lodgepole pines for a nest site. The female incubates then broods the young until they are about 5 days old, and she is fed by the male during this time. Nestlings are fed regurgitated seeds by their parents.

The young likely fledge at about 15–25 days. Their bills gradually become crossed as they are fed by their parents, perhaps up to 33 days. The female may have a second brood, while the male feeds the young from the first brood.[16]

## MOLT

Not well studied. In this species, adults have a complete molt after breeding mainly in July–August. Second-year males tend to replace orange with red feathers at this time.

## CONSERVATION

The Cassia Crossbill was described as a new species in 2017, and therefore its conservation status has not been fully assessed yet. However, the 2022 State of the Birds report listed Cassia Crossbill as a "tipping point" species, "species on a trajectory to lose another 50% of their remnant populations in the next 50 years, or already have perilously small populations and continue to face high threats."[17]

Its habitat has been degraded by mountain pine beetle and recent fires. With increasing global warming, hotter temperatures can mimic heat from fire and cause the lodgepole pines to shed some seeds sooner and more rapidly, depleting the bird's food source. It's estimated that this caused an 80% decline in Cassia Crossbill from 2003 to 2011. Climate change is likely to cause the decline of lodgepole pine in the South Hills and Albion Mountains, resulting in the possible extinction of the Cassia Crossbill this century, unless the birds can adapt and relocate elsewhere.[18]

# WHITE-WINGED CROSSBILL

*Loxia leucoptera leucoptera*

> *The morning was intense at the dunes of Tadoussac. It was a river of groups of more than 100 White-winged Crossbills going SW between 7:30 and 9:00, where 16,400 individuals passed by, almost all counted by 10s with a hand counter . . . The most numerous group of 420 birds, made a front covering the sky. These fronts often extended over several hundred meters.*
>
> —Jessé Roy Drainville, October 20, 2021[1]

## QUICK TAKE

The Observatoire d'Oiseaux de Tadoussac, which sits at the mouth of the St. Lawrence River in Quebec, is one of the premier spots in North America to see migrating finches. Jessé Roy Drainville, the official counter on October 21, 2021, is an expert at counting migrating birds. He finished the day with a record-breaking number of White-winged Crossbills counted: 23,357.[2] This single day's count destroyed the previous record of 6,666 set just the day before.[3] A sea of red avian torpedo-shaped beauty, hallmarked by white bars on black wings, passed before his eyes. Where did they come from and where were they going?

About 3.5 million years ago, crossbills diverged from redpolls. Less than 1 million years ago, White-winged Crossbills diverged from Red Crossbills. A sister species recognized in 2003, the Hispaniolan Crossbill (*Loxia megaplaga*), was marooned in the cool mountain forests of Hispaniola when the last ice age ended and the Caribbean warmed. There are two subspecies of White-winged Crossbill: The Two-barred Crossbill (*Loxia leucoptera bifasciata*) lives in Eurasia, from Scandinavia to Siberia. The White-winged Crossbill (*Loxia leucoptera leucoptera*) lives in North America, primarily in the continuous boreal coniferous forest from Newfoundland to Alaska, the upper Northeast, and down to the Washington Cascades and central Rockies. Its cousin, the Red Crossbill, generally lives more south, with a montane range down to Mexico and beyond.

Chasing conifer cone-crop abundance defines the life of a White-winged Crossbill, and its incredible seed-extracting bill is its lifeline to survival and reproduction. Possessing an uncanny ability to find, assess, then calculate when to move, White-winged Crossbills feed on the most profitable conifer cone crops. Profitability is measured by the rate at which crossbills can open a cone, husk, then eat a seed, the "dry mass of seed kernel consumed per second" according to C. W. Benkman's 1987 study.[4] Crossbills appear to "talk" to one another about how profitable a conifer cone crop is by watching and listening to feeding neighbors. If it's "don't-talk-with-your-mouth-full" quiet, crossbills continue munching. When profitability falls, calling begins, signaling the flock to move on.[5]

White-winged Crossbill flight, dunes of Tadoussac 10/20/21

Conifers have a phenology (schedule) of cone ripening, opening, and dropping seeds, though regional weather and climate conditions affect this schedule. They are most profitable when their seeds are mature and cones just opening. Like surfers, White-winged Crossbills ride this moving wave of conifer profitability. Across most of their range, they forage on white spruce and tamarack, then move to black spruce, whose seeds remain on the tree longer and open later, in late winter through spring, when the others have dropped their seed. In the West, they mostly ride the Engelmann cone crop wave south in the mountains.[6]

However, like the best Vegas gamblers, White-winged Crossbills can hedge their bets. Even when cone yields may be high, White-wings can sense that it might not last and may search for another cone crop.[7] If there is a large-scale crop failure, White-wings can oscillate across the boreal forest belt from one side of North America to the other, assessing the spruce and tamarack crops. If there is not enough food or too many crossbills due to a banner breeding year, they may flee or irrupt to areas well south of their normal range.

Like a constant wheel in motion, White-wings only set down when there is sufficient food based on profitability rates, that program overriding anything else. When they breed in the middle of winter, fire meets ice. Red beacons of hormonal fecundity broadcast their elaborate songs, throwing down a gauntlet to the weather gods. Breeding individuals triumph in the depth of wintertide.

Every *Loxia*-phile (crossbill-loving) birder would have traded their best binoculars to be Jessé Roy Drainville that October day. To be engulfed by a tsunami of crossbills might be nirvana. Could this happen again? The answer might be yes. Those White-winged Crossbills likely fled poor cone crops, in this case exacerbated by a record number of fires in Canadian forests. White-winged Crossbills are indelibly nomads, moving to find survival. But as the earth warms and fires become more frequent and severe, crossbills may not just be nomads, but, like other living things, climate migrants, moving to escape the devastation of once-reliable habitats. The planet could see a greater temperature increase in the next fifty years than it did in the last six thousand years combined.[8] Will wings be enough?

## DEEPER DIVE

All ages and sexes of White-winged Crossbills, all year, have yellow carotenoid pigments in their blood plasma (derived from food), which can create yellow feather color. However, during feather growth September–November, adult males have higher blood plasma levels of the less common plasma carotenoids (B-cyproxanthin, rubixanthin, and gazaniaxanthin), which are the precursors of their bright-red color.[28] Males may forage at this time for these pigments or have a special ability to metabolically produce them when in molt to create the bright red.

## IDENTIFICATION

**Size:** L 6.5"

**Shape:** Fairly small, short-tailed (although longest-tailed of the crossbills relative to body size) short-legged, big-headed, broad-necked bird with a distinctive fairly thin bill with tips that cross each other. Tail deeply notched; primary projection very long (2.5 x bill length).

**Both Sexes:** Two broad, well-defined white wingbars; white-tipped tertials (lacking on Red Crossbill).

**Adult Male:** Head, rump, and most underparts pinkish-red; back all black to mostly red; rear flanks paler and strongly to indistinctly streaked darker.

**Adult Female:** Variably faintly greenish (sometimes yellowish) on crown, back, rump, and breast; otherwise, grayish-brown upperparts and darkly streaked with brown.

**1st Year:** M. mixed brown with pinkish-red or orangish yellow; f. brownish or faintly greenish.

**Juv:** (Jan.–Oct.) (can breed in winter) Brownish overall with heavy brown streaking on whitish underparts; occasionally greenish or yellowish feathers, whitish wingbars. May breed in this plumage.

### *SUBSPECIES*

Two subspecies, White-winged Crossbill (*L. l. leucoptera*) in North America and Two-barred Crossbill, (*L. l. bifasciata*) across Eurasia. White-winged Crossbill is larger, has less black on back and wing coverts, has a larger, deeper bill. Based on bill structure which is tied to foraging rates, and differences in calls and ecology, the two subspecies might warrant full species status with more research.[9]

### *SIMILAR SPECIES*

The only other species in the United States and Canada with a crossed bill are the Red Crossbill (*L. curvirostra*) and Cassia Crossbill (*L. sinesciuris*). The White-winged Crossbill has a slightly thinner-based bill (for bill size comparisons see Red Crossbill Call Types Bill Sizes on page 125), a longer tail, and two broad, well-defined white wingbars and white-tipped tertials. The adult male White-winged Crossbill is more pinkish-red in fall to a deeper scarlet red as feather barbules wear off in spring. If bill is not seen well, male could be confused with male Pine Grosbeak, but that species is much larger, stocky with gray underparts, less bold white wingbars, and the bill is bluntly conical and not crossed.

### FUN FACT

**The bills of White-winged Crossbills cross left over right in a 3:1 ratio, whereas with individuals of the Red Crossbill it is a 1:1 ratio. It is believed that diet plays a role in the species' differences.**

Adult m. NY/03

Adult f. AK/02

1st yr. m. Ak/02

1st yr. f. WI/12

## DISTRIBUTION

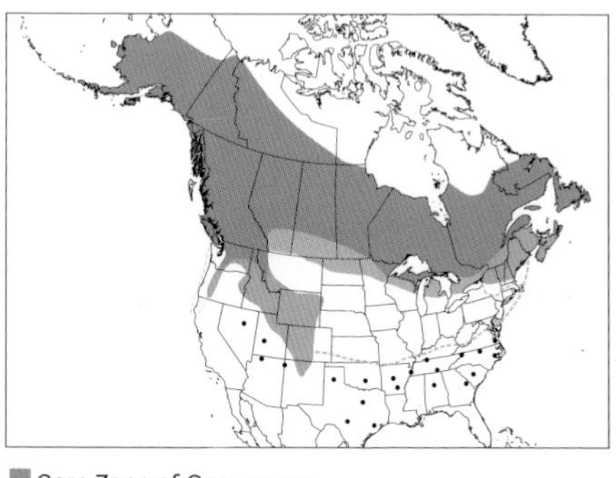

Core Zone of Occurrence
Secondary Zone of Occurrence
Primary Zone of Irruption

Highly irregular even within their normal range. They live and breed in the continuous boreal forest of Canada, associating with white spruce (*Picea glauca*), black spruce (*P. mariana*), and tamarack (*Larix laricina*.) They also occur and breed in open boreal (pockets of boreal habitat mixed with other forest types) containing red spruce, black spruce, white spruce, and tamarack from the Adirondacks of New York State east to (mainly northeast) Vermont, New Hampshire, Maine, New Brunswick, and Nova Scotia. They breed in the Upper Peninsula (rarely Lower Peninsula) and Isle Royale in Michigan and northern parts of Wisconsin and Minnesota.[10]

In the West they mostly live and breed in Engelmann spruce forests in Cascade Mountains to central Oregon, the Rocky Mountains to southern Colorado and down to northern New Mexico, but can also occasionally occur in British Columbia Douglas fir forests and coastal Sitka spruce forests to southeast Alaska and British Columbia.[11] During irruptions they go as far as the Carolinas, the plains states, Texas, Georgia, and California. The nonbreeding range is very like the breeding ranges except in big irruptions it may extend as far south as Texas and Florida.

## LANGUAGE

### *MALE*

Song is a very long, loud series of a number of types of dry trills on varying pitches. Can have a shorter version with a lesser number of trills. Sings a much louder song than Red Crossbill, which is related to having much larger-sized testes (Tom Hahn, personal communication).

### *FEMALE*

Sings, but less frequently than males. "The degree of sexual dimorphism in crossbills is similar to that in other species in which females sing, but less often and with a smaller song repertoire than males."[12]

### *MALE AND FEMALE*

Flight call is a chattering, mechanical, and relatively complex *jit-jit,* or *chet-chet-chet.* There is a second call of White-winged Crossbills that could be confused with Red Crossbill flight call types and is usually given by perched birds, the *toop* call; it's a sharper, quicker, and thinner *veet-veet-veet* than any of the Red Crossbill types. There is also a trumpeting nasal *zree* similar to Goldfinch.

### *IMITATION/MIMICRY*

When singing will imitate other finches like Pine Siskin and Type 3 Red Crossbill. More study is needed.

## HABITAT AND DIET

As a conifer seed specialist, White-winged Crossbills associate primarily with those conifers in their main living and breeding distribution areas, especially tamarack, white and black spruce (see Distribution). On southward irruptions, they use a wider variety of conifers such as pines and spruces of cemeteries and plantations, and hemlock (*Tsuga* spp.).

White-winged Crossbills feed by holding cones with the foot opposite the side the bill crosses, insert their bill, spread the cone scales, remove and secure the seed in a groove in their upper palate, then husk and eat the seed.

In spring and summer, they eat spiders, insects, especially spruce budworm and coneworm, and a variety of deciduous buds and seeds from trees and weeds.

## AT YOUR FEEDER

Rare, but slightly increasing feeder use perhaps due to habitat loss from fires and logging. Possibly young learn feeder use from their parents (Tom Hahn, personal communication). Feeder preferences: black oil sunflower, especially hulled sunflower seed at tube, hopper, or platform feeders. Eats salt, grit, and snow.

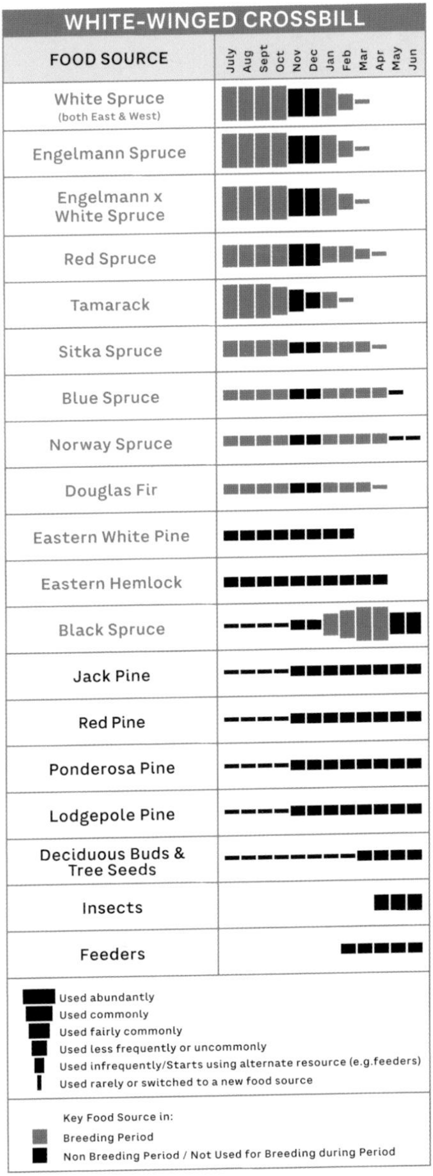

**WHITE-WINGED CROSSBILL**

| FOOD SOURCE | July | Aug | Sept | Oct | Nov | Dec | Jan | Feb | Mar | Apr | May | Jun |
|---|---|---|---|---|---|---|---|---|---|---|---|---|
| White Spruce (both East & West) | | | | | | | | | | | | |
| Engelmann Spruce | | | | | | | | | | | | |
| Engelmann x White Spruce | | | | | | | | | | | | |
| Red Spruce | | | | | | | | | | | | |
| Tamarack | | | | | | | | | | | | |
| Sitka Spruce | | | | | | | | | | | | |
| Blue Spruce | | | | | | | | | | | | |
| Norway Spruce | | | | | | | | | | | | |
| Douglas Fir | | | | | | | | | | | | |
| Eastern White Pine | | | | | | | | | | | | |
| Eastern Hemlock | | | | | | | | | | | | |
| Black Spruce | | | | | | | | | | | | |
| Jack Pine | | | | | | | | | | | | |
| Red Pine | | | | | | | | | | | | |
| Ponderosa Pine | | | | | | | | | | | | |
| Lodgepole Pine | | | | | | | | | | | | |
| Deciduous Buds & Tree Seeds | | | | | | | | | | | | |
| Insects | | | | | | | | | | | | |
| Feeders | | | | | | | | | | | | |

Used abundantly
Used commonly
Used fairly commonly
Used less frequently or uncommonly
Used infrequently/Starts using alternate resource (e.g.feeders)
Used rarely or switched to a new food source

Key Food Source in:
Breeding Period
Non Breeding Period / Not Used for Breeding during Period

## MOVEMENTS AND IRRUPTIONS

White-winged Crossbills are opportunistic breeders that can make large-scale movements depending on conifer cone-crop abundance, swinging back and forth across the boreal forest or irrupting southward when they have a large population but there are insufficient cone crops. Sometimes the irruptions reach historic proportions when, for example, over 20,000 individuals moved through in a day at the Observatoire d'Oiseaux de Tadoussac at the mouth of the St. Lawrence River in Quebec in October 2021.

Generally, movement occurs three or even more times a year depending on cone crops and where there is sufficient food for breeding.

- Mid-May–July: Move to areas with large ripening white spruce and tamarack crops, and breeding can then take place July–October/November.

- Late October–December: As spruce and tamarack begin dropping seeds, White-wings can move, unless crops are plentiful.[13] As the season progresses, they will look for the last remaining white spruce crops in the boreal, red spruce in the Northeast, Engelmann spruce in western mountains, Sitka spruce in the northwest coastal areas, or Douglas fir in northwest British Columbia. Winter breeding can ensue from January to April or longer if crops are estimated sufficient to feed nestlings through the first three weeks.

- February: Move when the previously mentioned conifers have dropped seeds, and White-wings are on the hunt for black spruce, which reliably holds its seeds longest and may provide an opportunity to breed in black spruce forests into June.

The White-winged Crossbill moved south in higher numbers than usual in 1961, 1964, 1965, 1966, 1970, 1972, 1976, 1978, 1981, 1982, 1985, 1988, 1990, 1993, 1995, 1996, 1997, 1998, 2001, 2004, 2009, 2010, 2012, 2013, and 2021.[14]

## BREEDING BEHAVIOR

### *TERRITORY*

Like many other finch species, males defend a floating territory centered on the female's movements, rather than defending and remaining at a fixed location, a reasonable strategy for a species that relies on a food supply that is concentrated, variable and not readily defended. Groups often nest semi-colonially. Feeding territories are not defended.

White-winged Crossbills on white spruce

### *COURTSHIP*

Courtship activities include males singing from treetops or with slow circling flight, singing in a small area, allowing females to size them up, and chasing females through trees.[15] Touching and nibbling bills proceed to the male feeding the female by regurgitating spruce or other conifer seeds. He then follows and watches over his mate closely, being especially vigilant when she is egg-laying.[16]

A study of banded birds in northern Utah[17] found that adult males and all females bred, nonbreeding first-year males continued to sing, and mated adult males ceased singing.

The arrangement of cones on a conifer species influences crossbill behavior, as when White-wings feed on black spruce, a conifer they specialize in, and whose cones are compactly clustered at the top of the tree. Packed-together crossbills then become more aggressive to one another, and adult males dominate females and immatures. Female feeding rates decline, which can lead to female mortality and a skewed sex ratio of more males than females, 1.30 males to 1 female according to one study.[18] Fewer females in the population means significant male competition for those females. The females choose among competing males, preferring those more richly colored with more elaborate displays. This drives the evolution of those traits and leads to White-winged Crossbill adult males who are more colorful and have bigger testes[19] than Red Crossbills. When it comes time to mate, the large testes size in adult male White-wings may indicate high rates of extrapair copulations.[20] Thus, the young in a nest could have different parents. More study is needed.

### *NESTING*

**Timing:** Mainly breeds in 2 cycles, July–October and January–April.
**Nest:** Cup, outside diameter about 4 in. (bigger in winter than summer), made of conifer twigs, grass and plant stems, bark, lichens, lined with finer, softer materials such as moss, lichens, feathers, bark shreds, cocoons. Placed 9–65 ft. high concealed on conifer limbs, sometimes near trunk.
**Eggs:** 2–4, pale bluish-white, with lavender and chocolate marks at larger end
**Incubation:** 14–16 days, by female
**Nestling period:** Little information. About 40 days between start of egg-laying and fledging.[21]
**Broods:** Usually 1–2, possibly up to 4

Crossbills will breed only when they find cone crops large enough and sense when their food intake rates will sustain them through egg-laying and, most importantly, through raising the nestlings three weeks later.[22] Crossbills may begin and then stop breeding if food intake rates decline rapidly. When a big cone crop is located, they may have a second brood.

The female incubates and the male feeds her regurgitated seeds, calling when he arrives. The female broods the young continuously in cold weather. In one study, the male and female fed the hatched young regurgitated seed kernels in a viscous bolus, at intervals of 15 to 45 minutes for nestlings that were six days old.[23] The parents ate the fecal sacs of the young. Young from an earlier nest may help adults feed the young of a later nest, as happens in Red Crossbills (Tom Hahn, personal communication).

When adult White-winged Crossbills have feeding intake rates sufficient to feed fledglings, both males and females do so. However, when intake rates are good enough to allow just one parent to feed the fledglings, only the male does so. The female leaves and presumably renests, possibly with another male,[24] though that is unconfirmed. If she did mate with a different male, it would be serial polyandry,[25] which has been documented in American Goldfinches and Common Redpolls.

Fledgling crossbills at first remain in trees and parents feed them, but can fly well after about a week. After about two weeks their bill becomes crossed and they gradually learn the skill of extracting conifer seeds, becoming more proficient by 60 days. Fledged young follow their parents and may join up with other crossbill families.[26]

## MOLT

White-winged Crossbill adults molt once a year and do not have a second molt into breeding plumage. Males initially look pinkish-red but have tiny uncolored parts of their feathers (unpigmented barbules) that wear off, revealing a brilliant deep-scarlet plumage by spring.

The timing of molt varies given some opportunistic breeding, but molt is primarily in fall, September to November. Adult males that molt in late summer

to autumn acquire red plumage. They have higher blood levels of diet-derived carotenoid-based red pigments at this time.[27] Females and most immatures are usually streaked brown with some greenish/yellowish, though immature males may show some pinkish or orange-yellow.

## CONSERVATION

Listed as Least Concern on the IUCN Red List and 6 out of 20 on the Partners in Flight Continental Concern Score. Their population trend appears stable, but breeding bird surveys may not accurately reflect the White-winged Crossbill trend because the surveys often occur south of their main distribution or at a time when birds might not be obvious. New research suggests a significant downward population trend.

# EUROPEAN GOLDFINCH

*Carduelis carduelis*

*The finches keep calling me.*
—Lillian Quinn Stokes

## QUICK TAKE

It was a rainy, foggy, morning in Massachusetts on December 7, 2021. On a hunch, I checked the MassBird listserv of birds being seen in my area, and a rare European Goldfinch was being discussed. What? I was just about to write this chapter on the European Goldfinch in this book! I looked up the sighting's map and next to the area it was being seen, the road sign said Lillian Rd. No way, you can't make this stuff up. Was this to be one of those special finch moments I keep having, like the moment I had when I met my coauthor, Matt, in person, for the first time, Red Crossbills descended on us, and as I drove away the road sign said Lillian's Way?

I loaded the car with binoculars and cameras and took off, hoping for clearing weather. When we arrived, the rain had stopped but the wind began. The area was Lexington Community Farm, a large area with back woods and lots of weeds and tangles. A birder walking toward me said that he had seen the bird earlier, but it had flown. I had that feeling that birders get, the you-should-have-been-here-an-hour-ago sinking feeling in the pit of your stomach. I desperately wanted to see and photograph this bird. It took a few hours and five birders. First, a pair of birders saw it briefly, down low and back in tangles, but it flew. The wind was likely keeping it well under cover, and deterring it from vocalizing. Then Don briefly spotted a bird with black and white that flew. Then Dave saw it, and he and I moved a bit and got on it. To my astonishment, this European Goldfinch proceeded to feed on burdock, in front of me, visible without much-obscuring vegetation. I became lost in an altered state of consciousness through my camera lens. I call it "becoming one with the bird," as I fired and got as many photos as possible.

Wow! At an especially challenging time in my life, I just had an uplifting, almost spiritual experience in which the stars aligned and I connected with this amazing finch who lifted my spirits. What a gift.

Lessons from finches: experiences like this are open to all who trust the improbable is possible. Yes, finches keep calling me, and I keep answering.

A European Goldfinch is not a native bird to the United States and Canada. It is native to Europe, northern Africa, and western Asia, and likely does not cross the Atlantic. Many thousands are captured in the wild each year in their native lands and exported; some are bred in captivity and sold. In the United States and Canada, European Goldfinches are sold as caged birds, may be bred in aviaries, and often can escape or be released and live in the wild. There have been times when European Goldfinch populations have bred in the wild and then diminished. More recently, in Wisconsin and Illinois, European Goldfinches are establishing self-sustaining populations that seem to be taking off. This Massachusetts European Goldfinch was thought to be an escapee. However, finches are full of surprises. They can move great distances. Who knows how the future will play out for this species?

## IDENTIFICATION

**Size:** L 4.7–5.3"

**Shape:** Fairly small, slim, somewhat small-headed bird with a fairly long notched tail and rather long, very pointed bill.

**Adult Male:** Unmistakable dramatic head pattern, head black and white with face deep red; red extends to just behind eye; black lore; bill whitish, conical, long, and pointed, with dark tip in nonbreeding; black nasal bristles protrude onto bill; tan upperparts; wings jet-black with broad yellow wingbar; black greater coverts; white uppertail coverts; buff-tan on sides of breast and flanks; white below; tail black, broadly tipped with white spots.

**Adult Female:** Similar to male; but red on face does not extend behind eye; buff on sides of face; bill with tan (not black as in male) nasal bristles protruding onto it; buff on breast often a complete band; less white in tail. Note: Distinguishing the sexes is not always reliable in the field.

**Juv:** (up to late summer and autumn) Head grayish-brown with diffuse streaks; no black and white on head with red face; streaking on upperparts and breast, tail, and upperwing like adults.

### *SUBSPECIES*

There are two groups: the European, *Carduelis carduelis* (*carduelis* group; Europe east to western central Asia, northern Africa, and introduced to the Azores, Cape Verde Islands, New Zealand, Tasmania, Australia, Uruguay, Argentina, Bermuda, and parts of the United States) with 10 recognized subspecies; in the eastern part of their range, Eastern, *Carduelis carduelis* (*caniceps* group; western and central Asia) with 4 recognized subspecies. The Eastern, *caniceps* group differs in having gray head with no black and white markings, longer bill, grayer upperparts, and sides of breast.[1]

### *SIMILAR SPECIES*

Juvenile American Goldfinch has browner upperparts, no streaking on head and breast, beige wingbars, and lacks the black wings with broad yellow wingbar of juvenile European Goldfinch.

## DISTRIBUTION

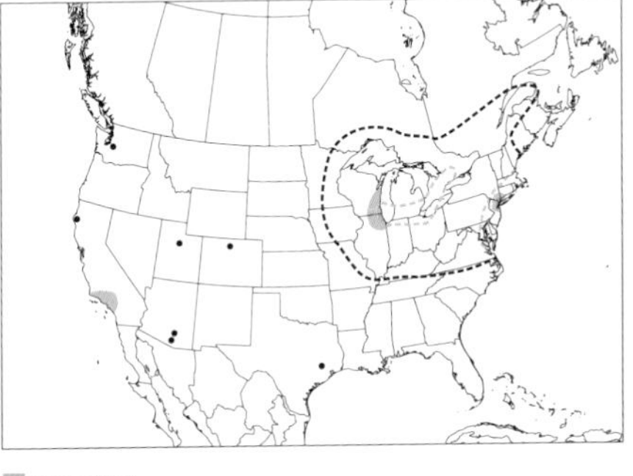


European Goldfinches have been reported in the United States and Canada for many years. The birds are of multiple subspecies that were wild-caught or raised by exporters who sell them to dealers. Then they escape captivity or may be intentionally released. In some cases, people buy and release birds to honor certain cultural or religious beliefs.

These birds have been kept in captivity since the 1600s. In North America, they have been introduced a number of times, in different places, from about the 1840s on. They became temporarily established but eventually died out. The first known intentional introduction was in Green-Wood Cemetery in Brooklyn, New York. Thomas S. Woodward imported 48 European Goldfinches in 1852, kept them over the winter, then released the surviving 16 finches on April 20, 1853.[2]

A look at eBird sightings maps for 2020–2023 shows scattered reports mainly of single birds.[3] Of note is a somewhat bigger cluster of sightings in the greater New York City area, especially in Brooklyn's Prospect Park and nearby Green-Wood Cemetery. While European Goldfinches might be breeding there, this population is likely being augmented by released captive birds.

By far the largest population is now in southeast Wisconsin and northern Illinois. The genesis of that story goes back 20 years when Julie Craves, then director of the Rouge River Bird Observatory at the University of Michigan-Dearborn, discovered a European Goldfinch in Dearborn. After asking for sightings of European Goldfinches in a post on the RRBO web page, between 2002 and 2006 she got over 400 records, mostly of birds sighted at feeders, from 20 states and 5 provinces, with 298 of the records from the western Great Lakes in Illinois, Wisconsin, Indiana, and Michigan.

Many of the reports coming from the Great Lakes region were thought to be a large number of releases from one Illinois breeder and importer.[4]

In 2023 Craves and Nicholas Anich published a more complete look at the European Goldfinch (*Carduelis carduelis*) in the western Great Lakes region.[5] They described the bird's "distribution, breeding status, nesting phenology, and natural food sources" as well as possible origins and ecological impact.

Lillian photographing the European Goldfinch in weedy habitat

They reviewed an astounding 7,000 plus sightings from across North America 2001–2021 garnered from multiple sources—eBird, iNaturalist, Project FeederWatch, reports to Craves, online sites, and other places. They found "since about 2018 records were concentrated between the cities of Milwaukee, Wisconsin and Chicago, Illinois, mostly within 15 km of Lake Michigan." They concluded that European Goldfinches "have been breeding in this area continuously since 2003 and the number of reported observations has increased in recent years."

The Wisconsin second Breeding Bird Atlas, completed in 2019, also documents European Goldfinches breeding in the state. Nicholas Anich is the coordinator for the atlas, and he and Craves estimated from several hundred "to the low thousands" of European Goldfinches breeding in the western Great Lakes area.[6]

In the western Great Lakes, many European Goldfinch eBird records are marked with an asterisk indicating their eBird status as "Naturalized: exotic population is self-sustaining, breeding in the wild, persisting for many years, and not maintained through ongoing releases (including vagrants from Naturalized populations). These count in official eBird totals and, where applicable, have been accepted by regional bird records committee(s)." In other locations a few European Goldfinch eBird records are considered Provisional but most are designated Escapee: Exotic species known or suspected to be escaped or releases, including those that have bred but don't yet fulfill the criteria for Provisional.[7] You can contribute to efforts to further understand European Goldfinches by noting them on your eBird checklists and including, when possible, photos and breeding status.

## LANGUAGE

### *MALE*

Song consists of rapid twitters and trills, continuously or with short breaks, but characteristically with interspersed harsher notes.

### *FEMALE*

Song similar to males but less frequent and not as long or vigorous.[8]

### *MALE AND FEMALE*

Call is a melodic 3-syllable *tickelitt, telitt,* or *tee-tuu,* heard from feeding flocks. Alarm note is a harsh, repeated *weeju* or *zeez*.

## HABITAT AND DIET

Found in open woodlands, riparian areas, gardens, fields, and farmlands with weedy areas. European Goldfinches eat a wide variety of seeds mainly from weeds, especially composites, and can hang upside down to access them. They seem to prefer nonnative plants, such as ones found in their native range, like burdock, thistle, and teasel. Buds and tree seeds may be eaten. They consume very few insects.

## AT YOUR FEEDER

European Goldfinches can thrive in the wild, even in cold weather. They readily come to feeders, often in the company of American Goldfinches, and sometimes Pine Siskins and House Finches. They do not seem to be very aggressive toward other species. European Goldfinches like black oil sunflower seeds, hulled sunflower, Nyjer®, and finch mixes.

European Goldfinch feeding on burdock

## MOVEMENTS AND IRRUPTIONS

There is small evidence that European Goldfinches, presumably those who once lived in captivity, and true to finch character, may move distances during spring and fall migratory time. One such bird (eastern group, *Carduelis carduelis caniceps*) was banded at Manomet Bird Observatory, Plymouth County, Massachusetts, April 22, 2016.[9] Although presumed to be an escapee, it was netted with American Goldfinches and "seemed to be migrating with other birds and had a fair amount of sub-dermal fat build-up," an indication of migration readiness.

## BREEDING BEHAVIOR

### *TERRITORY*

Breeding usually takes place from March to May, mostly earlier than the American Goldfinch. The European Goldfinch may maintain a territory of up to 250 square meters for nesting and mating but will forage outside of this area. Nests singly or loosely colonially.[10]

### *COURTSHIP*

Pairs are formed in winter flocks. European Goldfinches are seemingly monogamous. Mates display to one another face to face, with bodies swinging side to side. As in many other finch species, singing; slow, stiff-winged display flights with song; chases; and repeated bill touching are part of courtship. The male feeds the female during incubation and while she is brooding the nestlings.[11]

***NESTING***

**Timing:** Mostly March through May and occasionally up to July in the western Great Lakes region.[12]
**Nest:** Deep cup, made of plant fibers, with a lining of downy materials like thistle or cattail, secured to twigs with spider silk. Placed 9–68 ft. in branches of bush or pine or deciduous tree.
**Eggs:** 4–6, whitish or pale bluish, with violet or reddish splotches
**Incubation:** 9–13 days, by female
**Nestling period:** 13–18 days
**Broods:** Usually 1, possibly 2

Both parents care for the young and feed them for at least 10 days after they fledge. The young are fed mainly regurgitated seeds.

## MOLT

Juveniles get the red on their face by molting into their first-winter plumage from August to September.[13] Adults molt once after breeding and may look a little duller until the new feather tips wear off.

## CONSERVATION

European Goldfinches breed earlier than American Goldfinches and do not appear to be hybridizing with them. The nonnative plant foods they thrive on (various weed seeds and composites) are proliferating, which is a plus and may help their populations expand. However, it is unknown what effects will occur if they continue to become established. More research is needed.

### FUN FACT

**The very long, pointed bill of European Goldfinches allows them to extract seeds from the heads of teasel. They are one of the few birds that can do so.**

# PINE SISKIN

*Spinus pinus*

PINE SISKINS HAVE TAKEN OVER THE COUNTRY
*From coast to coast the species has irrupted in astounding numbers*

—*Audubon Magazine*, October 23, 2020

## QUICK TAKE

Who knew what was coming . . .

On March 11, 2020, the World Health Organization declared COVID-19 a pandemic. Like a 10 on the Richter scale, the crisis shook humanity and in a fear landscape like a floor undulating beneath them, humans reached out to a different landscape, an ancient, nurturing anchor. Through the magnifying lens of their pandemic isolation, people's backyards became their universe. Large numbers of people stayed at home and found sanctuary in nature outside. Viewing beautiful birds, and hearing their sounds, lifted the spirits of millions. Sales in bird seed and feeders skyrocketed. Millions of birders were then to get a surprise bonus.

By May 2020, a parallel but different crisis for birds was brewing in the vast boreal forest of North America, the green incubator of avian DNA. By summer 2020, high populations of finches in the boreal were fueled by ample conifer seed crops and spruce budworm outbreaks. When foods were finally depleted, this large population of finches, facing a massive food shortage, were to "irrupt" or flee to find life-sustaining food elsewhere.

By July and August 2020, the vanguard started with Purple Finches moving around in the border states, and the superflight proceeded. Evening Grosbeaks moved in their largest numbers in twenty years, redpolls had their biggest push in almost ten years, and the Pine Siskin irruption was off the charts.[1]

By October 2020, Pine Siskin became the poster child for the superflight, descending in numbers so large that *Audubon Magazine* declared Pine Siskins had taken over the country.[2]

While siskins usually irrupt about every two to three years, this was another order of magnitude. Matt Young described it as "epic, one for the record books." The bird reporting database, eBird, showed an enormous purple map of Pine Siskin sightings, covering the country. Siskins were reported as far as Miami, Florida; New Orleans, Louisiana; South Padre Island, Texas; San Diego, California; and even as

far away as Bermuda. On October 25, official counter Daniel Irons and birders at Higbee Beach WMA, Dike/Morning Flight Songbird Count in Cape May, New Jersey reported a flight of over eleven thousand Pine Siskins.[3] Tim Spahr, astronomer and field ornithologist, even recorded something practically never reported before: a flight of over five hundred Pine Siskins, usually a diurnal migrant, migrating at night! This was postulated as a sign of severe food shortage. Birder and science writer Ryan Mandelbaum reported that "clouds of Siskins seem to outnumber goldfinches in my native New York City's parks."[4] Other birders had hundreds of Pine Siskins at their feeders throughout the irruption, and some siskins even stayed in those areas to breed.

Pine Siskins are streak lightning bundles of energy that explode and dance over the sky, their fine bills leading striated brown plumage. Birders look for a golden treasure in the flock, the rare Pine Siskin "green morph" where in a small percent of the population, siskins are more extensively colored yellow over brown with yellow shadings on the wing, sides of the neck, and undertail coverts, giving them a greenish-yellow appearance.

Siskins usually live in boreal and montane coniferous and mixed coniferous-deciduous forests across North America from Alaska across Canada, and also in the Appalachians and montane western regions. Not picky eaters, they may have the most generalist palate of their relatives. They have redpolls' penchant for feeding on birch and alder catkins, crossbills' love for feeding on conifer seeds, goldfinches' taste for weed seeds, and Evening Grosbeaks' enthusiasm for spruce budworm caterpillars.

When siskins descend on feeders, the seed level goes down and budget goes up while other birds take a side seat. So, birders at the end of the superflight, while still thrilled with having seen Pine Siskins, may not entirely have been sorry to see them go. Finches are obvious drivers of seed sales when they visit feeders in such numbers.

This amazing event, the superflight of 2020–2021, incredibly brought birders the healing power of the excitement of birds at the best possible moment. Stars of the superflight, Pine Siskins returned to their breeding areas in spring and summer, but one thing is certain: the eBird map of their sightings will light up purple across much of North America once again in the next big irruption.

## FUN FACT

**The Pine Siskin's scientific name is *Spinus pinus, pinus* being Latin for "pine tree." Many people think of conifers as just pines, but the Pine Siskin feeds more on the soft-coned conifers such as Douglas fir, hemlocks, cedars, and spruces, for which its small, pointed bill is better adapted rather than hard-coned trees like lodgepole pine in the West or red pine in the East.**

## IDENTIFICATION

**Size:** L 5"

**Shape:** Small, slim, fairly small-headed bird with a short, well-notched tail and slender, fine-pointed, somewhat conical bill with straight culmen (rarely slightly decurved).

**Adult:** Head and body finely streaked with brown; underparts dull whitish with streaking across breast and along flanks; yellow edges to primaries and secondaries. Two thin buffy to white wingbars on median and greater coverts (greater coverts have yellow edges, and base of secondaries underneath is also yellow, so that when white to buffy wingbars wear off the greater coverts, the bird can appear to have a wide lower wing bar that is yellowish). There is great variation in the amount of yellow on individuals. The amount and brightness of yellow on the bases of the primaries and retrices is more on adults and young males than on young females and might be used to distinguish up to 35% of males and females when combined with measurements. Occasionally, Pine Siskins (the "green morph") can show abnormal amounts of yellow in the plumage.[5]

**Juv:** (June–Aug.) Streaked brown overall: wide buffy wingbars with buffier and slightly more yellowish upperparts.

### *SUBSPECIES*

(1) *S. p. pinus* (breeds and winters N. Am–s.c. Mex). Birds that breed in n.c. Mex and may winter to AZ–NM (*"macropterus"*) can be somewhat larger with finer streaks and more yellow by age/sex.

### *SIMILAR SPECIES*

Might be confused with goldfinches, but goldfinches lack the streaks of Pine Siskin. Streaky females of House, Cassin's, and Purple Finches are larger with a shorter tail notch. Redpolls are streaked but have a red forehead to forecrown. F. Pine Siskin distinguished from rare Eurasian Siskin by having thin whitish wingbars; little or no yellow on eyebrow and face; streaked whitish underparts; white undertail coverts (can be yellowish in green morph Pine Siskin) while f. Eurasian Siskin has yellow wingbars, sparser streaks on belly. Male Eurasian Siskin has black cap and chin, yellow face and breast.

## DISTRIBUTION

Range is in boreal and montane coniferous and mixed coniferous-deciduous forests across North America from central and southeastern Alaska, across Canada to Newfoundland, south to the northern United States border states, and south down the Appalachians in the East to the Carolinas, and in western interior mountain ranges south to Guatemala. Winter range includes the southern half of Canada, depending on food crops, and across the entire Lower 48 states. After irruptions siskins may stay and breed in southern areas where typically they are only seen in winter. Due to these irruptive tendencies, distribution can be erratic; they may be found in some breeding and wintering areas one year, but not the next.

Adult "green morph"

## LANGUAGE

### *MALE*

Song is a long, variable mixture of single notes and a series of notes, which can last up to 20 seconds or more. Can include imitations of other species, and can give a shorter disjunct song.

### *MALE AND FEMALE*

Most common vocalizations are a somewhat raspy flight call, *klee-u, tee-u* or *jirp, jirp,* and a distinctively long, gradually rising, coarse *zrreeee* or *dzzzzeee* call. These calls sometimes included in song, and *zrreee* may sometimes indicate aggression.[6]

### *IMITATION/MIMICRY*

Long song version can include imitations of calls of Evening Grosbeak, redpolls, American Robin, bluebird, shorebirds, Type 3 and Type 4 Red Crossbill, White-winged Crossbill, and many other species (Matt Young, personal observation).

## HABITAT AND DIET

Pine Siskins' main breeding habitat is in coniferous forests of boreal and montane regions of North America where they inhabit open softer-coned forests of spruces, cedars, hemlocks, some pines, and Douglas fir. Opportunists that they are, they will also breed in ornamental conifers and deciduous trees of suburban areas.

Pine Siskins can feed in large flocks, and even nesting birds may join into flocks. They forage in grasslands, weedy fields, roadsides, scrub, and chaparral as well as conifers. Of all the finches, they are the true diet generalist. They consume conifer seeds, alder and birch catkins, buds, flowers, weed seeds such as thistles, dandelions and composites, leaves and stems of plants, and insects including spruce budworm, which they feed to their young.

## AT YOUR FEEDER

Pine Siskins may mob the feeders, and are not choosy, feasting on Nyjer®, finch mixes, black oil sunflower, and hulled sunflower.

A study of Pine Siskins at feeders with American Goldfinches and Purple Finches in Wisconsin showed that the goldfinches and Purple Finches were wary and scanned more when feeding with the siskins, possibly because the siskins were dominant, aggressive, and more of a threat to displace them at the feeder.[7]

Pine Siskins are unfortunately susceptible to salmonella, which can be transmitted between birds in close contact, so feeder cleanliness is important. See the Feeding and Attracting Finches chapter for how to keep feeders clean and prevent diseases.

## MOVEMENTS AND IRRUPTIONS

Pine Siskins might just win the most erratic finch award; it's difficult to predict where and when they will show up. There is usually at least a small movement of Pine Siskins between northwest and southwest North America every fall, but in the less irruptive years they mostly remain in the boreal forest across Canada or montane areas of the West. In general, their larger southward irruptions are thought to occur every two to three years and are due to poor cone crops in their boreal range. However, a few times or less in a decade, a big population fueled by conifer crops and spruce budworm outbreaks, followed by a severe food shortage, may cause them to irrupt in extremely large numbers south and flood the entire country.

In the very largest of irruptions, siskins have been documented migrating at night, such as in 2008[8] and 2020 (Tim Spahr, personal communication, 2020). One hypothesis is that nocturnal migration may be a facultative strategy in years of large irruptive movements and that during these very large flights, birds stack up in such large numbers, especially along the coast, that eventually they fly at night (William Evans, personal communication, 2020).

In western North America there is less data available, though some impressive southbound movements have occurred, such as on November 7, 2002, at Ucluelet Harbour on Vancouver Island, BC, when over 2,500 siskins were observed in a little over an hour.[9]

Pine Siskins at tray feeder

The direction pattern of migrations varies and can be erratic, often more latitudinal in the East but altitudinal in western regions in spring and fall. One exceptional record of Pine Siskin movement was a bird banded in Maryland in 2020 and later recovered 2,403 miles away in British Columbia![10]

The largest eastern irruptions over the last 60 years were 1961, 1963, 1964, 1966, 1969, 1970, 1972, 1973, 1974, 1976, 1978, 1981, 1985, 1987, 1988, 1990, 1992, 1993, 1994, 1995, 1996, 1998, 2005, 2009, 2012, 2013, 2015, 2016, 2018, and 2021. Averages irrupting every 2 years, but can go several years in a row without irrupting or can irrupt several years in a row as in the 1970s and 1990s.[11]

## BREEDING BEHAVIOR

### *TERRITORY*

Large flocks in winter may be present with some birds remaining to breed and others moving north. A 1941 study noted "Thousands of siskins were present during winter and spring of 1941 throughout New England . . . there was a general tendency to nest by small portions of these spring flocks."[12] A pair of siskins in this study, prior to egg-laying, defended a territory of about 3–6 feet from other siskins and other birds. Another pair nested 60 yards from another pair.

May breed in late winter while feeding in the last remaining conifer seed crops from previous summer, and then two to three months later on herbaceous seeds in subalpine habitat.

### *COURTSHIP*

Pairing occurs while still in flocks, and they may breed in loose colonies or in pairs. When it comes to mate choice, females may prefer a familiar male over a new guy, even if the new male has similar-sized wing patches or even larger ones than the familiar male. So familiarity may trump the appeal of "sexual ornaments" (male yellow wing patches) for female siskins.[13] Males perform courtship flight displays of singing while fluttering wings, revealing the yellow wing patches. Males also chase females while singing. Courtship feeding of the female can precede copulation and continue through incubation into nesting.

### *NESTING*

**Timing:** Wide range from late February to early August, more usually March–June
**Nest:** Cup, 2.5–6 in. diameter, saucer of twigs, grasses, leaves, weeds, rootlets, bark strips, lichens, cloth strips, and string, lined with soft, insulating material such as hair, fur, feathers, moss, plant down; placed at height of 3 to 50 ft. concealed on a limb in conifers such as hemlock, spruce, redwood, cedar, or various trees and shrubs, such as maple, oak, cottonwood, box elder, lilac, serviceberry.
**Eggs:** 3–5, pale blue-green with splotches of reddish-brown, lavender
**Incubation:** 13 days
**Nestling period:** 13–17 days, usually about 15 days
**Broods:** 1–2

The male follows and guards the female and sings during nest building. The female builds the well-insulated nest concealed in the foliage of conifers or in deciduous trees. Nest material may be stolen from the nests of other birds like orioles and other siskins. The male feeds her during incubation. She broods the nestlings for 7–8 days almost continuously while the male delivers food to her and she, in turn, feeds the nestlings. After that, both parents feed the nestlings a thick yellowish or greenish paste by regurgitation.[14]

The young are fed for 3 weeks or more postfledging, and including more whole food items such as aphids.[15] Fledglings may remain in the area of the nest for a few weeks, or depart soon with adults and other family groups.

## MOLT

Pine Siskin adults have a complete molt once a year, mainly July–October, and may have a spring molt to replace some feathers of the throat and crown, but this needs more study.

## CONSERVATION

Their conservation status is Least Concern. According to Partners in Flight, while somewhat common, Pine Siskin populations declined by 69% from 1966 to 2019. On the Continental Concern Score, the Pine Siskin rates a 10 out of 20 and is considered a Common Bird in Steep Decline. Pine Siskins are vulnerable to habitat loss and also salmonella outbreaks, thus feeder cleanliness is important.

### DEEPER DIVE

Pine Siskins have impressive abilities to withstand severe winter temperatures. One study found they could augment their body heat production in February to withstand -70 degrees C / -94 degrees F for up to 6–8 hours.[16]

# LESSER GOLDFINCH

*Spinus psaltria*

> *In any weedy border of neglected fields small birds with yellow underpart, and white patches in their wings fly off when disturbed, with a little shivering note like the jarring of a cracked piece of glass. The spring flocks gather in trees near their feeding ground and keep up a concert of twittering song.*
>
> —Ralph Hoffmann, 1927[1]

## QUICK TAKE

There's nothing lesser about Lesser Goldfinches, especially if you live in the West and encounter a large foraging flock. This bouncing ball of energy might catch your eye or blow your bird seed budget if they arrive at your feeders to relish gourmet Nyjer® seed.

While often compared to American Goldfinches, who dazzle with bright beauty and are found coast to coast, the Lesser Goldfinch is a western treat unto themselves. Though petite, the smallest of the North American finches, their intriguing story is large. First of all, the males come in two plumages, easily field identifiable; while yellow below with black caps, the males in the western part of the range from Washington south through California are mostly green-backed with greenish cheeks; males in the eastern part of the range, Colorado, New Mexico to Texas, are increasingly black-backed and black-cheeked. Females all look similar and are brownish above, yellow below with females in the southeastern part of the range slightly larger.

On deeper inspection, there's an intergrade of male plumage, from birds that have all green backs, through those with some black on back, to birds with all black backs. Whether the Green-back and Black-backed Lesser Goldfinches are different subspecies, color morphs, or even separate species is debatable.

Then there's the distribution of this species. Range maps are always slightly behind the times because birds are on the move, especially where welcome mats prevail and new food and habitats open up. Lesser Goldfinch populations expanded in the northern parts of their range in the 1990s possibly due to an increase in winter bird feeding in those areas.[2]

Speaking of distribution, the Lesser Goldfinch was first called the Arkansas Goldfinch although not normally occurring in Arkansas. Before the state of Arkansas even became a state, the first known Lesser Goldfinch was collected on the banks of the Arkansas River between Colorado Springs and Pueblo, Colorado, during an 1819–1820 expedition. This type specimen was a green-backed bird although Colorado was in the range of the black-backed, so it was given the nominate subspecies name at the time for the black-backed, *psaltria*. For 135 years it was commonly known as the Arkansas Goldfinch until the fifth edition of the AOU checklist (1957) made it officially Lesser Goldfinch. The epithet *psaltria* is an ancient Greek word for female harpist.

Whether you think the song of the Lesser Goldfinch is heavenly harp music or the opening act for a Grateful Dead concert, one thing stands out. This bird is an accomplished mimic. Research done in the western range of Lesser Goldfinch documents it copying the vocalizations of 32 other species ranging from American Kestrels to Rock Wrens to American Robins to Yellow-rumped Warblers and American Goldfinches.[3] Mimicked phrases constituted up to 50% of Lesser Goldfinch songs in another study, the other phrases being call notes, unrecognized mimicry, modified mimicry, or uniquely goldfinch with phrases rarely repeated.[4]

The next time anyone diminishes Lesser Goldfinch as less than, show some LEGO (LEsser GOldfinch, the US Bird Banding code for common names of bird species using four letters) pride and say, No, this is a really cool, complex bird. It has two choices of plumage, an expanding range, and its chorus in numbers might just land it a concert gig.

## IDENTIFICATION

**Size:** L 4.5"

**Shape:** Small, slender, small-headed bird with a fairly deep-based conical bill. Proportionately shortest tail of our three goldfinches.

**Adult Male:** Underparts, including undertail coverts, plain yellow; black cap and dark back (either all dark or greenish or may have dark streaks; back, crown, and ear regions vary in darkness; ears usually not darker than rest); large white patch at base of primaries; 1 white wingbar, white patches in tail on outer 3–4 retrices, not on tip.

**Adult Female:** Bill dark grayish; bright to dull yellow underparts, including undertail coverts; no black on forehead and crown, olive upperparts; very small white patch at base of primaries; 1 whitish wingbar on greater coverts (a second indistinct bar on median coverts sometimes hidden); little to no white on tail.

**1st Winter:** Male: like ad. f. but mixed with some black feathers in forehead and crown, contrast between black tertials and brownish wings, and large white patch at base of primaries. Female: like adult f.

**Juv:** (May–Aug.) Like ad. f. but washed with buff overall, wingbars buffy, white primary patch small or absent.

### *SUBSPECIES*

Discussion is ongoing as to whether the green-backed and black-backed Lesser Goldfinches in North America (there are 3 subspecies from Mexico to South America) are different subspecies, color morphs, or even two different species. To add confusion, the first specimen collected in Colorado was green-backed, as mentioned, but given the subspecies name for the black-backed, *psaltria*, by Harry Oberhosler in 1903, since it was collected where black-backs occur.

Currently, Peter Pyle's *Identification Guide to North American Birds*, 2022, lists the green-backed as subspecies *S. p. hesperophilus* (breeds and winters WA–UT to Baja CA–n.w. Mex), adult m. with back and auriculars olive with dusky streaking or black mottling (rarely almost all black in s.e. UT–s.w. CO to e. AZ–w. NM), f. and imm. with upperparts greener and brighter; black-backed as *S. p. psaltria* (breeds and winters CO–OK to s.c. Mex), adult m. back and auriculars all black (or mixed with green in n.w. area of range), f. and imm. upperparts more olive, duller.[5] The Cornell Lab of Ornithology Birds of the World account similarly lists them as *hesperophilus* (n.e. UT–s.e. AZ and west) and *psaltria* (CO–s.w. NM and east).[6]

Researcher Ernest Willoughby developed a color scoring system from birds with the lightest green backs, heads, and cheeks to those with all black backs, heads, and cheeks, and examined 963 museum study skins for color, measurements, molt, and plumage wear.[7] He determined that Lesser Goldfinch color varied clinally (gradually changed across their range) from west to east with the darkest male birds in the southeast part of their range. He concluded color difference was likely genetic polymorphism not justifying subspecies distinctions based on color, or even measurements.

Recently, Sean Cozart looked at 360 photos of Lesser Goldfinch males on eBird, 30 from each state they bred in, and rated them according to Willoughby's scoring

Adult m., *psaltria* TX/06

Adult m., *psaltria* AZ/06

Adult m., *hesperophilis* CA/04

Adult f. CA/04

1st winter m., *hesperophilis* CA/03

Adult f. AZ/09

system. He found that birds with entirely dark upperparts were rare and occurred primarily in Texas. In the other states where black-backed birds supposedly occur, about half the Lessers were green-backed. Not only that, he estimated intergrades were only 1% of the population.[8]

Where does this leave things? Rounding out the picture as to the status of the green-backed and black-backed, as Sean points out, is the fact that they breed, molt, and may migrate at different times. Green-backed birds mainly breed April–July and are largely nonmigratory. Black-backed birds breed July–October and may migrate to Texas and Mexico.

Clearly, sorting out the subspecies issue for Lesser Goldfinch needs more work, including genetic research. The story continues to be written.

### *SIMILAR SPECIES*

Similar f. American Goldfinch is larger, lacks large white patch on primaries, has pinkish bill in summer, white undertail coverts, 2 well-defined wingbars.

## DISTRIBUTION

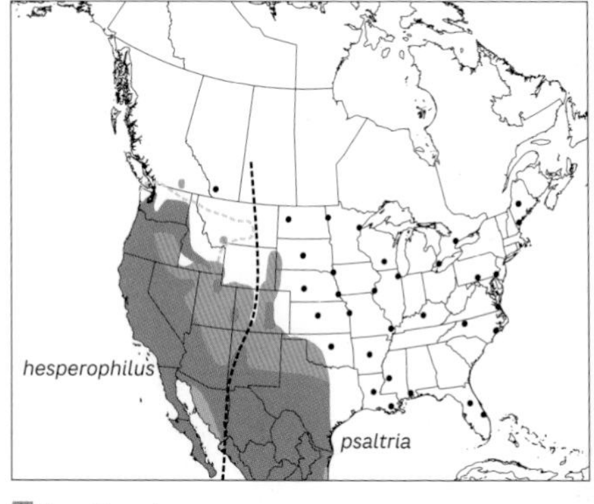


Occurs from southwest Washington, western Oregon, northern California, northern Utah, central Colorado, northwest Oklahoma, down through southern Texas, Mexico, Central America into South America, with breeding expansion into Washington, Idaho, and with records from British Columbia, Montana, and Wyoming.[9]

eBird data during breeding time from April to October in 2020–2022 shows Lesser Goldfinch from Washington, Montana, Wyoming, Colorado, to Texas and west.

In the eBird checklist reports with photos, many show Lesser Goldfinches at feeders eating Nyjer® or hulled sunflower seeds, and proliferation of bird feeding may explain some of their expansion. Within all-time eBird records are extralimital reports from a number of states outside of its usual range, as far east as Maine. eBird winter data November to March for 2020–2022 shows their presence in much of western North America, from British Columbia, Alberta, down through Montana, Wyoming, Colorado, New Mexico, and Texas, with a few reports as far east as Illinois, Alabama, even Arkansas.[10] The greatest abundance at that time is in California, Arizona, and Texas.

## LANGUAGE

### *MALE*

Song consists of a long series of twittering notes that, in addition to phrases uniquely its own, appropriates the vocalizations of many species, including Lawrence's and American Goldfinch. Song may intergrade into a disjunct song of various 1–2 note phrases at intervals. A courtship call like *tee-year* (falling pitch) or *tee-yee* (rising pitch) is given by male to attract a female. Heard early in season and regularly after. This call can be part of song, begin before song, or complete on its own.[11] Might be incorporated in disjunct song but needs more study.

### *FEMALE*

Female courtship call is a continuous series that begins with six to eight notes then ends as a single note. Given by female just preceding copulation.

Feeding call begins as a loud *pee-ee* or *tee-tee* as male approaches the nest. Increases in intensity and becomes almost continuous *tee-tee-tee* just before he feeds her.[12]

### *MALE AND FEMALE*

Their distinct *jeet-jeet-jeet* fight/contact call is given all year, higher pitched and more metallic than Pine Siskin's.[13]

Calls given in alarm include *dee-ree, bay-bee, bee-ee;* in aggression, a variable *dzik*.

### *IMITATION/MIMICRY*

Appropriates the vocalizations of 30 or more species.

## HABITAT AND DIET

Lesser Goldfinches live in a wide range of habitats, including riparian habitats with cottonwoods and willows, open woodlands, pine groves, weedy fields, chaparral, desert oasis, suburban residential areas, and agricultural lands.

They are agile, acrobatic feeders and eat the seeds of over 50 plant species, occasionally insects such as aphids, and also fruits and tree buds. Their longer more pointed bill than Lawrence's enables them to eat a wide range of bigger seeds, Napa thistle being a common choice. Lesser Goldfinches are highly dependent on water and during breeding drink in small flocks at streams alongside Lawrence's Goldfinches.

The style of feeding of the Lesser Goldfinch may be more grab-and-go at the takeout window than dine in. One study[14] found that Lesser Goldfinches tended to dominate Lawrence's while feeding in a lab environment and in limited observations in the field, but their feeding styles were different. Lessers flit about in constant activity from seed source to perching while Lawrence's Goldfinches fed for a longer time in one place then had quiet time. Speculation is this style may diminish competition in the wild since both species feed on similar plants in their overlap range.[15]

## AT YOUR FEEDER

Roll out the welcome mat with bird feeders, but don't be surprised if sometimes in summer Lesser Goldfinches retreat to breeding areas with plentiful wild seeds. Lesser Goldfinches dine with American Goldfinches, Lawrence's Goldfinches, Pine Siskins, House Finches, and others. At feeders, they relish Nyjer®, black oil sunflower, or hulled sunflower. They may sip from your hummingbird feeder too.

## MOVEMENTS AND IRRUPTIONS

More research is needed on the movements and migrations of Lesser Goldfinches, including the different subspecies.

In general, Lessers can sometimes be wide-ranging and nomadic but are thought to be resident in much of their range. Some populations in the eastern part of their range may move south in winter. However, populations can be unpredictable in winter areas, making it difficult to know whether movement there is because of migration, partial migration, postbreeding dispersal, or for postreproductive molt.

Lessers may be an altitudinal migrant in California and elsewhere, with populations moving down from higher elevation breeding locations to lowlands in winter. Some spring migration is reported along the inner Coast Ranges of central California, along the coast, and to California islands.[16]

Female on Napa thistle

## BREEDING BEHAVIOR

The study of Lesser Goldfinch breeding behavior is a bit like a tale of two cities. There are two different stories, but more chapters need to be written because only a few main studies have been done: one on the black-backed in the foothills around Boulder, Colorado;[17] and two on the green-backed in Placerita Canyon[18] and Hastings Natural History Reservation,[19] both in California.

### *TERRITORY*

In southern California's Placerita Canyon, breeding began for the green-backed after they arrived in flocks and quickly formed pairs in about 10–14 days. There was increasingly aggressive behavior by both sexes, especially males, who flew upwards grappling in aggressive encounters. After pairing, the male formed a territory of about 30 meters in diameter around the female and nest and defended it from other males with singing and flight displays with spread wings and tail, showcasing his white wing areas. Females also defended the nest, but from other females. This territoriality served to isolate the nesting pair. Males would leave the territory to feed. Territoriality waned after the eggs hatched.

The Colorado black-backed study was in ponderosa pines foothills in Boulder, where breeding began about 2 months later than green-backed, and clutch sizes were smaller. Quite social, these Lessers mostly nested colonially in small groups (some nests were 17 meters apart in an area less than 17 hectares) and did not show much territorial behavior. During nest building, pairs interacted with some aggressive encounters and chases, but during the whole breeding period the goldfinches moved about and fed together.

### *COURTSHIP*

In the Placerita Canyon study, after the flock began to break up, males spaced themselves about 20 meters apart in tall trees and gave short songs. The male's courtship calls attracted females, then high-speed chases ensued, the female usually leading and the male giving courtship song. Next came bill touching and courtship feeding, with both birds quivering wings and the male regurgitating food to the female. In the Hastings Natural History Reservation study, green-backed Lessers had a long breeding season, about March to July and sometimes later. Males engaged in courtship flights of high circles with wings and tail spread, exposing the white wing markings.

### NESTING

**Timing:** Breeding takes place for the green-backed April through early July in California with a peak mid-May to mid-June, but late records noted in September to October and November.[20] Breeding in the range of the black-backed takes place from about June to September and October.
**Nest:** Diameter about 3 in., of plant fibers, oak leaves, grasses, lichens, cocoons, webs, lined with hair, feather, fur, cottonwood seed fibers, 3.5–45 ft. or higher, shaded by leaves or vegetation, placed in a tree fork, 3–6 ft. from main branch. Black-backed study nests faced south or east, midway up pines in thick clusters of pine needles out toward tips of long branches.
**Eggs:** 3–6, pale bluish-white, may have a few small spots
**Incubation:** 12–15 days
**Nestling period:** 11–15 days
**Broods:** 1, possibly 2

In Placerita Canyon, the female explored potential real-estate nest sites with the male staying close, then constructed the nest in sycamores, shrubs, or large oaks. The females laid 3–5 eggs, one egg per day, and began the 12–13 day incubation period after laying the third egg. During this time until the young were about 5 days old, the male supplied almost all the food to the female in the form of regurgitated seeds. For the rest of the nestling phase, both parents fed the nestlings seeds and occasionally insects. At first the young's fecal sacs were eaten by the parents, but then the young defecated on the nest rim, which was not an issue since the nest was not reused. At 12–15 days the young fledged and after about a week were following adults giving begging calls. At the end of the season, family groups joined into larger flocks.

In the black-backed study, females sat tight on the nest, barely leaving, and they and the young were fed by the males until the young were 4–6 days old. Then both parents fed the young. The female's constant presence on the nest meant nesting success was high overall, 62% in three years of study. There was less predation and only one instance of cowbird parasitism (a low occurrence for goldfinches since cowbirds cannot survive on a strictly seed diet).

## MOLT

Molt in this species is complicated and needs more study. Continuing the tale of two cities theme, the black-backed and green-backed subspecies have their own molt strategies depending on location, habitat, and rainfall. Adult appearances basically remain the same. The male's black head, cheek, and black back feathers (where applicable) are fringed green when fresh, but these eventually wear off, making those areas appear darker.

In general, in its western range (Washington, Oregon, California, Nevada), green-backed adult birds molt completely postbreeding. Prebreeding, females molt

partially; most body feathers, not many flight feathers, and males do not molt or molt just a few body feathers.

In its eastern range (Utah, western Colorado, eastern Arizona, western New Mexico, and Texas), which includes black-backed birds as well as intermediate, prebreeding molt may be complete or incomplete.[21] After breeding, these birds molt again.

Some Lesser Goldfinches may undergo a "molt migration," stopping to primarily molt at the summer monsoon regions of Arizona, Sonora, and Baja California, depending on food resources, before continuing to winter grounds.[22]

## CONSERVATION

Partners in Flight rates them Low Concern, 7 out of 10 on the Continental Concern Score. Their populations are stable or slightly increasing. Human development, plantings, and irrigation have benefited Lesser Goldfinches.

# LAWRENCE'S GOLDFINCH*

*Spinus lawrencei*

## QUICK TAKE

Q: Why do they call you Lawrence's Goldfinch?

A: Glad you asked! Quite frankly, I never really felt my name reflected, you know, the real me. I was named after George Newbold Lawrence, a bird lover who lived in the nineteenth century and co-wrote *Birds of North America* with fellow ornithologists Spencer Fullerton Baird and John Cassin in 1860. So his buddy, John Cassin, decided to honor him by naming my common and scientific name, Lawrence's Goldfinch, *Spinus lawrencei* in 1852. I get why Cassin wanted to honor his buddy, but I'm not sure

* On November 1, 2023, the American Ornithological Society committed to changing all English-language names of birds within its geographic jurisdiction that are named directly after people, and that may affect this species. For more information, see How to Use This Guide, page xii.

naming birds after people who came from a tradition of sometimes naming animals after themselves was the best idea . . . just sayin'.

Q: I hear you and I want you to know that there is a serious movement in today's birding world to rename birds that have eponymous names with more fitting names. So, what would you like to be called?

A: Greatest Goldfinch of All Time!

Q: OK, but what would the other goldfinches think? That sounds a tad competitive and aren't you in some sort of "clade" (closely related in the same genus with a common ancestor) with American Goldfinch and Lesser Goldfinch? I thought you all got along.

A: Well, we try and work things out where we have to compete in the same habitats by using different feeding methods and different call notes but, quite frankly, American gets all the press, and Lesser can be a bit of a bully at feeders.

Q: Let's move on. What would you suggest as another name?

A: Greatest Mimic of All Time!

Q: Isn't that challenging the Northern Mockingbird? Do you really want to go there?

A: Have you heard me sing? I appropriate the vocalizations of at least forty-six other species of birds, including the Northern Mockingbird, and a Pacific Treefrog as well! So, move over mockingbird! Even though other finches are known as mimics, including Lesser Goldfinch and Pine Siskin—and don't even get me started on Pine Siskin, who is just meh—my repertoire totally rocks!!

Q: So why do you do this? What is its function?

A: I don't do it to exclude competitors. Think of it more as my vocal repertoire is a measurement of fitness. When it comes to female Lawrence's Goldfinches, size matters. Of course, female Lawrence's Goldfinches sing a bit as well, and scientists are starting to pay more attention to song in female birds.

Q: Very interesting. But let's try this again. What do you want your name to be?

A: How about Masked Goldfinch?

Q: It makes sense to name you after one of your plumage features, which are all beautiful. I also hear you acquire a bigger yellow patch in breeding by unique wearing off of gray plumage. But only the male Lawrence's Goldfinch has a mask, so that leaves out the female Lawrence's Goldfinch. It's good to have a name be inclusive of every age and sex of your species.

A: You're right! Those butterbutts have it easy, Yellow-rumped Warblers of all ages and sexes all have yellow rumps! This naming thing is harder than I thought.

Q: Not sure they'd like you calling them butterbutts. However, tell me some other things you would like the readers of this guide to know about you.

A: We like it hot, and we like it dry. We are nomads who wander throughout our range, breeding mainly in California and rarely in Arizona. We're a bit of a foodie and will travel during breeding to source our most favorite delectable food, *Amsinckia* spp., known as fiddleneck to you.

Q: Sounds good. What does it taste like?

A: It has a nutty, floral quality with a hint of pyrrolizidine alkaloid. Goes well with a Groth Vineyards California cabernet sauvignon.

Q: Thanks for the interview, you've given me a lot to think about, and please get back to me on the name. Maybe something about your beautiful golden yellow wing patches which make you unique from the other goldfinches . . .

A: I *am* stunningly beautiful, now that you mention it. Will do and thanks for asking.

Lawrence's Goldfinch on common fiddleneck

## IDENTIFICATION

**Size:** L 4.5"

**Shape:** Small, slim, small-headed bird with a short, notched tail and short, fairly deep-based conical bill.

**Both Sexes:** Gray body, golden patch on breast; black wings with golden wingbars (or whole wing coverts); golden edges to primaries and secondaries; pinkish bill.

**Adult Male:** Black foreface and forecrown; bright and extensive golden on breast and wings, expanding by wear through the breeding season.

**Adult Female:** All-gray head; reduced and duller golden on breast and wings.

**1st Winter:** M. similar to ad. m. but with partial black on foreface and forecrown; f. like ad. f.

**Juv:** (May–Aug.) Like ad. but with brownish wash overall; indistinct dusky streaking on breast and belly.

### *SUBSPECIES*

Monotypic

### *SIMILAR SPECIES*

Female American and Lesser Goldfinches are similar to Lawrence's females but lack the golden edges to primaries.

## DISTRIBUTION

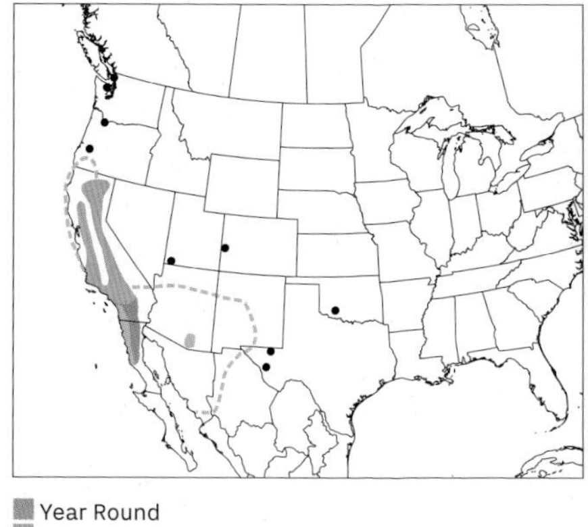


Main distribution is in California, making them practically endemic to the state. They breed largely in open dry woods and semiarid foothills, with water nearby, occurring generally from west of the Sierra Nevada/Cascade Mountain axis, in foothills of the Central Valley, through the southern Coastal Range, southern California, and down into Baja California.[1]

Breeding is unpredictable and opportunistic, and occurs where rainfall and a good food supply exist. However, Lawrence's Goldfinches have been confirmed as steady and reliable breeders for 30 years in Williamson Valley, San Benito County, California (Debi Love Shearwater, personal communication). Lawrence's are there year-round and in winter, along with other finches, feed on the hillsides of chamise. Debi had a day-high count of 589 birds in one area in winter 2016, and there could have been a large number on nearby inaccessible land. eBird records from April to July over the last ten years show multiple records of Lawrence's Goldfinch in Arizona. Winter range includes southern and central Arizona, central and southern New Mexico, and western Texas.

Adult m. CA/02

Adult f. CA/02

Adult m. CA/04

1st yr. m. CA/08

## LANGUAGE

### *MALE*

Song is complex, long, and high-pitched, with upward and downward notes. Has a more musical quality but is weaker than American and Lesser Goldfinches. Incorporates notes of a wide range of other species. Song may intergrade into a disjunct song of multiple short different phrases.[2] Song can also include contact calls and courtship calls. The male *teer* or *tee-yer* courtship call is given by males and attracts nearby females.

### *FEMALE*

Females occasionally sing a short song.[3] The female's *tee-tee* call, which increases in intensity, is given just before she is fed by the male precopulation.

### *MALE AND FEMALE*

The contact/flight *teet-tip, teeter-tip,* or *teetoo* call is soft and brief, and bell-like (versus lower-pitched and harsher in Lesser Goldfinch). It is given all year. The *dee-ree* alarm call increases in intensity to *bee-ee* in extreme alarm or distress. An aggressive call is a harsh sound like a snarl that increases in intensity and volume according to the degree of aggressiveness.

### *IMITATION/MIMICRY*

Lawrence's is an accomplished mimic. Most notes in its song are excellent copies of a wide range of at least 46 other species, including American Robin, Western Wood-Pewee, Rock Wren, American and Lesser Goldfinches, and Northern Mockingbird.[4]

## HABITAT AND DIET

Lawrence's Goldfinches prefer arid habitats of open oak woodlands, brushy areas, weedy fields, dry slopes with weedy patches, and chaparral. They are also found in coastal scrub, coniferous open forests, and pinyon-juniper habitats. A constant water source for drinking and bathing, such as streams, lakes, ponds, and irrigated areas, is a necessity. During nonbreeding, they frequent similar habitats and wander to river floodplains, arroyos, cultivated fields, and suburban gardens and parks.

Lawrence's Goldfinches eat a wide variety of seeds and sometimes plant buds and fruits, rarely insects. The seeds of fiddlenecks (genus *Amsinckia*) and others in the Boraginaceae (forget-me-not) family are important food sources. Chamise, mistletoe, coffeeberry, pigweed, inkweed, and thistles are also consumed. During breeding, Lawrence's may leave the nesting area and feed elsewhere. In winter they often forage with other finches and sometimes in very large flocks of 500–700.

## AT YOUR FEEDER

Lawrence's Goldfinches come to feeders, often with other finches, and many Southwest winter records document them at feeders. Nyjer® and sunflower top the menu. Lesser Goldfinches usually dominate Lawrence's in feeding situations by displacing them from perches and with aggressive displays.[5]

## MOVEMENTS AND IRRUPTIONS

Lawrence's Goldfinches are nomadic in their limited range and there is much to learn about their movements, which are complex and unpredictable, and defy the usual concept of a species migrating north to south on a fixed schedule. When and in what direction movement occurs depends on the seasonal abundance of food and availability of water. They are more likely to move east to west, or even altitudinally, where some birds move to higher elevations in fall if there is a drought.

In general, most of the population from northern, central, and inland California moves to southeastern California, southern Arizona and sometimes New Mexico, and far western Texas into Sonora and Chihuahua, Mexico, in winter. In some years it is a large-scale movement, perhaps due to successful breeding and a high population.[6] In other winters fewer birds are seen in the United States, possibly wintering in Mexico. Migrants return in March to southern California and in early April to northern areas of California.

Lawrence's Goldfinch flock at a pond

Adult male in April

## BREEDING BEHAVIOR

### *TERRITORY*

Lawrence's Goldfinches generally breed in loose colonies. At the start of breeding, courtship takes place in flocks. A territory is established after pairing occurs and the nest site is chosen. Thus, the function of the territory is more to isolate the pair just for nesting in this highly flocking species. While the female defends mainly the nest area, the male defends a rather small area of about 10–15 meters in diameter around the nest.[7] He mainly gives loud songs at male intruders, rarely chasing them. Territorial defense diminishes as nesting progresses.

### *COURTSHIP*

Lawrence's Goldfinches are reportedly monogamous. There are more males than females in the population, with a reported sex ratio of 58% males and 42% females.[8] During courtship, larger flocks of about 10–15 birds break into smaller groups of about 5–6 that include males and females, and noisy activity ensues for several days. Males sing and aggressively face one another with an elongated body, fluffed throat feathers, wings down, spread and raised tail, and pivot back and forth. The male's head-forward posture highlights his black face with pale bill and makes for an intimidating display to a rival.[9] Males supplant one another and may even fly up vertically when fighting. They also may do flight displays with spread wings and tail. Females, for the most part, look quietly on. Males give courtship calls that attract a female, then feed the female with regurgitated seeds. This continues through early nesting.

### *NESTING*

**Timing:** Mid-March to late July, but primarily mid-April to early July
**Nest:** Cup, outside diameter 3 in., of grasses, forbs, bits of lichens, plant fibers and down, feathers, fur, sometimes insect webs, placed in the fork of trees such as oaks or shrubs, sometimes in mistletoe clumps or lace lichen, 10–40 ft. high.
**Nesting:** Eggs, 4–5, sometimes 3–6, white, rarely light blue
**Incubation:** 12–13 days
**Nestling period:** 12–15 days
**Broods:** 1

The female explores widely for just the right nest site, inspecting potential tree or shrub crotches for a location. Her mate follows her closely during this time, often singing. Once the nest site is chosen, the territory is established.

The female builds the nest in 4–8 days. After the second to third egg is laid, she sits almost constantly on the nest for about 2 weeks, while the male makes trips, about once an hour, to feed her a regurgitated paste of partly digested seeds. The female broods the hatched young for 4–5 days while the male brings in food. After that, both parents go collect food and feed the young a thick seed paste.

After the young fledge from the nest, they remain nearby for several days and give begging calls, quivering their wings when hungry or when the adults return. Sometimes the adults transfer seeds directly from a plant to nearby perched young or feed them by regurgitation. By 5–7 days postfledging, the young move around with adults to feed, then remain as a family group until joining up in large flocks before migration begins.[10]

## MOLT

Lawrence's Goldfinches have one complete molt per year, postbreeding. However, an illusory change occurs in spring when the yellow breast patch of the male seems to grow bigger as breeding nears. In the past, that was thought to be caused by a prebreeding molt. The secret is the special adaptations of both the yellow and gray feathers on the male's (not the female's) breast that involve the actual structures of the feathers themselves. The yellow feathers are especially wear-resistant, but the gray feathers are more prone to abrasion, so they wear off and expose the bright yellow breast. The male also develops a yellow center of the back when the brownish tips of surrounding feathers wear off.[11]

## CONSERVATION

Since Lawrence's Goldfinch is nomadic, with small populations and not commonly seen, a thorough study of its population dynamics and demographics is needed. Partners in Flight ranks it 15 out of 20 for a Continental Concern Score and includes it on their Yellow Watch List: species that are highly vulnerable due to ecological specialization and require constant care and long-term assessment to prevent declines.

# AMERICAN GOLDFINCH

*Spinus tristis*

> *Panoplied in jet and gold the merry care-free Goldfinches in cheery companies flit in the summer sunshine.*
>
> —Edward Howe Forbush, 1929[1]

## QUICK TAKE

The American Goldfinch's buttery yellow beauty and ubiquitous presence at bird feeders earn them their name. Just about every bag of finch bird seed sold in the popular $2.2 billion wild bird products industry promotes their image.

The heart of the story behind this beautiful finch lands on the word gold. American Goldfinches are the only finches in North America that change clothes twice. From their brown-gray winter plumage Houdini act that has feeder watchers asking where have my goldfinches gone, they transform into their golden breeding plumage.

The transformation begins in spring, with a somewhat long, energy-demanding molt of body feathers. The molt length may allow time to slowly meet their protein demands of molt because their diet is low-protein seeds. Plumage color comes from eating plants rich in carotenoids, whose pigments produce the golden yellow feathers of their stunning breeding color. But the gold is more than a pretty color, it conveys vital information about a potential breeding partner's fitness and ability. There are no dating apps for finches!

Females assess potential males for their ability to feed females and young during nesting and beyond. Females prefer the most colorful males, whose vivid yellow signifies that he's an accomplished forager on carotenoid-rich plants.[2] Brighter plumaged males and females tend to breed with one another.

Ticktock, goldfinches race against time to produce offspring and pass on their genes to the next generation. Their July and August short breeding season coincides with the blooming and seed production of thistles and composite flowers, essential for food for young and fluff for nests. Goldfinches also do not come into breeding condition until their long spring molt is nearing completion. Experienced birds come into condition first. The most colorful gold males get to breed early with able and ready females, a good deal. Experienced females, if they've chosen wisely, get a good provider during incubation and the early nestling phase.

Female collecting nest material

Most goldfinches are monogamous, having one brood per season. But researchers discovered a bonus American Goldfinch strategy called polyandry.[3] In a small percentage of cases, the female leaves her mate to raise the nestlings, and she starts a new nest with a different male. The story goes deeper, for American Goldfinches have a skewed sex ratio: there are more males than females. Polyandry provides a payoff pot of gold for all players. The first male acquires a breeding opportunity with an experienced female. The second male also gets to breed. The female has two broods and thus produces more offspring carrying her genes.

Then presto, both sexes change into their brown-gray winter wardrobe. Goldfinches flock together, wandering to source the seed bounty of their survival. They may migrate or show up at your feeders. Now you know their secret. They're still here, just in their winter disguise!

## IDENTIFICATION

**Size:** L 5"
**Shape:** Slender, small finch that is somewhat small-headed with a fairly long, notched tail and short conical bill.
**Adult Male Spring/Summer:** Bill orange; black cap includes lore, forehead, and crown; body color varies from bright yellow to almost yellowish-orange; white undertail and uppertail coverts; black wings with worn white tips; lesser coverts partly to entirely yellow; median coverts white-tipped; greater coverts white-tipped; white covert tips create the appearance of 2 white wingbars, sometimes hard to see because the lesser coverts may obscure the median coverts; tail black with white patches on inner webs of tail feathers that extend to tip of tail; legs and feet pinkish-brown.
**Adult Female Spring/Summer:** Brighter than in nonbreeding plumage; bill orange; greenish-yellow crown; dusky yellow upperparts and yellow underparts; whitish uppertail and undertail coverts; dark-brown wings with worn white edges; lesser coverts brown; median and greater coverts white-tipped, producing wingbars; tail dark brown with white patches on inner webs of tail feathers that extend to tips; legs and feet pinkish-brown.
**Adult Fall/Winter:** Variably pale grayish to brownish-yellow; white undertail coverts; dark gray bill.
**Adult Male Fall/Winter:** Some bright yellow on throat; lesser coverts yellowish; black wings with whitish wingbars.
**Adult Female Fall/Winter:** Lesser coverts olive; dark-brown wings; whitish or buff wingbars.
**1st Year:** Like adults in each season, up to 10 inner greater wing coverts are replaced and darker with broader whitish tips.
**Juv:** (July–Oct.) Brownish-yellow; dark-brown wings with wide buffy wingbars and edges to tertials and secondaries; whitish undertail coverts. Males with slightly darker wings than females; yellow on male's throat gets brighter with age.

### *SUBSPECIES*

(3) *tristis* (breeds cent. ON–e. CO to Nfl–SC, winters to TX–FL) medium-sized: summer m. with extensive black cap and bright yellow body; *salicamans* (breeds and winters coastal s.w. BC–n.w. Baja CA) small: darker, browner, summer m. pale yellow with smaller black cap. Birds breeding in s.w. BC–s.w. OR (*"jewetti"*) may be browner; *pallidus* (breeds interior s. BC–NV to w. Ont–w. NE winters to AZ–TX) larger: more brown-olive on upperparts, summer m. smaller cap.

### *SIMILAR SPECIES*

Females may be confused with female Lesser and Lawrence's Goldfinches. American Goldfinch is slightly larger and has white undertail coverts (Lesser has yellow) and the white tail spots on the inner web of the outer tail feathers go to the tip of tail; Lesser and Lawrence's female tails have white spots on the center of the tail, and the tail tip is all dark. Lawrence's female has yellow wingbars.

Adult m. NH/06

Adult f. NH/06

Adult m. NH/04

Adult m. NH/04

Adult m., molting MA/04

Juv. MA/09

## DISTRIBUTION

Summer breeding range (including year-round range) goes across North America, from Newfoundland to British Columbia south through Washington, central Oregon, northeastern California, central Nevada, Utah, eastern Colorado, through Oklahoma, to northern Louisiana and across to North Carolina. Winter range extends beyond the year-round area to the West Coast, Gulf Coast, through the Southeast, and on to Mexico.

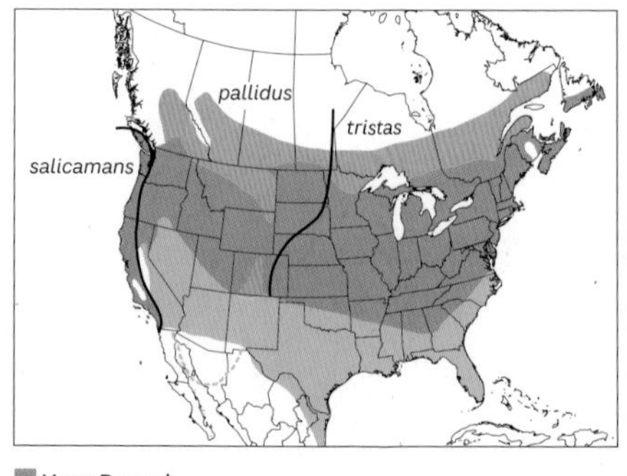


Year Round
Breeding
Non-Breeding

## LANGUAGE

### *MALE*

Song consists of a long, random, variable warbling, reminiscent of a canary's song, that lasts up to 20 seconds or more, includes couplet series strung together continuously. It is a continuum ranging from a longer song to short song, a version of 2–4 series given at intervals, to a so-called disjunct song, consisting of 1–2 note individual phrases mixed with call notes. This disjunct song can be given between counter-singing males.[4] Song can include within it the flight call and courtship call notes. Courtship call lasts for 2–3 seconds with intervals of 5 seconds. It may be part of the disjunct song but needs more research on the differentiation. It can be given alone or at the beginning of song, or included in song. May function to attract females early in the breeding season. After pairs are formed, it may help maintain pair bond.

### *FEMALE*

A high-pitched *tee-tee* call of 2–8 notes at short intervals is given during courtship and precedes copulation. At higher intensity becomes a high-pitched fast series of whistles that sounds like *teeteeteetee*. A similar very fast series of whistles is given from the nest, which may prompt the male to fly down and feed her.

### *MALE AND FEMALE*

Flight call is a distinctive phrase with three or four syllables. The sound has been represented by the written description *perchicoree* or the more memorable *po-ta-to-chip*. This most commonly identified sound accompanies almost all flying adults; it's also given in foraging flocks to stay in contact and by the male with deep-looping flight during breeding. Other calls include *sweeyeet*, a short ascending whistle, given when there may be danger or in conflicts with another goldfinch; *bearbee*, a 2–3 syllable phrase, usually repeated, an alarm for more dangerous situations, especially near the nest; *dzik*, a short buzzy call given in threat agonistic encounters, chases, and spring feeding flocks. The fledgling *chipee, chipee, chipeepee* is a 2-part call with the accent on the second part. It's heard incessantly as fledglings follow adults after leaving the nest, begging for food.

## HABITAT AND DIET

American Goldfinches live in open weedy areas with trees and shrubs for shelter and nesting. This includes streamsides, shrub thickets, open woodland edges, orchards, and suburban yards. Evergreen areas are used for roosting, and spruce and cedar, in masting years, for foraging. In California and the Southwest, they utilize streamside areas with willows. In winter, they flock to feeders or move to southern areas with appropriate habitats. Midwest goldfinches may use grassland fields in winter.

There's no low-carb diet for the seed- and grain-loving American Goldfinch. Their buffet includes dandelions, ragweed, mullein, grasses; flowers, especially the Compositae family, such as purple coneflower, sunflower, and thistle; trees, such as birch, elms, alder, cedar, spruce, and hemlock; sometimes tree buds. Goldfinches gymnastically sidle up weed stalks, weighing them down to feast on the seeds. American Goldfinches also eat grit to help them process seeds.

Male on purple coneflower

## AT YOUR FEEDER

American Goldfinches prefer Nyjer®, finch mixes, and hulled or in-shell black oil sunflower. Look for social interactions between goldfinches at feeders. In general, males are dominant over females during nonbreeding, but females are dominant over males during breeding. In antagonistic encounters, birds fly vertically upward with wings fluttering and beaks open, chase or posture with head forward and bill gaping. An aggressive bird may also fly at and take the perch of another bird. This behavior reaches an intensity during breeding.

Male at finch tube feeder

### FUN FACTS

**The American Goldfinch is the state bird of Iowa, New Jersey, and Washington. American Goldfinches can live to be 11 years old.**

## MOVEMENTS AND MIGRATIONS

Where you see goldfinches may depend on your location and, to some extent, the weather. American Goldfinches migrate in mid-April to early June and late October to mid-December and even early January. In winter, they leave the most northern part of their breeding range and move south in flocks. If they stay in northern areas, they'll hustle to bird feeders once wild foods are depleted or covered with snow and ice. Age and sex decide which finches go where. Banding studies have shown that immature males wintered north of adult males and did not move far from breeding grounds,[5] and adult males wintered north of females. Even if you have finches at your feeders, they may be replacements; your breeding finches may have taken a winter vacation and gone south, while finches to your north find your feeders just fine. However, they may feeder-hop and move several miles between feeders.

Then there are the significant migration years with large-scale finch movement such as the superflight of 2020–2021. The eBird database showed birders in the East reporting American Goldfinches on a higher percentage of their checklists in the Southeastern Coastal Plain region on irruption years in falls of 2016, 2018, 2020 than nonirruption years falls of 2015, 2017, and 2019.[6] Irruption years mean more American Goldfinches in the Southeastern Coastal Plain between December and March. In northern states like Maine (Atlantic Northern Forest), irruption years start with birders seeing more American Goldfinches than usual in the fall at their feeders and maybe visible diurnal flights. Still, they thin out in late fall. Soon, there are fewer American Goldfinches than usual until the following May, when southern birds come back (Joe Gyekis, personal communication).

In migration, American Goldfinches from New England and eastern Canada may concentrate along the coast, but birds in the center of the United States and Canada may concentrate along the Mississippi flyway. Western goldfinches may move through major valleys and along the coast.

## BREEDING BEHAVIOR

### *TERRITORY*

Goldfinches can pair within flocks before arrival on breeding grounds and before the formation of territories. Thus, a territory may function more to isolate a nesting area for a pair of goldfinches.[7]

Some researchers have described goldfinches going to nesting areas just before nest building[8] or earlier[9] with males and females defending a territory, including the nest, of a quarter acre to an acre or more. In general, males defend a territory from other males; females defend the nest area from females. Male defense of territory takes the form of chasing intruders, also making circling flights, flying in a flat line and giving long song. Males also perform circling deep-loop-flight displays around the territory boundary with the flight call.

Males in aggressive encounter

Goldfinches may travel distances to feed from nesting areas of a half mile or more to prime food sources, or their nesting areas may contain prime foods of composite plants. When incubation starts, territorial boundaries lessen.

### *COURTSHIP*

Pair bonds may form in the flock before establishing a nesting territory, or in cases of migration, where males arrive ahead of females, females may choose a mate after arriving. Courtship behavior can take several forms. Males vocalize with flight displays and give long song from exposed perches, especially in late spring. Unpaired females may approach the singing males at this time. Males also give courtship calls to attract a mate and later to maintain the pair bond. During courtship, look for females flying in a zig-zag pattern being chased closely by one or more males. Several males may also display over suitable breeding areas together doing a flat flight, flying without dips in a circular pattern with a stalling, butterfly-like pattern. One theory is this is a type of lek behavior where males gather together to court females.[10] Females visit the lek for one purpose: to choose a mate.

Male singing

Once paired, males feed females by passing them partly digested seeds. Mating occurs with female crouching, tail up with wings quivering, giving her courtship call, a rapid, high-pitched *teeteeteetee*. The male sings later while the female is building the nest, and song and courtship calls may stimulate the female to ovulate. When nest building is complete, the role of song changes to defend and advertise the territory and maintain a bond with the female.[11]

American Goldfinches are monogamous and usually have one brood per season. One study showed that in cases where the first brood fails due to predation, the female renests but may mate with another male in addition to her original mate. Thus, the young in the nest result from different fathers. This needs additional research.[12]

Even when a first brood is successful, female American Goldfinches may not stay paired with their mate for a second brood. In the polyandry study[13] mentioned in the Quick Take of this account, research on color-banded American Goldfinches showed that experienced females mated with a different male for a second brood in 4.9% of nests studied. The new male may not be a stranger, and the research revealed he might have visited and even fed the female while she was at her first nest. Usually, the new polyandrous relationship continued and produced a new brood. In a few cases, her original mate persisted and helped raise these young.

### *NESTING*

**Timing:** In the West, the subspecies, *S. t. salicamans*, is the earliest breeder, starting the end of April and stopping in July. The subspecies *S. t. pallidus* nests from May to mid-August. In the East, for *S. t. tristis* nesting is June to September.
**Nest:** Outside diameter 3 in., tightly woven bowl of plant fibers, lined with downy material usually from thistle (*Cirsium discolor* or *Cirsium arvense*) or other wind-dispersed seeds such as cattail, willow, poplar, or dandelions, attached to supports with webbing from caterpillars or spiders. Placed in the forks of upright shrubs, trees, or herbaceous plants, 4–20 ft. high, usually near marshy areas or water.
**Eggs:** 2–7, pale bluish-white with a few small spots
**Incubation:** 12–14 days
**Nestling period:** 11–17 days
**Broods:** 1–2

While both pair members may explore potential sites, the female chooses the final location and builds the nest secretively, flying silently. The male will stay with her or remain near the nest. She incubates after the second or third egg, remarkably spending about 95% of her time on the nest. The male feeds her about once per hour. She will call from the nest, and the male arrives and provides her large quantities of partially digested seeds while she crouches and quivers her wings.

Female at nest

The nestlings give quiet calls and reach up with open mouths for the first week in the nest when the parent arrives with food. They defecate in the nest, and the parents eat or carry away these white fecal sacs. During the nestling phase up until they are 4 days old, the female stays on the nest and broods; the male brings all the food, giving the regurgitated seeds to the female, who then feeds it to the young. After that, both parents make feeding trips. By week 2, the nestlings are calling upon parent arrival and defecate on the nest rim. Just before they fledge, their calls become the loud *chipee, chipee, chipee.*

The fledgling stage can last for about 3 weeks, after which the young are on their own and cease giving the *chipee* call. Young goldfinches join with other goldfinch flocks but may remain in the northern parts of their range in winter, while older goldfinches move south.

### DEEPER DIVE

**Recent research on female goldfinches has revealed that female bill color is a status signal. Females with the most colorful orange bills are dominant in interactions with other female goldfinches over food, thereby settling disputes with a visual signal instead of fighting and risking injury. Bright bills were not a factor in mate choice by males in this study.[17]**

## MOLT

American Goldfinches, unlike other finches, have two prolonged molts per year, pre- and postbreeding. Just about the only time they are not molting is during nesting. You can see the changes in each season as the new feathers grow in, creating a strange mottled appearance.

In spring, they replace just the body feathers. Both males and females become brighter yellow with orange bills. The change is the most dramatic for the more colorful yellow male, who also acquires his black cap. The yellow plumage and orange bill in adults come from carotenoid (red, orange, and yellow) pigments produced by plants. The intensity and hue of the male's yellow color rely on how well he can process and absorb carotenoid pigments. Carotenoid intake, food access, and parasite load affect the male's bill color, indicating his health state.[14] The male's cap size and blackness are not affected by these variables and comes from melanin pigmentation.[15] Females assess males on their plumage color, preferring to mate with more colorful males who may be better foragers. More colorful birds also tend to mate with one another, and yellow carotenoid color may be a factor in mate choice.[16] The yellow color on goldfinch body feathers is at the tip of the feather; the base is white.

After they breed in summer, goldfinches change again into their more subtle brownish-gray winter colors and put on their L.L.Bean parkas. Their feathers are now heavier and denser to insulate them better against cold. They also acquire dark bills, and males lose the black cap. Look for the changes at your feeder.

## CONSERVATION

Partners in Flight rates them 6 out of 20 on the Continental Concern Score and calls their status Low Concern. While common, goldfinch numbers declined somewhat from 1966 to 2019.

Attu

# VAGRANT FINCHES

*Vagrant: the wrong bird in the wrong place at the wrong time that has the potential to send birders into* mega *rarity delirium.*

—Lillian Quinn Stokes

## QUICK TAKE

***May 31, 2017***

"Number 643—Common Rosefinch!!!" Yve Morrell was doing an American Birding Association Big Year, the ultimate birding competition where birders, on an honor system, see how many species they can tally in North America in a calendar year. Immortalized in the movie *The Big Year* (2011), it is a competition of uber endurance, perseverance, luck, and skill.

The female Common Rosefinch Yve had just checked off her list as number 643 was a rare vagrant on Attu Island who had severely drifted off course during her spring migration, a journey of uber endurance, perseverance, luck, and skill.

Yve Morrell did not plan on doing a big year; she decided late in November that if there was a trip to Attu her big year was a go because to beat her competitors, she would have to eke out every last possible rare bird. In the movie, it was said that no birder could win a big year without going to Attu in May.

Attu is the stuff of legends. The last island in the Alaskan Aleutian chain and westernmost point in North America, it is *the* premier place to pick up numbers of stray migrating Eurasian species pushed off course, including vagrant finches. Birding is not easy there. Vast terrain, with snowcapped peaks leading down to treeless, spongy, wet tundra; nothing resembling a highway; and no transportation save bikes or hiking makes covering the 344.7 square miles herculean. At one time birders could stay in a defunct Coast Guard LORAN station. Yve looked at the names of former big year birders etched on its walls: Neil Hayward (2013 winner), John Weigel (2016 winner), and Sandy Komito, who won in 1998 competing heavily with two other birders, Al Levantin and Greg Miller. That real-life story became the basis for *The Big Year* book and movie starring Steve Martin, Jack Black, and Owen Wilson.

The island is uninhabited, so Yve's birding tour stayed on a boat. Good weather made favorable migrating conditions for birds with no stopping; bad weather was what birders prayed for. On May 28, the weather turned from mild and calm to strong winds.

Though there is no way to actually know, hypothetically this Common Rosefinch could have set out from Vietnam, where she wintered, and fueled up enough for her migration with ample reserves to arrive in breeding condition and produce her energy-demanding eggs, which would continue the life of her species. Her route to her breeding grounds in Russia, far east from Vietnam (close to four thousand miles), could have taken her out over water. Species who migrate offshore through East Asia encounter frequent eastward storms there in spring. If they have been flying for a long time and are tired, they can be drifted east to the Aleutians.[1]

The female Common Rosefinch was well into her journey and out over water for some time when she began to encounter strong winds, pushing her off course. As she battled onward, fatigue began to set into muscles that had been flapping for thousands of miles. She had a choice—continue or land—but there was no land in sight.

Common Rosefinch seen by Yve Morrell, May 31, 2017

She pressed on, using precious fuel reserves against the winds but gaining no ground. She then reached a tipping point, deciding to give in to the wind direction, and drifted in an airflow that landed her on Attu—a classic example of what is known as drift displacement. Exhausted, she rested, ate, and refueled, lucky to have found sanctuary, just as Yve was lucky to have seen her.

A vagrant is not easy to define, but in general, it could be thought of as a species that occurs when or where it should not be, or well beyond where most of the individuals in its range occur.[2] Detection plays a role; vagrant status is only based on what human observers have seen, not how many birds there actually are. Vagrants are usually found because they are in heavily birded areas, likely in terrain making them more visible, or they appear at bird feeders.

Vagrancy status is designated on a continuum from rare (species that occur annually but in low numbers), to casual (species that do not annually occur in North America but have occurred six or more times), to accidental (species seen fewer than five times outside their normal range).[3] The more rare, the more exciting. Birds seen for the first time in the Western Hemisphere could be inducted into a mythical mega rarity hall of fame, such as the Red-footed Falcon who made it across the Atlantic to a Martha's Vineyard airstrip in August 2004. Stampedes of birders from all over the country and media attention followed. But access matters: the first North American record of Pallas's Rosefinch in September 2015 on St. Paul Island, Alaska,[4] in the Bering Sea, was inaccessible to most birders.

Most vagrants are not, as is usually thought, hopelessly lost, wandering individuals—they think they know where they are going, but things go wrong, and sometimes badly awry. While there is still much to learn about migration, we do know that birds can migrate using the stars, sun, polarized light, long-distance low-frequency sound, in some cases smell, and, especially, an internal compass that senses magnetic north. Sometimes the ability to use these systems is flawed. New research reveals that birds may actually see geomagnetic fields. Disturbances to earth's magnetic field can lead birds off course, even during perfect weather, especially during fall migration, and affect both young and older birds.[5]

Young long-distance migrant birds undertaking their first migration use a genetically inherited compass and clock that help them know what direction to fly and when to stop.[6] However, they may not be able to know their exact location or change their flight direction due to wind drift, and wind up far off course.[7] They may also misorient—go in the wrong direction or fly too far—or even do "reverse migration" and fly in the exact opposite direction from a correct heading.

The majority of vagrant finch species are Asian migrants that occur in Alaska, but spring drift displacement also occurs in northeast North America but with fewer species. Birds taking off from Britain to Iceland may drift downwind and wind up in places like Newfoundland.[8] Drift can also occur in fall.

Vagrancy in finches can be a result of migratory mishaps, but finches also move distances due to irruptions caused by food shortages in their normal areas. That is why, for example, Pine Siskins were found in Bermuda in fall during the 2020–2021 superflight. In some cases, young finches move big distances due to dispersion from their natal areas.

Attu

While vagrancy has been thought of as an adverse thing for birds caused by external forces like weather, or internal errors, there is another side. In an article in *Scientific American*, ecologist Richard Veit of the College of Staten Island described vagrants as the expanding fringe of a growing population, and "vagrancy is condition-dependent, which can be linked to climate change," said researcher Frederic Jiguet.[9] So, to stretch it, perhaps vagrants could be thought of as Star Trek voyagers, exploring new worlds, and that could lead to future colonization.

---

As to the end of the Yve and the rosefinch story . . .

During her big year, Yve traveled all over North America, covering more than 127,000 miles by air, another 30,000 by car, not to mention an enormous number of miles hiked. She also spent twenty days at sea to find pelagic species. She made history, seeing 817 species in 2017 and becoming the first woman to win the Big Year competition. Winning was for Yve (and any big-year birder) a feat of uber endurance, perseverance, luck, and skill.

The Common Rosefinch, after resting, regaining energy, and refueling, continued on the path to her breeding grounds, and successfully produced four more Common Rosefinches. She then molted, refueled, and began her fall four-thousand-mile migration to her wintering grounds, a journey of uber endurance, perseverance, luck, and skill.

# COMMON CHAFFINCH

*Fringilla coelebs*

## IDENTIFICATION

**Size:** L 6"
**Shape:** Fairly small, deep-bellied, broad-necked bird with a slender conical bill and moderate-length notched tail. Crown rather flat when feathers are relaxed; peaked and triangular when raised.
**Both Sexes:** Closed wing patterned with 2 whitish wingbars (the upper one sometimes hidden) and small white patches at base of primaries. When flying, note white double wingbar, white sides to tail, greenish-gray rump.
**Adult Male:** (brightest in summer) Has gray crown and collar around rosy-brown face with small black forehead; back, breast, and belly rosy brown; outer tail feathers white.
**Adult Female:** Pale brown below, warm brown on back and crown, bold wing and tail pattern mentioned above, wingbar a bit more narrow than male's.
**Juv:** (Apr.–Sept.) Like adult female.

### *SUBSPECIES*

Records from North America are of *coelebs* group.

### *SIMILAR SPECIES*

Distinguished in all plumages from Brambling, which has little or no white on sides of tail and has whitish rump (may be yellowish on juvenile).

## STATUS AND DISTRIBUTION 4

Palearctic species. Casual vagrant to the northeastern United States and Canada. Common Chaffinches are kept as caged birds, and many sightings are likely of escapees, but some could be wild vagrants. Discussions about such matters are always ongoing, and each state bird records committee makes their own determinations. Sometimes there is no way to really know.

Although eBird designates many records of Common Chaffinch as Escapee ("known or suspected to be escaped"), there are Provisional records ("rarity of uncertain provenance, with natural vagrancy or captive provenance, both considered") from Nova Scotia, New Brunswick, Maine, Massachusetts, New Hampshire, and New Jersey.[1] A few records have been accepted by eBird from Newfoundland and Labrador, including a June 5, 2023 record.[2]

## LANGUAGE

### *MALE AND FEMALE*

Calls include a *yup* flight call, a loud *wheet* in spring, and variable *twit* call.

Adult m. HUN/05

Adult f., winter ITA/01

Male ITA/02

Note greenish-gray rump and white sides of tail distinguishing it in all plumages from Brambling, which has white rump

## HABITAT AND DIET

Open woods, gardens, and parks. Feeds on a variety of seeds, buds, small invertebrates. Comes to feeders.

# BRAMBLING

*Fringilla montifringilla*

## IDENTIFICATION

**Size:** L 6.25"
**Shape**: Fairly small, deep-bellied, broad-necked bird with a slender, conical bill and moderate-length notched tail. Crown rather flat when feathers are relaxed; peaked and triangular when raised. Long primary projection past tertials.
**Adult Spring/Summer:** Closed wing boldly patterned with 2 white-to-orangish wing-bars, small white patch at base of primaries, orangish lesser coverts; white rump.
**Male:** Black head and back, orangish-brown throat and breast, large dark spots along whitish rear flanks; bill black.
**Female**: Face plain grayish brown with dark brown lateral crown stripes continuing down nape; breast orangish; faint spots along flanks; bill black.
**Juv:** Similar to female but browner.
**Adult Male Fall/Winter**: Similar to summer, but pale edges to head and back feathers create mottled grayish appearance; bill dusky to pale with dark tip.
**Adult Female Fall/Winter:** Like summer female but bill orangish with dark tip.

### *SUBSPECIES*

Monotypic

### *SIMILAR SPECIES*

Distinguished in all plumages from Common Chaffinch by chaffinch's gray-green rump, white sides of tail, and underparts more uniformly pinkish or buffy (not the contrasting orange breast and white belly of Brambling).

## STATUS AND DISTRIBUTION 3

Widespread and common breeder in northern Europe and found across the Palearctic. Common but irregular migrant in the Aleutian Islands, rare in the Pribilof Islands and St. Lawrence Island, Alaska. Casual in rest of Alaska. Nesting has occurred on Attu.[1] There are many North American records from southern Canada and down across the United States to the Atlantic coast. Sightings have occurred as far east as Newfoundland and as far south as southern California, Arkansas, and North Carolina.[2] Flocks have been seen on the Aleutians, and one of the more notable records was a high count of 336 Bramblings on Shemya Island in May 2023.[3]

## LANGUAGE

### *MALE AND FEMALE*

Calls include a harsh *jeeak* or *te-chp* given in flight or perched, also clear *slit-slit-slit* notes in alarm.

Adult m., summer RUS/06

Adult m., winter ITA/02

Adult f., winter FIN/04

M. FIN/03

Note white rump, a distinguishing clue in all plumages from Common Chaffinch, which has gray-green rump

## HABITAT AND DIET

Open mixed coniferous and deciduous woods, and fields. Eats seeds and fruits, insects in summer.

# HAWFINCH

*Coccothraustes coccothraustes*

## IDENTIFICATION

**Size:** L 7"

**Shape:** Fairly large short-tailed finch with a large head, broad neck, and thick body. Strikingly large triangular bill is moderately long and very deep-based. Inner primaries have unusual extensions at tip, perpendicular to rest of feather.

**Adult Spring/Summer:** Brown head with distinctive black pattern enclosing eye, lore, base of bill, and chin. Underparts buffy brown; wings mostly black with a bluish sheen; primary greater coverts whitish at tips; secondary greater coverts warm brown with whitish bases. Bill grayish black with blue-gray base. Sexes alike except that female has grayish panel on secondaries. In flight, broad white wingbar, tail broadly tipped white.

**Adult Fall/Winter:** Like summer but slightly paler, bill pale yellow to pinkish.

**Juv:** Somewhat like adult but belly with dark spots.

### *SUBSPECIES*

(1) *japonicus*

### *SIMILAR SPECIES*

No very similar species in North America. The related Evening Grosbeak (*Cocothraustes vespertinus*), while also a large bird with big, deep-based conical bill, has extensive yellow in its plumage.

## STATUS AND DISTRIBUTION 4

Eurasian species. Mainly in spring, casual or rare on western and central Aleutian Islands and Bering Sea islands. Casual on western areas of the Alaska mainland where it has occurred in spring and winter.[1] There is a first Canadian record from Haines Junction, Yukon, Canada, of a Hawfinch discovered on December 14, 2020, seen in the general area by birders, then at a feeder.[2]

A more unusual occurrence was of a Hawfinch that landed in the Pacific Ocean on a container ship from China headed to California and rode aboard the ship for about 7 days. It was fed bird seed while aboard, preferring sunflower seeds. Multiple eBird reports from the ship track it across the Pacific, where it was last reported on May 17, 2016,[3] just as the ship was entering the Santa Barbara Ship Channel before arriving at Long Beach/San Pedro. The first eBird reports from the ship are designated Provisional; the last reports, nearing Santa Barbara, are designated Escapee, which includes birds that are ship assisted, fed, and likely could not reach their destination on their own wing power.

Adult ITA/12

Adult ITA/02

Adults, aggressive interaction ITA/02

## LANGUAGE

### *MALE AND FEMALE*

Most common call is a loud, sharp *piks*, often as double note; given in flight, perched, or on ground.

## HABITAT AND DIET

Deciduous and mixed woods, fruit trees. Massive, powerful bill that can generate over 50 kg of force[4] allows it to crack open fruit kernels such as cherries.

# COMMON ROSEFINCH

*Carpodacus erythrinus*

## IDENTIFICATION

**Size:** L 5.25"

**Shape:** Small, deep-bellied, broad-necked, fairly large-headed finch with a notched tail. Short, deep-based conical bill with a curved culmen. Primary projection past tertials about 2 x bill length. Fairly large dark eye.

**Adult Male:** Extensively deep rose-red on head, breast, back, and rump; little or no facial pattern; 2 whitish to reddish wingbars.

**Adult Female:** Streaked grayish brown overall with little contrast or facial pattern; 2 thin whitish wingbars. Both sexes lack pale eye-ring.

**1st Year:** Male mostly like adult female, but some have red feathers, acquire adult plumage by end of summer of second year.[1] Female similar to adult.

**Juv:** Like adult female but with some dull olive wash on face and upperparts.

### *SUBSPECIES*

(1) *grebnitskii*

### *SIMILAR SPECIES*

Females and young Common Rosefinch are rather uniformly brown, somewhat like House Sparrow, but have two pale wingbars and short, stout bill with curved culmen. Female House Finch has longer tail with less primary projection, extensive dusky brown streaks on underside. Cassin's and Purple Finches have more pattern on faces and straighter culmens.[2]

## STATUS AND DISTRIBUTION 4

Eurasian species. Occurs as rare, mainly spring migrant, western Aleutian Islands, also Bering Sea islands. Casual on the mainland of western Alaska.[3] There is a first state record for California, in fall 2007, from Southeast Farallon Island.[4]

## LANGUAGE

### *MALE AND FEMALE*

Calls include a short upslurred whistle *tooee*.

## HABITAT AND DIET

Wet woods, shrubby streamsides, parks. Diet is mainly seeds, buds, berries, and shoots, also some insects.

Adult m. FIN/06

F./1st yr. m. FIN/05

# PALLAS'S ROSEFINCH*

*Carpodacus roseus*

## IDENTIFICATION

**Size:** L 6.2–6.8"

**Shape:** Fairly small, deep-bellied, broad-necked bird with long notched tail. Deep-based conical bill with curved culmen.

**Both Sexes:** Pinkish-red rump and pale wingbars.

**Adult Male:** Deep pinkish-red head, nape, breast, with silvery tips on forehead, crown, throat; rest of upperparts pinkish with dark streaks; belly and flanks (flanks sometimes with grayish tips) and undertail coverts white to pinkish.

**Adult Female:** Brown and streaked; orange-buff wash on head and breast, whitish belly.

**1st Year:** Male lacks silvery tips on head and throat, buffy-brown tips to orange-pinkish head, breast feathers, pinkish mantle (acquires adult plumage summer–fall of second year); female like adult female but more heavily streaked; pinkish-orange tinge on head.[1]

**Juv:** Like adult female but lacks orange-buff on head and face.

### *SUBSPECIES*

(1) likely *roseus*

### *SIMILAR SPECIES*

Common Rosefinches have smaller heads, females are more plain brownish with weaker streaks, and males lack the striking silvery spangling on crown and throat.

## STATUS AND DISTRIBUTION 5

East Asian species. Winters south to China, Korea, northern Japan. There is one record of an immature male from September 20–24, 2015, on St. Paul Island, Alaska,[2] seen by a number of birders. This photograph of the Pallas's Rosefinch was taken September 21, 2015 by Tom Johnson, esteemed birder and guide for Field Guides Birding Tours. He passed away unexpectedly July 23, 2023, and is greatly missed by the worldwide birding community.

## LANGUAGE

### *MALE AND FEMALE*

Call a short *fee*, also single or double whistles.[3]

## HABITAT AND DIET

Boreal forest, boreal shrublands, open woods, and thickets, along rivers, sometimes in parks and gardens. Eats mainly seeds, sometimes insects.

---

* On November 1, 2023, the American Ornithological Society committed to changing all English-language names of birds within its geographic jurisdiction that are named directly after people, and that may affect this species. For more information, see How to Use This Guide, page xii.

Adult ITA/12

Adult ITA/02

Imm. male St. Paul Island, AK 9/21/2015

# EURASIAN BULLFINCH
*Pyrrhula pyrrhula*

## IDENTIFICATION
**Size:** L 6.5"
**Shape:** Fairly small, deep-bellied, very broad-necked finch with a very short deep-based bill. Culmen abruptly downcurved.
**Both Sexes:** Black cap and chin; gray back and nape; white rump and undertail coverts; black wings with broad whitish wingbar on greater coverts; black bill.
**Adult Male:** Rosy red chest and belly.
**Adult Female:** Grayish-buff chest and belly.
**Juv:** (Jun.–Oct.) Like ad. f. but with all-grayish-buff head (lacks black cap and chin).

### *SUBSPECIES*
(1) *cassinii*

### *SIMILAR SPECIES*
None

## STATUS AND DISTRIBUTION 4
Eurasian species. Casual migrant to western Aleutian Islands and Bering Sea islands and casual in winter on the Alaska mainland[1] including southeast as far as Petersburg, in March 2011.[2]

## LANGUAGE
### *MALE*
Song a slow, hesitant mixture of repeated low, fluted call notes sometimes mixed with higher-pitched notes.

### *FEMALE*
Sings but less frequently than male.

### *MALE AND FEMALE*
Call is a soft piping or tinny *peu*.[3]

## HABITAT AND DIET
Variable, mixed woods, conifers, gardens. Eats a variety of seeds, buds, shoots, berries, and insects.

Adult m. FIN/03

Adult f. ITA/01

Adult m. St. Paul Island, AK 9/13/22

# ASIAN ROSY-FINCH

*Leucosticte arctoa*

## IDENTIFICATION

**Size**: L 5.5–7"

**Shape:** Fairly small, deep-bellied, small-headed bird with a conical bill and fairly short notched tail.

**Adult Male:** Forehead and crown black, nape and sides of neck tawny-buff; upperparts chocolate brown tinged rusty; upper breast feathers black, tipped with gray or whitish; lower breast, belly, flanks blackish brown with white or pink tips; pink-suffused wings.

**Adult Female:** Paler than male, more gray-brown, pink in wings on outer median coverts, flight feathers with whitish edge.[1]

**Juv:** Paler, more overall brownish.

### *SUBSPECIES*

(1) *L. a. brunneonucha*

### *SIMILAR SPECIES*

Asian Rosy-Finch is related to the 3 North American rosy-finches: Black (*Leucosticte atrata*), Brown-capped (*Leucosticte australis*) and Gray-crowned Rosy-Finch (*Leucosticte tephrocotis*). From 1983 to 1993 they were lumped as one species but are currently recognized as separate species. Black and Gray-crowned Rosy-Finches have gray hindcrowns extending to eye (and sometimes cheek, on Gray-crowned); Brown-capped has black forehead blending into dark hindcrown and extending to eye, with brown cheek.

## STATUS AND DISTRIBUTION 5

Breeds in northeast and central Asia. Two North American records, both *L. a. brunneonucha*; one is an eBird record from Adak Island, Aleutian Islands, Alaska, December 30, 2011,[2] and another record is from Gambell, St. Lawrence Island, October 25–26, 2008.[3]

## LANGUAGE

### *MALE AND FEMALE*

Calls similar to North American rosy-finches. Main call is a repeated *chew* note.

## HABITAT AND DIET

Found in mountains on rocky slopes near glaciers, on alpine tundra, rocky shorelines, coastal plains. Eats variety of seeds, buds, berries, some insects.[4]

Adult m. JAP/01

Adult f. JAP/02

# ORIENTAL GREENFINCH

*Chloris sinica*

## IDENTIFICATION

**Size:** L 6"

**Shape:** Fairly small, deep-chested, broad-necked finch; deep-based conical bill with curved culmen and short notched tail.

**Both Sexes:** Dark brown or olive-brown overall with large yellow primary patch and largely white tertials on black wings; rump and base of outer tail feathers yellowish; bill pinkish.

**Adult Male:** Greenish face, grayish-olive crown and nape.

**Adult Female:** Brown crown and nape.

**Juv:** Like female but paler below and with dark streaks.

### *SUBSPECIES*

(1) *C. s. kawahiba*

### *SIMILAR SPECIES*

None

## STATUS AND DISTRIBUTION 4

Eurasian species. Casual, mostly in spring (sometimes fall) to western Alaska islands. Multiple records from outer Aleutians, a few from central Aleutians, one from the Pribilofs.[1] There is a first Canadian record November 9, 2015, from the Capital District, British Columbia[2] and a first Oregon record October 17, 2020, from Lane County.[3] There are December 1986–April 1987 records from Arcata Marsh, Humboldt County, California, of an Oriental Greenfinch seen by many birders and accepted by the California Bird Records Committee in 2018.[4]

## LANGUAGE

### *MALE AND FEMALE*

Calls include a high-pitched twittering and a buzzy *jweeee*.

## HABITAT AND DIET

Open woods, parks. Eats weed and shrub seeds, grains, and sometimes insects.

Adult m. *C. s. minor* JAP/05

Adult f. *C. s. minor* JAP/02

# EURASIAN SISKIN

*Spinus spinus*

## IDENTIFICATION

**Size:** L 5"

**Shape:** Small, slim, fairly small-headed bird with a short well-notched tail and slender, fine-pointed conical bill sometimes with a slightly decurved culmen.

**Adult Male:** Black cap and chin (partly veiled by gray in fresh plumage); unstreaked yellow face and breast; 2 broad yellow wingbars; slight dark streaking and yellow wash on flanks; gray bill.

**Adult Female:** 2 broad yellowish wingbars; yellowish eyebrow extends around dusky auricular and onto sides of breast; white underparts with fine dark streaking limited to sides of breast and flanks, leaving central underparts clear; bill gray; yellow wash to streaked rump; white undertail coverts.

### *SUBSPECIES*

Monotypic

### *SIMILAR SPECIES*

Similar female Pine Siskin has thin whitish wingbars; little or no yellow on eyebrow and face; defined dark streaks on whitish underparts; white undertail coverts (can be yellowish on green-morph Pine Siskin).

## STATUS AND DISTRIBUTION 5

Palearctic species. Breeds from western Europe across to eastern Russia and northern Japan, winters in Europe, Japan, and southeast China.[1] Accidental vagrant to western Alaska islands; 2 records, May 21–23, 1993,[2] and June 4, 1978, from Attu;[3] 1 record, February 25, 2015, from Unalaska Island,[4] and 1 record, June 6–7, 2023, from Shemya Island.[5]

Some records from northeastern areas of the United States and Canada may be of escaped birds.[6] The Chicago and Ontario areas are known to have had many releases by dealers and others of European finches such as Eurasian Siskin.[7] However, there are a few accepted records from Labrador and Newfoundland[8] and one in January 31, 2009, from Maine.[9]

## LANGUAGE

### *MALE AND FEMALE*

Calls include a downslurred *tiyoo* and a rising *toowee*.

## HABITAT AND DIET

Mixed and coniferous woods, woods edges, fields, feeders.

Adult m. ITA/02

Adult f. ITA/02

Adult f. FIN/05

Adult m. ITA/02

Hawai'i

# HAWAIIAN HONEYCREEPERS

*The beating wings onward and onward to*
*Strive and search and reach thru millennia*
*Dreaming of paradise awaiting them*
*Going beyond the known limits of flight*
*Arriving achieving radiation*
*Forms changing becoming new bird species*
*Paradise found but eventually lost*

—Lillian Quinn Stokes

## QUICK TAKE

### *7.2–5.8 million years ago*

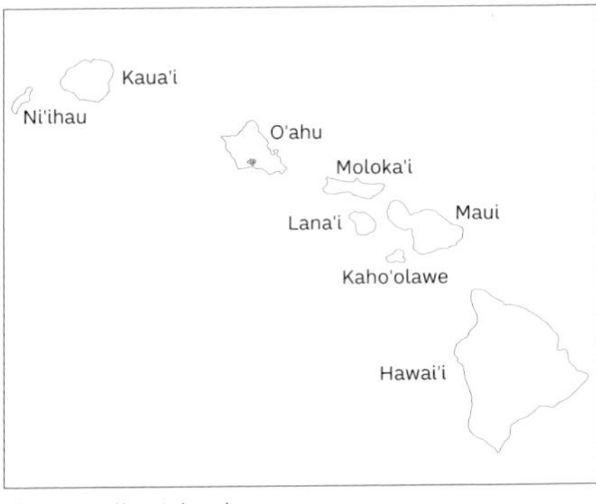


The Hawaiian Islands

A group of rosefinches (the common ancestor[1] of today's rosefinches and Hawaiian honeycreepers) from central Asia launched out over the Pacific Ocean, flew over 6,000 miles, and landed in Hawai'i. This may have happened more than once. We don't know how far a bird can fly. Model estimates from scientists suggest about 3,000 km (1,864 miles) for landbirds.[2] Clearly finches, whose middle name is "irruption," know more than scientists. Their ability to search for distant new opportunities when food supplies run out is nothing short of legendary. What these finches found was a Hawaiian tropical paradise. Hawai'i includes 137 volcanic islands spanning 1,500 miles. The main islands, from northwest to southeast, are Ni'hau, Kaua'i, O'ahu, Moloka'i, Lāna'i, Kaho'olawe, Maui, and Hawai'i (often called the Big Island to differentiate it from the name of the state). The islands abounded with an amazing variety of potential foods waiting to be eaten—seeds, insects, fruit, seabird eggs, nectar-producing flowers, and more—with few predators to threaten the finches.

In a process called adaptive radiation, similar to the story of Darwin's finches, these finches evolved into new species adapted to exploit these food resources. For example, the Palila on the cover of this guide developed a parrot-like, seed-cracking bill adapted to eat māmane seeds. The I'iwi looks nothing like a finch, but its long, decurved, pointed bill is perfect for accessing the sweet nectar of tree blossoms. This adaptive radiation got a turbo boost about 3.7–4 million years ago when the volcanic island of O'ahu emerged from the ocean, opening fertile ground for more colonization by the finches. Fast forward to about 1000–1200 CE, when Polynesians arrived. Birds became an important part of Hawaiian culture; their feathers were used in leis, and birds like the I'iwi were seen as family spiritual guides.[3] The first Europeans came in 1778 when British explorer James Cook landed (although there may have been Spanish arrival earlier).[4] Wave after wave of new settlers brought with them trouble for finches and other Hawaiian birds: rats, cats, pigs, mongooses; invasive plants and plant diseases; and most importantly, mosquitos carrying avian malaria. This spelled the decline of the honeycreepers from a high count of 54 species to now only about 16.[5] Some of the most endangered birds in the world are the Hawaiian honeycreepers, now forced to live at higher elevations to escape disease-carrying mosquitos moving upslope with the warming temperatures brought by climate change. Although what was once paradise for the finches now seems lost, not all is lost. The Hawaiian people's reverence for birds lives on. Conservationists, including the American Bird Conservancy and partners, have rallied and are implementing creative solutions to save the severely endangered honeycreepers. Learn more about these much-needed conservation efforts in the Research and Conservation chapter.

# 'AKIKIKI
*Oreomystis bairdi*

## IDENTIFICATION
**Size:** L 5″
**Shape:** Small honeycreeper with a relatively long, conical, slightly decurved bill.
**Adult Male:** Dark gray head, back, and flanks with contrasting off-white throat and underparts.
**Adult Female:** Same as male.
**Juv:** Similar to adults but with broad white eye-ring sometimes meeting the bill, and pale wingbars in some individuals.

### *SUBSPECIES*
Monotypic

### *SIMILAR SPECIES*
Pretty distinctive given range and overall gray color, but sometimes confused with Kaua'i 'Elepaio, an endemic flycatcher.

## DISTRIBUTION
Local and declining. Now considered effectively extinct in the wild. Was restricted to only about 15 square miles of Alaka'i Wilderness Preserve on Kaua'i.

## LANGUAGE
### *MALE*
Only male sings and is rarely ever heard, not necessarily due to how rare the species is, but because it is a songbird that just doesn't sing much. Song reported to be a "rarely uttered descending trill that trails off."[1]

### *MALE AND FEMALE*
Call notes are soft and variable, with most notable call being an upslurred *sweet,* sometimes referred to as a *cheep* or *chip* call.

## HABITAT AND DIET
Often found in pairs or family groups feeding or nesting in favored 'ōhi'a trees.

## CONSERVATION
Was listed as Endangered by the IUCN due to their small population size and restricted breeding distribution. Populations were decimated by avian malaria. Of the Hawaiian birds confirmed to be extant, it was thought to be the most endangered, with only 45 wild individuals known as of 2021. As of 2024 it is considered functionally extinct.

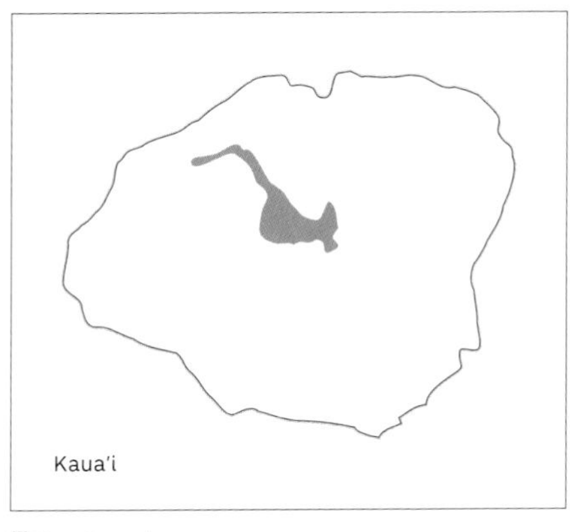


Year Round

## FUN FACT

'Akikiki is a unique, energetic, and special honeycreeper that feeds like a nuthatch.

# MAUI 'ALAUAHIO (MAUI CREEPER*)

*Paroreomyza montana*

## IDENTIFICATION

**Size:** L 4.5"
**Shape:** Small finch with a straight, warbler-like bill.
**Adult Male:** Olive-green above, yellow on head and underparts, with small dark spot in lore.
**Adult Female:** Duller gray-green with much less yellow than male.
**Juv:** Even less colorful than adult female.

### *SUBSPECIES*

Lāna'i subspecies *P. montana montana* extinct since 1930s. Now only *P. montana newtoni* survives on Maui.

### *SIMILAR SPECIES*

Pretty distinctive; could be confused with Hawai'i 'Amakihi, but straight bill distinctive. Males brighter yellow and lack narrow mask of that species.

## DISTRIBUTION

Fairly common in high-elevation native forest and tree plantations on Maui. Range has contracted, but birds can still be found in three disjunct populations above 2,952 feet. Easiest place to find them is Hosmer Grove, Haleakalā National Park, where they can be viewed around the picnic ground.

## LANGUAGE

### *MALE*

Perhaps two songs, one a varied series of notes that incorporates its most common vocalization, the *chip* note, at measured intervals; the second song is described as a "jumble warble very similar to the song of the House Finch but lacking the burry notes at the end."[1] Whisper song also incorporates the *chip* note.

### *MALE AND FEMALE*

Most frequent vocalization a *chip* that is sometimes described as a *cheek*, given by both sexes often as family groups forage.[2]

## HABITAT AND DIET

Higher elevation wet native forest and forest plantations. Gleans mostly arthropods in leaves or lichens of branches in the understory.

## CONSERVATION

Listed as Endangered by the IUCN due to their relatively restricted breeding distribution.

---

* For some species that have two recognized names, we list them in parentheses at the beginning of the account.

Adult m. HI/09

Adult f. HI/11

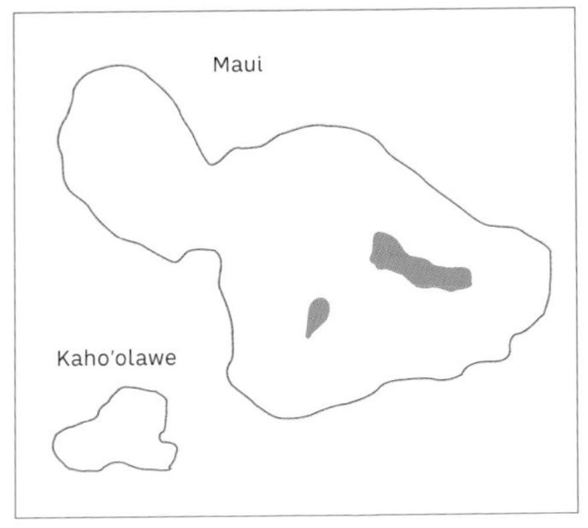

1st yr. HI/11

■ Year Round

## FUN FACT

**Inquisitive behavior makes them relatively easy to find, and second-year nonbreeding birds often act as helpers at nests by feeding the female during incubation.**

***Maui Forest Bird Recovery Project***

*"It's a delight to the observer to get 'MAALed.' That's a nickname for when a group of Maui 'Alauahio come in force, surrounding you and chipping excitedly. These curious fluff balls live in family groups and are fierce protectors. They will sound the alarm when there's a mongoose in the trees or when a Pueo is soaring over the forest or a biologist is walking by. The other honeycreepers seem to understand and also get agitated. The family group can also be seen allopreening, and sometimes you can catch a glimpse of a caterpillar that one of the birds has just pulled from the bark of a tree."*

# PALILA

*Loxioides bailleui*

## IDENTIFICATION

**Size:** L 7.5"

**Shape:** Large finch with an arched bill.

**Adult Male:** Yellow head and upper breast with gray back and pale gray to even perhaps whitish underparts.

**Adult Female:** Very similar to male but more lemon yellow than golden yellow of male.

**1st Year:** Crown of 1st-year females may be streaked with some gray.

**Juv:** Resembles adult female but with pale-green-tipped wingbars.

### *SUBSPECIES*

Monotypic

### *SIMILAR SPECIES*

Pretty distinctive given color and bill shape. While might seem similar to Laysan or Nihoa Finch, underparts are much paler than those two species, and Palila is not seen with them.

## DISTRIBUTION

Local and declining. Could go extinct in a few years without considerable conservation efforts. Fossil records indicate it occurred once upon a time on Kaua'i and O'ahu but today occurs only on Hawai'i Island.

## LANGUAGE

### *MALE*

Song often referred to as long, complex, and "canary-like with whistles, warbles, chirps and trills." Records of a "whisper song with mimicry" also noted.[1]

### *MALE AND FEMALE*

Typical call given by both sexes is translated as a sweet, warbled *pa-li-la*.

## HABITAT AND DIET

A specialist confined to 25 square miles of dry māmane-naio forest on the western slope of Mauna Kea, where it feeds mostly on māmane seeds extracted from green pods.

Year Round

## CONSERVATION

Listed as Critically Endangered by the IUCN due to their small population size, restricted breeding distribution, and diet preference for māmane seeds. This species was thought to be relatively safe for a decade or more, but populations have dipped quite a bit in recent years, and it could be lost soon unless considerable conservation actions take place.

### FUN FACT

**Most closely resembles bullfinches in Europe, which are most closely related to the Pine Grosbeak in the United States and Canada.**

***Dr. Patrick Hart, University of Hawai'i***

*"Appears to be declining despite apparent lack of mosquitoes in its high-elevation dry habitat. Perhaps rat predation on nests has increased over time but unclear. Māmane pod specialists require fruits to be available year-round, so they travel far across the landscape in search of ripe māmane."*

# LAYSAN FINCH ('AINOHU KAUO)

*Telespiza cantans*

## IDENTIFICATION

**Size:** L 6.5"
**Shape:** Medium to large finch with strongly overhanging grosbeak-like bill.
**Adult Male:** Golden-yellow finch above and below with gray and gold above.
**Adult Female:** Very similar to male but duller and more streaked throughout with gray back. Becomes less streaked with each molt.
**1st Year:** Slightly less heavily streaked than juv.
**Juv:** Yellow, heavily streaked on head, back, breast, and sides with dark brown.

### *SUBSPECIES*

Monotypic

### *SIMILAR SPECIES*

The Laysan Finch is larger, yellower, with a more strongly hooked bill when compared to the smaller Nihoa Finch.

## DISTRIBUTION

Local and declining. Fossil records show it once had a greater range that included the main Hawaiian Islands. Now only on Laysan Island and introduced to Pearl and Hermes Atoll. Population crashed in 1920s when introduced rabbits destroyed their shrub habitat.[1] The species survived by eating seabird eggs. Was also introduced to Midway Atoll, where it thrived for two decades only to succumb to rats that came ashore during World War II.

We don't show a map for Laysan Finch because Laysan Island, also known as Kauō, is small at only 1,016 acres and is more than 900 miles to the northwest of Honolulu, Oahu. Laysan Island is the second largest of the small islands and atolls of the northwestern Hawaiian islands. Hermes and Pearl Atolls, where Laysan Finch was introduced, are almost 1,300 miles from Honolulu.

## LANGUAGE

### *MALE AND FEMALE*

Both sexes can sing, but males more persistent.[2] Male song is a long, loud, twittering complex of vocalizations, "canary-like," and he is possibly a vocal mimic as well.[3] Calls are melodious, some resembling Palila's.[4]

Adult m. HI/03

## HABITAT AND DIET

Will forage in all vegetation types, especially scrub and beaches. Is even more of an omnivorous generalist than Nihoa Finch, as evidenced by the eating of eggs.

## CONSERVATION

Once thought to be abundant but now listed as Vulnerable by the IUCN due to range restriction and susceptibility to extreme weather events. Rising sea levels will likely continue to be a cause for concern for this species.

### FUN FACT

**The fossil record shows that the Laysan Finch once had a greater range in Hawai'i, reaching as far as O'ahu, and that birds on Laysan actually represent a relict population.**

# NIHOA FINCH

*Telespiza ultima*

## IDENTIFICATION

**Size:** L 6"

**Shape:** Medium-large finch with grosbeak-like bill less hooked than that of Laysan Finch.

**Adult Male:** Yellow head and breast, back blue-gray with gold patch in center, wing and tail feathers dark, edged gold, especially on secondary coverts. Flanks tinged blue-gray.

**Adult Female:** Duller and more heavily streaked with dark brown at all ages.

**1st Year:** Male less heavily streaked than adult female, with bold malar streak.

**Juv:** Male even less heavily streaked than 1st year.

### *SUBSPECIES*

Monotypic

### *SIMILAR SPECIES*

The Nihoa Finch is smaller overall than the Laysan Finch, including having a less hooked browner bill.

## DISTRIBUTION

Local and declining. Fossil records indicate it occurred once in the past on the main Hawaiian Islands, but is currently known only on Nihoa.

Was introduced to French Frigate Shoals in 1967, but attempt failed and birds were no longer present there by 1984.

We don't show a map for Nihoa Finch because Nihoa Island is very small at only 171 acres and is more than 200 miles to the northwest of Honolulu, Oahu. Nihoa Island is the tallest of the uninhabited northwestern Hawaiian islands.

## LANGUAGE

### *MALE AND FEMALE*

Both sexes can sing, but males more persistent.[1] Song is a long, loud, unhurried melodious complex of varied whistles. There are two different melodious calls, a 2-syllable upslurred call, and a 3-syllable call that goes up and then back down.

## HABITAT AND DIET

Omnivorous species of rocky scrubby shrub where it forages in the undercanopy. Eats a variety of insects and the seeds, flower heads, fruit, and leaves of ʻāweoweo, ʻihi, ʻilima, kakonakona, and ʻōhai.[2]

Adult m. HI/06

1st yr. HI/06

## CONSERVATION

Listed as Critically Endangered by the IUCN due to their small population size and restricted breeding distribution. Due to existing on only one very small island, population is especially susceptible to climate change and extreme climatic events. Translocation is still considered a viable conservation tool despite the failed attempt on French Frigate Shoals. High extinction risk due to population thought to number only 1,000–3,000.[3]

***Doug Pratt***

*"Introduction attempt on FFS [French Frigate Shoals] may have failed because of too few rocky potential nest sites. Birds nested in cinder blocks around research station, now abandoned."*

### FUN FACT

**Scientists in 1917 thought it would be the last described endemic species, hence the name *ultima*, but that turned out to be untrue with the discovery of the now-extinct Po'ouli in 1974.**

# 'ĀKOHEKOHE (CRESTED HONEYCREEPER)
*Palmeria dolei*

## IDENTIFICATION
**Size:** L 7"
**Shape:** Large honeycreeper with slightly decurved bill.
**Male:** Overall blackish with gray speckles on back, wings, and gray streaks on underparts. Prominent crest is pale gray to white. Orange surrounding eye and on nape.
**Female:** Sexes the same.
**Juv:** Duller with a reduced crest.

### *SUBSPECIES*
Monotypic

### *SIMILAR SPECIES*
Largest and unlike any of the other Hawaiian honeycreepers.

## DISTRIBUTION
Uncommon, local, and declining. Once found on Moloka'i until approximately 1944, but best and only place now to see it is on East Maui in wet forests above 5,000 feet on the slopes of Haleakalā. It is highly susceptible to avian malaria and lives only at higher elevations where it can evade the mosquitos that carry the disease.

## LANGUAGE
### *MALE*
Some suggest it has no song,[1] but Pratt describes highly varied array of territorial seasonal vocalizations consisting of harsh or screechy low-pitched dissonant sounds.[2]

### *MALE AND FEMALE*
Given by both sexes. Variable, but most common are an upslurred whistle or a guttural *ako-he-ko-he*.

## HABITAT AND DIET
Can be found in wet upland forests gathering nectar from ōhi'a most of the time, but also will feed on kolea, alani, kanawao,'ōhelo, pūkiawe, and 'ākala when in bloom. Pollinates trees and plants with its pom-pom-like crest.

## CONSERVATION
Listed as Critically Endangered by the IUCN due to their small population size and restricted breeding distribution. Climate change continues to be a threat, as mosquitoes carrying avian malaria are reaching higher elevations as the earth warms.

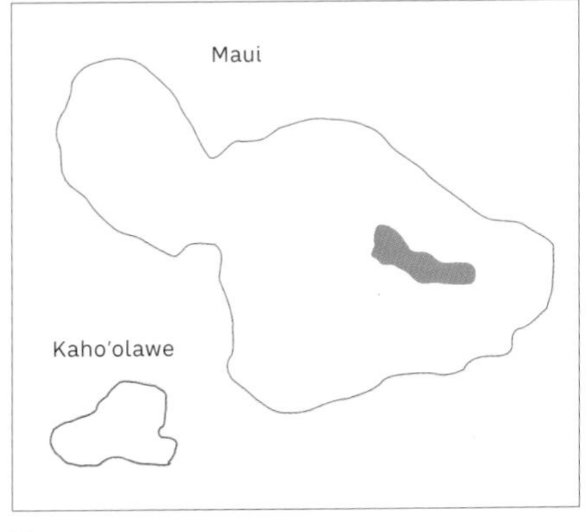


## FUN FACT

These finches are named honeycreepers due to several in the group having long downcurved bills used for nectaring that are similar to the cyanerpers honeycreepers of Mexico to Brazil. We now know from phylogenetics that they are actually finches despite the wide array of bill shapes and sizes, from short to long to curved to the more typical finch-like bill of the Palila.

***Maui Forest Bird Recovery Project***

*"For many birders, this is Hawai'i's most beautiful (or at least most flamboyant or punk-rock) extant bird."*

# 'APAPANE

*Himatione sanguinea*

## IDENTIFICATION

**Size:** L 5"

**Shape:** Small- to medium-sized honeycreeper with curved bill.

**Male:** Bright crimson red over most of head and body with black wings and white undertail coverts; bill and legs black.

**Female:** Sexes alike and only differentiable by measurements.

**Juv:** Mostly dull brown, with tawny or ocherous highlights; belly and undertail white.

### *SUBSPECIES*

Monotypic

### *SIMILAR SPECIES*

'I'iwi is also red but has long, decurved, red, sickle-shaped bill, white patch in tertials, and is more overall a darker crimson color.[1]

## DISTRIBUTION

Fairly common to common as they are the most abundant and widespread honeycreeper in Hawai'i. Can most commonly be found in 'ōhi'a habitat above 3,000 feet on Hawai'i and Maui, less so on Kaua'i. They are uncommon on O'ahu, rare on Moloka'i, and extirpated on Lana'i.

## LANGUAGE

### *MALE AND FEMALE*

Lots of different songs, with populations often singing the same one for a while and then changing to a different song. One sounds like a *tic-tic-tic-tic-tic-tic* of an old-fashioned rotary telephone dialing.[2] Vocalizations are a jumbled array of whistles, squeaks, chatters, and trills, but most common calls are descending *teerp* or *twep*. Gives a *cheep* call in flight as well. Both sexes produce a mechanical wing whir during flight, much like doves do.

## HABITAT AND DIET

Makes notably long flights from area to area in search of 'ōhi'a. Is a pollinator of 'ōhi'a, but also feeds in native koa, naio, māmane, kolea, kanawao, koki'o ke'oke'o, and ōlapa, as well as alien tagasaste, schefflera, and fuchsia.[3]

Adult HI/11

1st yr. HI/05

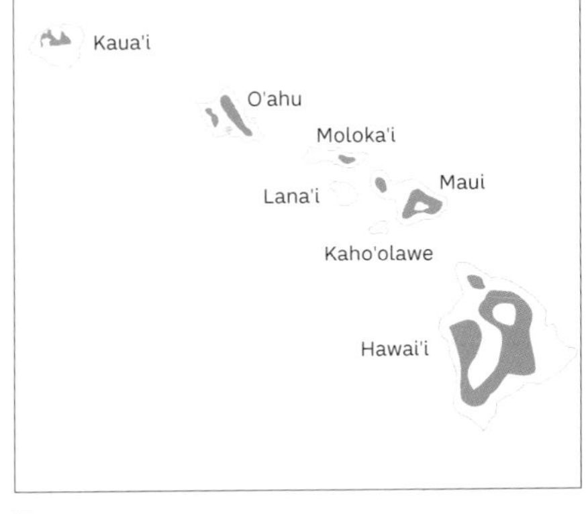


Year Round

## CONSERVATION

One of the few species not listed as endangered and is listed by the IUCN as Least Concern.

### FUN FACT

**Nectivorous like ʻIʻiwi and ʻĀkohekohe; often holds its tail cocked up like a wren. Since it is seen at lower elevation like Hawaiʻi ʻAmakihi, it might be forming or has formed some resistance to avian malaria (Gabrielle Names, personal communication).**

# 'I'IWI

*Drepanis coccinea*

## IDENTIFICATION

**Size:** L 6"

**Shape:** Chunky, medium-sized honeycreeper with long, thick, sickle-shaped (heavily decurved) bill.

**Adult Male:** Bright red with black wings and tail; reddish-orange bill and red legs. A flash of white in the tertials.

**Adult Female:** Sexes alike.

**Juv:** Mustard yellow speckled with black, bill dull yellow.

### *SUBSPECIES*

Monotypic

### *SIMILAR SPECIES*

Similar to 'Apapane but more orange red, white patch in tertials, and long, decurved red bill. 'Apapane is more crimson with white undertail.

## DISTRIBUTION

Once common across much of the main Hawaiian Islands, but now uncommon to fairly common. Best places to find now are the high-altitude native forests on Hawai'i Island and Maui where it seeks refuge from avian malaria. Declining and rare now on Kaua'i, almost extirpated on Moloka'i, and probably O'ahu, and no longer found on Lana'i.

## LANGUAGE

### *MALE AND FEMALE*

Highly variable repertoire of calls and songs that include "creaks, whistles, gurgles, and reedy notes, some resembling notes played on an old harmonica."[1] Some song is a halting series of whistles and mechanical sounds like a rusty hinge of a swing or gate, translated as *ii-wi* or *ee-vee* with an upward inflection. Pattern reminiscent of song of Yellow-breasted Chat. Unlike song of any other honeycreeper. Squared-off primaries make a sound in flight like that of 'Apapane.

## HABITAT AND DIET

Found in upland forests mainly gathering nectar from ōhi'a and māmane, but also feeds on a variety of native and introduced plants. Especially fond of invasive banana poka. Will also eat some insects.[2]

## CONSERVATION

Listed as Vulnerable by the IUCN. Climate change will continue to be a threat, as mosquitoes carrying avian malaria are reaching higher elevations as the earth warms.

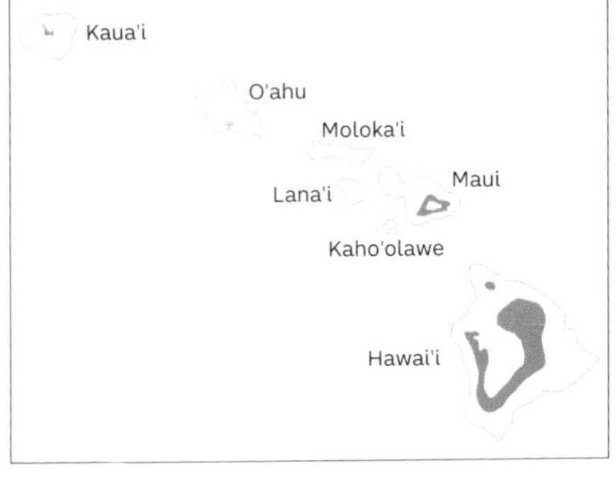


Year Round

## FUN FACT

Iconic species that is deeply entrenched in Hawaiian folklore. According to legend, ancient people could hear the sweet melodies of the 'I'iwi singing, but the only one who could see it was the demigod Maui, who had clear vision. Maui painted the 'I'iwi by hand, giving it a color that is as joyful to the eyes as its song is to the ears, and decided to unveil the beauty of the bird so all people could see it.

***Maui Forest Bird Recovery Project***

*"The forest is alive when you hear the 'I'iwi squawking and chasing each other. You know it's breeding season or soon to be. They are very active with their sounds and chasing. Oftentimes you see females or juveniles shadowing another individual and begging for food. Sometimes males will be seen fighting. They are a very engaging species to watch and very quick as they find nectar to drink. During the summer, outside of the breeding season, the forest is so quiet without all their boisterousness."*

*Rob Pacheco, veteran guide on the Big Island, calls this species "the essence of honeycreeperness."*

# MAUI PARROTBILL (KIWIKIU)

*Pseudonestor xanthophrys*

## IDENTIFICATION

**Size:** L 5.5"
**Shape:** Medium-sized honeycreeper with short tail and very large, parrot-like bill.
**Adult Male:** Olive-green above, bright yellow below with bright yellow face, throat, and eyebrow/superciliary stripe. Parrot-like overhanging upper mandible.
**Adult Female:** Duller and smaller than male, but similar in color to 1st-year male, which is intermediate between adult male and juv.
**Juv:** Similar to adults but mixed with more gray on underparts.

### *SUBSPECIES*

Monotypic

### *SIMILAR SPECIES*

Bill super distinctive and easily separates it from all other Hawaiian honeycreepers, but the bold, eye-catching yellow eyebrow is the easiest mark to see in forest understory.

## DISTRIBUTION

Scarce and local. At present can be found in only 19 square miles of East Maui where it is limited to forests above about 4,000 feet on the windward side of Haleakalā. The best place to see it, with permitted guide only, is the Waikamoi Preserve, owned by the Nature Conservancy.

## LANGUAGE

### *MALE*

Song is a descending series of short melodic warbles reminiscent of a Canyon Wren.[1] Whisper song is similar but much softer with a few short warbled whistles added at the end.[2]

### *MALE AND FEMALE*

Varied calls: one a loud *chet* or *chick;* another, given by 1st-year birds that follow their parents, *tseeop.*[3]

## HABITAT AND DIET

Wet, native upland forest of mainly ʻōhiʻa lehua where it uses its hooked bill to feed primarily on caterpillars, beetles, and other invertebrates.

## CONSERVATION

Listed as Critically Endangered by the IUCN due to their small population size and restricted breeding distribution. Numbers only 100–200 individuals, and a captive breeding program has been started. A translocation failed in 2019 when most of the birds died from avian malaria.

Mosquitoes continue to increase and climb in elevation, and the Maui Parrotbill may go extinct in the next few years without considerable conservation efforts. Given this plight, the Maui Forest Bird Recovery Project has put forth several plans, including at least temporarily fostering a sizable captive population at zoos in the mainland United States.

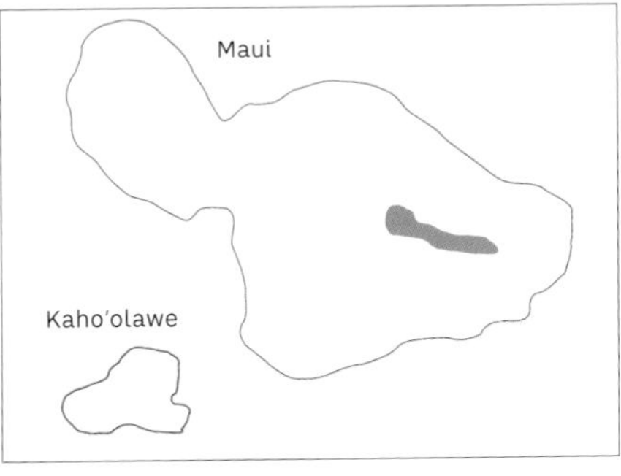


Year Round

## FUN FACT

**As far as anyone can determine, *Pseudonestor xanthophrys* had not historically had a common name in the Hawaiian language. The Hawaiian name Kiwikiu was developed by the Hawaiian Lexicon Committee, who was contacted by the Maui Forest Bird Recovery Project to select an appropriate name. A naming ceremony was held in the bird's habitat in September 2010.**

***Maui Forest Bird Recovery Project***

*"Along with its closest living relative, the 'Akiapōlā'au, the Maui Parrotbill has one of the slowest rates of reproduction among passerines. Nesting pairs can successfully fledge only one chick per year, and the fledgling is then dependent on its parents for many months afterwards. This period of dependency is necessitated by this species' foraging behavior. Successfully using the large, hooked bill to excavate beetle and moth larvae requires learned skills that young birds must practice before they are able to successfully forage. Parents must continue to feed the chick while it learns how to feed."*

# 'AKIAPŌLĀ'AU

*Hemignathus wilsoni*

## IDENTIFICATION

**Size:** L 5.5"
**Shape:** Medium-sized honeycreeper with short tail and one-of-a-kind bill with upper mandible long, thin, and curved, and lower mandible thicker and straight.
**Male:** Dull green above, yellow below; head mostly yellow with black lore, rather similar to coloration of Hawai'i 'Amakihi.
**Female:** Similar to male but with smaller bill and less yellow, mostly in the throat.
**Juv and 1st-Year:** Variable but similar to parents with even less yellow; sexes distinguishable by bill size. Yellow bill base darkens with age.

### *SUBSPECIES*

Monotypic

### *SIMILAR SPECIES*

The bill is super distinctive and easily separates it from all other Hawaiian honeycreepers.[1]

## DISTRIBUTION

Uncommon and local. Endemic to Hawai'i Island where less than 2,000 exist in native forests above 4,300 feet. The Hakalau Forest National Wildlife Refuge is perhaps the best place to observe one, but Pu'u Ō'ō Trail is more accessible.

## LANGUAGE

### *MALE*

Song is a loud warble of approximately 8 notes. Whisper song is a quieter version of its primary song.[2]

### *MALE AND FEMALE*

Most frequent call is a *chuwee*. Begging juveniles utter a "beacon call" similar to that of the House Sparrow.

## HABITAT AND DIET

Wet, native upland forest of mainly koa and 'ōhi'a lehua where it uses its combination-tool bill to feed on arthropods such as beetle larvae. With the upper mandible held out of the way, it hammers woodpecker-like at the bark with the lower mandible, then uses the upper to extract the larvae.

## CONSERVATION

This bird was included on the endangered species list in 1967 because of its fragmented populations, habitat loss, and low reproductive success (has a brood of 1) due to its young needing to learn to forage with adults for up to 9 months. Listed as

■ Year Round

Endangered by the IUCN due to small population size. Fewer than 2,000 birds exist within 4 populations. Efforts to save the species include reforestation, removal of feral ungulates, and perhaps starting a captive breeding population.

## FUN FACT

**This bill is an evolutionary wonder. The bird uses its lower mandible to peck open the bark and reach the larvae; it then uses its thin upper bill to probe out the meal and its lower bill to crush its meal. Despite the difference in length of the two mandibles, the tips can be brought together to pick up prey items thanks to an extra bone that allows the lower mandible to swing forward, unlike the way human jaws work.**

***Doug Pratt***

*"This is easily the most bizarre feeding adaptation of any Hawaiian honeycreeper. There is nothing like it among all the world's birds."*

# 'ANIANIAU

*Magumma parva*

## IDENTIFICATION

**Size:** L 4"
**Shape:** Very small honeycreeper with thin, short, slightly decurved, pinkish bill.
**Adult Male:** Bright yellow overall, darker on the back, with no black in the lore.
**Adult Female:** Slightly duller olive-green, but sexes very much alike.
**Juv:** Similar to female but even more muted olive-green.

### *SUBSPECIES*

Monotypic

### *SIMILAR SPECIES*

Can be confused with 'Akeke'e and Kaua'i 'Amakihi, but both have black lore and heavier bills.

## DISTRIBUTION

Kaua'i endemic. Uncommon and declining due to avian malaria as with many other honeycreepers. It can still be found in upland wet forests on Kaua'i, especially on the Alaka'i Swamp Trail.

## LANGUAGE

### *MALE*

Primary song is melodic trill of doubled or triple notes. Gives a whisper song like those of other honeycreepers.[1]

### *MALE AND FEMALE*

Gives varied calls like many of the honeycreepers, but most commonly gives a distinctive two-syllable *tew-weet*.

## HABITAT AND DIET

Wet, native upland forest where it mainly likes to sip nectar from native and introduced flowers but will also take invertebrates.

## CONSERVATION

Listed as Vulnerable by the IUCN. Populations have declined due to avian malaria as have many of the honeycreepers facing a conservation crisis.

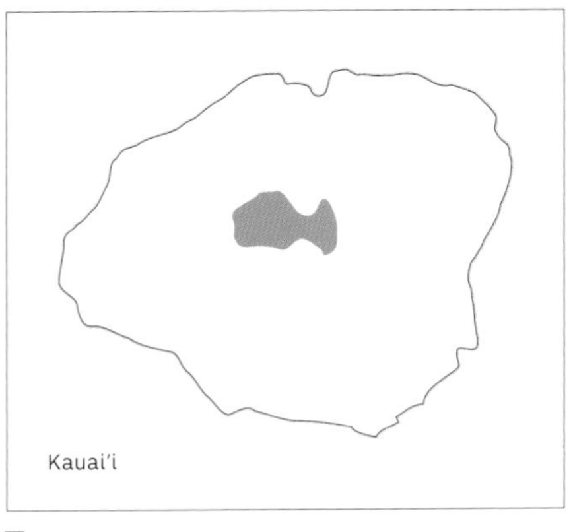


## FUN FACT

This species and Hawai'i 'Ākepa are close to a tie for smallest of the Hawaiian honeycreepers.

# HAWAI'I 'AMAKIHI

*Chlorodrepanis virens*

## IDENTIFICATION

**Size:** L 4.25"
**Shape:** Small finch with short tail and decurved bill.
**Adult Male:** Bright yellow-green overall, with black lore and thin decurved bill.
**Adult Female:** Similar to male but not as brightly colored.
**Juv:** Similar to female but even less yellow, often almost gray.

### *SUBSPECIES*

Monotypic

### *SIMILAR SPECIES*

Although similar to other two 'amakihi species, ranges set them apart. Could be confused with Maui 'Alauahio, but that species has a straight bill and only a small dark spot in lore. Also similar to Hawai'i Creeper, but Hawai'i Creeper is more olive with a broader mask and almost straight bill.

## DISTRIBUTION

Uncommon to common on Hawai'i, Maui, and Moloka'i, but can still be considered one of the most widespread honeycreepers on those islands. One of the best places to find it is Hosmer's Grove, Haleakalā National Park (Maui). Particularly numerous in māmane-naio forest on slopes of Mauna Kea (Hawai'i).

## LANGUAGE

### *MALE*

A loud, variable, ringing trill that tends to sound a bit louder as it continues.

### *MALE AND FEMALE*

Whisper song given by both sexes[1] is long and varied in male, less so in female. Calls are quite variable, but most common call is similar to the buzzy nasal *mew* of the Blue-gray Gnatcatcher.

## HABITAT AND DIET

Can be found in all forest and scrub types, both wet and dry, even at lower elevation. Generalist that feeds on nectar but eats insects, some fruit, and tree sap.

## CONSERVATION

Is one of only a few honeycreepers not listed as Endangered or Threatened.

Adult m. HI/04

Adult f. HI/04

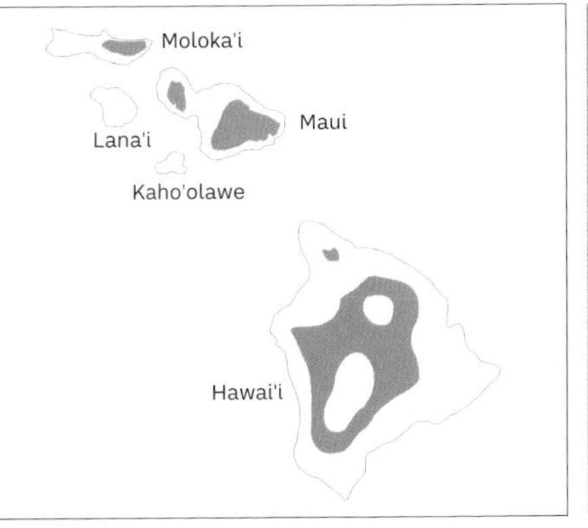

Year Round

1st yr. HI/08

## FUN FACT

**Appears to have developed a resistance to avian malaria and can therefore still be found at lower elevation. They also pollinate native plants with their bill.**

***Gabrielle Names, UC Davis PhD graduate who studied Hawai'i 'Amakihi***

*"This was the study species for my PhD and thus I have a strong attachment to this honeycreeper species. The 'Amakihi is sexually dimorphic, with males having bright yellow plumage and a black mask while females have more drab olive-colored plumage with a faint gray mask. Both have charismatically curved beaks that are adapted to their nectar diet. Resistant to malaria as they are the only honeycreeper species that has maintained stable populations at low elevation, where avian malaria is prevalent."*

# O'AHU 'AMAKIHI

*Chlorodrepanis flava*

## IDENTIFICATION

**Size:** L 4.25"

**Shape:** Small finch with short tail and decurved bill.

**Adult Male:** Bright yellow-green above, bright yellow below, with black lore and pale gray bill.

**Adult Female:** Similar to male but duller yellow-green with two fairly prominent cream-colored wingbars.

**Juv:** Similar to female but more greenish-gray above with two off-white wingbars.

### *SUBSPECIES*

Monotypic

### *SIMILAR SPECIES*

Similar to other two 'amakihi species, but more strongly two-toned, and females have wingbars. Of the three 'amakihi species, the male O'ahu 'Amakihi tends to be the brightest yellow throughout. On O'ahu, no other honeycreeper could be confused with the O'ahu 'Amakihi, but introduced Warbling White-Eye and Japanese Bush-Warbler present identification problems.

## DISTRIBUTION

Fairly common on O'ahu. One of the better places to see it is on the 'Aiea Loop Trail.

## LANGUAGE

### *MALE*

Loud repeated trill similar to that of the other two 'amakihi species, but tends to be slower with more notes.[1]

### *MALE AND FEMALE*

Whisper song given by both sexes is long and varied in male, less so in female. Variable calls, but most common call is a low-pitched mewing sound similar to Blue-gray Gnatcatcher call.[2] All three 'amakihi species give this call, but it is not the primary call for Kaua'i 'Amakihi.

## HABITAT AND DIET

Native and nonnative forests. Eats insects, but also feeds on nectar from native and nonnative trees such as kukui, golden shower tree, native hibiscus, and various eucalyptus.[3]

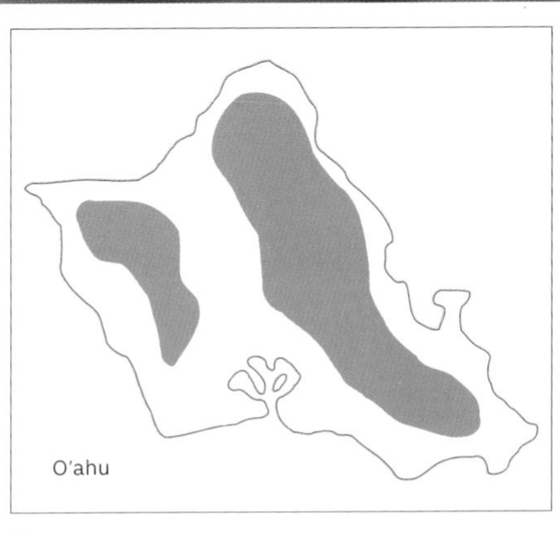


## CONSERVATION

Vulnerable. Likely the only surviving honeycreeper endemic to the island. Appears to be able to exist at lower elevations especially in winter, suggesting it might be developing resistance to avian malaria.

### FUN FACT

**Has been known to use sugar-water feeders.**

# KAUA'I 'AMAKIHI

*Chlorodrepanis stejnegeri*

## IDENTIFICATION

**Size:** L 4.5"
**Shape:** Small finch with short tail and medium-length decurved bill.
**Adult Male:** Bright yellow-green overall, with black lore and longer bill than the other two 'amakihi species' bills.
**Adult Female:** Similar to male but duller yellow-green.
**Juv:** Similar to female but more greenish-gray above.

### *SUBSPECIES*

Monotypic

### *SIMILAR SPECIES*

Differs from other 'amakihi species and other "little green birds" in having a strikingly larger, more decurved bill. Could be confused with 'Anianiau, which is much smaller with nearly straight bill and lacking dark lore, and 'Akeke'e, which has yellow forehead and rump visible in flight and conical bluish bill surrounded by black mask.

## DISTRIBUTION

Uncommon and local on Kaua'i. One of the best places to find it is Alaka'i Wilderness Preserve.

## LANGUAGE

### *MALE*

Starting with a distinctive introductory note, lacking in 'amakihi songs on other islands, male sings a loud, variable, and repeated trill that tends to drop in pitch as it continues.

### *MALE AND FEMALE*

Whisper song may include mimicry.[1] Calls are quite variable. Most common call is a *tseet*, but also gives nasally *mew* vocalization reminiscent of the Blue-gray Gnatcatcher that the other two 'amakihi species give as well.[2]

## HABITAT AND DIET

Upland native forests. A generalist that eats insects, but also feeds on nectar from 'ōhi'a, kanawao, 'ohe naupaka, Kaua'i koli'i, and more.[3] Pollinates these native plants by transferring pollen stuck to their feathers, or by shaking it loose by feeding motions.

Adult m.

HI/10

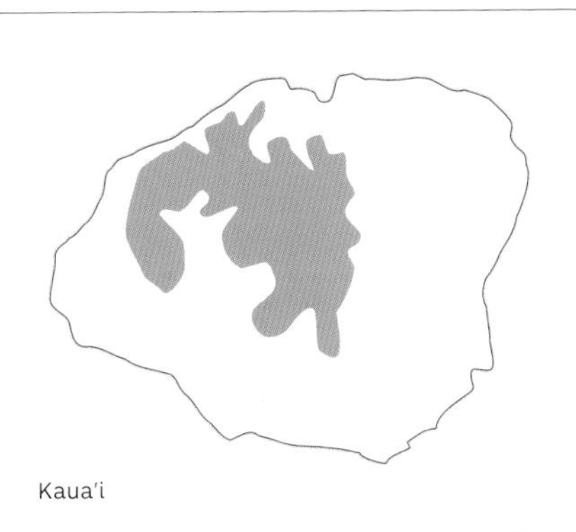

Adult f.

HI/10

Year Round

## CONSERVATION

Vulnerable, declining, and perhaps most restricted of the three 'amakihi species. Not found at lower elevations like the two other species, suggesting it remains susceptible to avian malaria.

### FUN FACT

**The largest of the three 'amakihis with the longest curved bill. Most readily distinguished from other "little green birds" by its longer, more decurved bill.[4]**

# HAWAI'I CREEPER ('ALAWĪ)

*Loxops mana*

## IDENTIFICATION

**Size:** L 4.25"

**Shape:** Small honeycreeper with a short tail and short, conical, ever so slightly decurved bill.

**Adult Male:** Olive-green above, yellowish-green below with white throat and triangular dark mask.

**Adult Female:** Very similar to male, sometimes a touch grayer.

**1st Year:** Intermediate in color, with yellowish superciliary.

**Juv:** Grayer than adults with no or reduced mask and a defined pale-white superciliary.

### *SUBSPECIES*

Monotypic

### *SIMILAR SPECIES*

Hawai'i 'Amakihi is similar, but the Hawai'i Creeper is more olive with broader mask and slightly straighter and paler bill.

## DISTRIBUTION

Uncommon in 4 disparate high-elevation locations above 5,000 feet on the island of Hawai'i. There is still a good chance of seeing them on a commercial tour of Hakalau Forest NWR (not open to public), less so on Pu'u Ō'ō Trail.

## LANGUAGE

### *MALE*

Song a relatively quiet, rattling, descending trill given faster than that of the other *Loxops* species. Whisper song is reported to be given on rare occasion and contains mimicry.[1]

### *MALE AND FEMALE*

Call is a slightly rising upslurred *sweet* or *cheit*. Juveniles following parents give short *whit* notes in syncopated bursts.

## HABITAT AND DIET

Native upland 'ōhi'a or koa forest, with the latter perhaps preferred.

## CONSERVATION

Listed as Endangered by the IUCN due to their small population size and restricted isolated breeding populations.

Adult HI/10

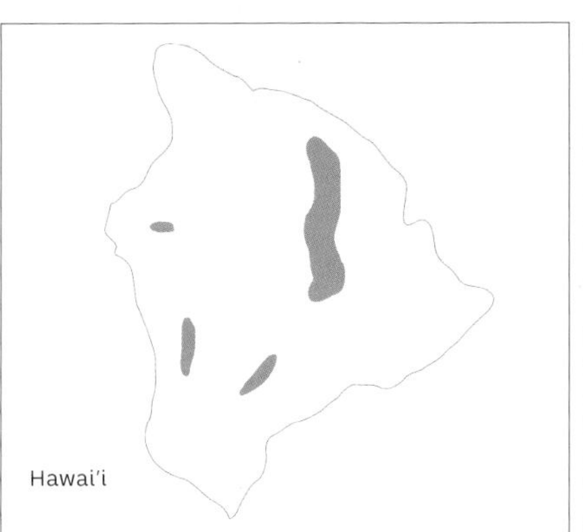

Juv./1st yr. HI/03

Year Round

## FUN FACT

**Movements resemble a nuthatch's when it forages by picking or pecking in crevices and cracks in bark of limbs and tree trunks.**

***Doug Pratt***

*"This species closely resembles the 'Akikiki in ecology, behavior (including nearly identical juvenile begging calls), and even anatomy as in identical tongue structure not found in other honeycreepers, but DNA has revealed that this is all the result of a remarkable example of evolutionary convergence and the two species are not closely related."*

# 'AKEKE'E

*Loxops caeruleirostris*

## IDENTIFICATION

**Size:** L 4.5"
**Shape:** Small honeycreeper with conical, cross-tipped bill, and notched tail.
**Adult Male:** A small olive above, yellow below finch of the unique genus *Loxops* that has slightly crossed mandibles. Black triangular mask, yellow rump, forehead, and crown, and sharp, pale-blue bill. Males take 3 years to reach adult plumage.
**Adult Female:** Slightly duller than male.
**1st Year:** Lacks mask, and duller than adults.

### *SUBSPECIES*

Monotypic

### *SIMILAR SPECIES*

'Anianiau and Kaua'i 'Amakihi are similar, but 'Anianiau has slightly curved warbler-like bill and no mask, and Kaua'i 'Amakihi has strongly curved bill and dark mask.

## DISTRIBUTION

Local and declining. Fewer than 1,000 individuals remain. Once found across Kaua'i, but only place to see them now is a 30-square-mile patch at higher elevations of the Alaka'i Wilderness Preserve.

## LANGUAGE

### *MALE*

A 2-part loud trill that "shifts gears" in the middle.

### *MALE AND FEMALE*

Most common call a loud upslurred *sweet* or *peek* that carries and pierces.

## HABITAT AND DIET

Wet, native upland forest. An 'ōhi'a specialist that searches for insect larvae by prying apart leaf buds that resemble tiny cones.

## CONSERVATION

Listed as Critically Endangered by the IUCN due to their small population size and restricted breeding distribution. It has been declining and could become extinct because of increasing prevalence of avian malaria.

Adult m. HI/04

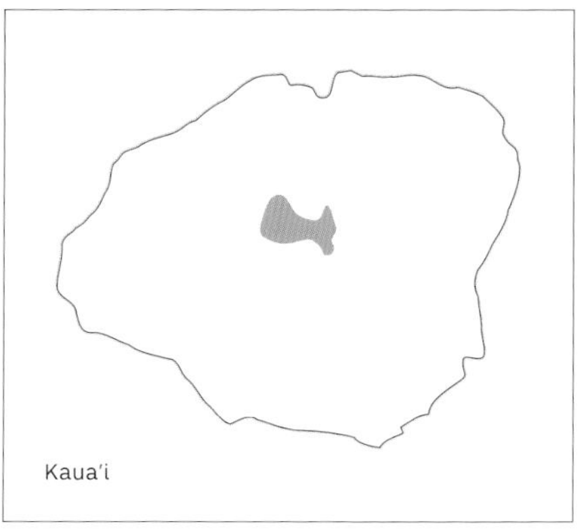

Adult f. HI/03

Year Round

**FUN FACT**

This bird builds nests primarily of twigs high up in trees, while the closely related 'Ākepa uses tree cavities.[1]

***Kaua'i Forest Bird Recovery Project***

*"This species has a specialized bill—with offset tips similar to those of mainland crossbill species—that allows it to pry open buds of 'ōhi'a leaves and flowers to search for invertebrates."*

# HAWAI'I 'ĀKEPA

*Loxops coccineus*

## IDENTIFICATION

**Size:** L 4"

**Shape:** Small honeycreeper with conical, cross-tipped bill, and notched tail.

**Adult Male:** A small red-orange songbird with slightly crossed mandibles reminiscent of the *Loxia* crossbills. Tail and wings are dusky black, bill is yellow and thin and like that of the Pine Siskin. Conical bill crosses either right or left like crossbills, too, but the crossing is not visible from any distance. Males take three years to reach adult plumage.

**Adult Female:** Gray-green or olive, paler below, with a broad yellow-orange breast-band and gray on front and on back. May have a diffuse supercilium.

**1st Year:** Same dull olive in both sexes, 2nd-year female yellowish, male not as bright as adult.

### *SUBSPECIES*

Monotypic but formerly included subspecies on Maui and O'ahu, both now given species status.

### *SIMILAR SPECIES*

Orange color of males distinctive, but females and juveniles may be confused with female and juvenile Hawai'i 'Amakihi and Hawai'i Creeper.

## DISTRIBUTION

Uncommon, local, and declining. Endemic to higher elevations of Hawai'i in upland wet or mesic forests on windward sides of island; most common in Hakalau Forest National Wildlife Refuge with a small population still in Ka'ū Forest Reserve. May be small relict populations declining on northern slope of Hualālai volcano and western slope of Mauna Loa volcano on leeward side.[1]

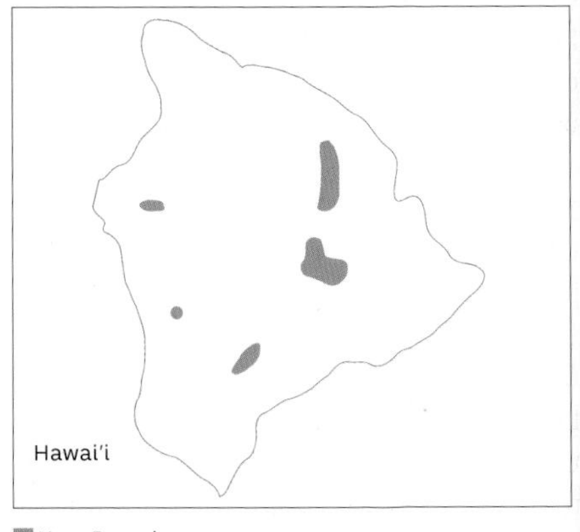


Year Round

## FUN FACT

**Unique among Hawaiian honeycreepers, the Hawai'i 'Ākepa nests exclusively in tree cavities.**

Adult m. HI/12

Adult f. HI/04

## LANGUAGE

### *MALE*

Male of Hawai'i 'Ākepa has an up-and-down 2–3 second rather lackadaisical song that ends with a slowing, descending trill. Overall descending quality of song is distinctive to the ear even if not clearly evident on spectrograms. Song is often transcribed as *TEEEDLE leeedle, leeedle, leeedle, leeedle.*[2]

1st yr. HI/05

### *MALE AND FEMALE*

Both sexes can give a whisper song characterized by short chirps and whistles with occasional mimicry of other species.[3] Calls consist of short, frequency-modulated whistles of 1–3 notes, typically a *teedle-lee* but also shorter versions.[4]

## HABITAT AND DIET

Upland ohi'a forest where it uses its unique bill to extract insects from leaf buds the way crossbills do with evergreen cones.

## CONSERVATION

Listed as Endangered by the IUCN due to their small population size and restricted breeding distribution. The Maui and O'ahu 'Ākepas are extinct, probably because of mosquito-borne diseases, with the last Maui 'Ākepa reported in 1988.

***Dr. Patrick Hart, University of Hawai'i***

*"Generally searches for insects on terminal leaf buds of "ōhi'a. Almost complete 'ōhi'a specialist. The only obligate cavity nester among the honeycreepers. Often forages in the vicinity of 'Alawī and forms large mixed species flocks with 'Alawī, 'Amakihi, and most other native forest birds after young have fledged (usually mid-June–July). Flocks contain many begging juveniles and appear to be a way to protect them from the Hawaiian Hawk, which seems to prefer young, tasty, naive fledglings."*

# FEEDING AND ATTRACTING FINCHES

*Look—flashing gold and black*
*See—wings descending*
*Watch—flocking seed seekers*
*Hear—chirping sleigh bells*
*Notice—Evening Grosbeaks feeding*
*Realize—you forgot . . . to worry . . . about . . . anything*

—Lillian Quinn Stokes

Bird feeding brings rewards to birds, but one of its biggest advantages is to connect you to something larger than yourself, the healing and wellness power of nature. Increasing scientific research supports what we may instinctively know—seeing the sights and hearing the sounds of beautiful birds is good for the body and good for the soul!

A recent study found that everyday encounters with birds resulted in improved mental well-being for healthy people but also for those who were depressed.[1] Another study revealed that people who lived in neighborhoods with more birds, shrubs, and trees had less stress, anxiety, and depression.[2]

What better way to reap these rewards than to create a finch-friendly habitat in your yard with the food and plantings finches seek and need? When we fill feeders and dig in the earth, we are nurturing and caring for other living things. In doing so we care for ourselves, and it is in that giving that we are rewarded.

Finches as a group have the largest number of species of feeder birds in the world. They're easy to attract and are among the top ten feeder birds in every area of the United States, according to Project FeederWatch (feederwatch.org).[3] Here is some of our best advice on how to feed finches and create habitats for them.

Evening Grosbeaks at feeder

# FEEDING FINCHES
***TYPES OF FEEDERS***

### FINCH TUBES, FINCH SOCKS, AND FINCH SCREEN FEEDERS

Finch tubes are cylindrical feeders with perches and very small openings for offering tiny Nyjer® seed. Finch socks are cloth mesh bags, and finch screen feeders are cylindrical screens made of a small-size mesh. Both styles allow finches to cling and pull out the Nyjer® seed. Do not put large seeds like sunflower seeds in these types of finch feeders—the finches will not be able to pull the large seeds through the small holes of the feeder.

### SEED TUBES AND SEED SCREENS

Seed tubes are plastic cylinders with perches and larger openings that are used for black oil sunflower or birdseed mixes. Seed screen sunflower feeders are cylindrical screens with large enough openings in the screen for birds to extract sunflower seeds. If there is a wide enough tray at the bottom of the tube or screen, larger birds like Evening Grosbeaks can feed.

### HOPPER FEEDERS

Hopper feeders have a large square or rectangular compartment usually enclosed by plastic panels, topped by a roof and with a tray below; the seed is dispensed into the tray out of a gap at the bottom of the plastic panels. Sometimes hopper feeders also have suet cages on their ends, primarily for other species, as finches rarely eat suet.

### TRAY AND PLATFORM FEEDERS

Tray and platform feeders are square or rectangular surfaces, made of wood, metal, or plastic, that can be hung or pole mounted. Platforms often have roofs over them to protect the seed from weather. They are the ultimate feeder for attracting larger finches like Evening and Pine Grosbeaks.

### FINCH BIRD BATHS

Birds need water to drink and bathe. Choose a bird bath with a nonslip surface that is not too deep (small birds prefer two inches or less) or at least has a gradual slope that provides more shallow areas. Locate the bath in the open but near cover so birds can flee predators. Adding a water dripper makes a bath even more appealing. Scrub away mold and mildew, and refill your bird bath frequently, at least daily in hot weather. Keep a brush nearby to make cleaning easy.

Purple Finch at bird bath

House Finch at seed tube feeder

American Goldfinches and Pine Siskin at finch tube

Purple Finch at hopper feeder

Purple Finches, Red-breasted Nuthatch, and Pine Siskin (behind feeder) at seed tube

Evening Grosbeaks at tray feeder

### *TYPES OF SEED*

### SUNFLOWER

Black oil sunflower has a higher oil content and thinner shell than gray-striped sunflower. Hulled black oil sunflower, also known as sunflower hearts, meaties, or sunflower chips if chopped up, is usually even more preferred. Gray-striped sunflower, a big seed with a tough shell, is eaten only by the largest finches like Evening Grosbeaks.

Black oil sunflower

***How to offer***

Trays, seed tubes with large openings, sunflower seed screen feeders, and hopper feeders.

***Finches attracted***

All species.

Hulled sunflower

***Pros & cons***

**Pro:** Number one choice of most birds, especially hulled, which leaves little mess.

**Con:** Shells can accumulate under the feeder. Hulled seed exposed to weather could mold, so offer in protected feeders.

### NYJER®

Nyjer® seed is a small black seed with high oil content, and its name is a registered trademark of the Wild Bird Feeding Institute. Sometimes called thistle, it is an imported seed (*Guizotia abyssinica*) from India, Ethiopia, and other areas, that is sterilized with intense heat to prevent germination of any additional seeds in it. It is not from the wildflower thistles in North America.

Nyjer® seed

***How to offer***

Finch tubes, finch screen, and finch socks.

***Finches attracted***

Mainly the smaller finches—goldfinches, redpolls, siskins, and to a lesser extent rosy-finches and House, Purple, and Cassin's Finches.

***Pros & cons***

**Pro:** Appealing to small finches.

**Con:** Expensive. Nyjer® can become rancid when stored for a long period, so it is best to buy it in smaller, fresh quantities more often.

## SAFFLOWER

This medium-sized white seed of an annual plant (*Carthamus tinctorius*) is widely commercially cultivated for vegetable oil.

Safflower

### *How to offer*

Seed tubes with large portals, seed screens, hopper and tray feeders.

### *Finches attracted*

In an informal survey of finch feeding on the Finches, Irruptions, and Mast Crops Facebook page, it was reportedly enjoyed by Evening Grosbeaks, Purple, and House Finches.

### *Pros & cons*

**Pro:** Appeals to medium and large finches.
**Con:** Not readily available, can leave shell mess.

Millet

## MILLET

White proso millet is a small, white, round seed and is mainly a component in finch and other birdseed mixes. It is not as easily obtained by itself, thus less commonly offered alone for feeding finches. There are other kinds of millet, such as red or golden millet, that may be used in finch mixes, but white proso millet seems to be the more popular addition.

Finch mix

### *How to offer*

If used alone, offer in finch tubes and finch screen feeders.

### *Finches attracted*

Not a top choice but eaten by smaller finches.

### *Pros & cons*

**Pro:** Some finches eat it.
**Con:** Often thrown out of feeder if part of a mix because it is less desirable.

## FINCH MIXES

There are many kinds of finch mixes available. They mainly contain Nyjer® and fine sunflower chips and sometimes white or red millet, canary seed, or peanut hearts. Nyjer® and sunflower chips top the list of finch favorites, so choose a mix that is either entirely composed of those seeds or they make up a large percentage of it.

The other seeds like millet or canary seed may be eaten but are sometimes thrown out of the mix.

*How to offer*
Finch tubes, finch screens, and finch socks.

*Finches attracted*
Mainly smaller finches.

*Pros & cons*
Pro: Very appealing to small finches especially if the mix only contains sunflower chips and Nyjer®.
Con: May contain less desirable seeds that finches will discard.

## BIRDSEED MIXES

There is an endless variety of birdseed mixes on the market. Almost all contain black oil sunflower, in shell or hulled, plus some percentage of other seeds like millet, cracked corn, peanuts and other nuts, and milo (generally one of the least preferred seeds). The better mixes contain a good percentage of black oil since it is the number one preference of most species of birds.

Bird seed mix with sunflower, safflower, and millet

*How to offer*
Seed tubes with large openings, seed screens, hoppers, and trays.

*Finches attracted*
All finches will be attracted to mixes containing sunflower, especially hulled sunflower.

*Pros & cons*
Pro: All finches are attracted to black oil sunflower.
Con: Less desirable seeds will be tossed out.

## *KEEPING SQUIRRELS OUT*

The number one complaint in bird feeding has not to do with birds but with furry-tailed thieves—squirrels! These seed-eating, seed-storing, seed-hoarding mammals may be cute to watch but not when treasured sunflower hearts are emptied out of the feeder. While it may not be 100% possible to outfox squirrels, there's a lot one can do to protect birdseed from them, if you want to.

Squirrel at squirrel-proof caged feeder

Sometimes the outfoxing game is just too engaging, and people want it to continue. Here are the best tips to protect feeders from squirrels.

Squirrel at squirrel feeder

**INSTALL A SQUIRREL-PROOF FEEDER**

There are many excellent squirrel-proof feeders. Most consist of a large cylinder with large portals designed to hold sunflower or seed mixes and have a mechanism that prevents a squirrel from accessing the seed. This mechanism may be a cage that surrounds the whole feeder that a squirrel cannot get through, a device that closes over the portal opening when a squirrel puts its weight on the landing perch, or the perch itself collapses under the weight of a squirrel. There are also hopper feeders that close the seed opening when a squirrel (but not a lighter-weight bird) lands on the perch. When hanging a squirrel-proof feeder from a pole, make sure it is out far enough from the pole that the squirrel cannot hold on to the pole with its back legs and only lightly put weight on the perch, which then does not trigger the mechanism to close the portal.

**INSTALL A SQUIRREL BAFFLE**

One of the best ways to deal with squirrels is to mount feeders either on top of or hanging from a pole and install a baffle on the pole below and close to the feeder to prevent squirrels from climbing up. Baffles come as a metal skirt or a metal stove pipe. The most important thing is to place the pole and feeders at least 12–15 feet or more from any place a squirrel could jump from!

If a feeder is hung from a wire or tree branch, a plastic dome-type baffle can be placed above the feeder to prevent the squirrel from climbing down to it. Just make sure the squirrel cannot jump from the ground up, or from a tree branch below the height of the baffle to the feeder.

**HAVE FUN WITH SQUIRREL DIVERSION**

Divert squirrels by giving them their own food away from the bird feeder—fun for squirrels, and entertainment for you! There is an endless array of cute styles of squirrel feeders, ranging from miniature picnic tables with a spike to hold a corn cob, to "squirrel boxes" that the squirrel learns to open, to rotating arms that hold corn cobs. Foods can include cracked corn, corn cobs, peanuts, and squirrel seed mixes.

**HOT AND SPICY**

Squirrel-deterring birdseed mixes are treated with hot pepper (which contains capsaicin) that theoretically squirrels don't like but birds can tolerate. However, there are many reports of squirrels not minding the taste and eating the seed. Few studies have been done on how capsaicin might affect birds. When we handle the treated seed, the hot pepper can get on our hands and could be a problem if it reaches our eyes or mouth. The preferred methods of deterring squirrels are using baffles and squirrel-proof feeders.

### *FINCH SAFETY AT FEEDERS*

**CLEAN, CLEAN, CLEAN!**

The best defense is a good offense. One of the best things you can do to keep birds safe is to clean your feeders and baths. Birds can transfer diseases to each other through droppings in food and water, direct contact, or even surfaces they have touched. Clean your feeders at least every two weeks or more often in summer. Use a mild dish detergent or, to more thoroughly disinfect, use one part bleach to nine to ten parts warm water or a mild 10% vinegar solution. Rinse well and let dry before refilling. Wear rubber gloves and wash your hands when handling bird feeders. Note: If you see any sick or dead birds at your feeders, take feeders down for several weeks or more to let sick birds disperse. Thoroughly disinfect feeders, rinse, and dry. Clean up seeds and shells under the feeder.

Purple Finches at feeder with seed mix

**PREVENT WINDOW STRIKES**

Bird collisions with glass are a significant cause of bird mortality, killing up to 1 billion birds in the United States yearly. Birds see the reflection of trees and sky in windows and fly into them. To prevent this, feeders can be moved away from windows and there are many effective products and solutions for homeowners that break up or cover the reflection on windows, usually placed on the outside of the glass. These include fiberglass screens, grids of tape or cords, window films, and closely spaced translucent UV decals. There are even options for bird-friendly glass for new or replacement windows. For more information, see abcbirds.org/solutions/prevent-home-collisions/.

**PREVENT DISEASE**

For the health of your backyard birds, keep those feeders clean. Do not handle sick birds. Do not handle dead birds without gloves. Report sick or dead birds to your local nature center or bird organization or Project FeederWatch. Note: It is illegal to possess wild birds without a permit, so do not attempt to keep sick birds or any other wild birds. These are the three main finch diseases:

### *Mycoplasmal conjunctivitis*

House Finch with mycoplasmal conjunctivitis

Often called House Finch eye disease because House Finches are so susceptible, it also can occur in goldfinches, Purple Finches, and Evening and Pine Grosbeaks. It is caused by the bacterium *Mycoplasma gallisepticum*, a pathogen found in domestic poultry. Discovered in the winter of 1993–1994, the disease spread rapidly in the eastern population of House Finches, severely impacting them, although they eventually somewhat recovered. In 2006 it spread to western House Finches. Symptoms are swollen, crusty, runny eyes that then shut, making the bird blind and susceptible to starvation or predators. A few birds may recover. Researchers in 2018 discovered the pathogen that caused House Finch eye disease has strengthened, even more reason to practice feeder safety.[4] This disease is strictly avian and will not affect humans or other mammals.

### *Salmonellosis*

This disease caused by *Salmonella* bacteria is transmitted from bird to bird through droppings and saliva. Pine Siskins are highly susceptible. Infected birds are tame and lethargic with ruffled feathers and swollen eyes. It can be transmitted to humans through direct contact with sick birds and their droppings, so wear gloves and wash your hands after handling feeders.

### *Trichomonosis*

Also known as trichomoniasis, canker, or frounce, this disease is caused by a protozoan parasite. It is usually found in Mourning Doves, wild pigeons, and birds of prey but can occur in other birds. In North American finches, it was first documented in 2007 and mainly affects Purple Finches and American Goldfinches found in the Canadian Maritime Provinces. Since 2005 it also has severely impacted greenfinches and chaffinches in the United Kingdom. It affects the crop and esophagus but can also affect other parts of the bird's body. Symptoms are fluffed-up feathers, lethargy, difficulty swallowing and closing the mouth, swollen neck, drooling or matted wet plumage on face, or regurgitated food around mouth. It is transmitted through food and water contaminated with saliva from infected birds, and also through regurgitation when they feed their young. This disease does not affect humans or pets. It is recommended that feeders be removed during a known outbreak. It is more common in summer than winter.

Large property with finch gardens and finch habitat

## GARDENING FOR FINCHES

Even a few planters on a patio can attract American Goldfinches

Whether your yard is a forty-acre landscape or planters on a patio, deck, or porch, there are many ways you can attract finches. Enhance your property with flowers that produce seeds, and trees and shrubs that produce seeds, fruits, cover, and structure for nesting. When possible, choose native species (get lists from your local agricultural or conservation organization) and avoid invasive species. Practice organic gardening and do not use pesticides. Most plants and flowers require sunlight to grow, so place them in sunny areas. If possible, let an area of lawn grow wild and tall to produce seeds; there may already be seed-producing wildflowers and grasses there that would attract finches. Mow at the very end of the season to keep out shrubs.

Following are some top finch-friendly blooms, trees, and shrubs.[5] For a more complete list, consult native plant groups, nurseries, or bird education and conservation organizations in your area.

Purple coneflower (*Echinacea purpurea*)

### *FLOWERS*

The main attractions of flowers are seeds for eating and fluff for goldfinch nests. Leave flower heads up as long as possible once they go to seed.

- Aster (*Aster* spp.)
- Black-eyed susan (*Rudbeckia* spp.)
- Blazing star (*Liatris* spp.)
- Coneflower (*Echinacea* spp.)
- Coreopsis (*Coreopsis* spp.)
- Cornflower (*Centaurea cyanus*)
- Cosmos (*Cosmos* spp.)
- Globe thistle (*Echinops* spp.)
- Goldenrod (*Solidago* spp.)
- Joe-pye weed (*Eupatorium* spp.)
- Marigold (*Tagetes* spp.)
- Mexican sunflower (*Tithonia rotundifolia*)
- Native thistle (*Cirsium* spp.) To make sure it's native, obtain it from a native plant nursery or organization.
- Sunflower (*Helianthus* spp.)
- Verbena (*Verbena bonariensis*)
- Zinnia (*Zinnia* spp.)

Grow sunflower for finches

American Goldfinch eating seeds of purple coneflower

## *TREES*

### SEED TREES

- Ash (*Fraxinus* spp.)
- Birch (*Betula* spp.)
- Fir (*Abies* spp.)
- Hemlock (*Tsuga* spp.)
- Larch (*Larix* spp.)
- Maple/box elder (*Acer* spp.)
- Pine (*Pinus* spp.)
- Spruce (*Abies* spp.)

### FRUIT TREES

- Cherry (*Prunus* spp.)
- Crabapple (*Malus* spp.)
- Dogwood (*Cornus* spp.)
- Hackberry (*Celtis* spp.)
- Hawthorn (*Crataegus* spp.)
- Mountain ash (*Sorbus* spp.)

### SHRUBS

- Agarita (*Mahonia trifoliolata*)
- Alder (*Alnus* spp.)
- Blackberry/raspberry (*Rubus* spp.)
- Blueberry (*Vaccinium* spp.)
- Dogwood (*Cornus* spp.)
- Elderberry (*Sambucus* spp.)
- Juniper (*Juniperus* spp.)
- Shadbush/serviceberry (*Amelanchier* spp.)
- Winterberry holly (*Ilex verticillata*)

Evening Grosbeak on spruce

Pine Grosbeak on crabapple

House Finch on agarita (*Mahonia trifoliolata*) shrub

Common Redpoll on alder

## TEN TIPS FOR FEEDING FINCHES

- Keep feeders full and keep multiple feeders near one another. Finches are flock species that like to feed together.
- Place feeders where you can enjoy them out your window.
- Keep binoculars and a field guide near the window for great looks and ID help.
- Store seed in closed containers in a cool place.
- Place feeders near cover so birds can hide from predators.
- Choose easy-to-clean feeders.
- Buy clean seeds free of sticks and debris.
- Take photos of feeder birds and share them.
- Finchscape your yard with plants that attract finches.
- Get kids involved in bird feeding.

Evening Grosbeaks in flight

# MOVEMENTS AND IRRUPTIONS

*It can be a long winter without finches around. During the dark cold days of winter, the colorful winter finches are a welcome sight to our backyards.*

—Ron Pittaway

It started on a midsummer day in the Adirondacks of New York while doing field work with noted crossbill researcher Jeff Groth, and Matt witnessed a number of Purple Finches moving in one direction southward. He wondered, Is that just local movement or are Purple Finches already moving or irrupting?

## WHAT IS AN IRRUPTION?

What is a "finch irruption"? Its simplest definition is when finches migrate out of the northern or montane areas they normally inhabit (boreal or coniferous forests across North America) and move into the very southern parts of their wintering range and beyond. Irruptions are facultative migrations; finches move some years but not others depending on food supplies, weather conditions, and population size. This is different from seasonal migrations, called obligate migration, which, according to Ian Newton "is considered 'hard-wired' in that the bird seems pre-programmed to leave its breeding area at a certain time each year, and to return at another time."[1] Think of irruptions as a "push-pull" system. Finches are pushed out of their area because of high population size and not enough food to support the population, and are pulled to make large-scale long-distance movements to relocate to another area where climate conditions have produced better food supplies.[2] Finches often appear to have uncanny abilities to know where to go. For a superflight to happen, there must be a widespread failure of food across much of their entire range, and it is during these years that nearly all of the irruptive finches move at once.

Not all finches make large-scale irruptions. Our common feeder finches, such as American Goldfinches, may make some minor migration but are often regular year-round in an area and delight us at our bird feeders. However, there is nothing like the excitement of seeing beautiful and rare northern finches such as Pine Grosbeaks and Hoary Redpolls driven to us by an irruption; that thrill erases any chill of a "bleak and gray" season. But for the finches, irruptions are serious business. Finding food for survival is their mission.

How and when do irruptions occur?

## THE DIFFERING IRRUPTIVE LANDSCAPES

### *WESTERN NORTH AMERICA*

Irruptions appear to be driven mostly by topography, which drives more microscale climatic patterns of precipitation that are tied to cone-crop production. These irruptions, or elevational movements, happen on a small scale, which makes them less noticeable or detectable. Western North America is dominated by mostly montane coniferous forests, from Yukon Territory and British Columbia to the southern United States, habitat used by many finch species, from crossbills, to grosbeaks, to the rosy-finches, and more. House Finches, and to a lesser degree the goldfinches, avoid conifer-dominated habitats. Some species like the rosy-finches and Pine and Evening Grosbeaks are most often found at elevation, and they only irrupt or move down into the valleys in the West in winter. These elevational movements are less obvious to detect except on a local scale.

### *EASTERN NORTH AMERICA*

Eastern North America isn't nearly as mountainous, and coniferous forests aren't nearly as extensive as those found in the West. Additionally, many songbirds found in the vast conifer-dominated boreal forest of Canada move from northwest to southeast, and therefore many naturally migrate through the eastern United States, staying east of the western mountains. In short, large-scale irruptions or movements are much more easily detected in the eastern part of the continent, hence why the Winter Finch Forecast first put out by Ron Pittaway, then Tyler Hoar and the Finch Research Network, has mostly focused on the eastern half of the United States and Canada from the upper Midwest and the Great Lakes eastward. It is also worth noting that there are more people to detect the birds in these more populated areas.

## THE MECHANISMS THAT DRIVE IRRUPTIONS

Finch irruptions can vary from year to year, and the winter locations of finches can be unpredictable depending on where the best food crops are. It is this interplay between population numbers and available food that drives these irregular incursions southward, but it's hard to know exactly how much one is driving the other.[3]

The primary mechanisms that drive these movements vary across species as well, depending on what that species eats—conifer seeds, deciduous seeds, or fruit. Crossbill movements are driven by cone crops. When there are great cone crops, crossbills will nest, even during winter when snow blankets the landscape, sometimes raising brood after brood in succession.[4] When these crops fail, crossbills have little choice but to move. Other species like redpolls are much more driven by willow, alder, and birch catkin crops, and when these produce plentiful crops they raise young with ease and stay in their preferred northern habitats across Canada. If the alder and birch crops fail, redpolls flood southern Canada and the northern-tier United States. Pine Grosbeaks are often tied to mountain-ash crops and other fruiting trees, and when these fail to produce fruit, Pine Grosbeaks come south as well. The cycles of good birch, alder, mountain ash, and conifer seed crops appear more regularly, occurring at intervals of every few years.

Red Crossbill, male

## PRIMARY DRIVERS OF WINTER FINCH IRRUPTIONS

### Conifer seeds

Red Crossbill

White-winged Crossbill

Pine Siskin

Common Redpoll

Evening Grosbeak

Purple Finch

### Deciduous seeds

Pine Siskin

Common Redpoll

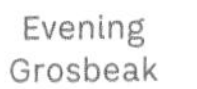

Evening Grosbeak

Purple Finch

### Fruit seeds

Pine Grosbeak

Pine Grosbeak, male on crabapples

With other species, irruptions are even more dynamic. Evening Grosbeaks, Purple Finches, and, to a lesser degree, Pine Siskins are known to be tied to spruce budworm outbreaks. These outbreaks can last for 10–20 years, with periods in between of little to no outbreaks sometimes lasting even longer. The outbreaks can kill conifers and thus cause widespread dieback of good finch breeding habitat, which can drive the finches less dependent on budworm, like the crossbills and Pine Grosbeak, southward. But these spruce budworm outbreaks also produce a protein-rich food source for nesting Evening Grosbeaks, Purple Finches, and other birds. Big budworm outbreaks lead to an increase in Evening Grosbeak and Purple Finch populations, which appears to increase the chances of them irrupting southward.

Interestingly, the sexes also appear to differentially migrate, with adult males staying more north, closer to their breeding grounds—it's not uncommon to see flocks of thirty to forty Evening Grosbeaks, especially when they first invade an area, to consist of only a handful or two of adult males. The sex differential can some years be even more dramatic for Pine Grosbeaks. During the superflight of 2020–2021, Matt viewed almost two hundred Pine Grosbeaks in three days from Brunswick, New York, to Bennington, Vermont, to Queensbury, New York, and points in between, and only five adult males were observed. But two years later in 2022–2023 on a trip to the Adirondacks, the ratio of adult males to the females/immatures was closer to one male to every four birds.

Given that their irruptions are driven by a combination of tree and conifer seed abundance and spruce budworm outbreaks, Evening Grosbeaks and Purple Finches tend to irrupt together. The Crossbills, both Red and White-winged, tend to irrupt together given their more obligate conifer seed-eating ways. The redpolls, driven most years by birch and alder crops, move together. And Pine Siskins, the generalists of the group, can irrupt with any of the above species.

## HISTORY OF IRRUPTIONS

### 1850–1959

For the charismatic Evening Grosbeak, the first noted irruption described at length in the literature was in 1854 when they were documented east of the Great Lakes to Toronto.[5] Additional eastward movements were well documented in 1878 and 1886–1887, but it wasn't until 1889–1890 that Evening Grosbeaks appeared in East Coast states. Invasions of the more tame but equally beautiful Pine Grosbeak are documented more than 125 years ago when they irrupted into southern parts of their wintering range in New England during the winters of 1869–1870, 1874–1875, 1892–1893, 1903–1904. A study by Spiers in 1939,[6] also from the Toronto area, finds Pine Grosbeak irruptions occurring at intervals of five to six years, and the same for the New England states during 1900–1950. From 1850 to 1932, flights of Red Crossbills to the East Coast were documented in 1850, 1870, 1875, 1882, 1884, 1887, 1896, 1900, 1903, 1907, 1919, and 1932.[7] Type 3 would be the most likely involved in these flights.

Major irruptions of Pine Siskins have not been noted as much, but their unpredictable appearances are mentioned. Redpoll movements are not well chronicled, though a noticeably large eastern flight was reported in 1947. During this time frame Evening Grosbeak irruptions continued to pick up, with flights becoming

Evening Grosbeak, male

biennial events by the 1940s, and East Coast states documenting breeding for the first time during the spruce budworm outbreak of 1945–1955.

### 1960–2000

Another spruce budworm outbreak, the largest of the twentieth century, raged on for as long as twenty years in the East, from 1965 to at least 1985. As the ornithological record-keeping process grew, it was easier to note when large finch irruptions took place synchronously. During the late 1960s through 1981, several "finch superflights" occurred, defined as years when at least seven of the eastern finches move en masse into the southern part of their wintering range.

From 1960–2000, eight superflight years were documented—1969, 1976, 1978, 1981, 1996, 1998—with eight species irrupting in 1972, and all nine species irrupting in 1970.[8] During this peak of the 1965–1985 spruce budworm outbreak, six of the eight superflights occurred in just thirteen years! In fact, six of the known ten superflights from 1960–2023 occurred between 1969 and 1981. It was also during this time period when the northeastern states saw their biggest movements of Boreal Chickadees and Black-backed Woodpeckers.[9]

### 2001–2023

As the popularity of the Winter Finch Forecast, which started in 1999, grew, eastern irruptions in general became small and more spaced.[10] From 1999 to 2013, a period of fifteen years, no superflights were reported until one occurred in 2013, and another again in 2021.[11] Not surprisingly, it was around 2014 when budworm outbreaks started occurring again in areas of the boreal forest in Quebec (Tyler Hoar, personal communication).

Purple Finch, male

Food crops tend to fluctuate on an every-other-year boom-bust cycle, with better than average crops forming one year and less than average crops produced the following year. Several factors need to come together for a finch superflight to materialize: higher population numbers across most or all of the finches; a year that finches are cyclically expected to irrupt due to the boom-bust cycle of crops forming; then wild cards like budworm outbreaks or ice storms that can help force the synchronization of species moving south in the same year.

Given the above conditions, some suites of species irrupt more with other species than not. Crossbills tend to be on their own cycles, and also Pine Grosbeaks, which are driven to an extent by fruiting crops of mountain ash and other trees. Evening Grosbeaks and Purple Finches tend to be driven by budworm outbreaks, and therefore irrupt together. The two redpoll species usually irrupt together, and the generalist Pine Siskin shares similarities with all the other species.

Common Redpoll, male

Leading up to the 2020–2021 superflight, there was an unusually large (once-in-a-generation or 20-year) cone crop across much of the eastern boreal forest in 2019–2020, which led to high reproductive success of both crossbill species and Pine Siskin. A continually expanded budworm outbreak was also occurring in the eastern boreal region, and populations of Evening Grosbeaks and Purple Finches were on the upswing for the first time in decades. It's hard to know exactly what drove the redpolls and Pine Grosbeaks to also irrupt south during the winter of 2021, but the likely cause was reduced fruit and alder/birch seed crops.

The 2020–2021 superflight will go down as the best in more than a generation, with the best redpoll flight in a decade materializing from the Great Lakes to the East Coast, and the best flight of Evening Grosbeaks, when a few birds were found all the way to Florida for the first time in more than thirty years. Pine Siskins were so numerous that, as stated in this book's Pine Siskin account, *Audubon Magazine* ran an article that said "they had taken over the country." Red Crossbills, particularly the newly described Northeastern Type 12, had first records coming from several southern states, and breeding was first confirmed in Pennsylvania. Purple Finches were found to the Gulf Coast by the end of October, with some occurring as far south as central Florida. And lastly, Pine Grosbeaks were seen in eastern New York and Connecticut in numbers for the first time since 2008.

The superflight irruption of finches in 2020–2021, though presumably a difficult event for finches, was a once-in-a-lifetime highlight for many birders as COVID kept us from connecting with one another. It brought the power of connection to birds and nature that helped us navigate that stressful time. Superflights will again occur, bringing magic to birders, but the mystery of when they will occur continues.

Evening Grosbeak, male

# RESEARCH AND CONSERVATION

*Will wings be enough?*
—Lillian Quinn Stokes

Today's threats to birds are many, and the list is only growing. Nearly three billion birds have been lost on the continent since the 1970s, according to a 2019 article in *Science* written with first author Ken Rosenberg, a research scientist at the Cornell Lab of Ornithology, and many others.[1] The alarm bells rang loud and clear especially within the research and conservation communities. What was particularly alarming were the massive losses chronicled across common species, including our beloved finches. One billion of those birds were lost across forest habitats that most finches call home.[2] Such a magnitude of loss among previously common species is a characteristic of an ongoing wave of potential extinction.

Vital research is needed to understand these losses and what we can do to help these species. Conservation is where the research rubber meets the road and where we can actually try to make a positive impact on turning around these trends.

At the top of the finch research and conservation list would be the finches of Hawai'i (a.k.a. the honeycreepers), the mountaintop-breeding rosy-finches, and the iconic Evening Grosbeak. Once a group of more than fifty species, now only about sixteen species of honeycreeper exist today, with some of them hanging in the balance if we don't do something immediately. Of the rosy-finches, the southern mountaintop-breeding Black and Brown-capped are especially imperiled due to climate change. The beloved Evening Grosbeak, a once-abundant sunflower-chomping bird feeder species, has seen the steepest decline of any species in North America—92% lost since 1970![3] Many organizations, including the Finch Research Network (FiRN), are interested in conserving these finch species.

## HAWAI'I'S FINCHES: THE HONEYCREEPERS

Flying under the radar are the beautiful finches of Hawai'i, known as the honeycreepers, a group that landed in Hawai'i some five to seven million years ago, adaptively radiated to over fifty new finch species, and now are down to only about sixteen species, some critically endangered (read more about this in the Hawaiian Honeycreepers chapter). Their declines are due to many factors: introduced predators such as rats and feral cats; goats and pigs that destroy habitat; introduced plants that degrade habitat by forming monocultures; avian pox virus; and the introduced house mosquito that carries deadly avian malaria. It's an all-hands-on-deck situation, but if we act now, some of the species can likely be saved. Conservationist groups and universities such as the American Bird Conservancy (ABC), Maui and Kaua'i Forest Bird Recovery Projects, the University of Hawai'i, and other agencies and organizations have rallied and are trying to implement creative solutions to save these magnificent birds. The two forest bird recovery teams are fast working on two high-profile captive conservation breeding and release programs. Over the last several years they've been the key players in saving the 'Akikiki and 'Akeke'e after population trends documented in 2012 surveys illustrated that extinction was imminent.[4] They are now investigating whether to translocate 'Akeke'es to higher elevations given that avian malaria is marching upslope as the climate continues to warm. As of January 2024, the 'Akikiki has become functionally extinct in the wild.

In addition to important duties such as habitat management on Maui and forest bird monitoring across the islands, the Maui Forest Bird Recovery Project is helping lead the efforts on saving the Kiwikiu (a.k.a. Maui Parrotbill). The critically endangered Kiwikiu, once found across much of Maui and Moloka'i, is now limited to eleven square miles of

Hawai'i 'Akepa, male

wet rainforest on windward east Maui. Its historic range covered multiple forested habitat types from high-elevation wet forests to lowland dry forests, but its range is now on the windward slopes of Haleakalā volcano, from the Nature Conservancy's Waikamoi Preserve in the east to the Manawainui Planeze in Haleakalā National Park. After a failed translocation and reintroduction attempt to Nakula Natural Area Reserve in 2019, it was determined that mosquitoes had invaded the area and the released birds (seven from the wild and seven from the captive breeding program) succumbed to avian malaria.

The initial introductions of avian malaria can be traced back to the early 1900s and led to honeycreeper declines and extinctions of multiple Hawaiian honeycreepers.[5] Fortunately, these impacts have largely been limited to birds living in habitats at low elevations because the malaria vector, the *Culex* mosquito, is cold intolerant, and development of malaria parasites is hampered in cold environments.[6] However, as temperatures increase and weather patterns become more variable with climate change, avian malaria threatens to invade the high-elevation refugia.[7]

'Akeke'e, male

"Birds, Not Mosquitoes" is a multiagency partnership initiative led by the American Bird Conservancy. They plan to use common, naturally occurring *Wolbachia* bacteria as "mosquito birth control" to suppress mosquito populations in Hawai'i. By introducing male mosquitoes with an incompatible *Wolbachia* stomach bacteria, females that mate with them will lay infertile eggs, thereby decreasing the density of mosquitoes on the islands.[8] The ABC and partners have been working hard to save these wonderful and unique birds. Some of the funding is in place to help release sterilized mosquitoes in 2024. At the end of 2023, a dozen researchers from the Kaua'i Forest Bird Recovery Project started to release incompatible male mosquitoes as part of pilot study to try to stop the extinction of four Native Hawaiian honeycreepers on the Alaka'i Plateau on Kaua'i. Raising awareness and securing funding will be key to all of the many conservation efforts to save the honeycreepers.

The University of Hawai'i, local conservationist Jack Jeffrey, and others are working on funding to preserve the Hakalau Forest, the last large, intact, high-altitude forest in Hawai'i, as this might end up being the last refuge to release any remaining honeycreeper species. There's also interest in engineering a GMO mosquito, which might be needed if current conservation efforts aren't as successful as hoped.

FiRN and Nathan Goldberg are helping to bring more awareness to the critical honeycreeper situation by offering presentations to organizations, agencies, and bird and nature groups across the continent.

Black Rosy-Finch, male

## THE ROSY-FINCH PROJECT

The stunningly beautiful rosy-finches are difficult to study because they nest in nearly inaccessible crags at high elevation, and their wandering winter flocks can be unpredictable. The Rosy-Finch Project is interested in all rosy-finches with an emphasis on the Black Rosy-Finch and Brown-capped Rosy-Finch because they are identified by the US Fish and Wildlife Service as Species of Concern. The IUCN also lists both the Black Rosy-Finch and Brown-capped Rosy-Finch as Endangered.

The Working Group formed in 2021 to expand collaboration and coordination among researchers, managers, and interested parties and to help fill in significant data gaps. This group has expanded to 85 members and helps address species research and conservation objectives. Group facilitators have included Janice Gardner of the Sageland Collaborative and Carl Brown from Biodiversity Research Institute, with chairperson Tempe Regan of the Idaho Department of Fish and Game. The project aims to address some of the following topics:

1. Seek funding to implement projects based on needs.

2. Develop strategies to conserve Rosy-Finches and their habitats.

3. Provide a forum of experts to respond to information needs.

4. Engage diverse stakeholders (such as scientists, managers, locals, and policymakers) using co-production and social science.

To date the group has:

- Developed a standardized rosy-finch monitoring protocol to address knowledge gaps in demographics.
- Coordinated and expanded winter banding and feeder watch programs.
- Used a Structured Decision Making process to help identify and rank potential conservation efforts.

## THE INTERNATIONAL EVENING GROSBEAK ROAD TO RECOVERY PROJECT

With a 92% decline since 1970, the Evening Grosbeak (*Coccothraustes vespertinus*) was cited as the steepest declining landbird in the continental United States and Canada in the Partners in Flight 2016 Landbird Conservation Plan. Causes for the decline are not fully understood, but may be a result of several factors, including spruce budworm (*Choristoneura* spp.) population cycles, forest alteration and loss, collision and disease mortalities, and climate change factors. Following several conservation listings, the Evening Grosbeak has garnered attention from the recently formed Road to Recovery (R2R) Initiative as it was called out as one of ninety-one bird species who are a tipping point species.[10]

In 2017, ornithologists from the Pennsylvania Natural Heritage Program at the Western Pennsylvania Conservancy (WPC) and Powdermill Avian Research Center at the Carnegie Museum of Natural History (CMNH) initiated the first migratory connectivity and tracking study on Evening Grosbeaks. This project aims to shed light on the species' annual cycle, local and widescale use of the landscape and habitats, linkages between winter and breeding populations, survival, and winter site fidelity.

This research was further bolstered in 2021 when WPC and CMNH teamed with the Finch Research Network to expand the scope of their Evening Grosbeak project and secured additional resources from the Knobloch Family Foundation through the Road to Recovery bird conservation initiative. Over the next few years, WPC, CMNH, and FiRN will collaborate to create an Evening Grosbeak Working Group focused specifically on developing conservation strategies and needs. As part of outreach for the project, FiRN has installed a feedercam with the help of Josh Stasik at Aspen Song Wild Bird Feed and Bill Sheehan in Woodland, Maine. See youtube.com/@FinchResearchNetwork/streams.

Evening Grosbeak, male

Evening Grosbeak, female

During the winters of 2021-22, 2022-23, and 2023-24, members of our team ventured into the field at Sax Zim Bog (Minnesota), Allegheny National Forest (Pennsylvania), the state forests of central New York and the Adirondacks of northern New York, and the northern Maine woods to study Evening Grosbeaks. As of winter 2024, we've color-banded 284 birds and deployed 55 satellite tags and 85 nanotags.

In order to address its rapid decline, additional study is needed to better understand the Evening Grosbeak's full annual cycle ecology—breeding, irruptive migration, and wintering—and identify limiting factors for its population. The overall need is to look into population declines, assortative mating, morphometrics, flight call variations, and genetics for all call types, but especially Type 1, which regularly overlaps with Types 2 and 4 and occasionally the other call types. Please contribute by recording Evening Grosbeaks wherever you encounter them, especially in the West, and then upload the recordings to eBird, Macaulay Library, or Xeno Canto. Smartphone recordings will work too if you don't have professional gear. The researchers plan to fundraise to continue to study and answer these main questions:

1. What is causing the declines? Disease, changes in habitat, climate change, collisions with cars, window strikes at feeder stations, pest outbreaks, logging, pest control, reduced survival and breeding due to neonics or some combination of these?

2. To what extent will Type 1 irrupt from year to year? Distance? Quantity?

3. How geographically isolated are the call types during the breeding season?

4. Do the call types overlap in parts of their range but only breed with the same type?

5. What other, more complex things may be happening on the breeding and wintering grounds?

More on the Evening Grosbeak Road to Recovery Project can be found on the FiRN website: finchnetwork.org/projects.

## RESEARCH TOPICS OF INTEREST ACROSS THE FRINGILLID FINCHES

1. On the topic of vocalizations or call types, calls given while in flight appear to be markers of such intraspecific diversity in certain bird lineages. The classic case of cryptic within-species diversity despite relatively minor variation in plumage is the Red Crossbill, where Type 9 has been recognized, at least for now, as a new species, the Cassia Crossbill. Could Type 1 and 2 Evening Grosbeaks possibly be different species? Have Type 1 and 2 Purple Finches diverged enough to be recognized at the species level? Is the same phenomenon going on across Eurasia with some finch species?

2. How much do Hoary and Common Redpolls, the three rosy-finches, and the Red Crossbill and Evening Grosbeak call types assortatively mate under changing environmental conditions? The latest genetic studies appear to show that the redpolls are one species, that there's a gene expression button pushed that makes birds lighter and frostier,[11] but we don't know to what level Common and Hoary Redpolls assortatively mate.

Red Crossbill, male

3. Additional genetic studies could also possibly reveal new species. The Pine Grosbeak on Haida Gwai might be monophyletic.[12] Could the same be happening with rosy-finches on the Alaskan islands? Has there been enough recent genetic work done on the two very different-looking Lesser Goldfinch subspecies, the nominate subspecies *psaltria* (the "Black-backed" Lesser Goldfinch) and subspecies *hesperophilus* (the "Green-backed" Lesser Goldfinch)? They appear to

possibly breed, molt, and perhaps migrate at different times of the year and are some of the least studied finches. Do we know if there are other cryptic finch species existing right under our noses, especially in Eurasia?

Lesser Goldfinch, male

4. The rosy-finch is for sure a very difficult species to study given its "cloudland" habitats. Why does it have a skewed sex ratio, with more males? This seems to be particularly evident, at least according to historical studies, in the "Aleutian" Gray-crowned Rosy-Finch. This also seems to exist in several other finches, from the rosy-finches to the Purple Finch to crossbills and the Evening Grosbeak. Could it be because of difference in behaviors, or is it something else, such as female survivorship compared with male survivorship?

5. Song: Mimicry or imitation appears to exist across several finch species. Why is this the case for Pine Siskin, Lesser Goldfinch, Lawrence's Goldfinch, Pine Grosbeak, Purple Finch, Cassin's Finch, and, to a degree, the crossbills, but not for the House Finch and American Goldfinch? And then there's the Evening Grosbeak, which has a vocalization that scientists even to this day are not 100% certain would be classified as a song. Song development and learning; open-ended versus critical-period learning; acquisition and function of imitated sounds are all areas that could be studied. There is also the issue of how much and under what conditions female finches sing, with more study needed.

6. How does logging affect species from area to area? It would seem to affect most finch species in deleterious ways, especially the crossbills, which rely on older growth trees that are more reliable at producing cone crops from year to year.[13]

7. What causes individuals of species with less fixed breeding periods, such as opportunistic breeders like crossbills and Pine Siskin, to decide to migrate to another area or stay to breed?[14]

8. It is thought that the main driving mechanism for finch irruptions is the interplay between population size and available food crops to support those populations as summer changes to fall and fall changes to winter. Do we know all the mechanisms driving these irruptions? Is climate change having an effect on them?

9. In how many species of fringillid finches do we see and hear females singing? How common is it, and what is its function?[15]

10. Overarching all the finch species is climate change, the existential threat of our time. How does climate change affect survivability and reproductive success (and timing of nesting for crossbills and siskins) of finches? How might warming trends decimate existing finch habitats? Does climate change cause more ice storms or rain events, which make it much harder for birds to thermoregulate, thus making it harder for crossbills and the Pine Siskin to breed during the colder months? Are increased forest fires and pest outbreaks leading to additive declines in some species? The Cassia Crossbill lives in an extremely restricted geographic area, and in the summer of 2020 as much as 40% of its habitat burned. Has climate change affected food crops in a way that trees produce less reliable food crops from year to year, making it harder to survive and breed? The Winter Finch Forecast put out by Tyler Hoar and the Finch Research Network hopes to expand the Winter Finch Forecasting Network as a way to hopefully better predict future irruptions of winter finches.

## HOW YOU CAN HELP

1. Be a citizen scientist. Please continue to record finches. Field recordings of Red Crossbills, Evening Grosbeaks, and other finches from around the world will add substantially to research and our understanding of their distribution, abundance, movements, vocalization repertoire, and more, and already has. This has been made possible with the help of all the scientists, birders, outdoor enthusiasts, sound recordists, and citizen scientists like you who are reading this book. Many of the recordings were taken by citizen scientists with smartphones, so don't think you can't be part of the growing "Finch Network" started by Ron Pittaway, the original Finch Forecaster here in North America, and by Ian Newton, author of the iconic book *Finches*, penned back in 1973. The Finch Research Network is dedicated to helping save the above species, and forming collaborative relationships with all the organizations and peoples listed in this book to help do so.

House Finch, female

2. Contribute your recordings and sightings to programs like Macaulay Library (macaulaylibrary.org) and Xeno-Canto (xeno-canto.org) and to projects like Merlin and BirdNet at the Cornell Lab of Ornithology (birds.cornell.edu).

3. Support and contribute to the many conservation and research organizations we have mentioned and others who work at local and national levels to conserve birds and their habitats.

4. Practice respect for birds and their existing environments, and educate others.

5. Enjoy finches and keep them safe at feeders (see the Feeding and Attracting chapter).

6. Participate in citizen-science projects at the local, state, and national level.

7. Join iNaturalist projects, the Finch Forecast Food Assessment: Become a Finch Forecaster and Red Crossbill and Evening Grosbeak Foraging Projects.

8. Given that watching birds can boost your overall mental health, adopt a Wellness for Finches, Wellness for You approach.

---

Finches may be more adaptable and resilient than we know, but will wings be enough to allow them to fly to better places to survive? The real question is if people will do enough to help them. The power of our connection to the beautiful finches and other birds we share the planet with is essential to our well-being, a concept dear to Lillian and Matt's hearts. If we all work together to save finches, it may just be enough—not only to save them, but also to save the planet's natural history.

# Acknowledgments

No book of this magnitude gets done without relying on the work of hundreds of people. We would first of all like to thank the many scientists, researchers, citizen-scientists, finch lovers, and others who over the years collected the information on which this book rests. It would not exist without them.

We would also like to thank our wonderful publishing team at Little, Brown and Company for accepting and producing this book: our editor Terry Adams, vice president, digital and paperback publisher; copyeditor Laura Whittemore; and designers Laura Lindgren, who created the initial beautiful design, and Ashley Prine of Tandem Books, who completed, enhanced, and brought it to fruition. A special shout-out goes to our cheerful and highly skilled production editor, Pat Jalbert-Levine, who always kept things progressing. We also thank Nyamekye Waliyaya, our production director, who oversaw the design work and the complex final production and printing steps.

We are grateful to our team of expert readers who took the time to carefully review the manuscript before it went to print and whose excellent suggestions helped improve the book: John C. Kricher read the entire manuscript; Tom Hahn read the Evening Grosbeak, Red Crossbill, Cassia Crossbill, White-winged Crossbill, Cassin's Finch, and Black, Brown-capped, and Gray-crowned Rosy-Finch accounts; Paul G. Rodewald read the Evening Grosbeak, Black Rosy-Finch, Purple Finch, Pine Siskin, Lesser Goldfinch, Lawrence's Goldfinch, and American Goldfinch accounts; W. Douglas Robinson read the Pine Grosbeak, Purple Finch, House Finch, Common Redpoll, and Hoary Redpoll accounts; Julie A. Craves read the European Goldfinch account; and H. Douglass Pratt read the Hawaiian Honeycreeper accounts.

In addition, we would like to thank others who contributed to the book in any way, especially those who significantly gave support, advice, information, and help in finding finches, and, in some cases, who went above and beyond what was asked of them: Meade Cadot (who led Lillian to the Red Crossbills in the first place), Tracy Behar, Sy Montgomery, Timothy Spahr, Tyler Hoar, Bill Sheehan, Nathan Pieplow, Josh Stasik, Bill Hilton, Shawn Carey, Ryan F. Mandelbaum, Ian Cruickshank, Patrick Franke, Matt Carey, Blair Dudeck, David Deifik, Jesse Roy Drainville, Debi Love Shearwater, Stephen Cox, Brian Small, Mark Guyt, Jack Jeffrey, Yve Morrill, Nicholas M. Anich, Joe Gyekis, Ryan Brady, Holger Klinck, Lynne Spriggs-O'Connor, Lisa Crupe, William R. Evans, Michael O'Brien, Ken Rosenberg, Jeffrey Wells, Christian Nunes, Caleb Centanni, Gabrielle Names, Eric VanderWerf, Patrick Hart, Mallory Sarver, Lucas DeGroote, Matthew J. Sarver, Matthew D. Medler, Matthew J. Williams, Ray Ackerman, Scott Spangenberg, Rich Frechette, David Young, Timothy Young, Michael Young, Sparky Stensass, Sean Cozart, Nathan Goldberg, Carl Brown, Tempe Regan, Janice Gardner, Konshau Duman, the Maui Forest Recovery Team, the Rosy-Finch Working Group, the Evening Grosbeak Working Group, the American Bird Conservancy, and the Cornell Lab of Ornithology.

We would like to thank Ron Pittaway and Jean Iron, who began the Winter Finch Forecast and grew the number of finch fans when they made it available to the masses in 1999. And we'd like to thank all the finch fans on the Finch-masters (Finch Research Network Finches, Irruptions and Mast Crops) Facebook group page, whose postings, photos, and recordings add much to collective finch knowledge and enthusiasm.

Special thanks go to Ken McEnaney for digitizing and assisting in the creation of the maps and to David Yeany II for assisting in the creation of the Red Crossbill foraging charts. We'd also like to thank Andrew Spencer for creating the Crossbill spectrograms and to the Cornell Lab of Ornithology for permission to use them.

We are enormously grateful to the many talented and amazing photographers whose photos grace these pages and bring to life the beauty of the finches. This book is greatly enhanced by their work. Their names and the photographs they took are listed in the photo credits.

We'd like to especially thank Jeffrey G. Groth, Craig W. Benkman, Tom Hahn, Jamie Cornelius, Heather Watts, Ian Newton, and Curtis Adkisson for laying much of the finch research groundwork that makes such a book possible and so rewarding for us to write.

Finally, we want to thank each other for the mutual support, respect, laughs, and working relationship that enabled us to complete this project. We hope our book makes you fall in love with finches.

# Notes


## HOW TO USE THIS GUIDE

1 American Ornithological Society, https://americanornithology.org/american-ornithological-society-will-change-the-english-names-of-bird-species-named-after-people/.

## MAIN BREEDING FINCHES

### *EVENING GROSBEAK*

1 Downs, E. H. (1956). "Evening Grosbeaks at South Londonderry, Vermont, 1954 and 1955." *Bird-Banding* 27: 166–170.

2 "Choristoneura fumiferana," Wikimedia Foundation, last modified 1 January 2023, at 15:39, https://en.wikipedia.org/wiki/Choristoneura_fumiferana.

3 MacLean, D. A. (1980). "Vulnerability of Fir-Spruce Stands During Uncontrolled Spruce Budworm Outbreaks: A Review and Discussion." *Forestry Chronicle* 56: 213–221.

4 "Boreal Forest," Boreal Songbird Initiative, accessed February 14, 2023, https://www.borealbirds.org/boreal-forest.

5 Grinnell, J. (1917). "The Subspecies of *Hesperiphona vespertina*." *Condor*. Vol. XIX 17–22.

6 Sewall, K., R. Kelsey, and T. P. Hahn (2004). "Discrete Variants of Evening Grosbeak Flight Calls." *Condor* 106: 161–65.

7 Haiman, A. N. K., "Levels of Variation in Evening Grosbeak" (master's thesis, University of California, Davis, 2011).

8 Gillihan, S. W. and B. E. Byers (2020). "Evening Grosbeak (*Coccothraustes vespertinus*)," version 1.0. In Birds of the World (A. F. Poole and F. B. Gill, Editors). Cornell Lab of Ornithology, Ithaca, New York. https://doi.org/10.2173/bow.evegro.01.

9 Pieplow, N. (2017). *Peterson Field Guide to Bird Sounds of Eastern North America*. Houghton Mifflin Harcourt: Boston, New York.

10 Gillihan and Byers, "Evening Grosbeak."

11 Sewall, Kelsey, and Hahn, "Discrete Variants of Evening Grosbeak Flight Calls."

12 Haiman, "Levels of Variation in Evening Grosbeak."

13 Gillihan and Byers, "Evening Grosbeak."

14 Bent, A. C., and collaborators (1968). *Life Histories of North American Cardinals, Grosbeaks, Buntings, Towhees, Finches, Sparrows, and Allies Order Passeriformes: Family Fringillidae Part One*. Smithsonian Institution Press: Washington, DC, 208.

15. Bolgiano, N. C. (2004). "Cause and Effect: Changes in Boreal Bird Irruptions in Eastern North America Relative to the 1970s Spruce Budworm Infestation." *American Birds* 58: 26–33.

16 Bolgiano, "Cause and Effect."

17 Bolgiano, "Cause and Effect."

18 Widick, I. V., M. A. Young, J. M. LaMontagne, C. Strong, and B. Zuckerberg (2023). "Poleward Shifts and Altered Periodicity in Boreal Bird Irruptions Over Six Decades." *Journal of Animal Ecology* 92(5): 1089–1101. https://doi.org/10.1111/1365-2656.13917.

19 eBird (2021). eBird: An online database of bird distribution and abundance [web application]. eBird, Cornell Lab of Ornithology, Ithaca, New York. Available: http://www.ebird.org. Accessed February 12, 2023.

20 eBird (2021).

21 Scott, A. C., and M. Bekoff (1991). "Breeding Behavior of Evening Grosbeaks." *Condor* 93: 71–81.

22 Bekoff, M., A. C. Scott, and D. A. Conner (1989). "Ecological Analyses of Nesting Success in Evening Grosbeaks." *Oecologia* 81: 67–74.

23 Gillihan and Byers, "Evening Grosbeak."

24 Bonter, D. N., and M. G. Harvey (2004). "Winter Survey Data Reveal Rangewide Decline in Evening Grosbeak Populations." *Condor* 110(2): 376–381.

25 North American Bird Conservation Initiative (2022). The State of the Birds, United States of America, 2022. StateoftheBirds.org.

26 Forbush, E. H. (1929). *Birds of Massachusetts and Other New England States*. Norwood Press: Norwood, Massachusetts, 3.

### *PINE GROSBEAK*

1 Young, M. A., and C. S. Adkisson (2020). "Pine Grosbeak (*Pinicola enucleator*)," version 2.0. In Birds of the World (P. G. Rodewald, B. K. Keeney, and S. M. Billerman, Editors). Cornell Lab of Ornithology, Ithaca, New York. https://doi.org/10.2173/bow.pingro.02.

2 Drovetski, S. V., R. M. Zink, P. G. P. Ericson, and I. V. Fadeev (2010). "A Multilocus Study of Pine Grosbeak Phylogeography Supports the Pattern of Greater Intercontinental Divergence in Holarctic Boreal Forest Birds Than in Birds Inhabiting Other High-Latitude Habitats." *Journal of Biogeography* 37: 696–706.

3 Young and Adkisson, "Pine Grosbeak."

4 Young and Adkisson, "Pine Grosbeak."

5 Pieplow, N. (2017). *Peterson Field Guide to Bird Sounds of Eastern North America*. Houghton Mifflin Harcourt: Boston, New York.

6 Young and Adkisson, "Pine Grosbeak."

7 Pieplow, *Peterson Field Guide to Bird Sounds of Eastern North America*.

8 Widick, I. V., M. A. Young, J. M. LaMontagne, C. Strong, and B. Zuckerberg (2023). "Poleward Shifts and Altered Periodicity in Boreal Bird Irruptions Over Six Decades." *Journal of Animal Ecology* 92(5): 1089–1101. https://doi.org/10.1111/1365-2656.13917.

9 French, N. R. (1954). "Notes on Breeding Activities and on Gular Sacs in the Pine Grosbeak." *Condor* 56: 83–85.

10 Pulliainen, E. (1979b). "On the Breeding of the Pine Grosbeak *Pinicola enucleator* in NE Finland." *Ornis Fennica* 56: 156–162.

11 Young and Adkisson, "Pine Grosbeak."
12 Young and Adkisson, "Pine Grosbeak."
13 French, "Notes on Breeding Activities."
14 Young and Adkisson, "Pine Grosbeak."
15 "Pine Grosbeak Life History." (2019). All About Birds (website). Cornell Lab of Ornithology, Ithaca, New York, accessed February 13, 2023, https://www.allaboutbirds.org/guide/Pine_Grosbeak/lifehistory.

### *GRAY-CROWNED ROSY-FINCH*

1 O'Connor, Lynne E. "The Finches of Cloudland: A Love of the Rosy-Finch." From *Elk Love: A Montana Memoir* (She Writes Press, 2024).
2 Johnson, R. E. (1965c). "Reproductive Activities of Rosy Finches, with Special Reference to Montana." *Auk* 82: 190–205.
3 Clemens, D. T. (1990). "Interspecific Variation and Effects of Altitude on Blood Properties of Rosy Finches (*Leucosticte arctoa*) and House Finches (*Carpodacus mexicanus*)." *Physiological Zoology* 63: 288–307.
4 MacDougall-Shackleton, S. A., R. E. Johnson, and T. P. Hahn (2020). "Gray-crowned Rosy-Finch (*Leucosticte tephrocotis*)," version 1.0. In Birds of the World (A. F. Poole and F. B. Gill, Editors). Cornell Lab of Ornithology, Ithaca, New York. https://doi.org/10.2173/bow.gcrfin.01.
5 Shreeve, D. F. (1980a). "Behaviour of the Aleutian Grey-crowned and Brown-capped Rosy Finches *Leucosticte tephrocotis*." *Ibis* 122: 145–165.
6 Shreeve, "Behaviour of the Aleutian Grey-crowned."
7 Gardner, J. H. (2022). "Rosy-Finch Literature Review & Bibliography. A Report to the Rosy-Finch Working Group." Sageland Collaborative, Salt Lake City, Utah. 37 pages.
8 Epanchin, P. "Indirect Effects of Nonnative Trout on an Alpine-Nesting Passerine Bird via Depletion of an Aquatic Insect Subsidy." (dissertation, University of California Davis, 2009).
9 Epanchin, P., R. Knapp, and S. Lawler. (2010). "Nonnative Trout Impact an Alpine-Nesting Bird by Altering Aquatic-Insect Subsidies." *Ecological Society of America* 91: 2406–2415.
10 Swenson, J., K. Jensen, and J. Toepfer. (1988). "Winter Movements by Rosy Finches in Montana." *Journal of Field Ornithology* 59: 157–160.
11 Shreeve, "Behaviour of the Aleutian Grey-crowned."
12 Johnson, R. E. (1983). "Nesting Biology of the Rosy Finch on the Aleutian Islands, Alaska." *Condor* 85: 447–452.
13 Gardner, "Rosy-Finch Literature Review & Bibliography."
14 Shreeve, D. (1980). "Differential Mortality in the Sexes of the Aleutian Gray-crowned Rosy Finch." *American Midland Naturalist* 104: 193–197.

### *BLACK ROSY-FINCH*

1 Brown, C. W., S. Patla, and R. E. Johnson. (2018). "Extension of the Breeding Range of the Black Rosy-Finch in Wyoming." *Western Birds* 49: 82–85; doi 10.21199/WB49.1.7.
2 Johnson, R. E. (2020). "Black Rosy-Finch (*Leucosticte atrata*)," version 1.0. In Birds of the World (A. F. Poole and F. B. Gill, Editors). Cornell Lab of Ornithology, Ithaca, New York. https://doi.org/10.2173/bow.bkrfin.01.
3 Kepple, Robyn (2019). "Rappelling for Rosy." Wyoming Wildlife, October 2019, accessed February 17, 2023, https://wgfd.wyo.gov/About-Us/Wyoming-Wildlife/Articles/Rappelling-for-Rosy.
4 Flair, Jeff (2019). "As the Rockies Melt, This Rare Nesting Bird Will Have Nowhere to Go." *Audubon Magazine*, Summer 2019, accessed February 17, 2023, https://www.audubon.org/magazine/summer-2019/as-rockies-melt-rare-nesting-bird-will-have.
5 Gardner, J. H. (2022). "Rosy-Finch Literature Review & Bibliography. A Report to the Rosy-Finch Working Group." Sageland Collaborative, Salt Lake City, Utah. 37 pages.
6 Gardner, J. H., "Rosy-Finch Literature Review & Bibliography."
7 Pieplow, N. (2017). *Peterson Field Guide to Bird Sounds of Eastern North America*. Houghton Mifflin Harcourt: Boston, New York.
8 Johnson, "Black Rosy-Finch."
9 Johnson, "Black Rosy-Finch."
10 Johnson, "Black Rosy-Finch."
11 French, N. R. (1959). "Life History of the Black Rosy Finch." *Auk* 76: 159–180.
12 Johnson, "Black Rosy-Finch."
13 "Tracking the Black Rosy-Finch: Hidden Treasure and Higher Learning in North America's Alpine Zone." National Science Foundation, July 30, 2004, accessed February 18, 2023, https://beta.nsf.gov/news/tracking-black-rosy-finch-hidden-treasure-higher.
14 French, "Life History of the Black Rosy Finch."
15 Gardner, J. H., "Rosy-Finch Literature Review & Bibliography."
16 French, "Life History of the Black Rosy Finch."

### *BROWN CAPPED ROSY-FINCH*

1 Johnson, R. E., P. Hendricks, D. L. Pattie, and K. B. Hunter (2020). "Brown-capped Rosy-Finch (*Leucosticte australis*)," version 1.0. In Birds of the World (A. F. Poole and F. B. Gill, Editors). Cornell Lab of Ornithology, Ithaca, New York. https://doi.org/10.2173/bow.bcrfin.01.
2 "Brown-capped Rosy-Finch," accessed February 18, 2023, https://www.audubon.org/field-guide/bird/brown-capped-rosy-finch.
3 Gardner, J. H. (2022). "Rosy-Finch Literature Review & Bibliography. A Report to the Rosy-Finch Working Group." Sageland Collaborative, Salt Lake City, Utah. 37 pages.
4 Shreeve, D. F. "Behaviour of the Aleutian Grey-crowned and Brown-capped Rosy Finches *Leucosticte tephrocotis*." *Ibis* 122: 145–165.
5 Shreeve, "Behaviour of the Aleutian Grey-crowned."
6 Gardner, "Rosy-Finch Literature Review & Bibliography."
7 Johnson, "Brown-capped Rosy-Finch."
8 Colorado Research and Rehabilitation Institute, Rosy-Finch Research, accessed February 18, 2023. http://www.carriep.org/rosyfinch-research.

9 Gardner, "Rosy-Finch Literature Review & Bibliography."
10 Shreeve, "Behaviour of the Aleutian Grey-crowned."
11 Hendricks, D. (1978). "Notes on the Courtship Behavior of Brown-capped Rosy Finches." *Wilson Bulletin* 90: 285–287.
12 Shreeve, "Behaviour of the Aleutian Grey-crowned."
13 DeSaix, M. G., T. Luke George, Amy. E. Seglund, Garth M. Spellman, Erika S. Zavaleta, and Kristen C. Ruegg (2022). "Forecasting Climate Change Response in an Alpine Specialist Songbird Reveals the Importance of Considering Novel Climate." August 25, 2022, Wiley Online Library, accessed February 18, 2023. https://onlinelibrary.wiley.com/doi/full/10.1111/ddi.13.

### *HOUSE FINCH*

1 The Hollywood Sign, accessed February 18, 2023. https://hollywoodsign.org/.
2 Elliott, J. J., and R. S. Arbib Jr. (1953). "Origin and Status of the House Finch in the Eastern United States." *Auk* 70: 31–37.
3 Elliott, "Origin and Status of the House Finch."
4 Elliott, "Origin and Status of the House Finch."
5 Badyaev, A. V., V. Belloni, and G. E. Hill (2020). "House Finch (*Haemorhous mexicanus*)," version 1.0. In Birds of the World (A. F. Poole, Editor). Cornell Lab of Ornithology, Ithaca, New York. https://doi.org/10.2173/bow.houfin.01.
6 Mundinger, P. C. (1975). "Song Dialects and Colonization in the House Finch." *Condor* 77: 407–422.
7 Bitterbaum, E., and L. F. Baptista (1979). "Geographical Variation in Songs of California House Finches (*Carpodacus mexicanus*)." *Auk* 96: 462–474.
8 Mundinger, "Song Dialects and Colonization in the House Finch."
9 Thompson, W. L. (1960a). "Agonistic Behavior in the House Finch. Part I: Annual Cycle and Display Patterns." *Condor* 62: 245–271.
10 Thompson, W. L. (1960b). "Agonistic Behavior in the House Finch. Part II: Factors in Aggressiveness and Sociality." *Condor* 62: 378–402.
11 Shedd, D. H. (1990). "Aggressive Interactions in Wintering House Finches and Purple Finches." *Wilson Bulletin* 102: 174–178.
12 Badyaev et al., "House Finch."
13 Thompson, "Agonistic Behavior in the House Finch. Part I."
14 Mennill, D. J., A. V. Badyaev, L. M. Jonart, and G. E. Hill. (2006). "Male House Finches with Elaborate Songs Have Higher Reproductive Performance." *Ethology* 112: 174–180.
15 Mundinger, P. C. (1975b). "Song Dialects and Colonization in the House Finch, *Carpodacus mexicanus*, on the East Coast." *Condor* 77: 407–422.
16 Badyaev et al., "House Finch."
17 Thompson, "Agonistic Behavior in the House Finch. Part I."
18 Hill, G. E. (1991). "Plumage Coloration is a Sexually Selected Indicator of Male Quality." *Nature* 350: 337–339.
19 Badyaev, A. V., and G. E. Hill. (2002). "Parental Care as a Conditional Strategy: Distinct Reproductive Tactics Associated with Elaboration of Plumage Ornamentation in the House Finch." *Behavioral Ecology* 13: 591–597.
20 Badyaev et al., "House Finch."
21 Badyaev, A. V., G. E. Hill, P. O. Dunn, and J. C. Glen. (2001a). "Plumage Color as a Composite Trait: Developmental and Functional Integration of Sexual Ornamentation." *American Naturalist* 158: 221–235.
22 Badyaev et al., "House Finch."
23 Stein, L. R., K. P. Oh, and A. V. Badyaev. (2010). "Fitness Consequences of Male Provisioning of Incubating Females in a Desert Passerine Bird." *Journal of Ornithology* 151: 227–234.
24 Badyaev et al., "House Finch."
25 Hill, G. E. et al. (2019). "Plumage Redness Signals Mitochondrial Function in the House Finch." *Proceedings of the Royal Society B: Biological Sciences* 286: 20191354. http//dx.doi.org/10.1098/rspb.2019.1354.
26 Hill, "Plumage Redness Signals Mitochondrial Function."
27 Inouye, C. Y., G. E. Hill, R. D. Stradi, and R. Montgomerie. (2001). "Carotenoid Pigments in Male House Finch Plumage in Relation to Age, Subspecies, and Ornamental Coloration." *Auk* 118: 900–915.
28 Hill, "Plumage Redness Signals Mitochondrial Function."

### *PURPLE FINCH*

1 Abramov I., J. Gordon, O. Feldman, and A. Chavarga (2012). "Sex and Vision II: Color Appearance of Monochromatic Lights." *Biology of Sex Differences* Sep 4;3(1): 21. doi: 10.1186/2042-6410-3-21.PMID: 22943488. https://pubmed.ncbi.nlm.nih .gov/22943488/.
2 Macfarlane, C. B. A., L. Natola, M. W. Brown, and T. M. Burg (2016). "Population Genetic Isolation and Limited Connectivity in the Purple Finch (*Haemorhous purpureus*)." *Ecology and Evolution*, 6: 8304–8317. doi: 10.1002/ece3.2524.
3 Hahn, T. P., Y. Kuang, L. M. Wigger, K. P. Kreuger, and M. A. Young (2021). Eastern and western Purple Finches (*Haemorhous purpureus*) produce categorically distinct flight calls. Poster for The Society of Integrative and Comparative Biology.
4 Hahn et al., Eastern and western Purple Finches.
5 Pieplow, N. (2017). *Peterson Field Guide to Bird Sounds of Eastern North America*. Houghton Mifflin Harcourt: Boston, New York.
6 Wootton, J. T. (2020). "Purple Finch (*Haemorhous purpureus*)," version 1.0. In Birds of the World (A. F. Poole and F. B. Gill, Editors). Cornell Lab of Ornithology, Ithaca, New York. https://doi.org/10.2173/bow.purfin.01.
7 Stratton, L. (1967). "Notes on Nesting of Purple Finch at Oxford." *Kingbird* 17: 19.
8 Wootton, "Purple Finch."
9 Pieplow, *Peterson Field Guide to Bird Sounds of Eastern North America*.
10 Pieplow, *Peterson Field Guide to Bird Sounds of Eastern North America*.

11 Shedd, D. H. (1990). "Aggressive Interactions in Wintering House Finches and Purple Finches." *Wilson Bulletin* 102: 174–178.
12 Popp, J. W. (1987a). "Agonistic Communication among Wintering Purple Finches." *Wilson Bulletin* 99: 97–100.
13 Widick, I. V., M. A. Young, J. M. LaMontagne, C. Strong, and B. Zuckerberg (2023). "Poleward Shifts and Altered Periodicity in Boreal Bird Irruptions Over Six Decades." *Journal of Animal Ecology* 92(5): 1089–1101. https://doi.org/10.1111/1365-2656.13917.
14 Wootton, "Purple Finch."
15 Bent, A. C. (1968). "Life Histories of North American Cardinals, Grosbeaks, Towhees, Finches, Sparrows, and Allies (Part 1)." United States National Museum Bulletin 237.
16 Wootton, "Purple Finch."

### CASSIN'S FINCH

1 "Essence," Wikimedia Foundation, last modified February 10, 2023, 3:59. https://en.wikipedia.org/wiki/Essence.
2 Hahn, T. P. (2020). "Cassin's Finch (*Haemorhous cassinii*)," version 1.0. In Birds of the World (A. F. Poole and F. B. Gill, Editors). Cornell Lab of Ornithology, Ithaca, New York. https://doi.org/10.2173/bow.casfin.01.
3 Pieplow, N. (2017). *Peterson Field Guide to Bird Sounds of Western North America*. Houghton Mifflin Harcourt: Boston, New York.
4 Samson, F. B. (1978). "Vocalizations of Cassin's Finch in Northern Utah." *Condor* 80: 203–210.
5 Mundinger, P. C. (1975b). "Song Dialects and Colonization in the House Finch, *Carpodacus mexicanus*, on the East Coast." *Condor* 77: 407–422.
6 Samson, "Vocalizations of Cassin's Finch in Northern Utah."
7 Pieplow, N. (2017). *Peterson Field Guide to Bird Sounds of Western North America*. Houghton Mifflin Harcourt: Boston, New York.
8 Hahn, "Cassin's Finch."
9 Hahn, "Cassin's Finch."
10 Bennetts, R. E., and R. L. Hutto. (1985). "Attraction of Social Fringillids to Mineral Salts: An Experimental Study." *Journal of Field Ornithology* 56: 187–189.
11 Herson, Kathryn Julia, "An Analysis of Salt Eating in Birds" (master's thesis, Western Michigan University, 1980). https://scholarworks.wmich.edu/masters_theses/1909.
12 Samson, F. B. (1977). "Social Dominance in Winter Flocks of Cassin's Finch." *Wilson Bulletin* 89: 57–66.
13 Hahn, "Cassin's Finch."
14 Mewaldt, L. R., and J. R. King. (1985). "Breeding Site Faithfulness, Reproductive Biology, and Adult Survivorship in an Isolated Population of Cassin's Finches." *Condor* 87: 494–510.
15 Samson, F. B. (1976b). "Territory, Breeding Density, and Fall Departure in Cassin's Finch." *Auk* 93: 477–497.
16 Samson, "Territory, Breeding Density, and Fall Departure in Cassin's Finch."
17 Samson, "Vocalizations of Cassin's Finch in Northern Utah."
18 Mewaldt and King, "Breeding Site Faithfulness."
19 Samson, "Territory, Breeding Density, and Fall Departure in Cassin's Finch."
20 Samson, "Vocalizations of Cassin's Finch in Northern Utah."
21 Samson, "Vocalizations of Cassin's Finch in Northern Utah."
22 Samson, "Territory, Breeding Density, and Fall Departure in Cassin's Finch."
23 Samson, "Social Dominance in Winter Flocks of Cassin's Finch."
24 Mewadlt and King, "Breeding Site Faithfulness."
25 Hahn, "Cassin's Finch."

### COMMON REDPOLL

1 Knox, A. G., and P. E. Lowther (2020). "Common Redpoll (*Acanthis flammea*)," version 1.0. In Birds of the World (S. M. Billerman, Editor). Cornell Lab of Ornithology, Ithaca, New York. https://doi.org/10.2173/bow.comred.01.
2 Knox and Lowther, "Common Redpoll."
3 Pieplow, N. (2017). *Peterson Field Guide to Bird Sounds of Eastern North America*. Houghton Mifflin Harcourt: Boston, New York.
4 Pieplow, *Peterson Field Guide to Bird Sounds of Eastern North America*.
5 Knox and Lowther, "Common Redpoll."
6 Centanni, Caleb. "Oregon (and Other Western States) Is Seeing Great Numbers of Crossbills and Common Redpolls This Fall," accessed February 21, 2023. https://finchnetwork.org/oregon-and-other-western-states-is-seeing-great-numbers-of-crossbills-and-common-redpolls-this-fall.
7 Widick, I. V., M. A. Young, J. M. LaMontagne, C. Strong, and B. Zuckerberg (2023). "Poleward Shifts and Altered Periodicity in Boreal Bird Irruptions Over Six Decades." *Journal of Animal Ecology* 92(5): 1089–1101. https://doi.org/10.1111/1365-2656.13917.
8 Knox and Lowther, "Common Redpoll."
9 Dilger, W. C. (1960). "Agonistic and Social Behavior of Captive Redpolls." *Wilson Bulletin* 72: 115–132.
10 Dilger, "Agonistic and Social Behavior of Captive Redpolls."
11 Knox and Lowther, "Common Redpoll."
12 Seutin, G., P. T. Boag, B. N. White and L. M. Ratcliffe. (1991). "Sequential Polyandry in the Common Redpoll (*Carduelis flammea*)." *Auk* 108: 166–170.
13 All About Birds (website). Cornell Lab of Ornithology, Ithaca, New York. https://www.allaboutbirds.org. Accessed February 22, 2023.
14 Shackford, John. "Common Redpoll." Oklahoma City Audubon Society. https://okc-audubon.org/common-redpoll/.

### HOARY REDPOLL

1 Cell Press (2006). "Pure Novelty Spurs the Brain." ScienceDaily, August 27, 2006. Accessed February 22, 2023. https://www.sciencedaily.com/releases/2006/08/060826180547.htm.
2 Mason, N. A., and S. A. Taylor (2015). "Differentially Expressed Genes Match Bill Morphology and Plumage Despite Largely Undifferentiated Genomes

in a Holarctic Songbird." *Molecular Ecology* 24(12): 3009–3025.

3 Funk, E. R., N. A. Mason, S. Pálsson et al. (2021). "A Supergene Underlies Linked Variation in Color and Morphology in a Holarctic Songbird." *Nature Communications* 12, 6833. https://doi.org/10.1038/s41467-021-27173-z.

4 Mason and Taylor, "Differentially Expressed Genes Match Bill Morphology."

5 Funk et al., "A Supergene Underlies Linked Variation."

6 Knox, A. G., and P. E. Lowther (2020). "Hoary Redpoll (*Acanthis hornemanni*)," version 1.0. In Birds of the World (S. M. Billerman, Editor). Cornell Lab of Ornithology, Ithaca, New York. https://doi.org/10.2173/bow.hoared.01.

7 Knox and Lowther, "Hoary Redpoll."

8 Knox and Lowther, "Hoary Redpoll."

9 Alsop, F. J., III (1973). "Notes on the Hoary Redpoll on its Central Canadian Arctic Breeding Grounds." *Wilson Bulletin* 85: 484–485.

10 Knox and Lowther, "Hoary Redpoll."

11 Knox and Lowther, "Hoary Redpoll."

12 Brooks, W. S. (1968). "Comparative Adaptations of the Alaskan Redpolls to the Arctic Environment." *Wilson Bulletin* 80: 253–280.

### *RED CROSSBILL*

1 Groth, J. G. (1993). *Evolutionary Differentiation in Morphology, Vocalizations, and Allozymes among Nomadic Sibling Species in the North American Red Crossbill (*Loxia curvirostra*) Complex*. University of California Press: Berkeley.

Benkman, C. W. (1993a). "Adaptation to Single Resources and the Evolution of Crossbill (*Loxia*) Diversity." *Ecological Monographs* 63: 305–325. https://doi.org/10.2307/2937103.

Parchman, T. L., C. W. Benkman, and S. C. Britch. (2006). "Patterns of Genetic Variation in the Adaptive Radiation of New World Crossbills (Aves: Loxia)." *Molecular Ecology* 15: 1873–1889.

2 Groth, *Evolutionary Differentiation in Morphology.*

3 Benkman, C. W., and M. A. Young (2020). "Red Crossbill (*Loxia curvirostra*)," version 1.0. In Birds of the World (S. M. Billerman, B. K. Keeney, P. G. Rodewald, and T. S. Schulenberg, Editors).

4 Irwin, K. (2010). "A New and Cryptic Call Type of the Red Crossbill." *Western Birds* 41: 10–25.

5 Young, M., and T. Spahr. (2017). "Crossbills of North America: Species and Red Crossbill Call Types." eBird [online]. https://ebird.org/news/crossbills-of-north-america-species-and-red-crossbill-call-types/.

6 Young et al. in review (2023). "A New Red Crossbill Call Type, Type 12, the 'Old Northeastern Subspecies of the Red Crossbill.'" *Frontiers in Bird Science.*

7 Benkman, "Adaptation to Single Resources."

8 Benkman and Young, "Red Crossbill."

9 Benkman and Young, "Red Crossbill."

10 Pieplow, N. (2017). *Peterson Field Guide to Bird Sounds of Eastern North America.* Houghton Mifflin Harcourt: Boston, New York.

11 Groth, J. G. (1993a). "Call Matching and Positive Assortative Mating in Red Crossbills." *Auk* 110: 398–401.

12 Benkman, C. W. (1987b). "Food Profitability and the Foraging Ecology of Crossbills." *Ecological Monographs* 57: 251–267.

13 Benkman, C. W. (1999). "The Selection Mosaic and Diversifying Coevolution between Crossbills and Lodgepole Pine." *American Naturalist* 153: S75–S91. https://doi.org/10.1086/303213.

14 Benkman, "Food Profitability and the Foraging Ecology of Crossbills."

15 Benkman, C. W., and R. E. Miller (1996). "Morphological Evolution in Response to Fluctuating Selection." *Evolution* 50: 2499–2504.

16 Smith, J. W., C. W. Benkman, and K. Coffey (1999c). "The Use and Misuse of Public Information by Foraging Red Crossbills." *Behavioral Ecology* 10: 54–62.

17 Benkman and Young, "Red Crossbill."

18 Cornelius, J. M., T. P. Hahn, A. R. Robart, B. J. Vernasco, J. L. Zahor, K. J. Glynn, J. Corrie, C. J. Navis, and H. E. Watts (2021). "Seasonal Patterns of Fat Deposits in Relation to Migratory Strategy in Facultative Migrants." *Frontiers in Ecology and Evolution* 9: 691808. https://doi.org/10.3389/fevo.2021.691808.

19 Young, M. A., K. Blankenship, M. Westphal, and S. Holzman (2011). "Status and Distribution of Type 1 Red Crossbill (*Loxia curvirostra*): An Appalachian Call Type?" *North American Birds* 65(3): 554–561.

20 Benkman, C. W. (2007). "Red Crossbill Types in Colorado: Their Ecology, Evolution, and Distribution." *Colorado Birds* 41(3): 153–163.

21 Young, M. A. (2011). "Red Crossbill (*Loxia curvirostra*) Call-Types of New York: Their Taxonomy, Flight Call Vocalizations, and Ecology." *The Kingbird* 61(2): 106–123.

22 Benkman, "Red Crossbill Types in Colorado."

23 Caleb Centanni, W. Douglas Robinson, and Matthew A. Young, in review (2023). "Is Specialization the Key?: Ecology and Distribution of Red Crossbill." *Frontiers in Bird Science.*

24 Centanni et al., "Is Specialization the Key?"

25 Benkman, "Red Crossbill Types in Colorado."

26 Brady R. S., N. M. Anich, and M. A. Young (2019). "Wisconsin's Red Crossbill Irruption of 2017–18: Distribution, Abundance, and Breeding Behavior of Multiple Call Types." *Passenger Pigeon* 81: 215–240.

27 Centanni et al., "Is Specialization the Key?"

28 Benkman, "Red Crossbill Types in Colorado."

29 Benkman, "The Selection Mosaic and Diversifying Coevolution."

30 Young, M. A. (2010). "Type 5 Red Crossbill (*Loxia curvisrotra*) in New York: First Confirmation East of the Rocky Mountains." *North American Birds* 64: 343–346. http://blog.aba.org/wp-content/uploads/2018/01/Type5RedCrossbill-NAB.pdf.

31 Benkman, "Red Crossbill Types in Colorado."

32 Young and Spahr, "Crossbills of North America."

33 Griscom, L. (1937a). "A Monographic Study of the Red Crossbill." *Proceedings of the Boston Society of Natural History* 41: 77–210.

34 Tremblay, J. A., M. Robert, D. P. Hynes, M. A. Young, and B. Drolet. (2018). "Range Extension of the Threatened Red Crossbill (*Loxia curvirostral percna*) in Canada: New Insights from Anticosti Island, Québec." *Avian Conservation and Ecology*13(1): 10.

35 Parchman, T. L., and C. W. Benkman (2002). "Diversifing Coevolution Between Crossbills and Black Spruce on Newfoundland." *Evolution* 56 (8): 1663–1672.

36 Young, M. A., D. A. Fifield, and W. A. Montevecchi (2012). "New Evidence in Support of a Distinctive Red Crossbill (*Loxia curvirostra*) Type in Newfoundland." *North American Birds* 66: 29–33.

37 Benkman, C. W., J. W. Smith, P. C. Keenan, T. L. Parchman, and L. Santisteban (2009). "A New Species of the Red Crossbill (Fringillidae: *Loxia*) from Idaho." *Condor* 111(1): 169–176.

38 Benkman et al., "A New Species of the Red Crossbill."

39 Mandelbaum, Ryan. (2020). Intense Idaho Wildfires Are Threatening this Brand New Finch Species. Finch Research Network. https://finchnetwork.org/conservation-news-intense-idaho-wildfires-are-threatening-this-brand-new-finch-species.

40 Nunes, Christian. (2021). Cassia Crossbill in Colorado. Finch Research Network. https://finchnetwork.org/cassia-crossbill-in-colorado.

41 Pieplow, Nathan. (2022). Cassia Crossbills in Colorado—The Mystery Deepens. Finch Research Network. https://finchnetwork.org/cassia-crossbills-in-colorado-the-mystery-deepens.

42 Benkman et al., "A New Species of the Red Crossbill."

43 Irwin, "A New and Cryptic Call Type."

44 Young and Spahr, "Crossbills of North America."

45 Benkman and Young, "Red Crossbill."

46 Young et al. in review (2023). "A New Red Crossbill Call Type, Type 12, the 'Old Northeastern Subspecies of the Red Crossbill.'" *Frontiers in Bird Science.*

47 Kelsey, T. R. "Biogeography, Foraging Ecology, and Population Dynamics of Red Crossbills in North America" (doctoral dissertation, University of California, Davis, December 2008).
Cornelius J. M., H. E. Watts, H. Dingle, T. P. Hahn. "Obligate Versus Rich Patch Opportunism: Evolution and Endocrine Mechanisms." *Gen Comp Endocrinol.* Sept. 1, 2013; 190:76-80. doi: 10.1016/j.ygcen.2013.04.003. Epub April 20, 2013. PMID: 23612018.

48 Snowberg, L. K., and C. W. Benkman (2007). "The Role of Marker Traits in the Assortative Mating within Red Crossbills, *Loxia curvirostra* complex." *Journal of Evolutionary Biology* 20: 1924–1932. https://doi.org/10.1111/j.1420-9101.2007.01372.x.

49 Keenan, P. C., and C. W. Benkman (2008). "Call Imitation and Call Modification in Red Crossbills." *Condor* 110: 93–101. https://doi.org/10.1525/cond.2008.110.1.93.

50 Smith, J. W., and C. W. Benkman. (2007). "A Coevolutionary Arms Race Causes Ecological Speciation in Crossbills." *American Naturalist* 169: 455–465. https://doi.org/10.1086/511961.

51 Young et al. in review (2023). "A New Red Crossbill Call Type, Type 12, the 'Old Northeastern Subspecies of the Red Crossbill.'" *Frontiers in Bird Science.*

52 Snowberg, L. K., and C. W. Benkman (2009). "Mate Choice Based on a Key Ecological Performance Trait." *Journal of Evolutionary Biology* 22: 762–769. https://doi.org/10.1111/j.1420-9101.2009.01699.x.

### *CASSIA CROSSBILL*

1 Benkman, C. W., W. C. Holimon, and J. W. Smith (2001). "The Influence of a Competitor on the Geographic Mosaic of Coevolution Between Crossbills and Lodgepole Pine." *Evolution* 55: 282–294.

2 Benkman, C. W., and C. K. Porter (2020). "Cassia Crossbill (*Loxia sinesciuris*)," version 1.0. In Birds of the World (P. G. Rodewald, Editor). Cornell Lab of Ornithology, Ithaca, New York. https://doi.org/10.2173/bow.redcro9.01.

3 Benkman, C. W., J. W. Smith, P. C. Keenan, T. L. Parchman, and L. Santisteban (2009). "A New Species of the Red Crossbill (Fringillidae: *Loxia*) from Idaho." *Condor* 111: 169–176. https://doi.org/10.1525/cond.2009.080042.

4 Parchman, T. L., C. A. Buerkle, V. Soria-Carrasco, and C. W. Benkman (2016). "Genome Divergence and Diversification within a Geographic Mosaic of Coevolution." *Molecular Ecology* 25: 5705–5718.

5 Benkman et al. "A New Species of the Red Crossbill (Fringillidae: *Loxia*) from Idaho."

6 Pieplow, N. "Cassia Crossbills in Colorado—The Mystery Deepens." Finch Research Network, accessed February 23, 2023. https://finchnetwork.org/cassia-crossbills-in-colorado-the-mystery-deepens.

7 Benkman and Porter, "Cassia Crossbill."

8 Benkman and Porter, "Cassia Crossbill."

9 Nunes, Christian (2021). eBird Checklist: https://ebird.org/checklist/S9185548. eBird: An online database of bird distribution and abundance [web application]. eBird, Ithaca, New York. Available: http://www.ebird.org. Accessed February 23, 2023.

10 Pheneger, Luke (2022). eBird checklist: https://ebird.org/checklist/S115435367. eBird: An online database of bird distribution and abundance [web application]. eBird, Ithaca, New York. Available: http://www.ebird.org. Accessed February 23, 2023.

11 Pieplow, N., "Cassia Crossbills in Colorado."

12 eBird (2021). eBird: An online database of bird distribution and abundance [web application]. eBird, Cornell Lab of Ornithology, Ithaca, New York. Available: http://www.ebird.org. Accessed February 23, 2023.

13 Pieplow, N., "Cassia Crossbills in Colorado."

14 Snowberg, L. K., and C. W. Benkman (2009). "Mate Choice Based on a Key Ecological Performance Trait." *Journal of Evolutionary Biology* 22: 762–769. https://doi.org/10.1111/j.1420-9101.2009.01699.x.

15 Benkman and Porter, "Cassia Crossbill."

16 Benkman and Porter, "Cassia Crossbill."

17 North American Bird Conservation Initiative (2022). The State of the Birds, United States of America, 2022. StateoftheBirds.org.

18 Benkman, C. W. (2016). "The Natural History of the South Hills Crossbill in Relation to its Impending Extinction." *American Naturalist* 188: 589–601.

### *WHITE-WINGED CROSSBILL*

1 Jessé Roy Drainville. "The morning was intense at the dunes of Tadoussac. It was a river of groups of more than 100 white-winged crossbills going SW between 7:30 and 9:00." Finches, Irruptions, and Mast Crops Facebook page. October 20, 2021. https://www.facebook.com/groups/3015382321871572/posts/4286336541442804.

2 Trektellen.org count data from Observatoire d'oiseaux de Tadoussac—Dunes (QC), October 20, 2021. https://www.trektellen.org/count/view/2880/20211020.

3 Trektellen.org count data from Observatoire d'oiseaux de Tadoussac—Dunes (QC), October 19, 2021. https://www.trektellen.org/count/view/2880/20211019.

4 Benkman, C. W. (1987). "Food Profitability and the Foraging Ecology of Crossbills." *Ecological Monographs* 57: 251–267.

5 Benkman, C. W. (2020). "White-winged Crossbill (*Loxia leucoptera*)," version 1.0. In Birds of the World (S. M. Billerman, Editor). Cornell Lab of Ornithology, Ithaca, New York. https://doi.org/10.2173/bow.whwcro.01.

6 Benkman, "Food Profitability and the Foraging Ecology of Crossbills."

7 Benkman, "Food Profitability and the Foraging Ecology of Crossbills."

8 Lustgarten, Abraham (2020). "The Great Climate Migration Has Begun." *New York Times Magazine*, July 23, 2020. https://www.nytimes.com/interactive/2020/07/23/magazine/climate-migration.html.

9 Benkman, "White-winged Crossbill."

10 Benkman, "White-winged Crossbill."

11 Benkman, "White-winged Crossbill."

12 MacDougall-Shackleton, S. A., P. J. Deviche, R. D. Crain, G. F. Ball, and T. P. Hahn. (2001). "Seasonal Changes in Brain GnRH Immunoreactivity and Song-Control Nuclei Volumes in an Opportunistically Breeding Songbird." *Brain, Behavior and Evolution* 58 (1): 38–48.

13 Benkman, "Food Profitability and the Foraging Ecology of Crossbills."

14 Widick, I. V., M. A. Young, J. M. LaMontagne, C. Strong, and B. Zuckerberg (2023). "Poleward Shifts and Altered Periodicity in Boreal Bird Irruptions Over Six Decades." *Journal of Animal Ecology* 92(5): 1089–1101. https://doi.org/10.1111/1365-2656.13917.

15 Coady, G. (2001). "First Nest Record of White-winged Crossbill in the Greater Toronto Area." *Ontario Birds* 19 (3): 101–111.

16 Benkman, "White-winged Crossbill."

17 Smith, K. G. (1978). "White-winged Crossbills Breed in Northern Utah." *Western Birds* 9: 79–81.

18 Benkman, C. W. (1997). "Feeding Behavior, Flock-Size Dynamics, and Variation in Sexual Selection in Crossbills." *Auk* 114: 163–178.

19 Manville, R. H. (1941). "Crossbills Breeding in Northern Michigan." *Wilson Bulletin* 53: 240–241.

20 Benkman, "White-winged Crossbill ."

21 Benkman, "Feeding Behavior, Flock-Size Dynamics, and Variation."

22 Benkman, C. W. (1990). "Intake Rates and the Timing of Crossbill Reproduction." *Auk* 107: 376–386

23 Coady, "First Nest Record of White-winged Crossbill in the Greater Toronto Area."

24 Benkman, C. W. (1989a). "Breeding Opportunities, Foraging Rates, and Parental Care in White-winged Crossbills." *Auk* 106: 483–485.

25 Benkman, "White-winged Crossbill."

26 Benkman, "White-winged Crossbill."

27 Deviche, P., K. J. McGraw, and J. Underwood (2008). "Season-, Sex-, and Age-Specific Accumulation of Plasma Carotenoid Pigments in Free-Ranging White-winged Crossbills *Loxia leucoptera*." *Journal of Avian Biology* 39 (3): 283–292.

28 Deviche et al., "Season-, Sex-, and Age-Specific Accumulation."

### *EUROPEAN GOLDFINCH*

1 Clement, P., J. del Hoyo, N. Collar, and G. M. Kirwan (2020). "European Goldfinch (*Carduelis carduelis*)," version 1.0. In Birds of the World (S. M. Billerman, B. K. Keeney, P. G. Rodewald, and T. S. Schulenberg, Editors). Cornell Lab of Ornithology, Ithaca, New York. https://doi.org/10.2173/bow.eurgol.01.

2 Craves, J. A., and N. M. Anich (2023). "Status and Distribution of an Introduced Population of European Goldfinches (*Carduelis carduelis*) in the Western Great Lakes Region of North America." *NeoBiota* 81: 129–155. https://doi. org/10.3897/neobiota.81.97736.

3 eBird (2021). eBird: An online database of bird distribution and abundance [web application]. eBird, Cornell Lab of Ornithology, Ithaca, New York. Available: http://www.ebird.org. Accessed February 12, 2023.

4 Craves, J. A. (2008). "Current Status of European Goldfinch (*Carduelis carduelis*) in the Western Great Lakes Region." *North American Birds* 62: 2–5.

5 Craves and Anich, "Status and Distribution of an Introduced Population of European Goldfinches."

6 Smith, D. (2022). "European Goldfinches Make Themselves at Home in Southeast Wisconsin." April 20, 2022, Wisconsin Public Radio, accessed February 26, 2023, https://www.wpr.org/european-goldfinches-makes-themselves-home-southeast-wisconsin.

7 eBird (2021). eBird: An online database of bird distribution and abundance [web application]. eBird, Cornell Lab of Ornithology, Ithaca, New York. Available: http://www.ebird.org. Accessed February 12, 2023.

8 Clement et al., "European Goldfinch."

9 Dalton, Evan (2021). eBird Checklist: https://ebird.org/checklist/S39404946. eBird: An online database of bird distribution and abundance [web application]. eBird, Ithaca, New York. Available: http://www.ebird.org. Accessed February 26, 2023.

10 Clement et al., "European Goldfinch."

11 Clement et al., "European Goldfinch."

12 Craves and Anich, "Status and Distribution of an Introduced Population of European Goldfinches."

13 Clement et al., "European Goldfinch."

### *PINE SISKIN*


1 Mandelbaum, R. "Irruption Alert: Astonishing Pine Siskin Nocturnal Migration." Finch Research Network, accessed February 23, 2023. https://finchnetwork.org/irruption-alert-astonishing-pine-siskin-nocturnal-migration.

2 Del-Colle, A. (2020). "Pine Siskins Have Taken Over the Country," October 23, 2020, Audubon, accessed February 23, 2023. https://www.audubon.org/news/-pine-siskin-finch-irruption-fall-2020.

3 Trektellen.org count data from Cape May Bird Observatory: Morning Flight (NJ), accessed February 23, 2023. https://www.trektellen.org/count/view/1746/20201025.

4 Mandelbaum, "Irruption Alert."

5 Pyle, P. (2022). *Identification Guide to North American Birds, Part I*. 2nd ed. Slate Creek Press: Point Reyes Station, CA.

6 Pieplow, N. (2017). *Peterson Field Guide to Bird Sounds of Eastern North America*. Houghton Mifflin Harcourt: Boston, New York.

7 Popp, J. P., "Scanning Behavior of Finches in Mixed-Species Groups." *Condor* 90: 510–512.

8 Michael L. Watson, Jeffrey V. Wells, and Ryan W. Bavis (2011). "First Detection of Night Flight Calls by Pine Siskins." *The Wilson Journal of Ornithology* 123(1): 161–164. https://doi.org/10.1676/09-171.1.

9 Young, M. A., and R. Mandelbaum (in progress). "Pine Siskin (*Spinus pinus*)," version 1.0. In Birds of the World (A. F. Poole, Editor). Cornell Lab of Ornithology, Ithaca, New York. https://doi.org/10.2173/bow.pinsis.01.

10 Mandelbaum, R. (2022). "Why Did the Siskin Cross the Continent?" July 21, 2022, Audubon, accessed February 24, 2023. https://www.audubon.org/news/why-did-siskin-cross-continent.

11 Widick, I. V., M. A. Young, J. M. LaMontagne, C. Strong, and B. Zuckerberg (2023). "Poleward Shifts and Altered Periodicity in Boreal Bird Irruptions Over Six Decades." *Journal of Animal Ecology* 92(5): 1089–1101. https://doi.org/10.1111/1365-2656.13917.

12 Weaver, R. L., and P. H. West (1943). "Notes on the Breeding of the Pine Siskin." *Auk* 60: 492–504.

13 Senar J. C., F. Mateos-Gonzalez, F. Uribe, and L. Arroyo (2013). "Familiarity Adds to Attractiveness in Matters of Siskin Mate Choice." *Proceedings of the Royal Society B: Biological Sciences* 280: 20132361. http://dx.doi.org/10.1098/rspb.2013.2361.

14 Rodgers, T. L. (1937). "Behavior of the Pine Siskin." *Condor* 39: 143–149.

15 Rodgers, T. L. (1937). "Behavior of the Pine Siskin." *Condor* 39: 143–149.

16 Dawson, W. R., and C. Carey (1976). "Seasonal Acclimatization to Temperature in Cardueline Finches. I. Insulative and Metabolic Adjustments." *Journal of Comparative Physiology* 112: 317–333.


### *LESSER GOLDFINCH*


1 Hoffmann, R. (1927). *Birds of the Pacific States*. Houghton Mifflin Co.: Boston, New York.

2 Versaw, A. (2000). "Winter Range Expansion of Lesser Goldfinches." *Journal of the Colorado Field Ornithologists* 34(2): 91–97.

3 Remsen, J. V., K. Garrett, and R. A. Erickson (1982). "Vocal Copying in Lawrence's and Lesser Goldfinches." *Western Birds* 13: 29–33.

4 Goldwasser, S. "Vocal Appropriation in the Lesser Goldfinch" (master's thesis, University of Arizona, Tucson, 1987).

5 Pyle, P. (2022). *Identification Guide to North American Birds, Part I*, 2nd ed. Slate Creek Press: Point Reyes Station, CA.

6 Watt, D. J., and E. J. Willoughby (2020). "Lesser Goldfinch (*Spinus psaltria*)," version 1.0. In Birds of the World (A. F. Poole, Editor). Cornell Lab of Ornithology, Ithaca, New York. https://doi.org/10.2173/bow.lesgol.01.

7 Willoughby, E. J. (2007). "Geographic Variation in Color, Measurements, and Molt of the Lesser Goldfinch in North America Does Not Support Subspecific Designation." *Condor* 109 (2): 419–436.

8 Cozart, S. (2021). "Populations of the Lesser Goldfinch, with New Discussion about Subspecies." Finch Research Network, June 29, 2021. https://finchnetwork.org/?s=Lesser+Goldfinch.

9 Watt and Willoughby, "Lesser Goldfinch."

10 eBird (2021). eBird: An online database of bird distribution and abundance [web application]. eBird, Cornell Lab of Ornithology, Ithaca, New York. Available: http://www.ebird.org. Accessed February 12, 2023.

11 Coutlee, E. L. (1971). "Vocalizations in the Genus *Spinus*." *Animal Behaviour* 19: 556–565.

12 Coutlee, "Vocalizations in the Genus *Spinus*."

13 Pieplow, N. (2017). *Peterson Field Guide to Bird Sounds of Western North America*. Houghton Mifflin Harcourt: Boston, New York.

14 Coutlee, E. L. (1968). "Maintenance Behavior of Lesser and Lawrence's Goldfinches." *Condor* 70: 378–384.

15 Coutlee, "Maintenance Behavior of Lesser and Lawrence's Goldfinches."

16 Watt and Willoughby, "Lesser Goldfinch."

17 Prather, J. W., L. M. Munger, and A. Cruz. (2002). "Breeding Biology of the Black-Backed Lesser Goldfinch in Ponderosa Pine Forests on the Colorado Front Range." *Wilson Bulletin* 114 (2): 192–196.

18 Coutlee, E. L. (1968). "Comparative Breeding Behavior of Lesser and Lawrence's Goldfinches." *Condor* 70: 228–242.

19 Linsdale, J. M. (1957). "Goldfinches on the Hastings Natural History Reservation." *American Midland Naturalist* 57: 1–119.

20 Linsdale, "Goldfinches on the Hastings Natural History Reservation."

21 Watt and Willoughby, "Lesser Goldfinch."

22 Watt and Willoughby, "Lesser Goldfinch."


### *LAWRENCE'S GOLDFINCH*


1 Watt, D. J., P. Pyle, M. A. Patten, and J. N. Davis (2020). "Lawrence's Goldfinch (*Spinus lawrencei*)," version 1.0. In Birds of the World (P. G. Rodewald, Editor). Cornell Lab of Ornithology, Ithaca, New York. https://doi.org/10.2173/bow.lawgol.01.

2 Pieplow, N. (2017). *Peterson Field Guide to Bird Sounds of Western North America*. Houghton Mifflin Harcourt: Boston, New York.
3 Watt et al., "Lawrence's Goldfinch."
4 Remsen, J. V., K. Garrett, and R. A. Erickson (1982). "Vocal Copying in Lawrence's and Lesser Goldfinches." *Western Birds* 13: 29–33.
5 Coutlee, E. L. (1968). "Maintenance Behavior of Lesser and Lawrence's Goldfinches." *Condor* 70: 378–384.
6 Watt et al., "Lawrence's Goldfinch."
7 Coutlee, E. L. (1968). "Comparative Breeding Behavior of Lesser and Lawrence's Goldfinches." *Condor* 70: 228–242.
8 Watt et al., "Lawrence's Goldfinch."
9 Coutlee, "Comparative Breeding Behavior of Lesser and Lawrence's Goldfinches."
10 Coutlee, "Comparative Breeding Behavior of Lesser and Lawrence's Goldfinches."
11 Willoughby, E. J., M. Murphy, and H. L. Gorton. (2002). "Molt, Plumage Abrasion, and Color Change in Lawrence's Goldfinch." *Wilson Bulletin* 114 (3): 380–392.

### *AMERICAN GOLDFINCH*

1 Forbush, E. H. (1929). *Birds of Massachusetts and Other New England States*. Vol. 3. Massachusetts Department of Agriculture.
2 McGraw, K. J., and A. L. Middleton (2020). "American Goldfinch (*Spinus tristis*)," version 1.0. In Birds of the World (P. G. Rodewald, Editor). Cornell Lab of Ornithology, Ithaca, New York. https://doi.org/10.2173/bow.amegfi.01.
3 Middleton, A. L. A. (1988). "Polyandry in the Mating System of the American Goldfinch, *Carduelis tristis*." *Canadian Journal of Zoology* 66: 296–299.
4 Pieplow, N. (2017). *Peterson Field Guide to Bird Sounds of Eastern North America*. Houghton Mifflin Harcourt: Boston, New York.
5 Middleton, A. L. A. (1978). "The Annual Cycle of the American Goldfinch." *Condor* 80: 401–406.
6 eBird (2021). eBird: An online database of bird distribution and abundance [web application]. eBird, Cornell Lab of Ornithology, Ithaca, New York. Available: http://www.ebird.org. Accessed February 12, 2023.
7 Coutlee, E. L. (1967). "Agonistic Behavior in the American Goldfinch." *Wilson Bulletin* 79: 89–109.
8 Stokes, A. W. (1950). "Breeding Behavior of the Goldfinch." *Wilson Bulletin* 62: 107–127.
9 Coutlee, "Agonistic Behavior in the American Goldfinch."
10 McGraw and Middleton, "American Goldfinch."
11 Coutlee, E. L. (1971). "Vocalizations in the Genus *Spinus*." *Animal Behaviour* 19: 556–565.
12 Gissing, G. J., T. J. Crease, and A. L. A. Middleton (1998). "Extrapair Paternity Associated with Renesting in the American Goldfinch." *Auk* 115 (1): 230–234.
13 Middleton, "The Annual Cycle of the American Goldfinch."
14 Murphy, T. G., M. F. Rosenthal, R. Montgomerie, and K. A. Tarvin (2009b). "Female American Goldfinches Use Carotenoid-Based Bill Coloration to Signal Status." *Behavioral Ecology* 20 (6): 1348–1355. https://doi.org/10.1093/beheco/arp140.
15 Hill, G. E., W. R. Hood, and K. Huggins (2009). "A Multifactorial Test of the Effects of Carotenoid Access, Food Intake and Parasite Load on the Production of Ornamental Feathers and Bill Coloration in American Goldfinches." *Journal of Experimental Biology* 212 (8): 1225–1233. https://doi.org/10.1242/jeb.026963.
16 MacDougall, A. K., and R. Montgomerie (2003). "Assortative Mating by Carotenoid-Based Plumage Colour: A Quality Indicator in American Goldfinches, *Carduelis tristis*." *Naturwissenschaften* 90(10): 464–467.
17 Murphy et al., "Female American Goldfinches."

## VAGRANT FINCHES

### *QUICK TAKE*

1 Howell, S. N. G., I. Lewington, W. Russell (2014). *Rare Birds of North America*. Princeton University Press: Princeton, New Jersey.
2 Howell et al., *Rare Birds of North America*.
3 American Birding Association Checklist Codes. https://www.aba.org/aba-checklist/.
4 eBird (2021). eBird: An online database of bird distribution and abundance [web application]. eBird, Cornell Lab of Ornithology, Ithaca, New York. Available: http://www.ebird.org. Accessed February 27, 2023.
5 "New Research into Vagrancy in Rare Birds," February 23, 2023, Birding Wire, Outdoor Wire Digital Network, accessed February 27, 2023. https://www.birdingwire.com/releases/a426eedf-5043-4a3c-b351-f7952c1c1367.
6 Lees, A., J. Gilroy (2021). *Vagrancy in Birds*. Princeton University Press: Princeton, New Jersey.
7 Howell et al., *Rare Birds of North America*.
8 Howell et al., *Rare Birds of North America*.
9 Ogden, L. E. "Vagrant Birds May Portend Species Distribution in Climate-Changed World." August 19, 2016, Scientific American, accessed February 27, 2023. https://www.scientificamerican.com/article/vagrant-birds-may-portend-species-distribution-in-climate-changed-world/.

### *COMMON CHAFFINCH*

1 eBird (2021). eBird: An online database of bird distribution and abundance [web application]. eBird, Ithaca, New York. Available: http://www.ebird.org. Accessed December 1, 2023.
2 Mactavish, B. (2021). eBird Checklist: https://ebird.org/checklist/S152224222. eBird: An online database of bird distribution and abundance [web application]. eBird, Ithaca, New York. Available: http://www.ebird.org. Accessed December 1, 2023.

### *BRAMBLING*

1 Dunn, J. L., and J. Alderfer (2017). *National Geographic Field Guide to the Birds of North America*, 7th ed. National Geographic: Washington, DC. 434.

2 eBird (2021). eBird: An online database of bird distribution and abundance [web application]. eBird, Cornell Lab of Ornithology, Ithaca, New York. Available: http://www.ebird.org. Accessed February 27, 2023.

3 Pohlen, Zak. eBird (2021). eBird Checklist: https://ebird.org/ak/checklist/S141574871. eBird: An online database of bird distribution and abundance [web application]. eBird, Cornell Lab of Ornithology, Ithaca, New York. Available: http://www.ebird.org. Accessed February 27, 2023.

### *HAWFINCH*

1 Dunn, J. L., and J. Alderfer (2017). *National Geographic Field Guide to the Birds of North America*, 7th ed. National Geographic: Washington, DC. 444.

2 Kloppers, Elsabe (2021). eBird Checklist: eBird: https://ebird.org/checklist/S82605935. eBird: An online database of bird distribution and abundance [web application]. eBird, Ithaca, New York. Available: http://www.ebird.org. Accessed February 28, 2023.

3 Leahy, Peter (2021). eBird Checklist: https://ebird.org/checklist/S29745290. eBird: An online database of bird distribution and abundance [web application]. eBird, Ithaca, New York. Available: http://www.ebird.org. Accessed February 28, 2023.

4 Clement, P., and D. A. Christie (2020). "Hawfinch (*Coccothraustes coccothraustes*)," version 1.0. In Birds of the World (J. del Hoyo, A. Elliott, J. Sargatal, D. A. Christie, and E. de Juana, Editors). Cornell Lab of Ornithology, Ithaca, New York. https://doi.org/10.2173/bow.hawfin.01.

### *COMMON ROSEFINCH*

1 Clement, P., and D. A. Christie (2020). "Common Rosefinch (*Carpodacus erythrinus*)," version 1.0. In Birds of the World (J. del Hoyo, A. Elliott, J. Sargatal, D. A. Christie, and E. de Juana, Editors). Cornell Lab of Ornithology, Ithaca, New York. https://doi.org/10.2173/bow.comros.01.

2 Howell, S. N. G., I. Lewington, and W. Russell (2014). *Rare Birds of North America*. Princeton University Press: Princeton, New Jersey.

3 Dunn, J. L., and J. Alderfer (2017). *National Geographic Field Guide to the Birds of North America*, 7th ed. National Geographic: Washington, DC. 434.

4 Tietz, Jim (2021). eBird Checklist: https://ebird.org/checklist/S52790856. eBird: An online database of bird distribution and abundance [web application]. eBird, Ithaca, New York. Available: http://www.ebird.org. Accessed February 28, 2023.

### *PALLAS'S ROSEFINCH*

1 Clement, P., and V. Arkhipov (2020). "Pallas's Rosefinch (*Carpodacus roseus*)," version 1.0. In Birds of the World (J. del Hoyo, A. Elliott, J. Sargatal, D. A. Christie, and E. de Juana, Editors). Cornell Lab of Ornithology, Ithaca, New York.

2 Gregory, Corey (2021). eBird Checklist: https://ebird.org/checklist/S25115167. eBird: An online database of bird distribution and abundance [web application]. eBird, Ithaca, New York. Available: http://www.ebird.org. Accessed February 28, 2023.

3 Clement and Arkhipov, "Pallas's Rosefinch."

### *EURASIAN BULLFINCH*

1 Dunn, J. L., and J. Alderfer (2017). *National Geographic Field Guide to the Birds of North America*, 7th ed. National Geographic: Washington, DC. 434.

2 Hunter, Brad (2021). eBird Checklist: https://ebird.org/checklist/S102040943. eBird: An online database of bird distribution and abundance [web application]. eBird, Ithaca, New York. Available: http://www.ebird.org. Accessed February 28, 2023.

3 Clement, P., and D. A. Christie (2020). "Eurasian Bullfinch (*Pyrrhula pyrrhula*)," version 1.0. In Birds of the World (J. del Hoyo, A. Elliott, J. Sargatal, D. A. Christie, and E. de Juana, Editors). Cornell Lab of Ornithology, Ithaca, New York. https://doi.org/10.2173/bow.eurbul.01.

### *ASIAN ROSY-FINCH*

1 Clement, P., and V. Arkhipov (2020). "Asian Rosy-Finch (*Leucosticte arctoa*)," version 1.0. In Birds of the World (J. del Hoyo, A. Elliott, J. Sargatal, D. A. Christie, and E. de Juana, Editors). Cornell Lab of Ornithology, Ithaca, New York. https://doi.org/10.2173/bow.asrfin1.01.

2 Helmericks, Isaac (2021). eBird Checklist: https://ebird.org/checklist/S44169856. eBird: An online database of bird distribution and abundance [web application]. eBird, Cornell Lab of Ornithology, Ithaca, New York. Available: http://www.ebird.org. Accessed February 12, 2023.

3 Dunn, J. L., and J. Alderfer (2017). *National Geographic Field Guide to the Birds of North America*, 7th ed. National Geographic: Washington, DC. 562.

4 Clement and Arkhipov, "Asian Rosy-Finch."

### *ORIENTAL GREENFINCH*

1 Dunn, J. L., and J. Alderfer (2017). *National Geographic Field Guide to the Birds of North America*, 7th ed. National Geographic: Washington, DC. 440.

2 Newell, Geoffrey (2021). eBird Checklist: https://ebird.org/checklist/S25768197. eBird: An online database of bird distribution and abundance [web application]. eBird, Ithaca, New York. Available: http://www.ebird.org. Accessed February 28, 2023.

3 Oregon Bird Records Committee (2021). eBird Checklist: https://ebird.org/checklist/S96627136). eBird: An online database of bird distribution and abundance [web application]. eBird, Ithaca, New York. Available: http://www.ebird.org. Accessed February 28, 2023.

4 California Birds Records Committee 1986-450A. *Western Birds* 49(4):252. https://californiabirds.org/queryDatabase.asp?species=Oriental+Greenfinch&county=hum

### *EURASIAN SISKIN*

1 Howell, S. N. G., I. Lewington, and W. Russell (2014). *Rare Birds of North America*. Princeton University Press: Princeton, New Jersey. 563.

2 Heinl, Steve (2021). eBird Checklist: https://ebird.org/checklist/S48922027. eBird: An online database of bird distribution and abundance [web application]. eBird, Ithaca, New York. Available: http://www.ebird.org. Accessed February 28, 2023.
3 Historical Data (2021). eBird Checklist: https://ebird.org/checklist/S90440233. eBird: An online database of bird distribution and abundance [web application]. eBird, Ithaca, New York. Available: http://www.ebird.org. Accessed February 28, 2023.
4 Puschock, John (2021). eBird Checklist: https://ebird.org/checklist/S52545445.
eBird: An online database of bird distribution and abundance [web application]. eBird, Ithaca, New York. Available: http://www.ebird.org. Accessed February 28, 2023.
5 Pohlen, Z. (2021). eBird Checklist: https://ebird.org/ak/checklist/S141575080. eBird: An online database of bird distribution and abundance [web application]. eBird, Ithaca, New York. Available: http://www.ebird.org. Accessed November 29, 2023.
6 eBird: An online database of bird distribution and abundance [web application]. eBird, Ithaca, New York. Available: http://www.ebird.org. Accessed February 28, 2023.
7 Craves J. A. (2008). "Current Status of European Goldfinch (*Carduelis carduelis*) in the Western Great Lakes Region." *North American Birds* 62: 2–5.
8 Newfoundland and Labrador Bird Records (2021). eBird Checklist: https://ebird.org/checklist/S32812280. eBird: An online database of bird distribution and abundance [web application]. eBird, Ithaca, New York. Available: http://www.ebird.org. Accessed February 28, 2023.
9 Vickery, Peter (2021). eBird Checklist: https://ebird.org/checklist/S6142175. eBird: An online database of bird distribution and abundance [web application]. eBird, Ithaca, New York. Available: http://www.ebird.org. Accessed February 28, 2023.

## HAWAIIAN HONEYCREEPERS

### 'AKIKIKI

1 Pratt, H. D. (2005). *The Hawaiian Honeycreepers: Drepanidinae*. Oxford University Press, Oxford.

### MAUI 'ALAUAHIO (MAUI CREEPER)

1 Pratt, H. D. (2005). *The Hawaiian Honeycreepers: Drepanidinae*. Oxford University Press, Oxford.
2 Pratt, *The Hawaiian Honeycreepers*.

### PALILA

1 Pratt, H. D. (2005). *The Hawaiian Honeycreepers: Drepanidinae*. Oxford University Press, Oxford.

### LAYSAN FINCH ('AINOHU KAUO)

1 Pratt, H. D. (2005). *The Hawaiian Honeycreepers: Drepanidinae*. Oxford University Press: Oxford.
2 Berger, A. J. (1981). *Hawaiian Birdlife*, 2nd ed. University Press of Hawaii: Honolulu.
3 Munro, G. C. (1960). *Birds of Hawaii*. Charles E. Tuttle Company: Rutland, Vermont.
4 Pratt, *The Hawaiian Honeycreepers*.

### NIHOA FINCH

1 Berger, A. J. (1981). *Hawaiian Birdlife*, 2nd ed. University of Hawaii Press: Honolulu.
2 Pratt, H. D. (2005). *The Hawaiian Honeycreepers: Drepanidinae*. Oxford University Press: Oxford.
3 Morin, M. P., and S. Conant (2002). "Nihoa Finch (*Telespiza ultima*)," version 1.0. In The Birds of North America (A. F. Poole, Editor). Cornell Lab of Ornithology, Ithaca, New York.

### 'ĀKOHEKOHE (CRESTED HONEYCREEPER)

1 Berlin, K. E., and E. M. VanGelder (1999). "'Akohekohe (*Palmeria dolei*)." No. 400 in: Poole, A. & Gill, F. eds. (1999). *The Birds of North America*. Vol. 10. The Birds of North America Inc.: Philadelphia, Pennsylvania.
2 Pratt, H. D. (2005). *The Hawaiian Honeycreepers: Drepanidinae*. Oxford University Press: Oxford.

### 'APAPANE

1 Pratt, H. D. (2005). *The Hawaiian Honeycreepers: Drepanidinae*. Oxford University Press: Oxford.
2 Pratt, *The Hawaiian Honeycreepers*.
3 Pratt, *The Hawaiian Honeycreepers*.

### 'I'IWI

1 Pratt, H .D. (2005). *The Hawaiian Honeycreepers: Drepanidinae*. Oxford University Press: Oxford.

### MAUI PARROTBILL (KIWIKIU)

1 Pratt, H. D. (2005). *The Hawaiian Honeycreepers: Drepanidinae*. Oxford University Press: Oxford.
2 Pratt, *The Hawaiian Honeycreepers*.
3 Pratt, *The Hawaiian Honeycreepers*.

### 'AKIAPŌLĀ'AU

1 Pratt, H. D. (2005). *The Hawaiian Honeycreepers: Drepanidinae*. Oxford University Press: Oxford.
2 Pratt, *The Hawaiian Honeycreepers*.

### 'ANIANIAU

1 Pratt, H. D. (2005). *The Hawaiian Honeycreepers: Drepanidinae*. Oxford University Press: Oxford.

### HAWAI'I 'AMAKIHI

1 Pratt, H. D. (2005). *The Hawaiian Honeycreepers: Drepanidinae*. Oxford University Press: Oxford.

### O'AHU 'AMAKIHI

1 Pratt, H. D. (2005). *The Hawaiian Honeycreepers: Drepanidinae*. Oxford University Press: Oxford.
2 Pratt, *The Hawaiian Honeycreepers*.
3 Pratt, *The Hawaiian Honeycreepers*.

### KAUA'I 'AMAKIHI

1 Pratt, H. D. (2005). *The Hawaiian Honeycreepers: Drepanidinae*. Oxford University Press: Oxford.

2 Pratt, *The Hawaiian Honeycreepers.*
3 Pratt, *The Hawaiian Honeycreepers.*
4 Pratt, *The Hawaiian Honeycreepers.*

### *HAWAI'I CREEPER ('ALAWĪ)*

1 Pratt, H. D. (2005). *The Hawaiian Honeycreepers: Drepanidinae.* Oxford University Press: Oxford.

### *'AKEKE'E*

1 Pratt, H. D. (2005). *The Hawaiian Honeycreepers: Drepanidinae.* Oxford University Press: Oxford.

### *HAWAI'I 'ĀKEPA*

1 Lepson, J. K., and L. A. Freed (2020). "Hawaii Akepa (*Loxops coccineus*)," version 1.0. In Birds of the World (A. F. Poole, Editor). Cornell Lab of Ornithology, Ithaca, New York. https://doi.org/10.2173/bow.akepa1.01
2 Pratt, H. D. (2005). *The Hawaiian Honeycreepers: Drepanidinae.* Oxford University Press: Oxford.
3 Pratt, *The Hawaiian Honeycreepers.*
4 Pratt, H. D. (1989b). "Species Limits in Akepas (Drepanidinae: Loxops)." *Condor* 91: 933–940.

## FEEDING AND ATTRACTING FINCHES

1 Hammoud, R., S. Tognin, L. Burgess et al. (2022). "Smartphone-based Ecological Momentary Assessment Reveals Mental Health Benefits of Birdlife." *Scientific Reports* 12, 17589. https://doi.org/10.1038/s41598-022-20207-6.
2 University of Exeter (2017). "Watching Birds Near Your Home is Good for Your Mental Health: People Living in Neighborhoods With More Birds, Shrubs and Trees Are Less Likely to Suffer from Depression, Anxiety and Stress." ScienceDaily, February 25, 2017. https//:www.sciencedaily.com/releases/2017/02/170225102113.htm.
3 Cornell Lab of Ornithology (2019). Project FeederWatch. Top 25 Birds. Cornell Lab of Ornithology, Ithaca, New York. https://feederwatch.org/pfw/top25. Accessed February 26, 2023.
4 Cornell Lab of Ornithology (2019). "House Finch Eye Disease: Increased Virulence as Disease Progresses." Cornell Lab of Ornithology, Ithaca, New York. https://feederwatch.org/blog/house-finch-eye-disease-increased-virulence-disease-progresses/. Accessed February 26, 2023.
5 Stokes, Donald and Lillian (1998). *Stokes Bird Gardening Book: The Complete Guide to Creating a Bird-Friendly Habitat in Your Backyard.* Little, Brown: New York.

## MOVEMENTS AND IRRUPTIONS

1 Newton, I. (2012). "Obligate and Facultative Migration in Birds: Ecological Aspects." *Journal of Ornithology* 153 (Suppl 1), 171–180. https://doi.org/10.1007/s10336-011-0765-3.
2 Lees, A., and J. Gilroy (2021). *Vagrancy in Birds.* Princeton University Press: Princeton, New Jersey. 51.
3 Bock, C. E., and L. W. Lepthien (1976f). "Synchronous Eruptions of Boreal Seed-Eating Birds." *American Naturalist* 110:559–571.
4 Benkman, C. W., and M. A. Young (2020). "Red Crossbill (*Loxia curvirostra*)," version 1.0. In Birds of the World (S. M. Billerman, B. K. Keeney, P. G. Rodewald, and T. S. Schulenberg, Editors). Cornell Lab of Ornithology, Ithaca, New York. https://doi.org/10.2173/bow.redcro.01.
5 Bent, A. C. (1968). "Life Histories of North American Cardinals, Grosbeaks, Towhees, Finches, Sparrows, and Allies (Part 1)." United States National Museum Bulletin 237.
6 Bent, "Life Histories of North American Cardinals, Grosbeaks, Towhees, Finches, Sparrows, and Allies."
7 Bent, "Life Histories of North American Cardinals, Grosbeaks, Towhees, Finches, Sparrows, and Allies."
8 Widick, I. V., M. A. Young, J. M. LaMontagne, C. Strong, and B. Zuckerberg. "Poleward Shifts and Altered Periodicity in Boreal Bird Irruptions Over Six Decades" (manuscript in review). *Journal of Animal Ecology*.
9 Bent, "Life Histories of North American Cardinals, Grosbeaks, Towhees, Finches, Sparrows, and Allies."
10 Widick et al., "Poleward Shifts and Altered Periodicity."
11 Widick et al., "Poleward Shifts and Altered Periodicity."

## RESEARCH AND CONSERVATION

1 Rosenberg, K. V., Adriaan M. Doktar, Peter J. Blancher, John R. Sauer, Adam C. Smith, Paul A. Smith, Jessica C. Stanton, Arvind Panjabi, Laura Helft, Michael Parr, and Peter P. Marra (2019). "Decline of the North American Avifauna." *Science* 365(6461). doi: 10.1126/science.aaw1313.
2 Rosenberg et al., "Decline of the North American Avifauna."
3 Rosenberg, K. V., J. A. Kennedy, R. Dettmers, R. P. Ford, D. Reynolds, J. D. Alexander, C. J. Beardmore, P. J. Blancher, R. E. Bogart, G. S. Butcher, A. F. Camfield, A. Couturier, D. W. Demarest, W. E. Easton, J. J. Giocomo, R. H. Keller, A. E. Mini, A. O. Panjabi, D. N. Pashley, T. D. Rich, J. M. Ruth, H. Stabins, J. Stanton, and T. Will (2016). Partners in Flight Landbird Conservation Plan. Partners in Flight Science Committee. https://partnersinflight.org/resources/the-plan/.
4 Paxton, Eben H., Richard J. Camp, P. Marcos Gorresen, Lisa H. Crampton, David L. Leonard Jr., and Eric VanderWerf. "Collapsing Avian Community on a Hawaiian Island." *Science Advances* 10.1126/sciadv.1600029. https://doi.org/10.1126/sciadv.1600029 2023/02/28.
5 Samuel, M. D., B. L. Woodworth, C. T. Atkinson, P. J. Hart, and D. A. LaPointe (2015). "Avian Malaria in Hawaiian Forest Birds: Infection and Population Impacts across Species and Elevations." *Ecosphere* 6(6), 1–21.
6 LaPointe, D. A., M. L. Goff, and C. T. Atkinson (2010). "Thermal Constraints to the Sporogonic Development and Altitudinal Distribution of Avian Malaria Plasmodium relictum in Hawai'i." *Journal of Parasitology* 96(2), 318–324.

7 Atkinson, C. T., K. S. Saili, R. B. Utzurrum, and S. I. Jarvi (2013). "Experimental Evidence for Evolved Tolerance to Avian Malaria in a Wild Population of Low Elevation Hawai 'i 'Amakihi (*Hemignathus virens*)." *EcoHealth* 10(4), 366–375.

8 "Birds, Not Mosquitoes: Endangered Hawaiian Birds," accessed February 28, 2023. https://www.birdsnotmosquitoes.org/.

9 Rosenberg et al. Partners in Flight Landbird Conservation Plan.

10 North American Bird Conservation Initiative (2022). The State of the Birds, United States of America, 2022. StateoftheBirds.org.

11 Funk, E. R., N. A. Mason, S. Pálsson, T. Albrecht, J. Johnson, S. A. Taylor (2021). "A Supergene Underlies Linked Variation in Color and Morphology in a Holarctic Songbird." *Nature Communications* 12 :6833 1–11. https://doi.org/10.1038/s41467-021-27173-z.

12 Young, M. A. and C. S. Adkisson (2020). "Pine Grosbeak (*Pinicola enucleator*)," version 2.0. In Birds of the World (P. G. Rodewald, B. K. Keeney, and S. M. Billerman, Editors). Cornell Lab of Ornithology, Ithaca, New York. https://doi.org/10.2173/bow.pingro.02.

13 Benkman, C. W. (1993b). "Logging, Conifers, and the Conservation of Crossbills." *Conservation Biology* 7: 473–479.

14 Cornelius, J. M., T. P. Hahn, A. R. Robart, B. J. Vernasco, J. L. Zahor, K. J. Glynn, J. Corrie, C. J. Navis, and H. E. Watts (2021). "Seasonal Patterns of Fat Deposits in Relation to Migratory Strategy in Facultative Migrants." *Frontiers in Ecology and Evolution* 9: 691808. https://doi.org/10.3389/fevo.2021.691808.

15 Webb, Wesley H., Dianne H. Brunton, J. David Aguirre, Daniel B. Thomas, Mihai Valcu, and James Dale (2016). "Female Song Occurs in Songbirds with More Elaborate Female Coloration and Reduced Sexual Dichromatism." *Frontiers in Ecology and Evolution* 4: 22. https://doi.org/10.3389/fevo.2016.00022.

# Codes for States, Provinces, and International Locations

**U.S. States and Territories**

AK – Alaska

AL – Alabama

AR – Arkansas

AZ – Arizona

CA – California

CO – Colorado

CT – Connecticut

DC – District of Columbia

DE – Delaware

FL – Florida

GA – Georgia

HI – Hawai'i

IA – Iowa

ID – Idaho

IL – Illinois

IN – Indiana

KS – Kansas

KY – Kentucky

LA – Louisiana

MA – Massachusetts

MD – Maryland

ME – Maine

MI – Michigan

MN – Minnesota

MO – Missouri

MS – Mississippi

MT – Montana

NC – North Carolina

ND – North Dakota

NE – Nebraska

NH – New Hampshire

NJ – New Jersey

NM – New Mexico

NV – Nevada

NY – New York

OH – Ohio

OK – Oklahoma

OR – Oregon

PA – Pennsylvania

PR – Puerto Rico

RI – Rhode Island

SC – South Carolina

SD – South Dakota

TN – Tennessee

TX – Texas

UT – Utah

VA – Virginia

VT – Vermont

WA – Washington

WI – Wisconsin

WV – West Virginia

WY – Wyoming

**Canadian Provinces**

AB – Alberta

BC – British Columbia

MB – Manitoba

NB – New Brunswick

NF&LB – Newfoundland and Labrador

NS – Nova Scotia

ON – Ontario

PE – Prince Edward Island

QC – Quebec

SK – Saskatchewan

**International Locations**

CRO – Croatia

FIN – Finland

HUN – Hungary

ITA – Italy

JAP – Japan

RUS – Russia

# Photo Credits

Numbers refer to pages; letters refer to relative positions on the page. Going down the page: T=top, M=middle, B=bottom. Going across the page: L=left, R=right.

**Dorian Anderson**
45BL, 45BR, 49, 53BL

**Deborah K. Beutler**
43

**Ryan Brady**
7BR, 12, 26, 95, 107TL, 107B, 108TL, 110, 156, 161BR, 165, 290

**Aidan Brubaker**
148, 150, 153TL

**Hannah Criswell**
56

**David Deifik**
172

**Blair Dudeck**
105TL, 105TR, 109TL

**Janice Gardner**
36

**Brian Genge**
149, 153BR

**Alain Ghignone/AGAMI.NL**
233TR

**Nathan Goldberg**
233B

**Melissa Groo**
11, 14, 79, 112

**Marc Guyt/AGAMI.NL**
223TL

**Beth Hamel**
198

**Bill Hilton Jr. (hiltonpond.org)**
285

**© JackJeffreyphoto.com**
FrontCoverTL, 243, 245TL, 245TR, 245BR, 247TL, 247TR, 247BR, 251TL, 251TR, 253TL, 253TR, 255TL, 255TR, 257TL, 257TR, 259TL, 259TR, 261TR, 261TL, 261BR, 263, 265TL, 265TR, 265BR, 267, 269T, 269BR, 271T, 271BR, 273T, 273BR, 275TL, 275TR, 275BR, 299, 300

**Ellen M. Jewett**
46, 55

**Tom Johnson**
231B

**Robby Kohley**
249

**Ralph Martin/AGAMI.NL**
171TR, 225TL

**Charles McCall Photography**
51

**Chris McCreedy**
28

**Jay McGowan**
7TR, 13, 16, 17, 105BR, 107ML, 108BL, 124, 277B

**Tamara McQuade**
39TL, 39TR, 153TR, 189TR

**Steven G. Mlodinow**
86, 87

**Yve Morrell**
218, 219, 221

**Alan Murphy Photography**
FrontCoverTR, FrontCoverML, FrontCoverBL, FrontCoverBR, 7ML, 21, 23ML, 25, 30, 33TL, 33TR, 35ML, 35MR, 35BR, 40, 41, 53BR, 61TL, 61MR, 63, 64, 66, 68, 73, 82, 83, 97, 98, 107MR, 109BL, 111, 161TR, 161BL, 179, 186, 189TL, 189ML, 189MR, 189BR, 195, 211, 288T, 288B, 289, 293ConiferSeeds, 293FruitSeeds, 298, 303, 306, 308, 330, 331

**Yann Muzika/AGAMI.NL**
231TL, 231TR

**© Jeff Nadler**
7MR, 75TL, 109BR, 119TR, 119MR, 161TL, 292, 293Row1M, 294, 295, 296, 297

**Daniele Occhiato/AGAMI.NL**
223TR, 223B, 225TR, 227TL, 227TR, 227B, 229T, 239TL, 239TR, 239BR

**Stuart Price/AGAMI.NL**
235T, 235B, 237T, 237B

**© Marie Read**
ii, 1, 2, 3, 4, 7TL, 7BL, 18, 58, 62, 65, 72, 77, 80, 81, 90, 96, 159, 167, 176, 181TL, 184, 207, 214, 215, 217, 276, 287M, 293DeciduousSeedsBottom

**Steve Rottenborn**
192, 197T, 197B, 199, 201BR, 203

**Jessé Roy Drainville**
157

**Brian E. Small**
FrontCoverMR, FrontInsideCover, 23TL, 23BL, 31, 33ML, 33MR, 35TL, 35TR, 42, 45TL, 45TR, 50, 53TL, 53TR, 57, 61TR, 61BL, 71ML, 71MR, 71BL, 71BR, 75BL, 75BR, 85TL, 85TR, 89, 93TL, 93ML, 100, 105ML, 105MR, 108TR, 108BR, 109TR, 119ML, 119BL, 146, 189BL, 196, 201TL, 201TR, 201BL, 204, 240, 301, 304, 305

**Lillian Stokes**
FrontCoverM, v, ix, 19, 20, 23TR, 23MR, 23BR, 27, 61ML, 61BR, 71TL, 71TR, 75TR, 78, 93TR, 93MR, 93BL, 93BR, 102, 103TL, 103TR, 107TR, 114, 116, 117, 119TL, 119BR, 144, 168, 169, 171TL, 173, 174, 177, 181TR, 181BR, 183, 206, 209TL, 209TR, 209ML, 209MR, 209BL, 209BR, 212, 213, 277T, 278, 279TL, 279TR, 279ML, 279BL, 279BR, 280T, 280M, 280B, 281T, 281M, 281B, 282T, 282B, 283, 284, 286T, 286B, 287T, 287B, 288M, 293Row1L, 293Row1R, 293Row2L, 293Row2M, 293Row2R, 293DeciduousSeedsTop, 293Row3L, 293Row3R, 293Row4L, 293Row4R, 293Row5L, 293Row5R

**Markus Varesvuo/AGAMI.NL**
225BL, 225BR, 229B, 233TL, 239BL

**Ben Vernasco**
33BR, 37, 38

**Mathew A. Young**
122, 302

# Index